COURT SYSTEM OF THE UNITED STATES: A BIBLIOGRAPHY

COURT SYSTEM OF THE UNITED STATES: A BIBLIOGRAPHY

D. ELLSWORTH BLANC (EDITOR)

Nova Science Publishers, Inc.
New York

Senior Editors: Susan Boriotti and Donna Dennis
Coordinating Editor: Tatiana Shohov
Office Manager: Annette Hellinger
Graphics: Wanda Serrano
Editorial Production: Vladimir Klestov, Matthew Kozlowski and Maya Columbus
Circulation: Ave Maria Gonzalez, Vera Popovich, Luis Aviles, Raymond Davis, Melissa Diaz, and Jeannie Pappas
Communications and Acquisitions: Serge P. Shohov
Marketing: Cathy DeGregory

Library of Congress Cataloging-in-Publication Data
Available Upon Request

ISBN 1-59033-533-3.

400 Oser Ave, Suite 1600
Hauppauge, New York 11788-3619
Tele. 631-231-7269 Fax 631-231-8175
e-mail: Novascience@earthlink.net
Web Site: http://www.novapublishers.com

Printed in the United States of America

CONTENTS

PREFACE

Courts play an integral in enforcing and interpreting the laws of the nation. While the legislatures are tasked with devising laws and the executive branch with carrying them out, it is the courts' job to determine the laws' meanings and applications. In the United States, this process involves an intricate and often complex set of differing levels and jurisdictions. These include district, circuit, and appeals branches. This judiciary break-down applies to both state and federal courts. Having one's case decided at one level is often not the end of the penal odyssey, as the possibility remains to appeal to the next highest court. Such a scenario is open all the way through the Supreme Court, but advancing that far is not a standard occurrence. Regardless, the courts are an important piece of the American way of life, holding the power to keep criminals from society and uphold the laws regulating daily life. In order to be a well-informed citizen and participant in U.S. society, one needs to have some knowledge of the court system.

This book meets that requirement by presenting a thorough and carefully selected list of literature pertaining to the American court system. The citations deal with the district, circuit, and appeals courts. (The Supreme Court is left out as it is the subject of its own Nova Science bibliography.) These divisions of the court system are often the least understood as they do not garner the national headlines of the Supreme Court, so this book makes for a critical tool in researching the U.S. courts. Further access to this important information comes via author, title, and subject indexes.

TITLE INDEX

#

A

B

C

D

E

F

G

H

I

J

L

M

N

O

P

T

U

V

W

BIBLIOGRAPHY

1977 supplement to Hart and Wechsler's The Federal Courts and the Federal system, second edition, by Paul M. Bator, Paul J. Mishkin, David L. Shapiro, Herbert Wechsler. Published/Created: Mineola, N.Y.: Foundation Press, 1977. Description: xii, 281 p.; 26 cm. Subjects: Courts--United States--Cases. Jurisdiction--United States--Cases. Series: University casebook series LC Classification: KF8718 .H32 1973 Suppl Dewey Class No.: 347/.73/2

A Blueprint for judicial reform / edited by Patrick B. McGuigan, Randall R. Rader. Published/Created: Washington, D.C. (721 Second St., N.E., Washington 20002): Free Congress Research & Education Foundation, c1981. Related Authors: McGuigan, Patrick B. Rader, Randall R. Description: ix, 382 p.; 23 cm. Notes: Erratum slip inserted. Includes bibliographical references. Subjects: Courts--United States. Justice, Administration of--United States. Political questions and judicial power--United States. Judicial review--United States. LC Classification: KF8700 .B55 Dewey Class No.: 347.73 347.307 19

A Comparative evaluation of stenographic and audiotape methods for United States District Court reporting / by J. Michael Greenwood ... [et al.]. Published/Created: Washington, D.C.: Federal Judicial Center, [1983] Related Authors: Greenwood, J. Michael. Federal Judicial Center. Description: xvi, 222 p.: ill.; 24 cm. Notes: "July 1983." Item 743-C-3 Includes bibliographical references. Subjects: Law reporting--United States--Data processing. Computer-aided transcription systems. Law reporting--United States. District Courts--United States. Series: FJC-R; 83-3 LC Classification: KF255 .C64 1983 Dewey Class No.: 347.73/13 347.30713 19 Govt. Doc. No.: Ju 13.10:83-3

A Conference on Judicial Reform: the proceedings: an edited transcript of a conference held by the Free Congress Research and Education Foundation on June 14, 1982 / edited by Patrick B. McGuigan and Claudia A. Keiper. Published/Created: Washington, D.C. (721 Second St., N.E., Washington 20002): The Foundation, c1982. Related Authors: McGuigan, Patrick B. Keiper, Claudia A. Free Congress Research and Education Foundation. Description: vii, 139 p.; 23 cm. Subjects: Courts--United States--Congresses. Justice, Administration of--United States--Congresses. Political questions and judicial power--United States Congresses. Series: Currents in judicial policy LC Classification: KF8700.A75 C66 1982 Dewey Class No.: 347.73 347.307 19

A Constitutional analysis of magistrate judge authority / prepared by the Magistrate Judges Division of the Administrative Office of the United States Courts under the supervision of the Judicial Conference Committee on the Administration of the Magistrate Judges System. Published/Created: Washington, D.C. (One

Columbus Circle, N.E., Washington 20544): The Division, [1993] Related Authors: United States. Administrative Office of the United States Courts. Magistrate Judges Division. Description: iii, 64 p.; 28 cm. Notes: "June 1993." Shipping list no.: 93-0400-P. Includes bibliographical references (p. 58-64). Subjects: United States magistrates. LC Classification: KF8792.Z9 C66 1993 Dewey Class No.: 347.7316 347.30716 20 Govt. Doc. No.: JU 10.2:C 76

A Court's heritage: the newsletter of the Historical Society of the United States District Court for the Eastern District of Pennsylvania. Published/Created: [Philadelphia, PA]: The Society, [c1985- Related Authors: Historical Society of the United States District Court for the Eastern District of Pennsylvania. Description: v.: ill.; 28 cm. Vol. 1, no. 1 (winter 1985)- ISSN: 1041-4932 Notes: Title from caption. SERBIB/SERLOC merged record Subjects: United States. District Court (Pennsylvania: Eastern District)--History--Periodicals. District Courts--Pennsylvania--United States--History--Periodicals. LC Classification: KF8755.P38 A133 Dewey Class No.: 347.73/22/09774805 347.307220974805 20

A Directory of oral history interviews related to the federal Courts / compiled and edited by Anthony Champagne, Cynthia Harrison, and Adam Land. Published/Created: Washington, DC (1520 H Street, N.W., Washington 20005): Federal Judicial History Office, Federal Judicial Center, 1992. Related Authors: Champagne, Anthony. Harrison, Cynthia Ellen. Land, Adam. United States. Federal Judicial History Office. Description: vi, 73 p.; 28 cm. Notes: Item 0743-C-03 Shipping list no.: 92-0392-P. Subjects: Courts--United States--History--Sources--Directories. Judges--Lawyers--United States--Interviews--Directories. Oral history--Archival resources--Directories. LC Classification: KF352 .D54 1992 Dewey Class No.: 347.73/2 347.3072 20 Govt. Doc. No.: Ju 13.14:H 62

A Framework for studying the controversy concerning the federal Courts and federalism. Published/Created: Washington, DC: Advisory Commission on Intergovernmental Relations, [1986] Related Authors: United States. Advisory Commission on Intergovernmental Relations. Description: xii, 75 p.; 28 cm. Notes: At head of title: An information report. Shipping list no.: 86-337-P. "April 1986." "M-149." Item 1049-D Bibliography: p. 67-75. Subjects: Courts--United States. Judicial power--United States. Judicial review--United States. Federal government--United States. LC Classification: KF8735 .F73 1986 Dewey Class No.: 347.73/1 347.3071 19 Govt. Doc. No.: Y 3.Ad 9/8:2 F 84

A friend to the Constitution. Published/Created: [n. p., 1801] Description: 60 p. 16 cm. Subjects: Courts, United States. United States--Politics and government--1801-1809. LC Classification: E331 .F91

A Guide to court systems. Edition Information: 2nd ed. Published/Created: New York, N.Y.: Institute of Judicial Administration, 1960. Related Authors: Schneider, Leon. Guide to court systems. Institute of Judicial Administration. Description: 50 p.: ill.; 21 cm. Notes: Cover title. Rev. ed. of: A guide to court systems / Leon Schneider. 1st ed. 1957. Subjects: Courts--United States. Courts--New York (State) LC Classification: KF8720 .I6 1960 Dewey Class No.: 347.73/1 347.3071 20

A Guide to court systems. Edition Information: 3rd ed. Published/Created: New York, N.Y.: Institute of Judicial Administration, 1962. Related Authors: Blasband, David. Institute of Judicial Administration. Description: 54 p.: ill.; 21 cm. Notes: Cover title. Materials added by David Blasband. Subjects: Courts--United States. Courts--New York (State) LC Classification: KF8720 .I6 1962 Dewey Class No.: 347.73/1 347.3071 20

A Guide to court systems. Edition Information: 5th ed. Published/Created: New York: Institute of Judicial Administration, 1971.

Related Authors: Institute of Judicial Administration. Description: 73 p.: ill.; 21 cm. Notes: Cover title. Subjects: Courts--United States. Courts--New York (State) LC Classification: KF8720 .I6 1971 Dewey Class No.: 347/.73/1

A Judicial odyssey: federal court in Santa Clara, San Benito, Santa Cruz, and Monterey counties / edited by Christian G. Fritz, Michael Griffith, Janet M. Hunter. Published/Created: San Jose: Advisory Committee--San Jose Federal Court, 1985. Related Authors: Fritz, Christian G., 1953- Griffith, Michael, 1948- Hunter, Janet M., 1951- Advisory Committee--San Jose Federal Court. Description: xv, 333 p.: ill.; 27 cm. ISBN: 0961369000: 0961369019 (pbk.) : Notes: Includes index. Bibliography: p. 291-313. Subjects: United States. District Court (California: Northern District)--History. Courts--California--History. Law--California--History. LC Classification: KF8755.C28 J83 1985 Dewey Class No.: 347.73/22 347.30702 19

A Manual for workshops on processing felony dispositions in limited jurisdiction Courts: improving the quality of justice while reducing delay / H. Clifton Grandy, project director ... [et al.]. Published/Created: [Williamsburg, Va.]: National Center for State Courts, [c1992] Related Authors: Grandy, H. Clifton. National Center for State Courts. Description: vii, 181 leaves: ill.; 29 cm. Notes: "Publication number WPO-033"--P. [i] Includes bibliographical references and index. Subjects: Criminal procedure--United States. Courts of special jurisdiction--United States. Plea bargaining--United States. Court congestion and delay--United States. LC Classification: KF9619 .M327 1992

A nation of states: federalism at the bar of the Supreme Court / edited with a preface by Kermit L. Hall. Published/Created: Brooklyn, N.Y.: Carlson Pub., 1996. Related Authors: Hall, Kermit. Description: p. cm. ISBN: 0926019961 (alk. paper) Notes: Includes bibliographical references and index. Subjects: United States. Supreme Courts--History. Federal government--United States. Constitutional history--United States. State rights--United States. Series: Equal justice under law; 4 LC Classification: KF8742.A45 E68 1996 vol. 4 KF4600 Dewey Class No.: 347.73/26 s 347.73/262 347.30735 s 347.307352 20

A study of the business of the federal Courts ... The American law institute ... Published/Created: Philadelphia, Pa., Executive office, The American law institute, 1934. Related Authors: United States. National commission on law observance and enforcement. Description: 2 v. tables (part fold.) diagrs., forms. 27 cm. Subjects: Courts--United States. Justice, Administration of--United States. Judicial statistics--United States. LC Classification: KF8719 .A84 Microfilm LL 1464 KF

Abbott, Benjamin Vaughan, 1830-1890. A treatise upon the United States Courts, and their practice: explaining the enactment by which they are controlled; their organization and powers; their peculiar jurisdiction; and the modes of pleading and procedure in them, with numerous practical forms. Edition Information: 3d ed. Published/Created: New York, Ward & Peloubet, 1877. Description: 2 v. 25 cm. Subjects: Courts--United States. LC Classification: KF8720 .A2 1877 Microfilm LL 847 KF

Abbott, Benjamin Vaughan, 1830-1890. A treatise upon the United States Courts, and their practice: explaining the enactments by which they are controlled; their organization and powers; their peculiar jurisdiction; and the modes of pleading and procedure in them, with numerous practical forms. Edition Information: 2d ed., rev. and cor. by Benjamin Vaughan Abbott. Vol. 1. Enactments, organization, jurisdiction. Published/Created: New York, Diossy & company, 1871. Description: xv, 639 p. 25 cm. Subjects: Courts--United States. LC Classification: KF8719 .A75

Abbott, Benjamin Vaughan, 1830-1890. A treatise upon the United States Courts, and their practice: explaining the enactments by which they are controlled; their organization and powers; their peculiar jurisdiction; and the modes of pleading and procedure in them, with numerous practical forms. By Benjamin Vaughan Abbott and Austin Abbott. Published/Created: New York, Diossy & company, 1869-71. Related Authors: Abbott, Austin, 1831-1896, joint author. Description: 2 v. 25 cm. Contents: v. 1. Enactments; organization; jurisdiction.--v. 2. Original suits; review forms. Subjects: Courts--United States. LC Classification: KF8719 .A74 Microfilm LL 352 KF

Abel, Charles F. In defense of political trials / Charles F. Abel & Frank H. Marsh. Published/Created: Westport, Conn.: Greenwood Press, 1994. Related Authors: Marsh, Frank H. Description: viii, 154 p.; 25 cm. ISBN: 0313251118 (alk. paper) Notes: Includes bibliographical references (p. 147-150) and index. Subjects: Courts--United States. Political questions and judicial power--United States. Law and politics. Series: Contributions in political science, 0147-1066; no. 336 LC Classification: KF8700 .A93 1994 Dewey Class No.: 347.73/1 347.3071 20

Abraham, Henry Julian, 1921- Courts & judges: an introduction to the judicial process / by Henry J. Abraham. Published/Created: New York: Oxford University Press, 1959. Description: vi, 58 p.; 26 cm. Notes: Includes index. Bibliography: p. [46]-56. Subjects: Judges. Courts. Courts--United States. Judicial review--United States. LC Classification: KF8720 .A27 Dewey Class No.: 347.9

Abraham, Henry Julian, 1921- The judicial process: an introductory analysis of the Courts of the United States, England, and France / Henry J. Abraham. Edition Information: 7th ed. Published/Created: New York: Oxford University Press, 1998. Description: xvi, 458 p.: ill., map; 24 cm. ISBN: 0195099877 (paper: acid-free paper) Notes: Includes bibliographical references (p. 421-431) and indexes. Subjects: Courts--United States. Courts--Great Britain. Courts--France. Judicial process. LC Classification: K2100 .A725 1998 Dewey Class No.: 347/.01 21

Abraham, Henry Julian, 1921- The judicial process: an introductory analysis of the Courts of the United States, England, and France / Henry J. Abraham. Edition Information: 6th ed. Published/Created: New York: Oxford University Press, 1993. Description: xvi, 415 p.; 24 cm. ISBN: 0195068017 (acid-free paper) Notes: Includes bibliographical references (p. 381-389) and indexes. Subjects: Courts--United States. Courts--Great Britain. Courts--France. Judicial process. LC Classification: K2100 .A725 1993 Dewey Class No.: 347/.01 342.71 20

Abraham, Henry Julian, 1921- The judicial process: an introductory analysis of the Courts of the United States, England, and France / Henry J. Abraham. Edition Information: 5th ed. Published/Created: New York: Oxford University Press, 1986. Description: xvi, 624 p.; 23 cm. ISBN: 0195037138 (pbk.: alk. paper) Notes: Includes indexes. Bibliography: p. [405]-598. Subjects: Courts--United States. Courts--Great Britain. Courts--France. Judicial process. LC Classification: K2100 .A725 1986 Dewey Class No.: 347/.01 342.71 19

Abraham, Henry Julian, 1921- The judicial process: an introductory analysis of the Courts of the United States, England, and France / Henry J. Abraham. Edition Information: 4th ed. Published/Created: New York: Oxford University Press, 1980. Description: xviii, 622 p.; 23 cm. ISBN: 0195026128 0195026136 (pbk.) Notes: Includes bibliographies and indexes. Subjects: Courts--United States. Courts--Great Britain. Courts--France. Judicial process. LC Classification: K2100 .A27 1980 Dewey Class No.: 347.01

Abraham, Henry Julian, 1921- The judicial process: an introductory analysis of the Courts of the United States, England, and France / Henry J. Abraham. Edition Information: 3d ed., rev. and enl.

Published/Created: New York: Oxford University Press, 1975. Description: xii, 543 p.; 24 cm. Notes: Includes indexes. Bibliography: p. 385-515. Subjects: Courts--United States. Courts--Great Britain. Courts--France. Judicial process. LC Classification: LAW Dewey Class No.: 347.01

Abraham, Henry Julian, 1921- The judicial process; an introductory analysis of the Courts of the United States, England, and France. Published/Created: New York, Oxford University Press, 1962. Description: xii, 381 p. 21 cm. Notes: Bibliography: p. 329-360. Subjects: Courts--United States. Courts--Great Britain. Courts--France. Judicial process. LC Classification: LAW Dewey Class No.: 347.9

Abraham, Henry Julian, 1921- The judicial process; an introductory analysis of the Courts of the United States, England, and France [by] Henry J. Abraham. Edition Information: 2d ed., rev. and enl. Published/Created: New York, Oxford University Press, 1968. Description: xiv, 496 p. 21 cm. Notes: Bibliography: p. 381-472. Subjects: Courts--United States. Courts--Great Britain. Courts--France. Judicial process. LC Classification: LAW Dewey Class No.: 347.9

Abraham, Henry Julian, 1921- The judiciary: the Supreme Court in the governmental process / Henry J. Abraham. Edition Information: 10th ed. Published/Created: New York: New York University Press, c1996. Description: xiv, 325 p.: ill., 1 map; 24 cm. ISBN: 0814706525 (cloth: alk. paper) 0814706533 (pbk.: alk. paper) Notes: Includes bibliographical references (p. 279-283) and indexes. Subjects: United States. Supreme Court. Civil rights--United States. Judicial power--United States. Courts--United States. LC Classification: KF8748 .A2 1996 Dewey Class No.: 347.73/26 347.30735 20

Accommodating the workload of the United States Courts of Appeals; report of recommendations. Paul D. Carrington, project director. Project advisory committee: Bernard G. Segal [and others] Published/Created: Chicago, 1968. Related Authors: Carrington, Paul D., 1931- Description: 8 p. 23 cm. Subjects: United States. Court of Appeals. LC Classification: KF8750 .Z9A5 Dewey Class No.: 347.99/73

Adams, Brooks, 1848-1927. The theory of social revolutions, by Brooks Adams. Published/Created: New York, Macmillan, 1913. Description: vii, 240 p. 19 cm. Contents: The collapse of capitalistic government. -The limitations of the judicial function. -American Courts as legislative chambers. -The social equilibrium. -Political Courts. -Inferences. Subjects: Revolutions. Courts--United States. United States--Politics and government. LC Classification: JC491 .A3

Adams, Eldridge. Courts and computers. Published/Created: Chicago, American Judicature Society [1972] Description: 159 p. illus. 23 cm. Notes: Bibliography: p. 149-159. Subjects: Court administration--United States. Information storage and retrieval systems--Law. LC Classification: KF8732 .A93 Dewey Class No.: 347/.73/130285

Administrative procedure. Published/Created: Washington, U.S. Govt. print. off., 1939. Related Authors: Woodall, Emery J. McGuire, Ollie Roscoe, 1892- Description: p. cm. Subjects: Administrative law--United States. Administrative Courts--United States. United States--Executive departments. LC Classification: KF5407.Z9 F4

Aikman, Alexander B. Friends of the court: lawyers as supplemental judicial resources / Alexander B. Aikman, Mary E. Elsner, Frederick G. Miller. Published/Created: [Williamsburg, VA]: National Center for State Courts, c1987. Related Authors: Oram, Mary Elsner, 1948- Miller, Frederick G. National Center for State Courts. Description: xxiii, 225 p.: ill.; 23 cm. ISBN: 0896560821 (pbk.) Notes: Includes bibliographies. Subjects: Courts--

United States--States--Officials and employees. Court administration--United States--States. Lawyers--United States--States. LC Classification: KF8795.Z95 A38 1987 Dewey Class No.: 347.73/1 347.3071 19

Alexander, Guy Scott, 1886- comp. Index to 364 depreciation cases decided by the United States Board of tax appeals and the United States Courts, Published/Created: Cincinnati, O., c1934. Related Authors: United States. Tax court. United States. Courts. Description: 1 p.l., 18 numb. l. 22 x 29 cm. Subjects: Income tax--United States--Cases. Depreciation. Annotations and citations (Law)--United States. LC Classification: KF6386.A54 A5

Alger, George William, 1872- The old law and the new order, by George W. Alger. Published/Created: Boston, New York, Houghton Mifflin Company, 1913. Description: 6 p. l., 3-295, [1] p., 1 l. 20 cm. Contents: Executive aggression.--The Courts and legislative freedom.--Treadmill justice.--The state as employer.--American discontent with criminal law.--Criticizing the Courts.--The police judge and the public.--Punishing corporations.--The law and industrial inequality.--The ethics of production. Notes: Partly reprinted from various periodicals. Subjects: Justice, Administration of--United States. Courts--United States. United States--Economic conditions. LC Classification: JK1544 .A6

Alterman, Irwin M. Michigan antitrust digest, Federal and State: chronological and topical index of the antitrust decisions of the Michigan Appellate Courts, the U.S. District Courts for Eastern and Western Michigan, and U.S. Court of Appeals for the Sixth Circuit, plus a statutory appendix of Federal and Michigan antitrust provisions / compiled by Irwin M. Alterman. Published/Created: [Ann Arbor, Mich.]: Institute of Continuing Legal Education, c1975- Related Authors: Institute of Continuing Legal Education (Mich.) State Bar of Michigan. Antitrust Law Section. Michigan. Laws, statutes, etc. Description: 1 v.; 26 cm. Notes: "The Antitrust Law Section of the State Bar of Michigan is pleased to make this digest available to the Michigan Bar." Loose-leaf for updating. Includes index. Subjects: Antitrust law--Michigan--Indexes. Antitrust law--United States--Indexes. LC Classification: KFM4431.A54 A38 Dewey Class No.: 343.774/072 19

Altschuler, Bruce E. Understanding law in a changing society / Bruce E. Altschuler, Celia A. Sgroi. Edition Information: 2nd ed. Published/Created: Upper Saddle River, N.J.: Prentice Hall, c1996. Related Authors: Sgroi, Celia A., 1949- Description: xxi, 527 p.; 24 cm. ISBN: 0134490193 Notes: Includes bibliographical references and index. Subjects: Law--United States. Courts--United States. Justice, Administration of--United States. LC Classification: KF385.A4 A45 1996 Dewey Class No.: 349.73 347.3 20

Altschuler, Bruce E. Understanding law in a changing society / Bruce E. Altschuler, Celia A. Sgroi. Published/Created: Englewood Cliffs, NJ: Prentice Hall, c1992. Related Authors: Sgroi, Celia A., 1949- Description: xix, 437 p.; 24 cm. ISBN: 013934134X Notes: Includes bibliographical references and index. Subjects: Law--United States. Courts--United States. Justice, Administration of--United States. LC Classification: KF385.A4 A45 1992 Dewey Class No.: 349.73 347.3 20

American court systems: readings in judicial process and behavior / edited and with introductory essays by Sheldon Goldman, Austin Sarat. Edition Information: 2nd ed. Published/Created: New York: Longman, c1989. Description: xi, 625 p.: ill.; 24 cm. ISBN: 0582286026 Notes: Includes bibliographies. Subjects: Courts--United States. Judicial process--United States. Judges--United States--Attitudes. LC Classification: KF8700.A7 A46 1989 Dewey Class No.: 347.73/1/09 347.307109 19

American court systems: readings in judicial process and behavior / edited and with introductory essays by Sheldon Goldman, Austin Sarat. Published/Created: San Francisco: W. H. Freeman, c1978. Related Authors: Goldman, Sheldon. Sarat, Austin. Description: xii, 648 p.: ill.; 24 cm. ISBN: 0716700611. 0716700603 Notes: Includes bibliographical references. Subjects: Courts--Judicial process--United States. Judges--United States--Attitudes. LC Classification: KF8700.A7 A46 Dewey Class No.: 347.73/1/09 347.307109 19

Amram, Philip Werner, 1900- Changes in practice resulting from the new Supreme court rules; Published/Created: [Philadelphia, c1939] Related Authors: United States. Supreme court. United States. District Courts. Description: 1 p. l., 15 p. 23 cm. Subjects: Court rules--United States. Civil procedure--United States. Civil procedure--Pennsylvania. LC Classification: KFP536.5 .A4

Amram, Philip Werner, 1900- The new Federal rules in Pennsylvania Published/Created: Philadelphia, Pa., 1938. Related Authors: United States. Supreme court. United States. District Courts. United States. District court. Pennsylvania. Description: 1 p.l., iii, 98 p. 23 cm. Subjects: Court rules--United States. Court rules--Pennsylvania. Civil procedure--United States. Civil procedure--Pennsylvania. Equity pleading and procedure--United States. Equity pleading and procedure--Pennsylvania. LC Classification: KFP530.Z9 A5

An act by which the "offices of judges" of the circuit and criminal Courts of the District of Columbia "be and the same are hereby forever abolished." Published/Created: [Washington, D.C.: s.n., ca. 1845] Related Authors: Joseph Meredith Toner Collection (Library of Congress) Description: 8 p.; 23 cm. Notes: Relates to a judiciary reform bill pending before the United States Senate at that time. Subjects: Courts--Judges--Law reform--Washington (D.C.) LC Classification: KFD1710.Z9 A27 1845

An evaluation of judicial case management under the Civil Justice Reform Act / James S. Kakalik ... [et al.]. Published/Created: Santa Monica, CA: RAND, c1996. Related Authors: Kakalik, James S. Institute for Civil Justice (U.S.) Judicial Conference of the United States. Description: xxxvii, 349 p.: ill.; 28 cm. ISBN: 0833024744 (alk. paper) Notes: "Rand Institute for Civil Justice." "Prepared for the Judicial Conference of the United States"--P. 2 of cover. "MR-802.0-ICJ"--P. 4 of cover. Includes bibliographical references (p. 321-332). Subjects: District Courts--United States--Administration. Justice, Administration of--United States--Evaluation. Costs (Law)--United States. Dispute resolution (Law)--United States. Court congestion and delay--United States. LC Classification: KF8754 .E93 1996 Dewey Class No.: 347.73/13 21

An Index-digest of all declarations approved by our Supreme and Appellate Courts. Published/Created: Centralia, Ill., Smith & co., 1907. Related Authors: Illinois. Supreme court. Illinois. Appellate court. Description: 30 p. 15 x 9 cm. Subjects: Law reports, digests, etc.--Illinois. LC Classification: LAW

An ordinance of His Excellency and Council for the establishing courts of judicature for the ease and benefit of each respective city, town and county within this province of New-York. Published/Created: [New York, Printed by William Bradford, 1699] Description: 4 p. 31 cm. Subjects: Courts--New York (State) LC Classification: LAW

Annual report. Published/Created: [Williamsburg, Va.: National Center for State Courts, Description: v.: ill.; 28 cm. 1973- ISSN: 0196-5433 Notes: Title from cover. SERBIB/SERLOC merged record Subjects: National Center for State Courts--Periodicals. Courts--United States--States--Periodicals. Court administration--United States--States--Periodicals. LC Classification: KF8736.A16 N37 Dewey Class No.: 347.73/3/06 347.307106

Appeals in all Courts: the arts and pitfalls of Appellate practice / sponsored by Advanced Legal Education, Hamline University, School of Law. Published/Created: St. Paul, Minn. (1536 Hewitt Ave., St. Paul 55104): ALE, [c1985] Related Authors: Hamline University. Advanced Legal Education. Description: 338 p.; 26 cm. Subjects: Appellate procedure--Minnesota. Appellate procedure--United States. LC Classification: KFM5955 .A96 1985 Dewey Class No.: 347.776/08 347.76078 19

Appeals to the Second Circuit / prepared by the Committee on Federal Courts of the Association of the Bar of the City of New York. Edition Information: 7th ed. Published/Created: New York, N.Y.: Record Press, 1993. Related Authors: Association of the Bar of the City of New York. Committee on Federal Courts. United States. Court of Appeals (2nd Circuit). Rules of the United States Court of Appeals for the Second Circuit. 1993. Description: vi, 246 p.: forms; 24 cm. ISBN: 0879450754 Notes: "Rules of the United States Court of Appeals for the Second Circuit": p. 67-110. Subjects: United States. Court of Appeals (2nd Circuit)--Rules and practice. Appellate procedure--United States. Court rules--United States. LC Classification: KF9054 2d .A4 1993 Dewey Class No.: 347.73/8 347.3078 20

Appeals to the Second Circuit / prepared by the Committee on Federal Courts of the Association of the Bar of the City of New York. Edition Information: 5th ed. Published/Created: New York, N.Y.: Record Press, 1984. Related Authors: Association of the Bar of the City of New York. Committee on Federal Courts. United States. Court of Appeals (2nd Circuit). Rules of the United States Court of Appeals for the Second Circuit. 1984. Description: iv, 179 p.: forms; 24 cm. ISBN: 087945041X (pbk.) : Notes: "Rules of the United States Court of Appeals for the Second Circuit": p. 53-92. Subjects: Appellate procedure--United States. Court rules--United States. LC Classification: KF9054 2d .A4 1984 Dewey Class No.: 347.73/8 347.3078 19

Appeals to the Second Circuit / prepared by the Committee on Federal Courts of the Association of the Bar of the City of New York. Published/Created: New York, N.Y.: Record Press, 1980. Related Authors: Association of the Bar of the City of New York. Committee on Federal Courts. United States. Court of Appeals (2nd Circuit). Rules of the United States Court of Appeals for the Second Circuit. 1980. Description: 163 p.: forms; 24 cm. Notes: "Rules of the United States Court of Appeals for the Second Circuit": p. 51-85. Subjects: Appellate procedure--United States. Court rules--United States. LC Classification: KF9054 2d .A4 1980 Dewey Class No.: 347.73/8 347.3078 19

Appeals to the Second Circuit. Published/Created: [New York, Distributed by Record Press] 1966. Related Authors: United States. Court of Appeals (2nd Circuit). Rules of the United States Court of Appeals for the Second Circuit. 1966. Description: v, 86 p. 23 cm. Notes: "Rules of the United States Court of Appeals for the Second Circuit": p. [39]-78. Bibliography: p. 37-38. Subjects: Appellate procedure--United States. Court rules--United States. LC Classification: KF9054 2d .A4 1966 Dewey Class No.: 347.99/73

Appellate court administration review. Published/Created: [s.l.] National Conference of Appellate Court Clerks, 1978- Related Authors: National Conference of Appellate Court Clerks. Description: no. ill. 28 cm. no. 1- ISSN: 0191-8524 Notes: "A publication of the National Conference of Appellate Court Clerks" SERBIB/SERLOC merged record Indexed entirely by: Legal resource index 1980- Subjects: Appellate Courts--United States--States--Periodicals. Court administration--United States--States--Periodicals. LC Classification: KF8750.A15 A66 Dewey Class No.: 347/.73/243

Appellate court performance standards / submitted to the State Justice Institute by National Center for State Courts and the Appellate Court Performance Standards Commission; Roger A. Hanson, project director. Published/Created: Williamsburg, VA: The Center, c1995. Related Authors: Hanson, Roger A. State Justice Institute (U.S.) National Center for State Courts. Description: viii, 22 p.; 23 cm. ISBN: 0896561615 Notes: "December 1995." Includes bibliographical references. Subjects: Appellate Courts--United States. Series: Publication (National Center for State Courts); R181. LC Classification: KF8750 .A98 1995

Appellate practice, Virginia and federal Courts. Edition Information: 3rd ed. Published/Created: [Charlottesville, Va.]: Virginia CLE Publications, c2001- Related Authors: Virginia CLE (Organization) Description: 1 v. (loose-leaf): forms; 30 cm. Notes: Includes bibliographical references and index. Subjects: Appellate procedure--Virginia. Appellate procedure--United States. Series: Virginia lawyers practice handbook LC Classification: KFV2955.Z9 A662

Appellate practice, Virginia and federal Courts. Edition Information: 2nd ed. Published/Created: [Richmond?]: Committee on Continuing Legal Education of the Virginia Law Foundation, c1992- Related Authors: Virginia Law Foundation. Committee on Continuing Legal Education. Description: 1 v. (loose-leaf): forms; 30 cm. Notes: Description based on: t.p., 1995 suppl. Includes bibliographical references and index. Subjects: Appellate procedure--Virginia. Appellate procedure--United States. Series: Virginia lawyers practice handbook LC Classification: KFV2955.Z9 A66 1992 Dewey Class No.: 347.755/08 347.55078 20

Appellate practice, Virginia and federal Courts. Published/Created: [Virginia]: Committee on Continuing Legal Education of the Virginia Law Foundation, c1988. Related Authors: Ney, R. Terrence. Kenny, Peter J., 1934- Virginia Law Foundation. Committee on Continuing Legal Education. Description: 1 v. (loose-leaf); 28 cm. Notes: Edited by R. Terrence Ney, with the assistance of Peter J. Kenny. "1986 edition with 1988 supplement." Includes bibliographical references. Subjects: Appellate procedure--Virginia. Appellate procedure--United States. Series: Virginia lawyers practice handbook LC Classification: KFV2955.Z9 A66 1988 Dewey Class No.: 347.755/08 347.55078 20

Apple, James G. Manual for cooperation between state and federal Courts / Federal Judicial Center, National Center for State Courts, State Justice Institute; by James G. Apple, Paula L. Hannaford, G. Thomas Munsterman. Published/Created: Washington, DC (One Columbus Circle, N.E., Washington 20002-8003): Federal Judicial Center, 1997. Related Authors: Hannaford, Paula L. Munsterman, G. T. Description: x, 248 p.; 23 cm. Notes: Shipping list no.: 97-0167-P. Subjects: Courts--Jurisdiction--Federal government--United States. State Courts--United States. LC Classification: KF8735 .A96 1997 Dewey Class No.: 347.73/1 21 Govt. Doc. No.: JU 13.8:C 83

April, Nathan, 1882- A guide to federal Appellate procedure; handbook for counsel about to engage in a federal appeal, Published/Created: New York, Prentice-Hall, inc., 1936. Related Authors: United States. Supreme court. United States. Circuit Courts of Appeals. Description: 8 p, l., v-xxx p., 1 l., 522 p. illus. 24 cm. Subjects: Appellate procedure--Court rules--United States. Forms (Law)--United States. LC Classification: KF9050 .A95

Armour, Elihu, 1912- Deputy United States marshal. Published/Created: [Brooklyn] c1942. Description: 75 l. 28 x 22 cm. Subjects: Courts----Officials and employees. Civil service--United States--Examinations. LC Classification: JK1599.M3 A7

Assisting in prosecution. Edition Information: 3rd ed. Published/Created: Evanston, Ill.: Traffic Institute, Northwestern University, 1985 printing, c1973. Related Authors: Northwestern University (Evanston, Ill.). Traffic Institute. Description: 7 p.: ill.; 28 cm. Notes: Bibliography: p. 7. Subjects: Traffic Courts--United States. Traffic violations--United States. Police--United States--Handbooks, manuals, etc. Series: Traffic law enforcement series Publication (Northwestern University (Evanston, Ill.). Traffic Institute)); no. 556. LC Classification: KF2232.Z9 A87 1985 Dewey Class No.: 345.73/0247 347.305247 19

Aumann, Francis Robert, 1901- The instrumentalities of justice: their forms, functions, and limitations. Published/Created: Columbus, Ohio State University Press, 1956. Description: ix, 137 p. Notes: Bibliography: p. [123]-131. Subjects: Justice, Administration of--United States. Courts--United States. Series: Ohio State University. Contributions in history and political science; no. 18. LC Classification: KF9223.Z9 A9

Automated information systems: planning and implementation guidelines: a monograph for court users / written by the staff of the State Judicial Information Systems Project. Published/Created: Williamsburg, Va.: National Center for State Courts, c1983. Related Authors: State Judicial Information Systems Project (National Center for State Courts) Description: 42 p.: ill.; 28 cm. ISBN: 0896560678 (pbk.) Notes: Bibliography: p. 42. Subjects: Information storage and retrieval systems--Court administration--United States. Information storage and retrieval systems--Criminal justice, Administration of--United States. Court administration--United States--Data processing. Series: Publication (National Center for State Courts); no. R077. LC Classification: KF242.C68 A94 1983 Dewey Class No.: 347.73/13/02854 347.3071302854 19

Auxiliary services to the courts of New York City; report. Published/Created: [New York] 1961. Description: 78 p. tables. 29 cm. Subjects: Courts--New York (State)--New York. Probation--New York (State)--New York. LC Classification: LAW

Baar, Carl. Separate but subservient: court budgeting in the American States / Carl Baar. Published/Created: Lexington, Mass.: Lexington Books, [1975] Related Authors: National Center for State Courts. Description: xi, 210 p.; 24 cm. ISBN: 0669001864 Notes: "A project of the National Center for State Courts." Includes bibliographical references and index. Subjects: Courts--United States--States--Finance. LC Classification: KF8732.5.Z95 B3 Dewey Class No.: 347/.73/13

Bacon, John, 1738-1820. The speeches of Mr. Bacon and Mr. Nicholson, in the national House of representatives, in defence of the bill received from the Seante, entitled, "An act to repeal certain acts respecting the organization of the Courts of the United States." Published/Created: Boston, Printed by Munroe & Francis, Half-court square, 1802. Related Authors: Nicholson, Joseph Hopper, 1770-1817. Miscellaneous Pamphlet Collection (Library of Congress) Description: 44 p. 22 cm. References: Shaw & Shoemaker 1794 Subjects: Courts--United States. LC Classification: JK1511 .B2

Bailey, Joseph W. (Joseph Weldon), 1863-1929. The American judiciary. Published/Created: Washington, Govt. print off., 1916. Description: p. cm. Subjects: Judges--United States. Courts--United States. LC Classification: JK1521 .B17

Bains, Rae. The Supreme Court / by Rae Bains; illustrated by Bob Dole. Published/Created: Mahwah, N.J.: Troll Associates, c1985. Related Authors: Dole, Bob, ill. Description: 29 p.: col. ill.; 24 cm. ISBN: 0816702721 (lib. bdg.): 081670273X (pbk.) : Summary: Explains the importance of the Supreme Court, which interprets the Constitution and makes decisions which establish precedents to gide all laws and legal action in the country. Subjects: United States. Supreme Court--Juvenile literature. United States. Supreme Court. Constitutional law--United States--Juvenile literature. Constitutional law--United States. Courts. Law. LC Classification: KF8742.Z9 B34 1985 Dewey Class No.: 347.73/26 347.30735 19

Baker, Thomas E., 1953- A primer on the jurisdiction of the U.S. Courts of Appeals / Thomas E. Baker. Published/Created: Washington, D.C.: Federal Judicial Center, 1989. Related Authors: Federal Judicial Center. Description: v, 99 p.; 24 cm. Notes: Shipping list no.: 88-728-P. "A report to the Federal Judicial Center"--Cover. "FJC-ETS-89-1"--T.p. verso. Item 743-C-4 Includes bibliographical references (p. 75-91). Subjects: Appellate procedure--United States. Appellate Courts--United States. Jurisdiction--United States. Series: Education and training series (Federal Judicial Center); 89-1. LC Classification: KF9052.Z9 B35 1989 Dewey Class No.: 347.73/08 347.3078 20 Govt. Doc. No.: Ju 13.9:89-1

Baker, Thomas E., 1953- Rationing justice on appeal: the problems of the U.S. Courts of Appeals / by Thomas E. Baker. Published/Created: St. Paul, Minn.: West Pub. Co., 1994. Related Authors: Justice Research Institute. Description: xxi, 445 p.; 23 cm. ISBN: 0314034943 (alk. paper) Notes: "A report of the Justice Research Institute." Includes bibliographical references (p. 303-426) and index. Subjects: Appellate Courts--United States. Appellate procedure--United States. Law reform--United States. LC Classification: KF8750 .B35 1994 Dewey Class No.: 347.73/24 347.3073 20

Baldwin, Simeon Eben, 1840-1927. A digest of all the reported cases decided in the Supreme court of errors and the Superior court of the state of Connecticut, and in the United States Courts for the district of Connecticut, down to those contained in vol. XLVII. Connecticut reports, and vol. XVII. Blatchford's Circuit court reports, inclusive. By Simeon E. Baldwin ... Published/Created: Boston, Little, Brown, 1871-82. Related Authors: Connecticut. Supreme court of errors. Connecticut. Superior court. United States. Courts. Description: 2 v. 27 cm. Notes: Includes index. Subjects: Law reports, digests, etc.--Connecticut. LC Classification: KFC3654 .B3 1871

Baldwin, Simeon Eben, 1840-1927. The American judiciary / by Simeon E. Baldwin. Published/Created: Littleton, Colo.: F.B. Rothman, 1992. Description: xiii, 403 p.; 22 cm. ISBN: 0837719224 (alk. paper) : Notes: Reprint. Originally published: New York: Century Co., 1905. (The American state series). Includes bibliographical references and index. Subjects: Courts--United States. Series: American state series LC Classification: KF8719 .B3 1991 Dewey Class No.: 347.73/1 347.3071 20

Baldwin, Simeon Eben, 1840-1927. The American judiciary / by Simeon E. Baldwin; with an introd. by Richard M. Pious. Published/Created: Farmingdale, N.Y.: Dabor Social Science Publications, c1978. Description: xiii, 403 p.; 22 cm. ISBN: 0895610809 Notes: Reprint of the 1905 ed. published by Century Co., New York, in Series: The American state series. Includes index. Subjects: Courts--United States. Law--United States--History. LC Classification: KF8719 .B3 1978 Dewey Class No.: 347/.73

Baldwin, Simeon Eben, 1840-1927. The American judiciary. Published/Created: New York, Century Co., 1905. Description: xiii, 403p. 20cm. Subjects: Law--United States--History. Courts--United States. LC Classification: KF8719 .B3

Ball, Howard, 1937- Courts and politics: the federal judicial system / Howard Ball. Edition Information: 2nd ed. Published/Created: Englewood Cliffs, N.J.: Prentice-Hall, c1987. Description: vi, 314 p.: ill.; 24 cm. ISBN: 0131846647 (pbk.)

Notes: Includes index. Bibliography: p. 299-308. Subjects: Courts--United States. Judicial process--United States. Political questions and judicial power--United States. Judges--United States. LC Classification: KF8700 .B33 1987 Dewey Class No.: 347.73/2 347.3071 19

Ball, Howard, 1937- Courts and politics: the Federal judicial system / Howard Ball. Published/Created: Englewood Cliffs, N.J.: Prentice-Hall, c1980. Description: xiv, 303 p.: ill.; 23 cm. ISBN: 0131846558 : Notes: Includes indexes. Bibliography; p. 281-290. Subjects: Courts--United States. Judicial process--United States. Political questions and judicial power--United States. Judges--United States. LC Classification: KF8700 .B33 Dewey Class No.: 347.73/2 347.3071 19

Barbour, Oliver L. (Oliver Lorenzo), 1811-1889. An analytical digest of the equity cases decided in the Courts of the several states, and of the United States; in the Courts of Chancery and Exchequer in England and Ireland, and in the English Privy Council and House of lords, since the year 1836. By Oliver L. Barbour. Published/Created: Springfield, Mass., G. and C. Merriam, 1843. Related Authors: United States. Courts. Great Britain. Court of Chancery. Great Britain. Court of Exchequer. Ireland. Court of Chancery. Ireland. Court of Exchequer. Great Britain. Parliament. House of Lords. Great Britain. Privy Council. Description: xxiii, 737 p. 25 cm. Subjects: Law reports, digests, etc.--United States. Law reports, digests, etc.--Great Britain. Equity. LC Classification: LAW

Barclay, Shepard, 1847- The American system of law, as a conservator of republican institutions Published/Created: [St. Louis? 1903] Description: p. cm. Subjects: Courts--United States. Law--United States. LC Classification: JK1544 .B3

Barnes, Patricia G. Congressional Quarterly's desk reference on American Courts / Patricia G. Barnes. Published/Created: Washington, D.C.: CQ Press, c2000. Description: ix, 301 p.: ill.; 25 cm. ISBN: 1568024355 (cloth) Notes: Includes bibliographical references (p. 283-284) and index. Subjects: Courts--United States--Popular works. Justice, Administration of--United States--Popular works. Series: Desk reference series LC Classification: KF8720 .B37 2000 Dewey Class No.: 347.73/1 21

Barrister of the state of Virginia. A summary review of the laws of the United States of North-America, the British provinces and West-Indies: with observations, precedents, &c. / by a Barrister of the state of Virginia. Published/Created: Edinburgh: Printed for T. and J. Ruddiman, and G.G.J. and J. Robinson, London, 1788. Description: iv, 103, [1] p.; 22 cm. (8vo) Notes: Signatures: pi² A-N4. References: Cohen, M. Bib. of early Amer. law, 5424 Subjects: Law--United States--Early works to 1800. Law--Great Britain--Early works to 1800. Courts--United States--Early works to 1800. Courts--Great Britain--Early works to 1800. Law--West Indies, British--Early works to 1800. LC Classification: KF68 .B37 1788

Barrow, Deborah J., 1952- The federal judiciary and institutional change / Deborah J. Barrow, Gary Zuk, and Gerard S. Gryski. Published/Created: Ann Arbor: University of Michigan Press, c1996. Related Authors: Zuk, Gary, 1950- Gryski, Gerard S. Description: xiv, 143 p.: ill.; 24 cm. ISBN: 0472106341 (hardcover: alk. paper) Notes: Includes bibliographical references (p. 103-138) and index. Subjects: Courts--United States--History. Coalition governments--United States--History. Law and politics--History. LC Classification: KF8719 .B35 1996 Dewey Class No.: 347.73/1/09 347.307109 20

Bartollas, Clemens. Participants in American criminal justice: the promise and the performance / Clemens Bartollas, Stuart J. Miller, Paul B. Wice, with chapters by Roy C. McLaren, William B. Sanders, William F. Wegener. Published/Created: Englewood Cliffs, NJ: Prentice-Hall, c1983. Related Authors: Miller, Stuart J., 1938- Wice, Paul B. Description: xvii, 380 p.: ill.; 24 cm. ISBN: 0136513492 : Notes: Includes bibliographies and index. Subjects: Criminal justice, Administration of--United States. Law enforcement--United States. Courts--United States. Corrections--United States. Series: Prentice-Hall series in criminal justice LC Classification: HV6789 .B33 1983 Dewey Class No.: 364/.973 19

Basic issues in Courts performance / Thomas J. Cook ... [et al.]. Published/Created: Washington, D.C.: U.S. Dept. of Justice, National Institute of Justice, 1982. Related Authors: Cook, Thomas J. Research Triangle Institute. National Institute of Justice (U.S.) Description: ix, 195 p.; 28 cm. Notes: "Project was supported by grant number 78-NI-AX-0113, awarded to the Research Triangle Institute by the National Institute of Justice "--T.p. verso. "July 1982." Item 718-A Includes bibliographical references. Subjects: Criminal Courts--United States--Evaluation. LC Classification: KF9223 .B34 1982 Dewey Class No.: 345.73/01 347.3051 19 Govt. Doc. No.: J 28.2:C 83

Batori, George J. No justice in any court: judges, clerks, and lawyers unmasked, an improved justice / by George J. Batori. Published/Created: Athol Springs, N.Y. (P.O. Box 443, Athol Springs 14010): Pro Patria, [1983] Description: 126 p.: ill.; 22 cm. Notes: Includes bibliographical references. Subjects: Justice, Administration of--United States. Courts--United States. LC Classification: KF8700.Z9 B35 1983 Dewey Class No.: 347.73/1 347.3071 19

Baum, Lawrence. American Courts: process and policy / Lawrence Baum. Edition Information: 5th ed. Published/Created: Boston: Houghton Mifflin Co., c2001. Description: xvii, 348 p.: ill., 1 map; 24 cm. ISBN: 0618122893 Notes: Includes bibliographical references and indexes. Subjects: Courts--United States. Judicial process--United States. LC Classification: KF8700 .B38 2001

Baum, Lawrence. American Courts: process and policy / Lawrence Baum. Edition Information: 4th ed. Published/Created: Boston, MA: Houghton Mifflin Co., c1998. Description: xvi, 363 p.: ill., 1 map; 24 cm. ISBN: 0395871050 Notes: Includes bibliographical references and indexes. Subjects: Courts--United States. Judicial process--United States. LC Classification: KF8700 .B38 1998 Dewey Class No.: 347.73/1 21

Baum, Lawrence. American Courts: process and policy / Lawrence Baum. Edition Information: 3rd ed. Published/Created: Boston: Houghton Mifflin, c1994. Description: xii, 369 p.: ill.; 24 cm. ISBN: 0395675391 Notes: Includes bibliographical references and index. Subjects: Courts--United States. Judicial process--United States. LC Classification: KF8700 .B38 1994 Dewey Class No.: 347.73/1 347.3071 20

Baum, Lawrence. American Courts: process and policy / Lawrence Baum. Edition Information: 2nd ed. Published/Created: Boston: Houghton Mifflin, c1990. Description: x, 374 p.: ill.; 24 cm. ISBN: 039543291X Notes: Includes bibliographical references. Subjects: Courts--United States. Judicial process--United States. LC Classification: KF8700 .B38 1990 Dewey Class No.: 347.73 20

Baum, Lawrence. American Courts: process and policy / Lawrence Baum. Published/Created: Boston: Houghton Mifflin Co., c1986. Description: xv, 343 p.: ill.; 24 cm. ISBN: 0395350042 (pbk.) Notes: Includes bibliographies and index. Subjects: Courts--United States. Judicial process--United States. LC Classification: KF8700 .B38 1986 Dewey Class No.: 347.73/1 347.3071 19

Baum, Lawrence. The Supreme Court / Lawrence Baum. Edition Information: 7th ed. Published/Created: Washington, D.C.: CQ Press, c2001. Description: xi, 297 p.: ill.; 24 cm. ISBN: 1568025246 (cloth) 1568025238 (pbk.) Notes: Includes bibliographical references (p. 276-279) and index. Subjects: United States. Supreme Court. Constitutional law--United States. Courts of last resort--United States. Judicial review--United States. LC Classification: KF8742 .B35 2001 Dewey Class No.: 347.73/26 21

Baum, Lawrence. The Supreme Court / Lawrence Baum. Edition Information: 6th ed. Published/Created: Washington, D.C.: CQ Press, c1998. Description: xi, 301 p.: ill.; 24 cm. ISBN: 1568023219 (cloth: alk. paper) 1568023200 (paper: alk. paper) Notes: Includes bibliographical references (p. 281-284) and indexes. Subjects: United States. Supreme Court. Constitutional law--United States. Courts of last resort--United States. Judicial review--United States. LC Classification: KF8742 .B35 1998 Dewey Class No.: 347.73/26 21

Bayard, James A. (James Asheton), 1767-1815. Speech of Mr. Bayard on the bill received from the Senate, entitled "An act to repeal certain acts respecting the organization of the Courts of the United States": delivered in the House of Representatives, Feb. 19, 1802. Published/Created: [Washington?: s.n., 1802?] Description: 34 p.; 22 cm. References: Shaw & Shoemaker 1850 Subjects: Courts--United States. LC Classification: KF8713.5 B39 1802

Bayard, James Asheton, 1767-1815. Speech of Mrs. Bayard, on the bill received from the Senate, Published/Created: [Washington? 1802] Related Authors: Miscellaneous Pamphlet Collection (Library of Congress) Description: 44 p. 22 cm. References: Shaw & Shoemaker 3443 Subjects: Courts--United States. LC Classification: JK1551 .B4

Bayard, James Asheton, 1767-1815. Speech of the Honorable James A. Bayard, of Delaware. Published/Created: Hartford, Printed by Hudson & Goodwin, 1802. Description: 48 p. 23 cm. Subjects: Courts--United States. LC Classification: JK1551 .B4 1802a

Benchbook for U.S. District Court judges. Edition Information: 4th ed. Published/Created: [Washington, D.C.]: Federal Judicial Center, 1996. Related Authors: Federal Judicial Center. Description: ix, 244 p.; 28 cm. Notes: Shipping list no.: 97-0140-P. Includes index. Subjects: Procedure (Law)--United States--Outlines, syllabi, etc. District Courts--United States--Rules and practice Outlines, syllabi, etc. Judges--United States--Handbooks, manuals, etc. LC Classification: KF8754.Z9 B46 1996 Dewey Class No.: 347.73/225 21 Govt. Doc. No.: JU 13.2:B 43

Benchmark Published/Created: Washington, D.C.: Center for Judicial Studies, c1984-c1993. Related Authors: Center for Judicial Studies (U.S.) Description: 5 v.; 26 cm. Introductory no., called Premier issue, issued in fall 1983. Vol. 1, no. 1 (Jan./Feb. 1984)-v. 5, no. 2 (winter 1993). ISSN: 0743-0310 Notes: Title from cover. SERBIB/SERLOC merged record Subjects: Constitutional law--United States--Periodicals. Courts--United States--Periodicals. LC Classification: KF4546.A3 B46 Dewey Class No.: 342.73/005 347.302005 19

Benson, Allan Louis, 1871-1940. The usurped power of the Courts, by Allan L. Benson. Published/Created: [New York] The Pearson publishing company, c1911. Description: 64 p. 20 cm. Subjects: Courts--United States. LC Classification: JK1541 .B4

Bent, James Appleton, 1853- The independent judiciary; a treatise on the reform of the judiciary by the nonpartisan selection of judges, by James A. Bent ... Published/Created: [Morgantown, W. Va., Morgantown printing & binding co., c1925] Description: 2 p.l., 3-115 p. 24 cm. Subjects: Courts--United States. Law reform--United States. Judges--United States. LC Classification: KF8700.Z9 B4 1925

Bentley, Elizabeth Petty. County courthouse book / Elizabeth Petty Bentley. Edition Information: 2nd ed. Published/Created: Baltimore, Md.: Genealogical Pub. Co., c1995. Description: viii, 397 p.; 28 cm. ISBN: 0806314850 Subjects: County Courts--United States--Directories. Courthouses--United States--Directories. Court records--Research--United States--Directories. United States--Genealogy. LC Classification: KF8700.A19 B46 1995 Dewey Class No.: 347.73/22/025 347.302025 20

Bentley, Elizabeth Petty. County courthouse book / Elizabeth Petty Bentley. Published/Created: Baltimore, Md.: Genealogical Pub. Co., c1990. Description: ix, 386 p.; 28 cm. ISBN: 080631284X : Notes: Includes bibliographical references (p. ix). Subjects: County Courts--Courthouses--Court records--Research--United States--Directories. United States--Genealogy. LC Classification: KF8700.A19 B46 1990 Dewey Class No.: 347.73/22/025 347.3072025 20

Berger, Raoul, 1901- Death penalties: the Supreme Court's obstacle course / Raoul Berger. Published/Created: Cambridge, Mass.: Harvard University Press, 1982. Description: vii, 242 p.; 25 cm. ISBN: 0674194268 Notes: Includes indexes. Bibliography: p. 205-216. Subjects: United States. Supreme Court. Capital punishment--United States. LC Classification: KF9227.C2 B47 1982 Dewey Class No.: 345.73/0773 347.305773 19

Berkson, Larry Charles. Court unification: history, politics and implementation / by Larry Berkson and Susan Carbon, with the assistance of Judy Rosenbaum. Published/Created: [Washington]: National Institute of Law Enforcement and Criminal Justice, Law Enforcement Assistance Administration, U.S. Dept. of Justice, 1978. Related Authors: Carbon, Susan J., joint author. Rosenbaum, Judith, joint author. Description: xii, 259 p.: ill.; 26 cm. Notes: Includes bibliographical references. Subjects: Courts--United States--States. LC Classification: KF8700.Z95 B47 Dewey Class No.: 347.73/1 19

Bermant, Gordon. Jury selection procedures in United States District Courts / by Gordon Bermant. Published/Created: Washington, D.C.: Federal Judicial Center, 1982. Related Authors: Federal Judicial Center. Description: iii, 60 p.; 24 cm. Notes: "June 1982." "FCJ-ETS-82-1"--t.p. verso. Item 743-C-4 Subjects: Jury selection--United States. District Courts--United States. Series: Education and training series (Federal Judicial Center); 82-1. LC Classification: KF8979 .B474 1982 Dewey Class No.: 347.73/752 347.307752 19 Govt. Doc. No.: Ju 13.9:82-1

Bermant, Gordon. The cases of the United States Court of Appeals for the District of Columbia Circuit / by Gordon Bermant, Patricia A. Lombard, and Carroll Seron; assisted by Rama Bar-Adon, Joseph Matta, and Sam Spina. Published/Created: Washington, D.C.: Federal Judicial Center, 1982. Related Authors: Lombard, Patricia A. Seron, Carroll. Federal Judicial Center. Description: xiii, 56 p.: ill.; 24 cm. Notes: "July 1982." Item 743-C-3 Includes bibliographical references. Subjects: United States. Court of Appeals (District of Columbia Circuit) Court congestion and delay--United States. Appellate Courts--United States. Series: FJC-R; 82-3 LC Classification: KF8727 .B47 1982 Dewey Class No.: 347.73/24/0264 347.307240264 19 Govt. Doc. No.: Ju 13.10:82-3

Bias in the court!: focusing on the behavior of judges, lawyers, and court staff in court interactions. Published/Created: [Williamsburg, VA]: National Center for State Courts, [c1997] Related Authors: National Center for State Courts. Description: 1 v. (various pagings); 28 cm. ISBN: 0896561763 Notes: Includes bibliographical references. Subjects: Court administration--United States. Conduct of court proceedings--United States. Bias (Law)--United States. Series: Access to justice for persons of color; model guide 2 Publication (National Center for State Courts); R-195. LC Classification: KF8720 .B47 1997 Dewey Class No.: 347.73/12 21

Bickford, Hugh Craig, 1900- Court procedure in federal tax cases, Edition Information: Rev. ed. Published/Created: New York, Prentice-Hall, inc., 1929. Description: xl, 440 p. 24 cm. Subjects: United States. Tax court. Circuit Courts of Appeals. District of Columbia. Court of appeals. District Courts. United States. Supreme court. Civil procedure--Appellate procedure--Court rules--Forms (Law)--United States. LC Classification: KF6320 .B48 1929

Biggs, James Crawford, 1872- Address by the president, J. Crawford Biggs, Published/Created: Wilmington, N.C., Wilmington stamp & printing co. [1915] Description: p.cm. Subjects: Courts-United States. LC Classification: JK1541 .B46

Biggs, James Crawford, 1872- The power of the judiciary over legislation. Address delivered beofre the North Carolina bar association at its seventeenth annual convention held in Asheville, N.C., on August 2, 1915, Published/Created: Washington, Govt. print. off., 1916. Description: 27 p. 23 cm Subjects: Courts--United States. LC Classification: JK1541 .B45

Biographical directory of the federal judiciary. Published/Created: Lanham, MD: Bernan, c2001- Description: v.; 29 cm. 1st ed. (1789-2000)- ISSN: 1530-9797 Subjects: Courts--United States--Directories. Judges--United States--Biography--Dictionaries. Courts--United States--Registers.

Biskupic, Joan. The Supreme Court at work. Edition Information: 2nd ed. / Joan Biskupic and Elder Witt. Published/Created: Washington, D.C.: Congressional Quarterly Inc., c1997. Related Authors: Witt, Elder. Description: vii, 402 p.: ill.; 28 cm. ISBN: 1568023235 (acid-free paper) Notes: Rev. ed. of: The Supreme Court at work. c1990. Includes bibliographical references (p. 381-382) and index. Subjects: United States. Supreme Court. Courts of last resort--United States. LC Classification: KF8742 .S912 1997 Dewey Class No.: 347.73/26 347.30735 20

Bissell, Josiah Hooker, 1845-1901, comp. Rules of all the Courts of record applicable in the city of Chicago, and the special practice acts for Courts in Cook county. Published/Created: Chicago, Callaghan & Cockcroft, 1869. Related Authors: United States. Courts. Illinois. Courts. Chicago. Courts. Description: 3 p.l., [3]-213 p., 1 l. 23 cm. Subjects: Court rules--Chicago. Court rules--Cook co., Ill. LC Classification: KFI1729 .A2 1869

Bizzell, William Bennett, 1876-1944. Judicial interpretation of political theory; a study in the relation of the Courts to the American party system, by William Bennett Bizzell. Published/Created: New York and London, G. P. Putnam's sons, 1914. Description: v, 273 p. 21 cm. Notes: "The contents of this volume consist in the main of a series of lectures delivered at the Illinois college of law in 1910." Subjects: Courts--United States. LC Classification: KF4575 .B5

Blachly, Frederick Frank 1880- Some consequences of judicial review Published/Created: Berlin und Leipzig, W. de Gryter co. 1929 Related Authors: Oatman, Miriam Eulalie, 1887- joint author. Description: [1], [500]-511 p. 27 cm. Subjects: United States. Supreme court. Courts--United States. United States--Constitutional law. LC Classification: LAW

Blachly, Frederick Frank, 1880- Federal regulatory action and control, by Frederick F. Blachly and Miriam E. Oatman. Published/Created: Washington, D.C., Brookings Institution, 1940. Related Authors: Oatman, Miriam E. (Miriam Eulalie), b. 1887, joint author Description: xviii, 356 p. 24 cm. Notes: "Published March 1940" Subjects: Administrative law--Executive departments--Executive power--Legislation--Courts--United States. Series: Studies in administration (Washington, D.C.) LC Classification: KF5402 .B53

Blachly, Frederick Frank, 1880- Working papers on administrative adjudication, by Frederick F. Blachly ... Published/Created:

[Washington] U.S. Govt Print Off., 1938. Description: 1 p. l., 170 p. 30 x 49 cm. Notes: At head of title: 75th Congress, 3d session. Committee print. Subjects: Administrative law--United States. Executive departments--United States. Administrative Courts--United States. LC Classification: KF5417 .B55

Blasi, Vince. Federal Courts. Published/Created: Austin, Institute for Texas Bar Review, inc. [1969] Related Authors: Institute for Texas Bar Review. Description: 33 l. 22 x 36 cm. Notes: Caption title. Subjects: Courts--United States--Compends. LC Classification: KF8720 .B5 Dewey Class No.: 347.99/73

Bliss, Philemon, 1814-1889. The Federal judiciary. Speech of Hon. Philemon Bliss, of Ohio, in the United States House of Representatives, February 7, 1859. Published/Created: [Washington, 1859] Description: 8 p. 26 cm. Notes: Caption title. Subjects: Courts--United States. Judges--United States. LC Classification: JK1507.1859 .B4

BNA's directory of state and federal Courts, judges, and clerks. Published/Created: Washington, D.C.: Bureau of National Affairs, c1992- Related Authors: King, Kamla J. Miller, Judith A. BNA Library (Washington, D.C.) Bureau of National Affairs (Washington, D.C.) Description: v.; 28 cm. Vols. for 1994-95- carry chronological designation only. 4th ed.- ISSN: 1078-5582 Notes: "A state-by-state and federal listing." Vols. for 1992-<1994-95 compiled by Kamla J. King and Judith Springberg with the BNA library staff. SERBIB/SERLOC merged record Subjects: Courts--United States--States--Directories. Judges--United States--States--Directories. Clerks of court--United States--States--Directories. Courts--United States--Directories. Judges--United States--Directories. Clerks of court--United States--Directories. LC Classification: KF8700.A19 B53 Dewey Class No.: 347.73/1/025 347.3071025 20

BNA's directory of state Courts, judges, and clerks. Published/Created: Washington, D.C.: BNA Books, c1986-c1990. Related Authors: King, Kamla J. Modlin, Marilyn J. Miller, Judith A. BNA Library (Washington, D.C.) Description: 3 v.; 28 cm. Vols. for 1988-1990 called 2nd ed.-3rd ed. [1st ed.]-3rd ed. Notes: Compiled, with the BNA Library Staff, by Kamla J. King and Marilyn J. Modlin, 1986; and by Kamla J. King and Judith Springberg, 1988-1990. "A state-by-state listing." SERBIB/SERLOC merged record Subjects: Courts--United States--States--Directories. Judges--United States--States--Directories. Clerks of court--United States--States--Directories. LC Classification: KF8700.A19 B53 Dewey Class No.: 347.73/1/025 347.3071025 20

Boardman, Henry A. (Henry Augustus), 1808-1880. The federal judiciary: a Thanksgiving discourse / by Henry A. Boardman. Published/Created: Philadelphia: W.S. & A. Martien, 1862. Related Authors: YA Pamphlet Collection (Library of Congress) Description: 54 p.; 22 cm. Notes: Cover title: The judiciary. Subjects: Judicial power--United States. Courts--United States. Thanksgiving Day addresses. LC Classification: KF8775.Z9 B6

Bonney, Charles Carroll, 1831-1903. The doctrine of judicial supremacy. Published/Created: Philadelphia, Press of G.S. Harris & sons, 1883. Description: 10 p. 23 cm. Subjects: Courts--United States. LC Classification: JK1541 .B6

Borah, Wayne G., 1891-1966. Papers of Wayne G. Borah, 1928-1950 (bulk 1947-1949) Description: 800 items. 3 containers. 1.25 linear feet. Summary: Case files, charges to juries, and reports of the U.S. Dept. of Justice examiners pertaining primarily to Borah's service (1928-1949) as judge on the U.S. District Court for the Eastern District of Louisiana. Relates chiefly to shipping disputes involving maritime vessels and railroad companies. Notes: Formerly part of: J. Skelly Wright papers. MSS80800 Subjects: United States.

District Court (Louisiana: Eastern District) District Courts--United States. Freight and freightage--United States. Railroads--United States--Traffic. Shipment of goods--United States. Shipping--United States. Jurists. Lawyers. Local Call/Shelving: MMC-3574

Bork, Robert H. Papers of Robert H. Bork, 1924-1987 (bulk 1962-1982) Description: 10,680 items. 31 containers plus 1 OV plus 1 CL. 14.2 linear feet. Summary: Personal and official correspondence, lectures, legal briefs and opinions, legal case files, memoranda, speeches, writings, research notes, and other papers documenting Bork's career as a lawyer, legal scholar, professor of law, and federal Appellate court judge. Includes material on antitrust law, legislative encroachments, the role of the Supreme Court in capitalist society, and the Watergate Affair (particularly Bork's firing of special prosecutor Archibald Cox); Bork's affiliation with Yale Law School, the U.S. Dept. of Justice, and the American Enterprise Institute for Public Policy Research; his association with Alexander M. Bickel and the Freedom of Information Act; and the failure of Bork's nomination to the Supreme Court in 1987. Correspondents include William J. Baroody, Alexander M. Bickel, James H. Billington, Hammond E. Chaffetz, Charles W. Colson, Edward De Grazia, Milton Friedman, Barry Goldwater, Alexander Meigs Haig, H. R. Haldeman, Howard G. Krane, Irving Kristol, Thomas B. Leary, Edward Hirsch Levi, Thurgood Marshall, Abner J. Mikva, Richard M. Nixon, Bernard J. Nussbaum, Benjamin H. Read, Donald H. Rivkin, Frederick M. Rowe, and Lawrence E. Walsh. Notes: MSS65871 Subjects: Baroody, William J., 1916-1980 --Correspondence. Bickel, Alexander M.--Correspondence. Billington, James H.--Correspondence. Chaffetz, Hammond E.--Correspondence. Colson, Charles W.--Correspondence. Cox, Archibald, 1912- De Grazia, Edward, 1927- --Correspondence. Friedman, Milton, 1912- --Correspondence. Goldwater, Barry M. (Barry Morris), 1909- Correspondence. Haig, Alexander Meigs, 1924- --Correspondence. Haldeman, H. R. (Harry R.), 1926- --Correspondence. Krane, Howard G.--Correspondence. Kristol, Irving--Correspondence. Learu. Thomas B. (Thomas Barrett), 1931- --Correspondence. Levi, Edward Hirsch, 1911- --Correspondence. Marshall, Thurgood, 1908-1993 --Correspondence. Mikva, Abner J.--Correspondence. Nixon, Richard M. (Richard Milhous), 1913-Correspondence. Nussbaum, Bernard J., 1931- --Correspondence. Read, Benjamin H. (Benjamin Huger), 1925-Correspondence. Rivkin, Donald H. (Donald Herschel), 1924- Correspondence. Rowe, Frederick M.--Correspondence. Walsh, Lawrence E.--Correspondence. American Enterprise Institute for Public Policy Research. United States. Dept. of Justice. United States. Freedom of Information Act. United States. Supreme Court. Yale Law School. Antitrust law--United States. Appellate Courts--United States. Capitalism--United States. Law--Study and teaching. Legislative power--United States. Watergate Affair, 1972-1974. Educators. Jurists. Lawyers. Local Call/Shelving: 0447C OVSD VAULT 0705C (Unprocessed ac. 22,097) 0706C (Unprocessed ac. 22,295)

Bortner, M. A., 1948- Inside a juvenile court: the tarnished ideal of individualized justice / M.A. Bortner. Published/Created: New York: New York University Press, 1982. Description: vii, 283 p.; 24 cm. ISBN: 0814710417 : Notes: Includes index. Bibliography: p. [271]-279. Subjects: Juvenile Courts--United States. Juvenile delinquency--United States. LC Classification: KF9794 .B67 1982 Dewey Class No.: 345.73/081 347.30581 19

Bosworth, Matthew H. Courts as catalysts: state supreme Courts and public school finance equity / Matthew H. Bosworth. Published/Created: Albany: State University of New York Press, c2001. Description: viii, 290 p.; 24 cm. ISBN: 0791450139 (HC: alk. paper) 0791450147 (PB: alk. paper) Notes: Includes bibliographical references (p. 263-280) and index. Subjects: Political questions and judicial power--United States States. Courts of last resort--United States.--States. Law reform--United States--States. Education--Finance--Law and legislation--United States States. Education--United States--Finance. LC Classification: KF8775 .B67 2001 Dewey Class No.: 344.73/076 21

Breckenridge, Ralph W., 1860- The Constitution, the court, and the people. Published/Created: Washington [Govt. print. off.] 1913. Description: 17 p. 24 cm. Subjects: United States. Constitution. Courts--United States. United States--Constitutional law. LC Classification: JK1544 .B7

Breckinridge, Sophonisba Preston, 1866-1948. Social work and the Courts; select statutes and judicial decisions, by Sophonisba P. Breckinridge. Published/Created: Chicago, Ill., The University of Chicago press [c1934] Description: xv, 610 p. 24 cm. Notes: The documents in this volume supplement the documents and the material presented in the courses on "Public welfare administration" and "The family and the state." cf. Introd. "A selected bibliography": p. 591-601. Subjects: Social service. Justice, Administration of--United States. Courts--United States. Legal aid--United States. LC Classification: Law Dewey Class No.: 361.8

Brewer, William E. Winning in small claims court: a step-by-step guide for citizen litigators / by William E. Brewer. Edition Information: 1st ed. Published/Created: Marietta, GA: Law Works Pub., 1995. Description: 216 p.: forms; 28 cm. ISBN: 0964678764 Notes: Includes index. Subjects: Small claims Courts--United States--Popular works. LC Classification: KF8769.Z9 B736 1995 Dewey Class No.: 347.73/28 347.3074 20

Brewer, William E. Winning in small claims court: a step-by-step guide for trying your own small claims cases / by William E. Brewer. Published/Created: Franklin Lakes, NJ: Career Press, c1999. Description: 185 p.: forms; 28 cm. ISBN: 1564143740 Notes: Includes index. Subjects: Small claims Courts--United States--Popular works. LC Classification: KF8769.Z9 B738 1999 Dewey Class No.: 347.73/28 21

Brewster, Stanley F. (Stanley Farrar), 1889- Federal procedure / by Stanley F. Brewster Published/Created: Chicago: Callaghan, 1940. Related Authors: United States. Supreme Court. United States. District Court (District of Columbia) Description: xxxvii, 769 p.; 26 cm. Contents: Federal jurisdiction -- Federal civil procedure -- Federal criminal procedure. Notes: "Table of cases": p. 701-731. "Federal bibliography": p. 84-88. Subjects: Courts--United States. Jurisdiction--United States. Civil procedure--United States. Criminal procedure--United States. Appellate procedure--United States. Equity pleading and procedure--United States. LC Classification: KF8840 .B7

Brewster, Stanley F. (Stanley Farrar), 1889- Twelve men in a box / by Stanley F. Brewster; with a foreword by Clarence E. Martin. Published/Created: Chicago: Callaghan, 1934. Description: xiii, 175 p.; 23 cm. Subjects: Jury--United States. Courts--United States. Justice, Administration of--United States. Civil procedure--United States. Criminal procedure--United States. Trial practice--United States. LC Classification: KF89720.Z9 B7

Brhel, Martin C. Courtroom survival for small claims court litigants / by Martin C. Brhel, Jr. Published/Created: [Palm Springs, CA: Copper Bible Bk. Co., c1989] Description: i, 131 p.; 28 cm. ISBN: 0944380018 Subjects: Small claims Courts--United States--Popular works. Civil procedure--United States. LC Classification: KF8769.Z9 B74 1989 Dewey Class No.: 347.73/04 347.73074 20

Brightly, Frank Frederick, 1845- A digest of the decisions of all the Courts of the state of New York, from the earliest period [1794] to the year 1892, Published/Created: New York, Albany,

Banks and brothers, 1893. Related Authors: New York (State) Courts. Description: 4 v. 28 cm. Subjects: Law reports, digests, etc.--New York (State) LC Classification: LAW

Brightly, Frederick C. (Frederick Charles), 1812-1888. A digest of the decisions of the federal Courts, from the organization of the government to the present time [1789-1870]. By Frederick C. Brightly ... Published/Created: Philadelphia, Kay & brother, 1868-70. Related Authors: United States. Courts. Description: 2 v. 27 cm. Notes: Vol. 1: 1789-1868; v. 2: 1868-1870. Subjects: Law reports, digests, etc.--United States. LC Classification: LAW

Brightly, Frederick C. (Frederick Charles), 1812-1888. A digest of the decisions of the federal Courts, from the organization of the government to the present time [1789-1873]. By Frederick C. Brightly ... Published/Created: Philadelphia, Kay & brother, 1868-73. Related Authors: United States. Courts. Description: 2 v. 27 cm. Notes: Vol. 2: 2d edition. Vol. 1: 1789-1868; v. 2: 1868-1873. Subjects: Law reports, digests, etc.--United States. LC Classification: LAW

Brightly, Frederick Charles, 1812-1888. A digest of the decisions of the Courts of the state of New York, from the earliest period 1794 to 1884, embracing not only all the reported cases contained in the regular series of reports, but also those in the Practice reports, and the legal periodicals of the day, with a table of overruled and reversed cases. Published/Created: New York, Albany, Banks & brothers, 1875-84. Related Authors: New York (State). Courts. Description: 3 v. 28 cm. Subjects: Law reports, digests, etc.--New York (State) LC Classification: LAW

Brindze, Ruth, 1903- All about Courts and the law. Illustrated by Leonard Slonevsky. Foreword by Erwin N. Griswold. Published/Created: New York, Random House [1964] Description: 138 p. illus. 24cm. Subjects: Justice, Administration of--United States--Juvenile literature. Courts--United States--Juvenile literature. LC Classification: KF8700.Z9 B67 Dewey Class No.: 347.90973

Brown, Arthur March, 1876- Guide to federal and bankruptcy practice; Published/Created: Albany, N.Y., M. Bender & company, incorporated, 1933. Related Authors: United States. Supreme court. United States. Circuit Courts of Appeals. Description: xxv, 1010 p. 26 cm. Subjects: Courts--United States. Jurisdiction--United States. Admirality--United States. Bankruptcy--United States. Civil procedure--United States. Criminal procedure--United States. Equity pleading and procedure--United States. Appellate procedure--United States. Forms (Law)--United States. LC Classification: KF1527 .B7

Brown, Henry Billings, 1836-1913. The new federal Judicial code; address by Justice Henry B. Brown ... before the American bar association, delivered at Boston, Massachusetts, August 30, 1911. Published/Created: [n.p., 1911?] Description: 22 p. 23 cm. Subjects: Courts--United States. LC Classification: KF8700.Z9 B7

Brown, James, 1766-1835. Papers of James Brown, 1765-1867 (bulk 1800-1810) Description: 500 items. 5 v. Summary: Correspondence, legal and commercial documents, pertaining to Brown's Louisiana law practice and his service as U.S. senator. Papers primarily concern legal practices and social conditions in Louisiana. Includes papers relating to the court-martial of U.S. Army officer, Thomas Butler (1804-1805). Correspondents include James's brother, U.S. Senator John Brown, and a second brother, Samuel. Notes: In English and Spanish. MSS14076 Subjects: Brown, John, 1757-1837. Brown, Samuel, 1769-1837. Butler, Thomas, 1748-1805. United States. Army--Officers. United States. Congress. Senate. Courts-martial and Courts of inquiry. Procedure (Law)--Louisiana. Louisiana--Politics and government. Louisiana--Social conditions.

Diplomats. Lawyers. Senators, U.S. Local Call/Shelving: MMC-3215

Browne, Joseph G. M. (Joseph Greengrass Maximillian), b. 1890. New York State Appellate practice and procedure: a practical discussion on the practice and procedure in the Appellate Courts of the State of New York: elements of jurisdiction, illustrative forms, rules of practice, tables of cases and general index / by Joseph G.M. Browne. Published/Created: Brooklyn: Federal Publications, 1932. Description: x, 261 p.: forms; 26 cm. Notes: Includes index. Subjects: New York (State). Court of Appeals--Rules and practice. New York (State). Supreme Court. Appellate Division. Rules and practice. Appellate procedure--New York (State) Court rules--United States. LC Classification: KFN6075 .B9

Bruce, Andrew A. (Andrew Alexander), 1866-1934. The American judge by Andrew Alexander Bruce Published/Created: New York The Macmillan company 1924 Description: 4 p. 1., 218 p. 20 cm. Subjects: Judges--United States. Courts--United States. Law reform LC Classification: KF8700 .B7

Buchanan, James, president, U. S., 1791-1868. Speech of Hon. James Buchanan, of Pennsylvania, Published/Created: Washington, Printed at the Globe office, 1842. Description: 16 p. 25 cm. Subjects: Courts--United States. LC Classification: JK1591 .B8

Bunn, Charles Wilson, 1855- A brief survey of the jurisdiction and practice of the Courts of the United States, Edition Information: 2d ed. Published/Created: St Paul, West publishing company, 1921. Description: vi, 3-143 p. 19 cm. Subjects: Courts--United States. LC Classification: KF8720 .B8

Bunn, Charles Wilson, 1855-1941. A brief survey of the jurisdiction and practice of the Courts of the United States. Edition Information: 5th ed., by Charles Bunn. Published/Created: St. Paul, West Pub. Co., 1949. Description: ix, 408 p. 20 cm. Subjects: Courts--United States. Jurisdiction--United States. LC Classification: KF8858.Z9 B8 1949

Bunn, Charles Wilson, 1855-1941. A brief survey of the jurisdiction and practice of the Courts of the United States, by Charles W. Bunn. Edition Information: 4th ed., by Charles Bunn. Published/Created: St. Paul, West publishing company, 1939. Related Authors: Bunn, Charles, 1893- ed. Description: ix, 257 p. 20 cm. Notes: "Table of statutes": p. 213-220. "Table of cases": p. 221-243. Subjects: Courts--United States. Jurisdiction--United States. LC Classification: KF8720 .B8

Bunn, Charles Wilson, 1855-1941. A brief survey of the jurisdiction and practice of the Courts of the United States / by Charles W. Bunn. Edition Information: 3rd ed. Published/Created: St. Paul: West Pub. Co., 1927. Description: viii, 169 p.; 20 cm. Notes: Spine title: United States Courts. Includes index. Subjects: Courts--United States. Jurisdiction--United States. LC Classification: KF8720 .B8 1927

Burges, Tristam, 1770-1853. Speech of Mr. Burges, of R. I., on the judiciary bill. Delivered in the House of representatives of the United States, Jan 23, 1826. Published/Created: Washington, Printed by Gales & Seaton, 1826. Related Authors: Miscellaneous Pamphlet Collection (Library of Congress) Description: 24 p. 20 cm. References: Shoemaker 23967 Subjects: Courts--United States. LC Classification: AC901 .M5 vol. 250, no. 11

Business equipment and the courts: guide for court managers / Courts' Equipment Analysis Project; project staff, J. Michael Greenwood, project director ... [et al.]. Published/Created: Denver: National Center for State Courts, 1977. Related Authors: Greenwood, J. Michael. Description: x, 46 p.: ill.; 28 cm. Notes: "Summarizes ... conclusions detailed in [the project's Business equipment and the courts: a reference manual." Subjects: Court administration--United States--

Equipment and supplies. Series: Publication (National Center for State Courts); R0030. LC Classification: KF8732.7 .C68 Dewey Class No.: 347/.73/1028

Butler, Rush Clark, 1871- Before the House Judiciary committee, Published/Created: [n. p., 1934] Related Authors: Hurd, Ferris Evans, 1905- American federation of utility investors, incorporated. Description: cover-title, iii, 46 p. 23 cm. Subjects: United States District Courts. Public utilities--United States. Public service commissions--United States. LC Classification: RH2103.Z9 B2

Cahan, Richard. A court that shaped America: Chicago's federal District Court from Abe Lincoln to Abbie Hoffman / Richard Cahan; with a foreword by Marvin E. Aspen. Published/Created: Evanston, Ill.: Northwestern University Press, 2002. Description: p. cm. ISBN: 0810119811 (pbk.: alk. paper) Notes: Includes bibliographical references and index. Subjects: United States. District Court (Illinois: Northern District)--History. District Courts--Illinois--Chicago Metropolitan Area History. LC Classification: KF8755.I48 C34 2002 Dewey Class No.: 347.73/22/0977311 21

Caldwell, Frederick Perry, 1875- Notes to the Kentucky reports; being an alphabetically arranged table of all Kentucky cases subsequently cited to the court of appeals of Kentucky, with parallel citations, and with notes showing the point on which each case has been affirmed, approved, disapproved, distinguished, explained, followed, limited, modified, overruled, questioned or reconciled, together with a complete judicial history of every Kentucky case carried to the Supreme court of the United States, Published/Created: Cincinnati, The W.H. Anderson company [c1939] Related Authors: Barker, Albert H., ed. Kentucky. Court of appeals. Kentucky. Courts. United States. Supreme court. Description: 1 p.l., v-viii, 2322 p. 26 cm. Subjects: Law reports, digests, etc.--Kentucky. Annotations and citations (Law)--Kentucky. LC Classification: KFK1259 .C3 1939

Caldwell, Frederick Perry, 1875- Notes to the Kentucky reports; being an alphabetically arranged table of all Kentucky cases with reference to each publication in which the case is reported, and with notes showing the point on which each case has been followed, affirmed, approved, cited, construed, critcised, disapproved, distinguished, explained, modified, questioned, or overruled. Published/Created: Cincinnati, O., The W. H. Anderson company, 1907- Related Authors: Kentucky. Courts. Kentucky. Court of appeals. United States. District court. Kentucky (Eastern district) Description: v. 24 cm. Subjects: Law reports, digests, etc.--Kentucky. Annotations and citations (Law)--Kentucky. Court rules--Kentucky. Court rules--United States. LC Classification: KFK1259 .C3

California perspectives: four leaders look at the state of the State / Charles Warren ... [et al.]. Published/Created: Berkeley: Institute of Governmental Studies, University of California, 1977. Related Authors: Warren, Charles, 1927- Description: vii, 52 p.; 23 cm. ISBN: 0877722471 Contents: Warren, C. Critical resource issues of 1976.--McWilliams, C. Is California still exceptional?--Mosk, S. The California judiciary.--Cranston, A. California: representing a nation in the United States Senate. Notes: Includes bibliographical references. Subjects: Courts--California. California--Politics and government--1951- California--Economic conditions. California--Social conditions. LC Classification: JK8719 .C3 Dewey Class No.: 309.1/794/05

Callahan, Michael. Entrapment and the federal Courts / by Michael Callahan. Published/Created: [Washington, D.C.]: U.S. Dept. of Justice, Federal Bureau of Investigation, [1984] Related Authors: United States. Federal Bureau of Investigation. Description: ii, 64 p.; 28 cm.

Notes: "November, 1984." Subjects: Entrapment (Criminal law)--United States. Defense (Criminal procedure)--United States. Courts--United States. LC Classification: KF9244 .A83 1984

Callender, Clarence Newell, 1887- American Courts; their organization and procedure, Edition Information: 1st ed. Published/Created: New York [etc.] McGraw-Hill book company, inc., 1927. Description: p. cm. Subjects: Justices of the Peace--United States. Courts--United States. Pleading--United States. Civil procedure--United States. Appellate procedure--United States. Equity pleading and procedure--United States. Probate law and practice--United States. Criminal procedure--United States. Arbitration and award--United States. Forms (Law)--United States. LC Classification: KF8719 .C3

Callison, Israel Putnam, 1870- Courts of injustice. Published/Created: New York, Twayne Publishers [1956] Description: 775 p. 24 cm. Subjects: Justice, Administration of--United States--States. Courts--United States--States. Judges--United States--States. LC Classification: KF8700.Z95 C3 Dewey Class No.: 347.98*

Carbon, Susan J. Literature on court unification: an annotated bibliography / by Susan Carbon and Larry Berkson. Published/Created: Washington: National Institute of Law Enforcement and Criminal Justice, Law Enforcement Assistance Administration, U.S. Dept. of Justice: for sale by the Supt. of Docs., U.S. Govt. Print. Off., 1978. Related Authors: Berkson, Larry Charles, joint author. Description: v, 38 p.; 27 cm. Notes: "June 1978." Includes index. Subjects: Courts--United States--States--Bibliography. Court administration--United States--States--Bibliography. LC Classification: KF8736.A1 C37 Dewey Class No.: 016.34773/1 19

Carp, Robert A., 1943- Judicial process in America / Robert A. Carp, Ronald Stidham. Edition Information: 5th ed. Published/Created: Washington, D.C.: CQ Press, c2001. Related Authors: Stidham, Ronald, 1940- Description: xvii, 425 p.: ill.; 23 cm. ISBN: 1568025092 (alk. paper) Notes: Includes bibliographical references and indexes. Subjects: Justice, Administration of--United States. Courts--United States. Judicial process--United States. LC Classification: KF8700 .C37 2001 Dewey Class No.: 347.73/1 21

Carp, Robert A., 1943- Judicial process in America / Robert A. Carp, Ronald Stidham. Edition Information: 4th ed. Published/Created: Washington, D.C.: CQ Press, c1998. Related Authors: Stidham, Ronald, 1940- Description: xvi, 408 p.: ill, map; 23 cm. ISBN: 1568023944 Notes: Includes bibliographical references and index. Subjects: Courts--United States. Judges--United States. Judicial process--United States. LC Classification: KF8700 .C37 1998 Dewey Class No.: 347.73/1 21

Carp, Robert A., 1943- Judicial process in America / Robert A. Carp, Ronald Stidham. Edition Information: 3rd ed. Published/Created: Washington, D.C.: CQ Press, c1996. Related Authors: Stidham, Ronald, 1940- Description: xvi, 432 p.: ill.; 23 cm. ISBN: 087187833X (alk. paper) Notes: Includes bibliographical references and index. Subjects: Courts--United States. Judges--United States. Judicial process--United States. LC Classification: KF8700 .C37 1996 Dewey Class No.: 347.73/1 347.3071 20

Carp, Robert A., 1943- Judicial process in America / Robert A. Carp, Ronald Stidham. Edition Information: 2nd ed. Published/Created: Washington, D.C.: CQ Press, c1993. Related Authors: Stidham, Ronald, 1940- Description: xvi, 421 p.: ill.; 23 cm. ISBN: 0871877074 : Notes: Includes bibliographical references (p. 393-402) and index. Subjects: Courts--United States. Judges--United States. Judicial process--United States. LC Classification: KF8700 .C37 1992 Dewey Class No.: 347.73/1 347.3071 20

Carp, Robert A., 1943- Judicial process in America / Robert A. Carp, Ronald Stidham. Published/Created: Washington, D.C.: CQ Press, c1990. Related Authors: Stidham, Ronald, 1940- Description: xiii, 393 p.; 23 cm. ISBN: 0871874857 : Notes: Includes bibliographical references (p. 367-375) and index. Subjects: Courts--Judges--Judicial process--United States. LC Classification: KF8700 .C37 1989 Dewey Class No.: 347.73/1 347.3071 20

Carp, Robert A., 1943- Policymaking and politics in the federal District Courts / Robert A. Carp and C.K. Rowland. Edition Information: 1st ed. Published/Created: Knoxville: University of Tennessee Press, c1983. Related Authors: Rowland, C. K., 1943- Description: xiv, 203 p.: ill.; 23 cm. ISBN: 0870493698 : Notes: Includes index. Bibliography: p. [188]-199. Subjects: Judicial process--United States. District Courts--United States. LC Classification: KF8775 .C37 1983 Dewey Class No.: 347.73/22 347.3072 19

Carp, Robert A., 1943- The federal Courts / Robert A. Carp, Ronald Stidham. Edition Information: 4th ed. Published/Created: Washington, D.C.: CQ Press, 2001. Related Authors: Stidham, Ronald, 1940- Description: xiv, 258 p.: ill.; 23 cm. ISBN: 1568025912 (alk. paper) Notes: Includes bibliographical references and index. Subjects: Courts--United States. Judges--United States. Judicial process--United States. LC Classification: KF8719 .C33 2001 Dewey Class No.: 347.73/2 21

Carp, Robert A., 1943- The federal Courts / Robert A. Carp, Ronald Stidham. Edition Information: 3rd ed. Published/Created: Washington, D.C.: CQ Press, c1998. Related Authors: Stidham, Ronald, 1940- Description: xiii, 236 p.: ill.; 23 cm. ISBN: 0871878208 Notes: Includes bibliographical references and index. Subjects: Courts--Judges--Judicial process--United States. LC Classification: KF8719 .C33 1998 Dewey Class No.: 347.73/2 21

Carp, Robert A., 1943- The federal Courts / Robert A. Carp, Ronald Stidham. Edition Information: 2nd ed. Published/Created: Washington, D.C.: CQ Press, c1991. Related Authors: Stidham, Ronald, 1940- Description: xi, 253 p.; 23 cm. ISBN: 0871875802 : Notes: Includes bibliographical references (p. 239-246) and index. Subjects: Courts--United States. LC Classification: KF8719 .C33 1990 Dewey Class No.: 347.73/2 347.3071 20

Carp, Robert A., 1943- The federal Courts / Robert A. Carp, Ronald Stidham. Published/Created: Washington, D.C.: CQ Press, c1985. Related Authors: Stidham, Ronald, 1940- Description: xi, 258 p.: ill.; 23 cm. ISBN: 0871873494 (pbk.) : Notes: Includes index. Bibliography: p. 239-246. Subjects: Courts--United States. LC Classification: KF8719 .C33 1985 Dewey Class No.: 347.73/2 347.3071 19

Carpenter, William Seal, 1890-1957. Judicial tenure in the United States, with especial reference to the tenure of federal judges Published/Created: New Haven, Yale university press; [etc., etc.] 1918. Description: vii p., 1 l., 234 p. 19 cm. Notes: 1.Judges--United States. Subjects: Courts--United States. LC Classification: KF8776 .C3

Carr, Wm. Wilkins (William Wilkins), b. 1853. Judicial interpretation by the United States Courts of the acts of Congress relating to the tariff / by Wm. Wilkins Carr. Published/Created: Philadelphia: Johnson, 1894. Description: vii, 631 p.; 24 cm. Subjects: Tariff--Law and legislation--United States. LC Classification: KF6659 .C3

Carrigan, Jim R. Inherent powers of the Courts. Text material prepared by Jim R. Carrigan. Published/Created: [Reno, Nev.] National College of the State Judiciary [1973] Related Authors: National College of the State Judiciary. Description: 26 p. 26 cm. Subjects: Court administration--United States. Judicial power--United States. LC Classification: KF8732.Z9 C3 Dewey Class No.: 347/.73/1

Carrington, Paul D., 1931- Justice on appeal / by Paul D. Carrington, Daniel J. Meador, Maurice Rosenberg. Published/Created: St. Paul: West Pub. Co., 1976. Related Authors: Meador, Daniel John, joint author. Rosenberg, Maurice, 1919- joint author. Description: xv, 263 p.; 24 cm. Notes: Includes bibliographical references and indexes. Subjects: Appellate Courts--United States. LC Classification: KF8750 .C3 Dewey Class No.: 347/.73/24

Carroll's federal directory including Congress [electronic resource]. Published/Created: Washington, D.C.: Carroll Pub., [1994?] Description: 1 computer laser optical disc; 4 3/4 in. Nov./Dec. 1994. Notes: Title from disc label. System requirements: IBM PC or compatible; CD-ROM drive with MS-DOS extensions; MS Windows 3.1 or higher; 4MB RAM; 8MB free hard disk space. SERBIB/SERLOC merged record Subjects: United States. Congress--Directories. United States. Congress--Officials and employees Directories. Government executives--United States--Directories. Administrative agencies--United States--Directories. Courts--United States--Directories. United States--Officials and employees--Directories. LC Classification: JK723

Carroll's federal directory. Edition Information: Library ed. Published/Created: Washington, DC: Carroll Pub., 1995-1997. Description: 3 v.: ill.; 29 cm. 1995-1997. ISSN: 1093-2089 Notes: SERBIB/SERLOC merged record Has a bimonthly edition. Carroll's federal directory 1080-4919 (DLC) 95648055 (OCoLC)31757791 Subjects: United States. Congress--Directories. Administrative agencies--United States--Directories. Government executives--United States--Directories. Courts--United States--Officials and employees Directories. LC Classification: JK723.E9 F37 NAL Class No.: JK723.E9F4 Dewey Class No.: 353/.00025 20

Carroll's federal directory: executive, legislative, judicial. Published/Created: Bethesda, Md.: Carroll Pub., c2002- Description: v.; 29 cm. 2002 annual ed.- ISSN: 1539-6320 Subjects: United States. Congress--Directories. Administrative agencies--United States--Directories. Government executives--United States--Directories. Courts--United States--Officials and employees Directories. Dewey Class No.: 353 13

Carroll's federal directory: executive, legislative, judicial. Published/Created: Washington, DC: Carroll Pub., 1995- Description: v.; 28 cm. Jan./Feb. 1995- ISSN: 1080-4919 Notes: SERBIB/SERLOC merged record Has an annual edition. Carroll's federal directory (Annual) 1093-2089 (DLC) 95644461 (OCoLC)32902153 Subjects: United States. Congress--Directories. Government executives--United States--Directories. Courts--United States--Officials and employees Directories. LC Classification: JK6 .F42 NAL Class No.: JK6.F43 Dewey Class No.: 353.002/05 20

Carroll's federal regional directory. Published/Created: Washington, D.C.: Carroll Pub. Co., c1995- Description: Mar./Aug. 1995- ISSN: 1082-3182 Notes: SERBIB/SERLOC merged record Subjects: United States. Congress--Directories. Government executives--Courts--United States--Directories. United States--Officials and employees--Directories. LC Classification: JK723.E9 F43 NAL Class No.: JK723.E9F44 Dewey Class No.: 353 12

Carroll's federal/federal regional directory. Edition Information: Annual ed. Published/Created: Washington, DC: Carroll Pub., c1998-2001. Description: 4 v.: ill.; 28 cm. 1998-2001. Notes: Split into: Carroll's federal regional directory (Annual), and: Carroll's federal directory (Annual: 2002). Subjects: United States. Congress--Directories. Administrative agencies--Government executives--United States--Directories. Courts--United States--Officials and employees Directories. LC Classification: JK723.E9 F37 Dewey Class No.: 353/.00025 20

Carson, Julia M. H. (Julia Margaret Hicks), 1899- The judicial system: a brief summary / by Julia M.H. Carson. Published/Created: Washington, D.C.: National League of Women Voters, [c1935] Related Authors: League of Women Voters (U.S.) Description: iv, 15 p.; 23 cm. Notes: "Published under the Belle Sherwin fund."--p. [2] of cover. Includes bibliographical references. Subjects: Courts--United States. LC Classification: KF8700.Z9 C3

Carter, Howard Marshall, 1869- The jurisdiction of federal Courts, as limited by the citizenship and residence of the parties. Published/Created: Boston, Little, Brown and company, 1899. Description: xxviii, 303 p. 25 cm. Subjects: Courts--United States. LC Classification: KF8858 .C3

Carter, Philip. Materials on the Courts and public law, by Philip Carter with James Rainey and Edward Bartoli. Published/Created: [n.p., c1966] Related Authors: Rainey, James. Bartoli, Edward. Description: 2 v. 28 cm. Notes: Cover title. Bibliographical footnotes. Subjects: Courts--United States. Jurisdiction--United States. Public law--United States--Cases. LC Classification: KF8720 .C3 Dewey Class No.: 347.99/73

Casenote legal briefs. Federal Courts: adaptable to courses utilizing Bator, Mishkin, Shapiro, and Wechsler's casebook on the federal Courts and the federal system / Dana L. Blatt, senior editor, Norman S. Goldenberg, senior editor, Peter Tenen, managing editor; staff writers, Jeremiah Flanigan, Terry Molloy, James I. Rosenthal. Published/Created: Beverly Hills, CA: Casenotes Pub. Co.; Gardena, Calif.: distributed by Law Distributors, c1977. Related Authors: Blatt, Dana L. Goldenberg, Norman S. Description: 132 p.; 28 cm. Subjects: Courts--Jurisdiction--United States--Cases. LC Classification: KF8718 .C37 Dewey Class No.: 347/.73/2

Casenote legal briefs. Federal Courts: adaptable to courses utilizing Bator, Mishkin, Shapiro, and Wechsler's casebook on the Federal Courts and the Federal System / Norman S. Goldenberg, senior editor; Peter Tenen, managing editor; Robert J. Switzer, editorial director; staff writers, Jean Christine Youker ... [et al.]. Published/Created: Santa Monica, CA: Casenotes Pub. Co., c1988. Related Authors: Goldenberg, Norman S. Tenen, Peter. Description: 130 p.; 28 cm. ISBN: 0874570867 Notes: "1360." Subjects: Courts--United States--Cases. Jurisdiction--United States--Cases. LC Classification: KF8718 .C37 1988 Dewey Class No.: 347.7/32/02648 347.302702648 20

Casenote legal briefs. Federal Courts: adaptable to courses utilizing Currie's casebook on Federal Courts / Norman S. Goldenberg, senior editor; Peter Tenen, managing editor; Robert J. Switzer, associate editor; staff writers Susan Yudelson ... [et al.]. Published/Created: Beverly Hills, CA: Casenotes Pub. Co.; Gardena, Calif.: Distributed by Law Distributors, c1985. Related Authors: Goldenberg, Norman S. Yudelson, Susan. Currie, David P. Federal Courts. Description: 3, 80 p.; 28 cm. ISBN: 0874570875 (pbk.) Subjects: Jurisdiction--United States--Cases. Courts--United States--Cases. LC Classification: KF8858.A7 C37 1985 Dewey Class No.: 347.73/2 347.3072 19

Casenote legal briefs. Federal Courts: adaptable to courses utilizing Low and Jeffries' casebook on federal Courts and the law of federal-state relations / Norman S. Goldenberg, senior editor; Peter Tenen, managing editor; Robert J. Switzer, editorial director; staff writer, Chris Youker. Published/Created: Beverly Hills, CA: Casenotes Pub. Co., c1990. Related Authors: Goldenberg, Norman S. Youker, Chris. Low, Peter, 1937- Federal Courts and the law of federal-state relations. Description: iii, 67 p.; 28 cm. ISBN: 0874571642 Notes: "1363." Subjects: Courts--Jurisdiction--Federal government--State action (Civil rights)--United States--Cases. LC Classification: KF8735.A7 C37 1990 Dewey Class No.: 347.73/2 347.3072 20

Casenote legal briefs. Federal Courts: adaptable to courses utilizing McCormick, Chadbourn, and Wright's casebook on federal Courts / Dana L. Blatt, senior editor, Norman S. Goldenberg, senior editor, Peter Tenen, managing editor; staff writers, Susan Ydelson ... [et al.]. Published/Created: Beverly Hills, CA: Casenotes Pub. Co.; Gardena, Calif.: distributed by Law Distributors, c1978. Related Authors: Blatt, Dana L. Goldenberg, Norman S. McCormick, Charles Tilford, 1889-1963. Cases and materials on federal Courts. Description: 129 p.; 28 cm. Subjects: Civil procedure--United States--Cases. Jurisdiction--United States--Cases. LC Classification: KF8839 .C35 Dewey Class No.: 347/.73/2

Casenote legal briefs. Federal Courts: adaptable to courses utilizing McCormick, Chadbourn, and Wright's casebook on federal Courts / Norman S. Goldenberg, senior editor, Peter Tenen, managing editor, Robert J. Switzer, associate editor; staff writers Susan Yudelson ... [et al.]. Published/Created: Beverly Hills, CA: Casenotes Pub. Co.; Gardena, Calif.: Distributed by Law Distributors, c1988. Related Authors: Goldenberg, Norman S. Tenen, Peter. Switzer, Robert J. Yudelson, Susan. McCormick, Charles Tilford, 1889-1963. Cases and materials on federal Courts. Description: 121 p.; 28 cm. ISBN: 0874570883 Subjects: Civil procedure--United States--Cases. Jurisdiction--United States--Cases. LC Classification: KF8839 .C35 1988 Dewey Class No.: 347.73/2 347.3072 19

Casenote legal briefs. Federal Courts: adaptable to courses utilizing McCormick, Chadbourn and Wright's casebook on federal Courts / Norman S. Goldenberg, senior editor, Peter Tenen, managing editor, Robert J. Switzer, associate editor; staff writers, Susan Yudelson ... [et al.]. Published/Created: Beverly Hills, CA: Casenotes Pub. Co.; Gardena, Calif.: Distributed by Law Distributors, c1983. Related Authors: Goldenberg, Norman S. Tenen, Peter. Switzer, Robert J. Yudelson, Susan. McCormick, Charles Tilford, 1889-1963. Cases and materials on federal Courts. Description: 127 p.; 28 cm. Subjects: Civil procedure--United States--Cases. Jurisdiction--United States--Cases. LC Classification: KF8839 .C35 1983 Dewey Class No.: 347.73/2 347.3072 19

Casenote legal briefs. Federal Courts: adaptable to courses utlizing Currie's casebook on Federal Courts / Dana L. Blatt, senior editor, Norman S. Goldenberg, senior editor, Peter Tenen, managing editor; staff writers, Susan Yudelson, James Rosenthal. Published/Created: Beverly Hills, CA: Casenotes Pub. Co.; Gardena, Calif.: distributed by Law Distributors, c1978. Related Authors: Blatt, Dana L. Goldenberg, Norman S. Currie, David P. Federal Courts. Description: 79 p.; 28 cm. Subjects: Jurisdiction--United States--Cases. Courts--United States--Cases. LC Classification: KF8858.A7 C37 Dewey Class No.: 347/.73/2

Cayton, Nathan, 1899- Small claims and conciliation courts, Published/Created: [Philadelphia? 1939?] Description: 8 p. 24 cm. Subjects: Courts--United States. LC Classification: KF8769.Z9 C39

Cecil, Joe S. Deciding cases without argument: a description of procedures in the courts of appeals / by Joe Cecil and Donna Stienstra. Published/Created: Washington, D.C.: Federal Judicial Center, 1985. Related Authors: Stienstra, Donna. Federal Judicial Center. Description: iv, 41 p.; 23 cm. Notes: Shipping list no.: 85-1179-P Item 743-C-3 Includes bibliographical references. Subjects: Oral pleading--United States. Appellate procedure--United States. Appellate Courts--United States. Series: FJC-R; 85-9 LC Classification: KF8870 .C37 1985 Dewey Class No.: 347.73/72 347.30772 19 Govt. Doc. No.: Ju 13.10:85-9

Cecil, Joe S. Deciding cases without argument: an examination of four courts of appeals / Joe S. Cecil and Donna Stienstra. Published/Created: Washington, D.C.: Federal Judicial Center, 1987. Related Authors: Stienstra, Donna. Federal Judicial

Center. Description: ix, 220 p.; 24 cm. Notes: Shipping list no.: 88-147-P. Item 743-C-3 Includes bibliographical references. Subjects: Appellate Courts--United States. Oral pleading--United States. Court congestion and delay--United States. LC Classification: KF8750 .C43 1987 Dewey Class No.: 347.73/24 347.3073 19 Govt. Doc. No.: Ju 13.10:87-5

Cecil, Joe S. Summary judgment practice in three district courts / Joe S. Cecil, C.R. Douglas. Published/Created: Washington, D.C.: Federal Judicial Center, 1987. Related Authors: Douglas, C. R. Federal Judicial Center. Description: vi, 13 p.; 24 cm Notes: Shipping list no.: 87-451-P. Item 743-C-3 Includes bibliographical references. Subjects: Summary judgments--United States. District Courts--United States. Series: FJC-R; 87-2 LC Classification: KF8999 .C43 1987 Dewey Class No.: 347.73/75 347.30775 19 Govt. Doc. No.: Ju 13.10:87-2

Center court. Published/Created: Williamsburg, Va.: National Center for State Courts, c1996- Related Authors: National Center for State Courts. Description: v.: ill.; 28 cm. Vol. 1, no. 1 (spring/summer 1996)- Notes: "For and about those who work in our state Courts." Caption title. SERBIB/SERLOC merged record Subjects: Courts--United States--States--Periodicals. Court administration--United States--States--Periodicals. LC Classification: KF8736.A15 C46 Dewey Class No.: 347.73/3/05 21

Chamberlain, Daniel Henry, 1835-1907. The state judiciary: its place in the American constitutional system. Published/Created: New York, London, 1889. Description: p. [237]-286. 22 cm. Subjects: Courts--United States--States. LC Classification: JK241 .M62

Chamberlain, Joseph Perkins, 1873-1951. The judicial function in Federal administrative agencies [by] Joseph P. Chamberlain, Noel T. Dowling [and] Paul R. Hays. Published/Created: Freeport, N.Y., Books for Libraries Press [1970, c1942] Related Authors: Dowling, Noel Thomas, 1885-1969, joint author. Hays, Paul R. (Paul Raymond), 1903- joint author. Description: xii, 258 p. 24 cm. ISBN: 0836954955 Notes: Bibliography: p. [235]-241. Subjects: Administrative law--United States. Executive departments--United States. Courts--United States. LC Classification: KF5417 .C43 1970 Dewey Class No.: 340

Chamberlain, Joseph Perkins, 1873-1951. The judicial function in Federal administrative agencies / Joseph P. Chamberlain, Noel T. Dowling, Paul R. Hays ... of the Legislative Drafting Research Fund, Columbia University. Published/Created: New York: Commonwealth Fund, 1942. Related Authors: Dowling, Noel Thomas, 1885-1969. Hays, Paul R. (Paul Raymond), 1903- Columbia University. Legislative Drafting Research Fund. Commonwealth Fund. Legal Research Committee. Description: xii, 258 p.; 24 cm. Notes: This study has been conducted under the auspices of the Legal Research Committee of the Commonwealth Fund. Cf. Foreword. Includes index. Bibliography: p. [235]-241. Subjects: Administrative law--United States. Executive departments--United States. Courts--United States. LC Classification: KF5417 .C43

Chambers handbook for judges' law clerks and secretaries / Federal Judicial Center. Published/Created: Washington, DC: The Center, 1994. Related Authors: Federal Judicial Center. Description: xi, 184 p.; 25 cm. Notes: Cover title. "Third printing of the Chambers handbook contains the Code of Conduct for Judicial Employees adapted ... September 19, 1995"--P. [i]. "Fourth printing"--P. [ii]. Includes bibliographical references. Subjects: Law clerks--United States--Handbooks, manuals, etc. Legal secretaries--United States--Handbooks, manuals, etc. Court administration--United States. Courts--United States--Officials and employees. LC Classification: KF8771 .C49 1994

Chemerinsky, Erwin. Federal jurisdiction / Erwin Chemerinsky. Edition Information:

3rd ed. Published/Created: Gaithersburg [Md.]: Aspen Law & Business, c1999. Description: xxiv, 1003 p.; 26 cm. ISBN: 0735500371 Notes: Includes index. Subjects: Jurisdiction--United States. Courts--United States. LC Classification: KF8858 .C48 1999 Dewey Class No.: 347.73/2 21

Chemerinsky, Erwin. Federal jurisdiction / Erwin Chemerinsky. Edition Information: 2nd ed. Published/Created: Boston: Little, Brown, c1994. Description: xxiv, 930 p.; 26 cm. ISBN: 0316137758 Notes: Includes the text of the Constitution and excerpts from the U.S. Code. Includes bibliographical references and index. Subjects: Jurisdiction--United States. Courts--United States. LC Classification: KF8858 .C48 1994 Dewey Class No.: 347.73/1 347.3071 20

Chemerinsky, Erwin. Federal jurisdiction / Erwin Chemerinsky. Published/Created: Boston: Little, Brown and Co., c1989. Description: xxv, 801 p.; 26 cm. ISBN: 0316137596 Notes: Includes the text of the Constitution and excerpts from the U.S. Code. Kept up to date by pocket parts and supplements. Includes bibliographical references. Subjects: Jurisdiction--United States. Courts--United States. LC Classification: KF8858 .C48 1989 Dewey Class No.: 347.73/12 347.30712 20

Chester, Alden. Courts and Lawyers of New York. A History 1809-1925. Published/Created: New York and Chicago, The American Historical Society, Inc., 1925. Description: p. cm. LC Classification: LAW

Citizen of Ohio. Strictures, upon the constitutional powers of the Congress and courts of the United States, over the execution laws of the several states in their application to the federal courts / by a Citizen of Ohio. Published/Created: Cincinnati: Morgan, Lodge and Fisher, printers, 1825. Description: 17 p.; 24 cm. References: Shoemaker 20796 Cohen, M. Bib. of early Amer. law, 2924 Subjects: United States. Congress. Executions (Law)--United States. Constitutional law--United States. Courts--United States. LC Classification: KF9025 .C58 1825

Citizens and their Courts: building a public constituency / developed by National Courts and Community Advisory Committee. Published/Created: Olympia, WA (PO Box 41170, Olympia 98504-1170): Office of the Administrator for the Courts, [1995] Related Authors: National Courts and Community Advisory Committee (U.S.) State Justice Institute (U.S.) Description: 30 p.; 22 cm. Notes: "Sponsored by: Conference of Chief Justices, Conference of State Court Administrators, [and the] National Center for State Courts". Funded by the State Justice Institute SJI-93-12A-A-067. Subjects: Courts--Public relations--United States--States. LC Classification: KF8736 .C57 1995

Citizens' forum on the Courts: a newsletter of the American Judicature Society. Published/Created: [Chicago, Ill.]: The Society, [c1984- Related Authors: American Judicature Society. Description: v.: ill.; 28 cm. Vol. 1, no. 1 (summer 1984)- ISSN: 0748-2000 Notes: Title from caption. SERBIB/SERLOC merged record Subjects: Courts--United States--Periodicals. LC Classification: KF8712 .C58 Dewey Class No.: 347.73/1/05 347.307105 19

Civil litigation management manual / Judicial Conference of the United States, Committee on Court Administration and Case Management. Published/Created: Washington, D.C.: Administrative Office of the United States Courts; Federal Judicial Center, Information Services Office, 2001. Description: xii, 463 p.: forms; 28 cm. Notes: Includes bibliographical references (p. 437-451) and index. Subjects: Court congestion and delay--Court administration--Costs (Law)--United States. LC Classification: KF8727 .C58 2001 Dewey Class No.: 347.73/13 21

Claghorn, Kate Holladay, 1863- ...The immigrant's day in court, by Kate Holladay

Claghorn. Edition Information: [1st ed.] Published/Created: New York and London, Harper & brothers, 1923. Description: xvi, 546 p. Subjects: Courts--United States. United States--Emigration and immigration. LC Classification: JV6455 .C5

Claghorn, Kate Holladay, 1863- The immigrant's day in court. Published/Created: New York, Arno Press, 1969. Description: xvi, 546 p. 21 cm. Notes: Reprint of the 1923 ed. Subjects: Courts--United States. United States--Emigration and immigration. Series: Americanization studies. LC Classification: JV6455 .C5 1969 Dewey Class No.: 342/.73

Claghorn, Kate Holladay, 1863-1938. The immigrant's day in court. With a new introd. by Ann S. Petluck. Published/Created: Montclair, N.J., Patterson Smith, 1971 [c1923] Description: xxxvi, 546 p. 22 cm. Notes: Includes bibliographical references. Subjects: Courts--United States. United States--Emigration and immigration. Series: Bernard, William Spencer, 1907- comp. Americanization studies: the acculturation of immigrant groups into American society, 9. LC Classification: JV6407 .B4 vol. 9 JV6455 Dewey Class No.: 342/.73/082

Clark, Lindley D. (Lindley Daniel), b. 1862. Labor laws that have been declared unconstitutional, by Lindley D. Clark. November, 1922. Published/Created: Washington, Govt. print. off., 1922. Description: 90 p. 23 cm. Notes: At head of title: U. S. Department of labor. James J. Davis, secretary. Bureau of Labor Statistics. Ethelbert Stewart, commissioner. Issued also as House doc. 418, 67th Cong., 3d sess. Bibliographical foot-notes. Subjects: Labor laws and legislation--United States. United States--Courts. LC Classification: HD8051 .A62 no. 321

Clark, Walter, 1846- Address to the law class at the University of North Carolina, Published/Created: [Raleigh, N.C., Mitchell printing co., 1919] Description: p. cm. Subjects: United States. Supreme court. Courts--North Carolina. LC Classification: JK1541 .C555

Clark, Walter, 1846-1924. Constitution. Article entitled "Back to the Constitution," by Walter Clark, L.L. D., Chief Justice of the Supreme Court of the State of North Carolina ... Published/Created: Washington [Govt. Print. Off.] 1916. Description: 13 p. 23 cm. Notes: Presented by Mr. La Follette. Ordered printed February 3, 1916. Reprinted from vol. III, no. 3, of the Virginia law review. Subjects: United States. Supreme Court. Courts--United States. LC Classification: JK1541 .C56

Clifford, Mary Louise. 1984 state trial court jurisdiction guide for statistical reporting: summary tables / Mary Louise Clifford and Robert T. Roper. Published/Created: [Williamsburg, Va.: National Center for State Courts, 1985?] Related Authors: Roper, Robert T., 1952- National Center for State Courts. Conference of State Court Administrators. National Center for State Courts. Court Statistics and Information Management Project. Description: vi, 110 p.: ill.; 28 cm. Notes: Cover title. "A joint effort of the Conference of State Court Administrators and the Court Statistics and Information Management Project of the National Center for State Courts." Subjects: Courts--United States--States--Statistical methods. LC Classification: KF8736 .C58 1985 Dewey Class No.: 347.73/1 347.3071 19

Clifford, Mary Louise. Court case management information systems manual: with model data elements, reporting forms, and management reports / by Mary Louise Clifford and Lynn A. Jensen; prepared by the State Judicial Information Systems Project and the National Court Statistics Project in cooperation with the Conference of State Court Administrators. Published/Created: [Williamsburg, Va.]: National Center for State Courts, c1983. Related Authors: Jensen, Lynn A. State Judicial Information Systems Project (National Center for State Courts) National

Court Statistics Project (U.S.) Conference of State Court Administrators. Description: xiii, 327 p.: ill., forms; 28 cm. ISBN: 0896560716 (pbk.) Notes: Bibliography: p. 319-327. Subjects: Court administration--United States. Court administration--United States--Statistical methods. LC Classification: KF8733 .C58 1983 Dewey Class No.: 347.73/1/068 347.3071068 19

Clinton, Robert N. Federal courts: theory and practice / Robert N. Clinton, Richard A. Matasar, Michael G. Collins. Published/Created: Boston: Little, Brown, c1996. Related Authors: Matasar, Richard A. Collins, Michael G. Description: xxxv, 1553 p.; 26 cm. ISBN: 0316263354 Notes: Includes bibliographical references (p. 1521-1541) and index. Subjects: Courts--United States--Cases. Judicial power--United States--Cases. Jurisdiction--United States--Cases. Procedure (Law)--United States--Cases. Series: Law school casebook series LC Classification: KF8718 .C58 1996 Dewey Class No.: 347.73/2 347.3072 20

Coffin, Frank Morey. On appeal: courts, lawyering, and judging / Frank M. Coffin; illustrations by Douglas M. Coffin. Edition Information: 1st ed. Published/Created: New York: W.W. Norton, c1994. Description: xix, 373 p.: ill.; 22 cm. ISBN: 0393035824 : Notes: Includes bibliographical references (p. [339]-354) and index. Subjects: Appellate Courts--United States. Appellate procedure--United States. Judicial process--United States. Lawyers--United States. LC Classification: KF8750 .C625 1994 Dewey Class No.: 347.73/8 347.3078 20

Cohen, Jonathan Matthew. Inside appellate courts: the impact of court organization on judicial decision making in the United States Courts of Appeals / Jonathan Matthew Cohen. Published/Created: Ann Arbor: University of Michigan Press, c2002. Description: xii, 231 p.; 24cm. ISBN: 0472112562 (cloth: acid-free paper) Contents: The bureaucratization of the U.S. Courts of Appeals -- The organizational character of the U.S. Courts of Appeals -- The formal features of the U.S. Courts of Appeals -- The internal structure of the appellate judicial chambers and the role of the law clerk -- Structure and the interaction among judicial chambers -- Organizational culture in the appellate judicial process -- Tilting the balance: organizational behavior and organizational change in the U.S. Courts of Appeals. Notes: Includes index. Subjects: United States. Court of Appeals. Judicial process--United States. Judgments--United States. Appellate Courts--United States. LC Classification: KF8775 .C64 2002 Dewey Class No.: 347.73/24 21

Commission on Structural Alternatives for the Federal Courts of Appeals: working papers. Published/Created: Washington, DC: The Commission, [1998?] Related Authors: United States. Commission on Structural Alternatives for the Federal Courts of Appeals. Description: 348 p.: ill.,; 28 cm. Notes: Cover title. Includes bibliographical references. Subjects: Appellate Courts--United States. Court administration--United States. Appellate procedure--United States. Judicial statistics--United States. LC Classification: KF8750 .C66 1998 Dewey Class No.: 347.73/24 21

Comparative analysis: Federal rules of criminal procedure and military practice and procedure / prepared by the Committee on Criminal Justice and the Military, Section of Criminal Justice, American Bar Association. Published/Created: [Washington, D.C.] (1800 M St., N.W., Washington 20036): The Section, c1982. Related Authors: American Bar Association. Committee on Criminal Justice and the Military. United States. Supreme Court. Rules of criminal procedure for the United States District Courts. 1982. Description: 131 p.; 28 cm. Notes: Cover title. Subjects: Courts-martial and Courts of inquiry--United States. Criminal procedure--United States. Court rules--United States. LC Classification: KF7625 .C65 1982 Dewey Class No.: 343.73/0143 347.303143 19

Compiled laws of Alaska, 1933, Published/Created: Alaska, Daily Alaska empire [1933?] Related Authors: Roden, Henry, ed. United States. Laws, statutes, etc. Alaska (Ter.) Courts. United States. Courts. ALaska. Law revision board. Description: 1224 p. 27 cm. LC Classification: KFA1230.1933 .A224

Computer-aided transcription in the Courts: a project of the National Center for State Courts. Published/Created: Williamsburg, Va. (300 Newport Ave., Williamsburg 23185): The Center, 1981. Related Authors: National Center for State Courts. Description: x, 259 p.: ill.; 28 cm. Subjects: Law reporting--United States--Data processing. Computer-aided transcription systems. Series: Publication (National Center for State Courts); R0057. LC Classification: KF255 .C65 Dewey Class No.: 347.73/1/0285 347.30710285 19

Computer-aided transcription in the Courts: executive summary: a project of the National Center for State Courts. Published/Created: Williamsburg, Va. (300 Newport Ave., Williamsburg 23185): The Center, 1981. Related Authors: National Center for State Courts. Description: xi, 36 p.: ill.; 28 cm. Subjects: Law reporting--United States--Data processing. Computer-aided transcription systems. Series: Publication (National Center for State Courts); no. R0058. LC Classification: KF255 .C66 Dewey Class No.: 347.73/1/0285 347.30710285 19

Conciliation Courts review. Published/Created: Los Angeles, Calif.: Conciliation Court of Los Angeles County, [1965-1988] Related Authors: Association of Family and Conciliation Courts. Conference of Conciliation Courts (U.S.) Description: 24 v.; 28 cm. Vol. 3, no. 1 (Jan. 1965)-v. 26, no. 2 (Dec. 1988). ISSN: 0588-9774 Notes: Title from cover. Issued by: Conference of Conciliation Courts, 1965-1976; Association of Family Conciliation Courts, 1977-1981; Association of Family and Conciliation Courts, 1982-1988. SERBIB/SERLOC merged record Subjects: Domestic relations Courts--United States--Periodicals. LC Classification: K3 .A43 Dewey Class No.: 346 11

Conductor generalis, or The office, duty and authority of Justices of the Peace, high-sheriffs, under-sheriffs, goalers, coroners, constables, jury men, over-seers of the poor: and also the office of clerks of assize and of the peace, &c. / collected out of all the books hitherto written on those subjects, whether of common or statute-law to which is added, a collection out of Sir Matthew Hales concerning the descent of lands. Published/Created: Union, N.J.: Lawbook Exchange, 2001. Related Authors: Hale, Matthew, Sir, 1609-1676. Description: p. cm. ISBN: 1584771232 (alk. paper) Notes: Originally published: [Philadelphia]: Printed and sold by Andrew Bradford in Philadelphia, 1722. Subjects: Justices of the peace--United States. Courts--United States--Officials and employees. Justices of the peace--Great Britain. Courts--Great Britain--Officials and employees. LC Classification: KF8800 .C58 2001 Dewey Class No.: 347.73/16 21

Conference on judicial administration, Published/Created: [Chicago, 1957] Description: 97 p. 24 cm. Subjects: Courts--United States. Series: Its Conference series, no. 16. LC Classification: KF8719.A2 C5

Conflict, Courts, and trials / authors, Linda Riekes ... [et al.]; editors, Dolores B. Malcolm, Michael A. Wolff; contributing editors, Miranda Duncan ... [et al.]. Edition Information: 3rd ed. Published/Created: St. Paul: West Pub. Co., c1991. Related Authors: Riekes, Linda. Malcolm, Dolores B. Wolff, Michael A., 1945- Riekes, Linda. Courts and trials. Description: v, 266 p.: ill. (some col.); 26 cm. + teacher's resource guide. ISBN: 0314473610 Summary: Examines the working of the United States court system and the ways Courts resolve disputes and conflicts. Readers learn how to conduct their own mock trials. Notes: Rev. ed. of: Courts and trials / Linda Riekes and Sally Mahe Ackerly. 2nd ed.

for teachers. c1980. Subjects: Courts--United States--Juvenile literature. Dispute resolution (Law)--United States--Juvenile literature. Mock trials--Juvenile literature. Courts. Trial practice. Series: Law in action series LC Classification: KF8700.Z9 C64 1991 Dewey Class No.: 347.73/1 347.3071 20

Congress and the Courts: a legislative history, 1787-1977: documents and materials regarding the creation, structure, and organization of Federal Courts and the Federal judiciary / compiled by Bernard D. Reams, Jr. and Charles R. Haworth. Published/Created: Buffalo: W. S. Hein, c1978. Related Authors: Reams, Bernard D. Haworth, Charles R. Description: 6 v. in 30; 26 cm. ISBN: 0930342569 (set) Notes: Kept up to date by supplements. Includes unnumbered index volume. Vol. 1 incluces bibliography. Subjects: Courts--United States. LC Classification: KF8713.8 1978 Dewey Class No.: 347.73/2 347.3071 19

Congress and the Courts: a legislative history, 1978-1984-[<1993-1998]: documents and materials regarding the creation, structure, and organization of federal Courts and the federal judiciary / [compiled] by Bernard D. Reams, Jr. Published/Created: Buffalo, N.Y.: W.S. Hein, 1985-<1999 Related Authors: Reams, Bernard D. Manz, William H. Description: v. <1-47, 50-52; 27 cm. ISBN: 0899414338 (set) Notes: On spine: Second series. Vols. <47, 50-52: [compiled] by William H. Manz. Vols. 23-46: the 99th through the 102d Congresses; v. <47, 50-51: the 103rd through the 105th Congresses. "Serves to expand and update Congress and the Courts: a legislative history, 1787-1977"--Introd. Includes bibliographical references. Subjects: Courts--United States. LC Classification: KF8713.8 1985 Dewey Class No.: 347.73/2 347.3071 19

Conkling, Alfred, 1789-1874. A treatise on the organization, jurisdiction and practice of the courts of the United States in suits at law, including municipal seizures and criminal prosecutions, with an appendix of practical forms. Edition Information: 5th ed., rev., Published/Created: Albany, W. C. Little & co., 1870. Description: xi, 946 p., 1 l. 24 cm. Subjects: Courts--United States. Court rules--United states. LC Classification: KF8719 .C6 1870 Microfilm LL 1414 KF

Conkling, Alfred, 1789-1874. A treatise on the organization, jurisdiction and practice of the courts of the United States, with an appendix of practical forms. Edition Information: 4th ed., rev., Published/Created: Albany, W. C. Little, 1864. Description: xi, [1], 882 p. 24 cm. Subjects: Courts--United States. Court rules--United States. LC Classification: KF8719 .C6 1864 Microfilm LL 407 KF

Conkling, Alfred, 1789-1874. The admiralty jurisdiction, Published/Created: Albany, W. C. Little & co.; 1848. Description: p. cm. Subjects: Admiralty. Courts--United States. LC Classification: KPH12 .50 1974

Conkling, Alfred, 1789-1874. A treatise on the organization, jurisdiction, and practice of the courts of the United States / by Alfred Conkling. Edition Information: 3rd ed., rev. and corr. Published/Created: Albany: W.C. Little and Co., 1856. Description: xiii, 926 p.; 23 cm. Notes: Spine title: Conkling's treatise. Includes appendix of rules and forms. Includes index. Subjects: Courts--United States. Court rules--United States. LC Classification: KF8719 .C6 1856

Conkling, Alfred, 1789-1874. A treatise on the organization, jurisdiction and practice of the courts of the United States: to which is added an appendix, containing rules and also a few practicle forms. By Alfred Conkling. Published/Created: Albany, W. & A. Gould & Co., New York, Gould, Banks & co.; 1831. Description: vii, [1], 538 p., 1 l. 22 cm. Subjects: Courts--United States Court rules--United States LC Classification: KF8719 .C6 1831

Conkling, Alfred, 1789-1874. A treatise on the organization, jurisdiction, and practice of the courts of the United States: with an appendix of practical forms / by Alfred

Conkling. Edition Information: 4th ed. / revised, corrected, and enlarged by the author. Published/Created: Holmes Beach, Fla.: Wm.W. Gaunt, 1987. Description: xi, 882 p.; 22 cm. ISBN: 0912004614 Notes: Reprint. Originally published: 4th ed. Albany: W.C. Little Law Booksellers, 1864. Includes bibliographical references and index. Subjects: Courts--United States. Court rules--United States. LC Classification: KF8719 .C6 1987 Dewey Class No.: 347.73/12 347.30712 19

Conlon, James. Federal tax procedure and appeals; a treatise on the statutes, regulations, court decisions, Board of tax appeals opinions, decisions, orders and forms, Treasury decisions, Internal revenue rulings, evidence, practice and procedure pertaining to income, estate and excise taxes and court and Board of tax appeals decisions on avoiding and minimizing taxes, by James Conlon. Published/Created: Washington, D.C., J. Conlon, 1933. Related Authors: United States. Laws, statutes, etc. United States. Tax Court. United States. Dept. of the Treasury. United States. Internal Revenue Service. United States. Courts. Description: xvi, 640 p. 24 cm. Subjects: Income tax--Law and legislation--United States. Inheritance and transfer tax--Internal revenue law--Law reports, digests, etc.--United States. LC Classification: KF6300 .C6 Dewey Class No.: 336.20973

Connecticut practice. Rules of court. Published/Created: St. Paul, Minn., West Pub. Co. Related Authors: West Publishing Company. Connecticut. Connecticut rules of court. Description: v. 25 cm. -1977. Summary: Includes some Federal rules. Includes amendments. Notes: SERBIB/SERLOC merged record Subjects: Court rules--Connecticut. Court rules--United States. LC Classification: KFC4129 .A193 Dewey Class No.: 347.746/051 347.460751

Connecticut rules of court. Published/Created: St. Paul, Minn. West Pub. Co. Related Authors: West Publishing Company. Description: v. 25 cm. 1978- Summary: Includes state and federal rules and amendments. Notes: SERBIB/SERLOC merged record Subjects: Court rules--Connecticut. Court rules--United States. LC Classification: KFC4129 .A193 Dewey Class No.: 347.746/051

Constitutional Courts in comparison: the U.S. Supreme Court and the German Federal Constitutional Court / edited by Ralf Rogowski and Thomas Gawron. Published/Created: New York: Berghahn Books, 2002. Related Authors: Rogowski, Ralf. Gawron, Thomas. Description: x, 262 p.; 23 cm. ISBN: 1571814779 (hardback: alk. paper) Notes: Includes bibliographical references and index. Subjects: United States. Supreme Court. Germany. Bundesverfassungsgericht. Constitutional Courts. Judicial review. LC Classification: KF8742 .C655 2002 Dewey Class No.: 347.73/26 21

Contemplating Courts / Lee Epstein, editor. Published/Created: Washington, D.C.: CQ Press, c1995. Related Authors: Epstein, Lee, 1958- Description: xix, 499 p.: ill.; 23 cm. ISBN: 0871879832 (cloth: alk. paper) 0871879824 (pbk.: alk. paper) Notes: Includes bibliographical references (p. 439-480) and index. Subjects: Judicial process--United States. Justice, Administration of--United States. Courts--United States. LC Classification: KF8700 .C66 1995 Dewey Class No.: 347.73/1 347.3071 20

Cookling, Alfred, 1789-1874. The admiralty jurisdiction, law and practice of the courts of the United States: with an appendix, containing the new rules of admiralty practice prescribed by the Supreme court of the United States, Edition Information: 2d ed., Published/Created: Albany, W. C. Little & co., 1857. Related Authors: United States. Supreme court. United States. Circuit court (2d circuit) United States. District court. New York (Northern district) Description: p. cm. Subjects: Admiralty--United States. Courts--United States. Court rules--United States. LC Classification: KF1112 .C6 1857

Cooper, Phillip J. Hard judicial choices: federal district court judges and state and local officials / Phillip J. Cooper. Published/Created: New York: Oxford University Press, 1988. Description: 374 p.: ill.; 25 cm. ISBN: 0195041917 (alk. paper) 0195041925 (pbk.: alk. paper) Notes: Includes index. Bibliography: p. [353]-361. Subjects: Judicial review of administrative acts--United States. District Courts--United States. Judicial process--United States. Remedies (Law)--United States. Abuse of administrative power--United States--States. Law and politics. LC Classification: KF5425 .C66 1988 Dewey Class No.: 347.73/5 347.3075 19

Cope, Alfred Haines, 1912- ed. Franklin D. Roosevelt and the Supreme Court. Edition Information: Rev. ed. Edited with an introd. by Alfred Haines Cope [and] Fred Krinsky. Published/Created: Lexington, Mass., Heath [1969] Related Authors: Krinsky, Fred, 1924- joint ed. Description: x, 115 p. 24 cm. Notes: Bibliography: p. [113]-115. Subjects: United States. Supreme Court. Judicial review--United States. Courts--United States. United States--Politics and government--1933-1945. Series: Problems in American civilization LC Classification: KF8748 .C57 1969 Dewey Class No.: 347.99/73

Cope, Alfred Haines, 1912- ed. Franklin D. Roosevelt and the Supreme Court, edited with an introd. by Alfred Haines Cope [and] Fred Krinsky. Published/Created: Boston, Heath [1952] Description: 109 p. 24 cm. Subjects: United States. Supreme Court. Judicial review--United States. Courts--United States. United States--Politics and government--1933-1945. LC Classification: KF8748 .C57 1952 Dewey Class No.: 347.99 347.972*

Copyright liability of states and the Eleventh Amendment, June 1988 / a report of the Register of Copyrights. Published/Created: [Washington, D.C.]: U.S. Copyright Office, Library of Congress: For sale by the Supt. of Docs., U.S. G.P.O., 1988. Description: xi, 105, 11, 23 p.; 28 cm. ISBN: 084440618X Subjects: Copyright infringement--United States--States. Government liability--United States--States. Courts--United States. Jurisdiction--United States. LC Classification: KF3080.Z95 L5 1988 Dewey Class No.: 346.7304/82 347.306482 19

Copyright record books of the District Courts, 1790-1870 [microform]. Published/Created: [1790-1870] Related Authors: Roberts, Martin Arnold, 1875-1940. Records in the Copyright Office deposited by the United States District Courts, covering the period 1790-1870. Library of Congress. Rare Book and Special Collections Division. Description: 321 v. Notes: Accompanied by reel index and printed guide with title: Records in the Copyright Office deposited by the United States District Courts, covering the period 1790-1870 / by Martin A. Roberts. Original record books housed in the Library of Congress Rare Book Collection. Master microform held by: DLC. Microfilm. Washington, D.C.: Library of Congress, Photoduplication Service, 1977. 76 microfilm reels; 35 mm. MicRR guide no.: 11 and Z642.R64 1939 . LC Classification: Microfilm 49541 (K)

Copyright title pages of the United States. Published/Created: 1790-1870. Related Authors: Early Copyright Records Collection (Library of Congress) Description: ca. 44,000 items. Summary: Title pages deposited in United States federal Courts by authors and publishers as evidence of intention to publish. Notes: Originally part of copyright deposit records maintained by the District Courts of the United States. Forms part of: Early Copyright Records Collection (Library of Congress). Subjects: Copyright--Titles--United States. Title pages--Specimens. Copyright--United States--History--Sources. United States--Imprints--History--Sources. LC Classification: Z649.T5 C67 1790

Copyright, unfair competition & trademark cases [electronic resource]. Notes: Copyright, trademark, and unfair competition case library

Published/Created: Conklin, NY: Matthew Bender, Related Authors: Matthew Bender (Firm) United States. Supreme Court. Description: computer laser optical discs; 4 3/4 in. Issues for issued on two discs. Each issue is cumulative. Summary: Contains decisions of the U.S. Supreme Court; the U.S. Court of Appeals; the U.S. Court of Appeals for the Federal Circuit; the U.S. Court of Customs and Patent Appeals; the U.S. Court of Federal Claims; the U.S. Customs Court; the U.S. Court of International Trade; the U.S. District Courts; the U.S. Bankruptcy Courts; and state Courts. Notes: "Folio infobase." At head of disc: Authority from Matthew Bender. Description based on: Release 2 (12/96); title from disc label. System requirements: 386 or higher IBM compatible; Microsoft Windows 3.1 or higher; DOS 3.1 or higher; 4MB RAM; 10MB hard drive space available; CD-ROM drive; mouse; color monitor. Quick install Windows version; Release notes; How to use the Authority case law update feature; Using the LEXIS-NEXIS online connection. Subjects: Copyright--United States--Cases--Databases. Competition, Unfair--United States--Cases--Databases. Trademarks--Law and legislation--United States--Cases Databases.

Cornelius, Kay. The Supreme Court / Kay Cornelius; Arthur M. Schlesinger, Jr., senior consulting editor. Published/Created: Philadelphia: Chelsea House Publishers, c2000. Related Authors: Schlesinger, Arthur Meier, 1917- Description: 64 p.: ill. (some col.); 24 cm. ISBN: 0791055329 (hc) Summary: Surveys the history, decisions, justices, and controversies of the highest court in the land. Notes: Includes bibliographical references (p. 62) and index. Subjects: United States. Supreme Court--Juvenile literature. United States. Supreme Court. Judicial power--United States--Juvenile Literature. Courts. Law. Series: Your government--how it works LC Classification: KF8742.Z9 C59 2000 Dewey Class No.: 347.73/26 21

Cosgrave, George, 1870-1945. Early California justice: the history of the United States District Court for the Southern District of California, 1849-1944 / George Cosgrave; edited by Roy Vernon Sowers. Published/Created: San Francisco: Grabhorn Press, 1948. Related Authors: Sowers, Roy Vernon, 1897- Description: 97 p.: facsims.; 30 cm. Notes: "Four hundred copies printed"--T.p. verso. Includes bibliographical references and index. Subjects: United States. District Court (California: Southern District) District courts--California--History. LC Classification: KF8755.C3 C66

Coudert, Frederic R. (Frederic René), 1871- Certainty and justice; studies of the conflict between precedent and progress in the development of the law, by Frederic R. Coudert. Published/Created: New York, London, D. Appleton, 1913. Description: vii, 319, [1] p. 20 cm. Contents: Certainty and justice.--The challenge to the Constitution.--What is the matter with the law?--Jury trial as an instance of constitutional development.--Criminal procedure and the Constitution.--The Constitution and our new peoples; citizens, subjects, nationals or aliens.--The law and our industrial development. "The rule of reason."--Perversion of precedent. Stare decisis. History misinterpreted.--Aliens and the progress of the law.--Progress of international law in treatment of political crime.--The crisis of the law; professional incompetency. Notes: Partly reprinted from various sources. Subjects: Law--United States. Courts--United States. United States--Constitutional law. LC Classification: KF389 .C6

Coudert, Frederic René, 1871- Certainty and justice; Published/Created: New York and London, D. Appleton and company, 1914. Description: vii, 319, [1] p. 20 cm. Subjects: Law--Addresses, essays, lectures. Courts--United States. United States--Constitutional law. LC Classification: KF213 .C6 1914

Court administration: issues and responses / edited by Charles R. Swanson and Susette

M. Talarico. Published/Created: Athens, Ga.: Carl Vinson Institute of Government, University of Georgia, c1987. Related Authors: Swanson, Charles R., 1942- Talarico, Susette M. Description: 113 p.: ill.; 26 cm. ISBN: 0898541190 (pbk.) Contents: Keeping pace / Herbert Jacob [et al.] -- The training of court managers / Harvey E. Solomon -- The judicial executive / E. Keith Stott -- User fees for the Courts / David Bresnick -- Providing information about witnesses / Robert C. Davis -- Using technology to improve the administration of justice in the federal Courts / Charles W. Nihan and Russell R. Wheeler -- Cutback management in the judicial branch / Harry O. Lawson and Barbara J. Gletne -- Judicial impact statements / Keith Boyum and Samuel Krislov -- Bureaucratization of the federal Courts / Alvin B. Rubin -- Justice Potter Stewart's philosophy of federal judicial administration / James A. Grazell. Notes: Includes bibliographies. Subjects: Court administration--United States. LC Classification: KF8732.A75 C68 1987 Dewey Class No.: 347.73/13 347.30713 19

Court attendant (New York state civil service) Published/Created: New York: Arco Civil Service Publications, [1940] Description: 118 l.; 28 cm. Notes: Leaves variously numbered. Subjects: Courts--New York (State) Civil service--New York (State)--Examinations. Civil service--United States--Examinations. LC Classification: KFN5985.A65 A96

Court houses and court rooms, United States and New Jersey: their history and literature. Published/Created: Jersey City, N.J.: [John Marshall College], 1937. Related Authors: McLoughlin, William G. Description: 26 p.; ill.; 28 cm. Notes: Cover title. "With the compliments of John Marshall College." "Historical accounts contributed by William G. McLoughlin of the law faculty": p. [2]. Subjects: Courthouses--New Jersey. Courthouses--United States. Courts--New Jersey. Courts--United States. LC Classification: NA4472.N5 J6

Court improvement bulletin. Published/Created: [Chicago, Ill.]: American Judicature Society, c1981-1988. Related Authors: American Judicature Society. Coordinating Council of National Court Organizations (U.S.) Description: v.; 28 cm. No. 1 (spring 1981)-no. 15 (fall 1988) ISSN: 0731-3624 Notes: Title from caption. Issued in cooperation with the Coordinating Council of National Court Organizations. SERBIB/SERLOC merged record Subjects: Courts--United States--Periodicals. LC Classification: KF8712 .C68 Dewey Class No.: 347.73/1/05 347.307105

Court management journal. Published/Created: Williamsburg, Va.: National Center for State Courts, c1978-1985. Related Authors: National Center for State Courts. Description: 8 v.; 28 cm. 1978- Ceased with: 1985? ISSN: 0276-1661 Notes: "A joint publication of the Federal Courts Association, National Association for Court Administration, National Association of Trial Court Administrators, National Conference of Appellate Court Clerks." SERBIB/SERLOC merged record Subjects: Court administration--United States--Periodicals. LC Classification: KF8732.A15 C68 Dewey Class No.: 347.73/013/05 347.3071305

Court reform in seven States / Lee Powell, editor. Published/Created: [Chicago?]: American Bar Association, 1980. Related Authors: Powell, Lee. Implementation of Standards of Judicial Administration Project. Description: vii, 158 p.; 23 cm. Notes: "Products of the Implementation of Standards of Judicial Administration (ISJA) Project." Subjects: Courts--United States--States--Addresses, essays, lectures. Court administration--United States--States--Addresses, essays, lectures. Series: Publication (National Center for State Courts); R0054. LC Classification: KF8720 .C68 Dewey Class No.: 347.73/1 19

Court technology reports / Technical Services. Published/Created: Williamsburg, Va.: National Center for State Courts, Related

Authors: National Center for State Courts. Technical Services. Description: v.: ill.; 28 cm. Began in 1988. ISSN: 1053-7716 Notes: Some issues have also distinctive titles. Description based on: 1989. SERBIB/SERLOC merged record Subjects: Information storage and retrieval systems--Court administration--United States. Court administration--United States--Data processing. Series: Publication (National Center for State Courts) LC Classification: KF242.C68 C67 Dewey Class No.: 025.0634773013 025.0634730713 20

Courts and criminal justice: emerging issues / edited by Susette M. Talarico. Published/Created: Beverly Hills, Calif.: Sage Publications, c1985. Related Authors: Talarico, Susette M. Academy of Criminal Justice Sciences. Description: 175 p.: ill.; 23 cm. ISBN: 0803924380 0803924399 (pbk.) Notes: "Published in cooperation with the Academy of Criminal Justice Sciences." Includes bibliographies. Subjects: Criminal Courts--Criminal justice, Administration of--United States. Series: Perspectives in criminal justice; 9 LC Classification: KF9223 .C69 1985 Dewey Class No.: 345.73/05 347.3055 19

Courts and diversion: policy and operations studies / edited by Patricia L. Brantingham and Thomas G. Blomberg. Published/Created: Beverly Hills, CA: Sage Publications, c1979. Related Authors: Brantingham, Patricia L. Blomberg, Thomas G. American Society of Criminology. Description: 144 p.: ill.; 23 cm. ISBN: 0803913214 0803913222 (pbk.) Notes: "Papers presented at the 30th annual meeting of the American Society of Criminology, held in Dallas, Texas, November 8-12, 1978." Includes bibliographies. Subjects: Criminal justice, Administration of--Criminal Courts--Pre-trial intervention--United States. Pre-trial intervention--Australia--South Australia. Series: Sage research progress series in criminology; v. 14 LC Classification: KF9223.A75 C69 Dewey Class No.: 345/.73/05

Courts and free markets: perspectives from the United States and Europe / edited by Terrance Sandalow and Eric Stein. Published/Created: Oxford: Clarendon Press; New York: Oxford University Press, 1982. Related Authors: Sandalow, Terrance, 1934- Stein, Eric. Description: 2 v. (xxxix, 600 p.); 24 cm. ISBN: 0198253664 (v. 1) 0198253923 (v. 2) Notes: Includes bibliographical references. Subjects: United States. Supreme Court. Court of Justice of the European Communities. Interstate commerce--Law and legislation--United States. Interstate commerce--European Economic Community countries. LC Classification: K1030.4 .C68 1982 Dewey Class No.: 338.5/22 19

Courts and judges / James A. Cramer, editor. Published/Created: Beverly Hills: Sage Publications, c1981. Related Authors: Cramer, James A. Description: 280 p.; 23 cm. ISBN: 080391640X 0803916418 (pbk.) Notes: Includes bibliographies. Subjects: Courts--United States--Addresses, essays, lectures. Judges--United States--Addresses, essays, lectures. Series: Sage criminal justice system annuals; v. 15 LC Classification: KF8719.A2 C68 Dewey Class No.: 347.73/1 347.3071 19

Courts and justice: a reader / [edited by] G. Larry Mays, Peter R. Gregware. Edition Information: 2nd ed. Published/Created: Prospect Heights, Ill.: Waveland Press, c2000. Related Authors: Mays, G. Larry. Gregware, Peter R. Description: xii, 561 p.; 23 cm. ISBN: 1577660722 Notes: Includes bibliographical references and index. Subjects: Courts--United States. Justice, Administration of--United States. LC Classification: KF8700.A7 C667 2000 Dewey Class No.: 347.73/1 21

Courts and justice: a reader / [edited by] G. Larry Mays, Peter R. Gregware. Published/Created: Prospect Heights, Ill.: Waveland Press, c1995. Related Authors: Mays, G. Larry. Gregware, Peter R. Description: xii, 545 p.; 23 cm. ISBN: 0881338613 Notes: Includes bibliographical references and index.

Subjects: Courts--United States. Justice, Administration of--United States. LC Classification: KF8700.A7 C667 1995 Dewey Class No.: 347.73/1 347.3071 20

Courts and the culture wars / edited by Bradley C. S. Watson. Published/Created: Lanham, Md.: Lexington Books, 2002. Related Authors: Watson, Bradley C. S., 1961- Description: p. cm. ISBN: 0739104144 (hardcover: alk. paper) 0739104152 (paperback: alk. paper) Contents: Courts and the culture wars / Robert H. Bork -- From Ockham to Blackmun: the philosophical roots of liberal jurisprudence / Francis Canavan -- The death of the legalized constitution and the specter of judicial review / Keith Whittington -- The right to life, the higher law, and the Courts / Charles E. Rice -- Who owns the right to privacy / Jeremy Rabkin -- Tolerance and American constitutionalism: the case of gay rights / Murray Dry -- Religious freedom without religious neutrality: our once and future constitutional common sense / Graham Walker -- The one-way ratchet and other problems of stare decisis for cultural conservatives / John C. Eastman -- The California Supreme Court in the culture wars: a cast study in judicial failure / Edward J. Erler -- Courts, culture, and community: rescuing constitutional supremacy from judicial supremacy / Christopher P. Manfredi -- The Voting Rights Act and the politics of multiculturalism: the challenge to commercial republicanism at century's turn / Anthony A. Peacock. Notes: Includes bibliographical references and index. Subjects: Political questions and judicial power--United States. Judge-made law--United States. Civil rights--United States. Culture and law. United States--Social life and customs. LC Classification: KF5130 .C68 2002 Dewey Class No.: 347.73/12 21

Courts and the political process: Jack W. Peltason's contributions to political science / edited by Austin Ranney. Published/Created: Berkeley, Calif.: Institute of Governmental Studies Press, University of California, Berkeley, 1996. Related Authors: Ranney, Austin. Description: viii, 139 p.; 23 cm. ISBN: 0877723699 Notes: Papers from a symposium held on September 27, 1995, at the Institute of Governmental Studies, University of California. "Bibliography of Jack W. Peltason": p. 137-139. Includes bibliographical references. Subjects: Peltason, J. W. (Jack Walter), 1923- -- Contributions in political science. Courts--United States. Judicial process--United States. Law and politics. LC Classification: KF8719.A2 C69 1996 Dewey Class No.: 347.73/1 347.3071 20

Courts in American politics: readings and introductory essays / Henry R. Glick [editor]. Published/Created: New York: McGraw-Hill, c1990. Related Authors: Glick, Henry Robert, 1942- Description: xi, 405 p.: ill.; 24 cm. ISBN: 0070234973 : Notes: Includes bibliographical references. Subjects: Courts--United States. Judicial process--United States. Law and politics. LC Classification: KF8700 .C68 1990 Dewey Class No.: 347.73/1 347.3071 20

Courts of limited jurisdiction: a national survey / edited by Karen Markle Knab. Published/Created: [Washington]: National Institute of Law Enforcement and Criminal Justice, Law Enforcement Assistance Administration, U.S. Dept. of Justice: for sale by the Supt. of Docs., U.S. Govt. Print. Off., [1977] Related Authors: Knab, Karen Markle. American Judicature Society. American Judges Association. Description: xiv, 423 p.; 28 cm. Notes: Conducted by the American Judicature Society in cooperation with the American Judges Association. Includes bibliographical references. Subjects: Courts of special jurisdiction--United States--States. LC Classification: KF8759.Z95 C68 Dewey Class No.: 347/.73/28

Courts, corrections, and the Constitution: the impact of judicial intervention on prisons and jails / edited by John J. DiIulio, Jr. Published/Created: New York: Oxford University Press, 1990. Related Authors: DiIulio, John J. Description: xii, 338 p.; 22 cm. ISBN: 0195061411 (alk. paper) Notes:

Includes bibliographical references and index. Subjects: Prisons--Law and legislation--United States. Correctional law--United States. Judicial process--United States. LC Classification: KF9730 .C68 1990 Dewey Class No.: 344.73/035 347.30435 20

Courts, health science & the law / Georgetown University Medical & Law Centers. Published/Created: Baltimore, MD: Williams & Wilkins, c1990-c1991. Related Authors: Georgetown University. Medical Center. Georgetown University. Law Center. Description: 2 v.: ill.; 28 cm. Vol. 1, no. 1 (July 1990)-v. 2, no. 1 (summer 1991). ISSN: 1043-8483 Notes: Title from cover. SERBIB/SERLOC merged record Has Supplement: Insight into Courts 1043-8467 (DLC) 90642763 (OCoLC)19579783 Subjects: Medical laws and legislation--United States--Periodicals. Medical policy--United States--Periodicals. Health Policy--United States--periodicals. Jurisprudence--United States--periodicals. Legislation, Medical--United States--periodicals. LC Classification: K3 .O93 Dewey Class No.: 344 11

Courts, judges & politics: an introduction to the judicial process / [edited by] Walter F. Murphy, C. Herman Pritchett, Lee Epstein. Edition Information: 5th ed. Published/Created: Boston: McGraw-Hill, c2002. Related Authors: Murphy, Walter F., 1929- Pritchett, C. Herman (Charles Herman), 1907- Epstein, Lee, 1958- Description: xxii, 770 p.; 24 cm. ISBN: 0070441677 (pbk.: alk. paper) Notes: Includes bibliographical references and index. Subjects: Justice, Administration of--United States. Judicial process--United States. Political questions and judicial power--United States. LC Classification: KF8700.A7 C67 2002 Dewey Class No.: 347.73/1 21

Courts, judges, and politics: an introduction to the judicial process / [edited by] Walter F. Murphy, C. Herman Pritchett. Edition Information: 4th ed. Published/Created: New York: Random House, c1986. Related Authors: Murphy, Walter F., 1929- Pritchett, C. Herman (Charles Herman), 1907- Description: xiv, 657 p.; 24 cm. ISBN: 0394347404 (pbk.) : Notes: Includes bibliographies and indexes. Subjects: Judicial process--United States. Law and politics. LC Classification: KF8700.A7 C67 1986 Dewey Class No.: 347.73/1 347.3071 19

Courts, law, and judicial processes / edited by S. Sidney Ulmer. Published/Created: New York: Free Press; London: Collier Macmillan Publishers, c1981. Related Authors: Ulmer, S. Sidney. Description: xii, 564 p.; 24 cm. ISBN: 0029329809 0029329701 (pbk.) Notes: Includes bibliographical references and index. Subjects: Courts--United States. Judicial process--United States. LC Classification: KF8700.A7 C68 Dewey Class No.: 347.73/1 19

Cousar, Robert Moore, 1853-1903, ed. Digest of the laws and decisions relating to the appointment, salary, and compensation of the officials of the United States courts, Published/Created: Washington, Govt. print. off., 1895. Related Authors: United States. Laws, statutes, etc. United States. Dept. of justice. Description: 300 p. 24 cm. Subjects: Courts--United States. United States--Officials and employees--Appointment, qualifications, tenure, etc. United States--Officials and employees--Salaries, allowances, etc. LC Classification: KF8770 .C6 Microfilm LL 1171 KF

Covering the Courts: free press, fair trials & journalistic performance / Robert Giles, Robert W. Snyder, editors. Published/Created: New Brunswick, N.J.: Transaction Publishers, c1999. Related Authors: Giles, Robert H., 1933- Snyder, Robert W., 1955- Description: xi, 146 p.: ill.; 23 cm. ISBN: 076580462X (pbk.: acid-free paper) Notes: Originally published in the Media studies journal, winter 1998. Includes bibliographical references (p. 139-141) and index. Subjects: Free press and fair trial--United States. Conduct of court proceedings--United States. Newspaper court reporting--

United States. Mass media and criminal justice--United States. Series: Media studies series LC Classification: KF9223.5 .C68 1999 Dewey Class No.: 347.73/12 21

Coxe, Brinton, 1833-1892. An essay on judicial power and unconstitutional legislation, being a commentary on parts of the Constitution of the United States. By Brinton Coxe ... Published/Created: Philadelphia, Kay and brother, 1893. Related Authors: Meigs, William Montgomery, 1852-1929. ed. Description: xvi, 415 p. 24 cm. Notes: Edited by William M. Meigs. Subjects: Courts--United States. United States--Constitution. LC Classification: KF4575 .C6 1893

Coxe, Richard S. (Richard Smith), 1792-1865. A digest of the decisions in the Supreme court, Circuit courts, and District courts of the United States. By Richard S. Coxe. Published/Created: Philadelphia, P. H. Nicklin, 1829. Related Authors: United States. Supreme Court. United States. Circuit Courts. United States. District Courts. Description: viii, 752 p. 23 cm. Notes: Book-plate of James Louis P-etigru. Subjects: Law reports, digests, etc.--United States. LC Classification: LAW

Cramer, Frank. The case of the people against the lawyers and the courts; interviews with an outdoor philosopher, reported by Frank Cromer. Published/Created: Palo Alto, Calif., F. Cramer, 1915. Description: 143 p. 20 cm. Subjects: Justice, Administration of--United States. Courts--United States. LC Classification: JK1544 .C7

Cratsley, John C. Inherent powers of the courts / by John C. Cratsley. Published/Created: Reno: National Judicial College, American Bar Association at University of Nevada, c1980. Related Authors: Carrigan, Jim R. Description: xi, 59 p.; 26 cm. Notes: Earlier ed. by J. R. Carrigan. Includes bibliographies and indexes. Subjects: Court administration--United States. Judicial power--United States. LC Classification: KF8732.Z9 C3 1980 Dewey Class No.: 347.73/12 19

Creation of the federal judiciary. A review of the debates in the federal and state constitutional conventions; and other papers. Prepared by G. J. Schulz, director, Legislative Reference Service, Library of Congress. Published/Created: Washington, U.S. Govt. Print. Off., 1938. Related Authors: Schulz, George J. Description: iii, 293 p. incl. tables. 24 cm. Notes: Presented by Mr. Sheppard. Referred to the Committee on Printing July 22 (calendar day, July 27), 1937. Subjects: Courts--United States. LC Classification: KF350 .S34 Dewey Class No.: 347.90973

Criminal Courts for the 21st century / [compiled by] Lisa Stolzenberg, Stewart J. D'Alessio. Edition Information: 2nd ed. Published/Created: Upper Saddle River, N.J.: Prentice Hall, c2002. Related Authors: Stolzenberg, Lisa. D'Alessio, Stewart J. Description: viii, 455 p.: ill.; 24 cm. ISBN: 0130912891 Notes: Includes bibliographical references and index. Subjects: Criminal justice, Administration of--United States. Criminal Courts--United States. Criminal procedure--United States. Series: Prentice Hall's contemporary justice series. LC Classification: KF9223 .C745 2002 Dewey Class No.: 345.73/01 21

Criminal Courts for the 21st century / [compiled by] Lisa Stolzenberg, Stewart J. D'Alessio. Published/Created: Upper Saddle River, N.J.: Prentice Hall, c1999. Related Authors: Stolzenberg, Lisa. D'Alessio, Stewart J. Description: viii, 429 p.: ill., forms; 24 cm. ISBN: 0130805491 Notes: Includes bibliographical references. Subjects: Criminal justice, Administration of--United States. Criminal Courts--United States. Criminal procedure--United States. Series: Prentice Hall's contemporary justice series LC Classification: KF9223 .C745 1999 Dewey Class No.: 345.73/01 21

Criminal justice in America: theory, practice, and policy / [edited by] Barry W. Hancock, Paul M. Sharp. Edition Information: 3rd ed. Published/Created: Upper Saddle River, NJ: Prentice Hall, 2004. Related Authors: Hancock, Barry W., 1954- Sharp, Paul M. Description: p. cm. ISBN:

0130984116 (alk. paper) Notes: Includes bibliographical references. Subjects: Criminal justice, Administration of--United States. Law enforcement--United States. Criminal Courts--United States. Corrections--United States. Juvenile justice, Administration of--United States. LC Classification: HV9950 .C746 2004 Dewey Class No.: 364.973 21

Criminal justice in America: theory, practice, and policy / [edited by] Barry W. Hancock, Paul M. Sharp. Edition Information: 2nd ed. Published/Created: Upper Saddler River, NJ: Prentice Hall, 2000. Related Authors: Hancock, Barry W., 1954- Sharp, Paul M. Description: p. cm. ISBN: 0130832294 Notes: Includes bibliographical references. Subjects: Criminal justice, Administration of--United States. Law enforcement--United States. Criminal Courts--United States. Corrections--United States. Juvenile justice, Administration of--United States. LC Classification: HV9950 .C746 2000 Dewey Class No.: 364.973 21

Criminal justice in America: theory, practice, and policy / [edited by] Barry W. Hancock, Paul M. Sharp. Published/Created: Upper Saddle River, NJ: Prentice Hall, c1996. Related Authors: Hancock, Barry W., 1954- Sharp, Paul M. Description: x, 437 p.: ill.; 24 cm. ISBN: 0134338715 Notes: Includes bibliographical references. Subjects: Criminal justice, Administration of--United States. Law enforcement--United States. Criminal Courts--United States. Corrections--United States. Juvenile justice, Administration of--United States. LC Classification: HV9950 .H36 1996 Dewey Class No.: 364.973 20

Cummings, Homer S. (Homer Stillé), 1870-1956. Progress of the President's plan for judicial reform. An address by Honorable Homer Cummings, attorney general of the United States. April 26, 1937. Broadcast over the network of the National broadcasting company... Published/Created: [Washington, U.S. Govt. Print. Off., 1937] Description: 9 p. 24 cm. Notes: Cover-title. "Reprinted in the Congressional record for April 27, 1937, p. 5064." Subjects: United States. Supreme Court. Courts--United States. LC Classification: JK1521 .C8 Dewey Class No.: 347.99 [353.5] Govt. Doc. No.: J 1.2:J 88/3

Cummings, Homer Stillé, 1870- Selected addresses of Homer Cummings, attorney general of the United States, 1933-1939. Published/Created: [Washington, D.C., U. S. Govt. print. off., 1939] Description: 1 v. plates, port. 23 cm. Subjects: United States. Dept. of justice. United States. Supreme court. Law--United States--Addresses, essays, lectures. Courts--United States. Crime and criminals--United States. LC Classification: KF213 .C8 1939

Current rules governing the courts of the State of New Jersey, amendments to September ... / with comments and annotations by Sylvia B. Pressler. Published/Created: Newark, N.J.: Gann Law Books, Related Authors: Pressler, Sylvia B. United States. District Court (New Jersey) Description: v.; 23 cm. Began with 1972 ed. ISSN: 1065-8963 Notes: "Complete text of Rules of United States District Court for the District of New Jersey." Description based on: 1984 ed. (1983). SERBIB/SERLOC merged record Subjects: Court rules--New Jersey. LC Classification: KFN2329 .A197 Dewey Class No.: 347 12

Currie, David P. Federal courts: cases and materials / by David P. Currie. Edition Information: 4th ed. Published/Created: St. Paul, Minn.: West Pub. Co., 1990. Description: xliii, 783 p.; 26 cm. ISBN: 0314744851 Notes: Includes bibliographical references and index. Subjects: Jurisdiction--United States--Cases. Courts--United States--Cases. Series: American casebook series LC Classification: KF8858.A7 C8 1990 Dewey Class No.: 347.73/2 347.3071 20

Currie, David P. Federal courts: cases and materials / by David P. Currie. Edition Information: 3rd ed. Published/Created: St. Paul, Minn.: West Pub. Co., 1982. Description: li, 1042 p.; 26 cm. ISBN:

0314675973 : Notes: Includes index. Bibliography: p. xliii-l. Subjects: Jurisdiction--United States--Cases. Courts--United States--Cases. Series: American casebook series LC Classification: KF8858.A7 C8 1982 Dewey Class No.: 347.73/2 347.3071 19

Currie, David P. Federal courts: cases and materials / by David P. Currie. Edition Information: 2d ed. Published/Created: St. Paul: West Pub. Co., 1975. Related Authors: United States. Judiciary Act of 1789. 1975. Description: xli, 1040 p.; 27 cm. Notes: "The Judiciary Act of 1789": p. 983-996. Includes index. Bibliography: p. xxxvii-xli. Subjects: Jurisdiction--United States--Cases. Courts--United States--Cases. Series: American casebook series LC Classification: KF8858.A7 C8 1975 Dewey Class No.: 347/.73/2

Currie, David P. Federal courts; cases and materials, by David P. Currie. Published/Created: St. Paul, West Pub. Co., 1968. Description: xxxii, 823 p. 27 cm. Notes: Bibliography: p. xxix-xxxii. Subjects: Courts--United States--Cases. Jurisdiction--United States--Cases. Series: American casebook series LC Classification: KF8858.A7 C8 Dewey Class No.: 347/.73/2

Currie, David P. Federal jurisdiction in a nutshell / by David P. Currie. Edition Information: 4th ed. Published/Created: St. Paul, Minn.: West Group, 1999. Description: 242 p.; 19 cm. ISBN: 0314243526 (alk. paper) Subjects: Jurisdiction--United States. Courts--United States. Series: Nutshell series. LC Classification: KF8858.Z9 C87 1999 Dewey Class No.: 347.73/202 21

Currie, David P. Federal jurisdiction in a nutshell / by David P. Currie. Edition Information: 3rd ed. Published/Created: St. Paul, Minn.: West Pub. Co., 1990. Description: xlv, 242 p.; 19 cm. ISBN: 0314751211 Notes: Spine title: Federal jurisdiction. Includes index. Subjects: Jurisdiction--United States. Courts--United States. Series: Nutshell series LC Classification: KF8858.Z9 C87 1990 Dewey Class No.: 347.73/202 347.30712 20

Currie, David P. Federal jurisdiction in a nutshell / by David P. Currie. Edition Information: 2nd ed. Published/Created: St. Paul, Minn.: West Pub. Co., 1981. Description: xxxix, 258 p.; 19 cm. Notes: Includes index. Subjects: Jurisdiction--United States. Courts--United States. Series: Nutshell series LC Classification: KF8858.Z9 C87 1981 Dewey Class No.: 347.73/202 347.30712 19

Currie, David P. Federal jurisdiction in a nutshell / by David P. Currie. Published/Created: St. Paul: West Pub. Co., 1976. Description: xxiv, 228 p.; 19 cm. Notes: Includes index. Subjects: Jurisdiction--United States--Compends. Courts--United States--Compends. LC Classification: KF8858.Z9 C87 Dewey Class No.: 347/.73/202

Curtis, Benjamin Robbins, 1809-1874. Jurisdiction, practice, and peculiar jurisprudence of the courts of the United States. Edition Information: 2d ed., Published/Created: Boston, Little, Brown, and company, 1896. Related Authors: Merwin, Henry Childs, 1858-1929, ed. Description: xxvi, 341 p. 20 cm. Subjects: United States. Supreme court. United States. Circuit courts. United States. District courts. Courts--United States. LC Classification: KF8858 .C77 1896 Microfilm LL 1276 KF

Curtis, Benjamin Robbins, 1809-1874. Jurisdiction, practice, and peculiar jurisprudence of the courts of the United States. Published/Created: Boston, Little, Brown, and company, 1880. Related Authors: Curtis, George Ticknor, 1812-1894, ed. Curtis, Benjamin Robbins, 1855-1891, joint ed. Description: xviii, 298 p. 20 cm. Subjects: United States. Supreme Court. United States. Circuit courts. United States. District courts. Courts--United States. LC Classification: KF8719.A21 C8 Microfilm LL 1301 KF

Curtis, Benjamin Robbins, 1809-1874. Jurisdiction, practice, and peculiar jurisprudence of the courts of the United States / by Benjamin Robbins Curtis; edited, with notes, by George Ticknor Curtis and Benjamin R. Curtis. Published/Created: Littleton, Colo.: F.B. Rothman, 1989. Related Authors: Curtis, George Ticknor, 1812-1894. Curtis, Benjamin Robbins, 1855-1891. Description: xviii, 298 p.; 18 cm. ISBN: 083772015X (alk. paper) : Notes: Spine title: Courts of the United States. Reprint. Originally published: Boston: Little, Brown, 1880. Subjects: Jurisdiction--United States. Courts--United States. LC Classification: KF8858 .C77 1989 Dewey Class No.: 347.73/12 347.30712 20

Curtis, George Ticknor, 1812-1894. Commentaries on the jurisdiction, Published/Created: Philadelphia, T. & J. W. Johnson, 1854. Description: xxiv, 635 p. 23 cm. Subjects: United States. Supreme court. Courts--United States. United States--Constitutional law. LC Classification: KF8742 .C87

Curtis, Russell Hurd, 1850-1897, ed. Important federal statutes annotated, Published/Created: Chicago, Callaghan and company, 1891. Related Authors: United States. Laws, statutes, etc. Description: iv, iva-ivb, [v]-vii, 203 p. 24 cm. Subjects: Courts--United States. LC Classification: KF8714 1891

Cyclopedia of Federal procedure. Edition Information: 2d ed. by Palmer D. Edmunds, Clark A. Nichols and the publisher's editorial staff. Published/Created: Chicago, Callaghan, 1943-44. Related Authors: Edmunds, Palmer Daniel, 1890- Longsdorf, George Foster. Description: 14 v. 25 cm. Notes: First ed., 1928-30, by G. F. Longsdorf. On t. p., v. 1-9: In twelve volumes. Kept up to date by pocket supplements and revised vols. Subjects: Civil procedure--United States. Criminal procedure--United States. Courts--United States. LC Classification: KF8840 .C92

Cyclopedia of federal procedure. Edition Information: 3rd ed. Published/Created: [St. Paul, Minn.]: West Group, 1951- Related Authors: West Group. Lawyers Co-operative Publishing Company. Callaghan and Company. Description: v. 25 cm. Notes: Published in Chicago and Wilmette, Ill. by Callaghan (1951-1991) and in Rochester, N.Y. by Lawyers Cooperative Pub. (1992-1997). Vol. 17 (1988-) now issued in loose-leaf format. Kept up to date by pocket supplements, revised volumes, and supplementary pamphlets (some issued as amendments). Includes unnumbered loose-leaf Criminal procedure volume. Description based on: t.p., 1998 rev. vol. 2. LC holdings recorded in Shelflist only. Subjects: Civil procedure--United States. Criminal procedure--United States. Courts--United States. Civil procedure--United States--Forms. Criminal procedure--United States--Forms. LC Classification: KF8840 .C93 Dewey Class No.: 347.73/5 347.3075 19

D.C. federal Courts handbook. Edition Information: 2nd ed. Published/Created: Englewood Cliffs, NJ: Prentice Hall Law & Business, c1991- Related Authors: Prentice Hall Law & Business (Firm) Description: 1 v. (loose-leaf): ill.; 26 cm. ISBN: 0132032414 Subjects: Court rules--United States--Washington (D.C.) Courts--Washington (D.C.)--Directories. Judges--Washington (D.C.)--Biography. LC Classification: KF8816 .A2 1991 Dewey Class No.: 347.73/205 347.30725 20

D.C. federal Courts handbook. Published/Created: Clifton, N.J.: Prentice Hall Law & Business, c1988- Related Authors: Prentice Hall Law & Business (Firm) Description: 1 v. (loose-leaf): ill.; 26 cm. ISBN: 0131988883 (loose-leaf) Notes: Rev. ed. of: D. C. Circuit handbook. c1980- Includes index. Subjects: Court rules--United States--Washington (D.C.) Courts--Washington (D.C.)--Directories. Judges--Washington (D.C.)--Biography. LC Classification: KF8816 .A2 1988a Dewey Class No.: 347.73/205 347.307205 20

Dabney, Walter D. (Walter Davis), 1853-1899. Outlines of federal jurisdiction and law procedure / prepared as a basis of lectures to law students at the University of Virginia, by W. D. Dabney. Published/Created: [Charlottesville]: W.W. Olivier [c1897] Description: 1 p.l., [5]-260 p.; 23 cm. Notes: Includes table of cases and index. Bryson: no. 306. Subjects: Jurisdiction--United States. Courts--United States. LC Classification: KF885 .D3

Dallas, Alexander James, 1759-1817. Reports of cases ruled and adjudged in the several courts of the United States, and of Pennsylvania: held at the seat of the federal government / by A.J. Dallas. Published/Created: Philadelphia: Printed for the reporter at the Aurora Office, 1798-1807. Description: 3 v.; 24 cm. Vol. 2-v. 4. Current Frequency: Irregular Notes: Commonly cited as v.2-4 of:United States reports Published: Philadelphia: J. Ormond, 1799; Philadelphia: Printed for P. Byrne by Fry and Kammerer, 1807. Commonly cited as v. 1 of: United States reports Includes reports of the Supreme Court of the U.S. from 1790-1800 and of other courts 1781-1806 Continued in 1804 by: United States. Supreme Court. Reports of cases argued and adjudged in the Supreme Court of the United States. Subjects: Law reports, digests, etc.--United States Law reports, digests, etc.--Pennsylvania. LC Classification: KF101 .A212

Data processing and the courts: guide for court managers / Courts' Equipment Analysis Project; project staff, J. Michael Greenwood ... [et al.]. Published/Created: Denver: National Center for State Courts, 1977. Related Authors: Greenwood, J. Michael. Description: x, 44 p.: ill.; 28 cm. Notes: Includes bibliographical references. Subjects: Information storage and retrieval systems--Court administration--United States--Data processing. Series: Publication (National Center for State Courts); R0033g. LC Classification: KF242.C68 C68 Dewey Class No.: 347/.73/130285

Dator, James Allen. Alternative futures for the State Courts of 2020 / James A. Dator, Sharon J. Rogers. Published/Created: [Washington, D.C.]: State Justice Institute; Chicago, IL: American Judicature Society, c1991. Related Authors: Rodgers, Sharon J. State Justice Institute (U.S.) American Judicature Society. Future and the Courts Conference (1990: San Antonio, Tex.) Description: x, 206 p.; 25 cm. ISBN: 0938870521 Notes: Report with abstract of papers of the Future and the Courts Conference held in San Antonio, Texas in May 1990. Includes bibliographical references (p.195-206). Subjects: Courts--United States--States--Congresses. Justice, Administration of--United States--States Congresses. Procedure (Law)--United States--States--Congresses. Judges--United States--States--Congresses. LC Classification: KF8700 .A17 1990 Dewey Class No.: 347.73/3/0112 347.30720112 20

Davis, Horace A. (Horace Andrew), b. 1870. The judicial veto, by Horace A. Davis. Published/Created: New York, Da Capo Press, 1971 [c1914] Description: vi, 148 p. 23 cm. ISBN: 030670093X Subjects: United States. Supreme Court. Judicial review--United States. Courts--United States. LC Classification: KF4575 .A75D3 1971 Dewey Class No.: 347/.7312

Davis, Horace A. (Horace Andrew), b. 1870. The judicial veto, by Horace A. Davis. Published/Created: Boston, New York, Houghton Mifflin Company, 1914. Description: vi p., 1 l., 148 p., 1 l. 19 cm. Contents: I. Extra-constitutional law.--II. Judicial review.--III. Annulment of legislation by the Supreme Court. Notes. Appendix: New York statutes adjudicated. Notes: Chapter III is republished with slight revision from the American Political Science Review. cf. Pref. Subjects: United States. Supreme Court. Courts--United States. United States--Constitutional history. LC Classification: KF4575.A75 D3

Dawson, John M. Felons sentenced to probation in state courts, 1986 / by John M.

Dawson. Published/Created: Washington, D.C.: U.S. Dept. of Justice, Office of Justice Programs, Bureau of Justice Statistics, [1990] Related Authors: United States. Bureau of Justice Statistics. Description: ii, 16 p.; 28 cm. Notes: "November 1990." "NCJ-124944." Includes bibliographical references. Subjects: Criminal statistics--United States--States. Probation--United States--States--Statistics. Courts--United States--States--Statistics. Sentences (Criminal procedure)--United States--States Statistics. LC Classification: KF183 .D38 1990 Dewey Class No.: 345.73/077 347.30577 20

DeMascio, Robert E. Fourteen years or life: the bankruptcy court dilemma / by Robert E. DeMascio, William L. Norton, and Richard Lieb; introduction by Strom Thurmond; preface by Peter W. Rodino, Jr. Published/Created: Washington, D.C.: National Legal Center for the Public Interest, 1983. Related Authors: Norton, William L. Lieb, Richard. National Legal Center for the Public Interest. Description: xii, 48 p.; 23 cm. ISBN: 0960389431 (pbk.) : Notes: Includes bibliographical references. Subjects: Bankruptcy--United States. Courts--United States. Separation of powers--United States. LC Classification: KF1524.3 .D36 1983 Dewey Class No.: 346.73/078 347.30678 19

Derden, James. Digest of the decisions of the Supreme court of New Mexico, volumes 1 to 14, inclusive, and all New Mexico decisions in Pacific reporter, 1 to 106, inclusive, with tables of cases and with rules of the Supreme and District courts, Published/Created: Denver, W. H. Courtright, 1910. Related Authors: New Mexico. Supreme court. New Mexico. District courts. Description: 520 p. 24 cm. Subjects: Law reports, digests, etc.--New Mexico. Court rules--New Mexico. LC Classification: LAW

Desty, Robert, 1827-1895 A manual of practice in the courts of the United States, embracing the Revised statutes of the United States, relating to federal courts and practice therein, together with the rules and orders promulgated by the Supreme court of the United States, and the latest amendments thereto. Published/Created: San Francisco, S. Whitney & co., 1877. Description: 77, 77a-77d, 78-372, 372a-372 l. 373-447 p. 15 cm. Subjects: Courts--United States. Civil procedure--United States. Criminal procedure--United States. LC Classification: KF8840 .D4 1877

Desty, Robert, 1827-1895. A manual of practice in the courts of the United States. Edition Information: 6th ed. Published/Created: San Francisco, Bancroft-Whitney co., 1887. Description: 1. Courts--United States. Subjects: Civil procedure--United States. Criminal procedure--United States. LC Classification: KF8815 .A2 1887

Desty, Robert, 1827-1895. A manual of practice in the courts of the United States, Published/Created: San Francisco, S. Whitney & co., 1881. Description: 77, 77a-77d, 78-372, 372a-372m, 375-447 p. 16 cm. Subjects: Courts--United States. Civil procedure--United States. Criminal procedure--United States. LC Classification: KF8815 .A2 1881

Desty, Robert, 1827-1895. A manual of practice in the courts of the United States. Embracing the provisions of the Constitution, the Revised statutes, and amendments thereto relating to federal courts, together with the rules promulgated by the Supreme court of the United States. Edition Information: 8th ed. Published/Created: San Francisco, Bancroft-Whitney co., 1893. Description: 2 v. 16 cm. Subjects: Courts--United States. Civil procedure--United States. LC Classification: KF8840 .D4 1893

Desty, Robert, 1827-1895. A manual of practice in the courts of the United States. Embracing the provisions of the Constitution, the Revised statutes, and amendments thereto relating to federal courts, together with the rules promulgated by the Supreme court of the United States. Edition Information: 7th ed.

Published/Created: San Francisco, Bancroft-Whitney co., 1889. Description: xxvii, 24, 24a-24h, [25]-884, 884a-884s, [885]-902, [1] p., 1 l., [925]-1010 p. 16 cm. Subjects: Courts--United States. Civil procedure--Criminal procedure--United States. Criminal procedure--United States. LC Classification: KF8840 .D4 1889

Desty, Robert, 1827-1895. A manual of practice in the courts of the United States, Embracing the Revised statutes of the United States, Published/Created: San Francisco, S. Whitney & co., 1875. Description: 77, 77a-77d, 78-372, 372a-372 l, 373-447 p. 16 cm. Subjects: Courts--United States. Civil procedure--United States. Criminal procedure--United States. LC Classification: KF8840 .D4 1875

Desty, Robert, 1827-1895. A manual of practice in the courts of the United States. Embracing the Revised statutes of the United States, Edition Information: 2d ed. Published/Created: San Francisco, S. Whitney & co., 1876. Description: 77, 77a-77d, 78-372, 372a-372, l, 373-477 p. 16 cm. Subjects: Courts--United States. Civil procedure--United States. Criminal procedure--United States. LC Classification: KF8815 .A2 1876

Desty, Robert, 1827-1895. Digest of decisions of U. S. Circuit and District courts reported in the Federal reporter, vols. 1-20. Published/Created: St. Paul, West publishing co., 1885. Related Authors: United States. Circuit courts. United States. District courts. Description: v, 1157 p. 23 cm. Subjects: Law reports, digests, etc.--United States. LC Classification: LAW

Desty, Robert, 1827-1895. The removal of causes from state to federal courts. Published/Created: San Francisco, S. Whitney & co., 1882. Description: 2 p.l., [vii]-xii, [13]-283 p. 16 cm. Subjects: Removal of causes. Jurisdiction--United States. United States--Circuit courts. LC Classification: KF8860 .D4 1882 Microfilm LL 556 KF

Desty, Robert, 1827-1895. The removal of causes from state to federal courts, with a preliminary chapter on jurisdiction of the Circuit courts of the United States. Edition Information: 2d ed. Published/Created: San Francisco, Bancroft-Whitney co., 1888. Description: 2 p.l., [vii]-xii, [13]-346 p. 15 cm. Subjects: United States. Circuit courts. Removal of causes. Jurisdiction--United States. LC Classification: KF8860 .D4 1888 Microfilm LL 1253 KF

Desty, Robert, 1827-1895. A manual of practice in the courts of the United States. Embracing the provisions of the Constitution, the Revised statutes, and amendments thereto relating to federal courts, together with the rules promulgated by the Supreme Court of the United States. With notes of decisions. By Robert Desty... Edition Information: 6th ed. rev. Published/Created: San Francisco, S. Whitney, 1884. Description: xxvii, 24, 24a-24h, [25]-934 p. 15 cm. Subjects: Courts--United States. Civil procedure--United States. Criminal procedure--United States. LC Classification: KF8815 .A2 1884

Desty, Robert, 1827-1895. A manual of practice in the courts of the United States. Embracing the provisions of the Constitution, the Revised statutes and amendments thereto relating to federal courts, together with the rules promulgated by the Supreme court of the United States. With notes of decisions. By Robert Desty. Edition Information: 9th ed. Rev. and brought to date, with the addition of the rules of the Circuit courts of appeals, the Bankruptcy act, and general orders in bankruptcy. By M. A Folsom .. Together with a volume of forms, adapted and referring to this manual. By C. H. Tebbs. Published/Created: San Francisco, Bancroft-Whitney Co., 1899. Description: 4 v. 18 cm. Notes: Vol. 4 has title: Forms of procedure in the federal courts of the United States, including the official forms under the Bankruptcy act, 1898, with notes and special references to 9th ed. of Desty's federal procedure, as revised by M. A. Folsom. Compiled and arranged by C.

Harding Tebbs ... Subjects: Courts--United States. Civil procedure--United States. Criminal procedure--United States. Forms (Law)--United States. LC Classification: KF8840 .D4 1899 Dewey Class No.: 347.90973

Directory of administrative hearing facilities. Published/Created: [Washington, D.C.?]: Administrative Conference of the United States, Office of the Chairman, 1981. Related Authors: Administrative Conference of the United States. Office of the Chairman. Description: 210 p.: maps; 28 cm. Notes: "February, 1981." Subjects: Administrative Courts--United States--Directories. LC Classification: KF5417 .D57 Dewey Class No.: 342.73/0664 347.302664 19 Govt. Doc. No.: Y 3.Ad 6:2 D 62

Directory of federal court guidelines / Christine Housen, editor. Published/Created: Englewood Cliffs, NJ: Aspen Law & Business, c1996- Related Authors: Housen, Christine. American Bar Association. Section of Litigation. Description: 3 v. (loose-leaf): ports.; 26 cm. ISBN: 1567062962 (two-vol. set) Notes: "Published in cooperation with the ABA Section of Litigation." Includes index. Subjects: District Courts--United States--Outlines, syllabi, etc. Procedure (Law)--United States--Outlines, syllabi, etc. Court rules--United States--Outlines, syllabi, etc. Judges--United States--Directories. LC Classification: KF8816 .D57 Dewey Class No.: 347.73/22 21

Directory of state court clerks & county courthouses. Published/Created: Washington, D.C.: WANT Pub. Co., c1989- Related Authors: Want Publishing Company. Description: v.; 28 cm. 1990 ed.- ISSN: 1042-4172 Notes: SERBIB/SERLOC merged record Companion publication to: Want's Federal-state court directory. Want's Federal-state court directory 0742-1095 (DLC) 88654741 (OCoLC)10296033 Subjects: Clerks of court--United States--States--Directories Periodicals. County Courts--United States--Directories--Periodicals. Courts--United States--States--Directories--Periodicals. Courthouses--United States--Directories--Periodicals. Series: Your nation's Courts series LC Classification: KF8700.A19 D574 Dewey Class No.: 347.73/02/025 347.3072025 20

Disability reference guide for federal judiciary employees. Published/Created: [Washington, D.C.]: Administrative Office of the U.S. Courts, Employee Relations Office, [2000] Related Authors: United States. Administrative Office of the United States Courts. Employee Relations Office. Description: vi, 76 p.; 26 cm. Notes: "March 2000." Subjects: Courts--United States--Officials and employees--Handbooks, manuals, etc. People with disabilities--Services for--United States Directories. LC Classification: KF8732.Z9 D57 2000

Disaster recovery planning for Courts: a guide to business continuity planning / National Association for Court Management. Published/Created: Williamsburg, VA: National Association for Court Management, 2000. Related Authors: National Association for Court Management (U.S.) Description: iii, 45 p.: ill.; 28 cm. Notes: Title from cover. "National Association for Court Management Mini-Guide, Summer 2000."--Cover Includes bibliographical references (p. 41-45). Subjects: Court administration--United States. Court records--Safety measures. Data processing service centers--Safety measures. Disasters.

Disorder in the court: legal laughs, court jests, and just jokes culled from the nation's justice system / with a foreword by Richard Lederer. Published/Created: Vienna, VA: National Court Reporters Association, c1996. Related Authors: Lederer, Richard, 1938- Description: vii, 298 p.: ill.; 14 cm. ISBN: 1881859118 Subjects: Courts--United States--Humor. Law--United States--Anecdotes. LC Classification: K184 .D57 1996 Dewey Class No.: 347.73/1/0207 21

District court caseload forecasting: an executive summary: a report / prepared by the Research Division of the Federal Judicial Center. Published/Created: [Washington]: The Center, 1975. Description: iii, 40, 16 p.: graphs; 27 cm. Notes: "FJC 75-7." Subjects: District Courts--United States. Court administration--United States. LC Classification: KF8754 .F4 Dewey Class No.: 347/.73/223

District court studies project: interim report / Federal Judicial Center; prepared by Steven Flanders. Published/Created: [Washington]: The Center, 1976. Related Authors: Flanders, Steven. Description: xi, 68, [44] p.; 27 cm. Notes: "Second printing, July 30, 1976." Subjects: District Courts--United States. LC Classification: KF8754 .A84 Dewey Class No.: 347/.73/22

Divisions between traditionalism and liberalism in the American Jewish community: cleft or chasm / edited by Michael Shapiro. Published/Created: Lewiston [N.Y.]: E. Mellen Press, c1991. Related Authors: Shapiro, Michael, 1938- Description: 115 p.; 23 cm. ISBN: 0773494421 Notes: Includes bibliographical references ([107]-110) and index. Subjects: Roth, Philip--Criticism and interpretation. Ozick, Cynthia--Criticism and interpretation. Jews--United States--Politics and government. Judaism--United States. Rabbinical Courts--United States. Orthodox Judaism--United States. Feminism--Religious aspects--Judaism. United States--Ethnic relations. LC Classification: E184.J5 D56 1992 Dewey Class No.: 323.1/1924073 20

Dobie, Armistead Mason, 1881- ed. Cases and materials on federal jurisdiction and procedure, Published/Created: St. Paul, Minn., West publishing co., 1940. Related Authors: Ladd, Mason, 1898- joint ed. United States. Supreme court. United States. Supreme court. Advisory committee on rules for civil procedure. United States. District courts. United States. Circuit courts of appeals. Description: 1 p. l., vii-lxiv, 1045, xxi, 149, 1047-1091 p. illus. (map) 26 cm. Subjects: Jurisdiction--United States--Cases. Civil procedure--United States--Cases. Courts--United States. Civil rules--United States. Forms (Law)--United States. LC Classification: KF8839 .D6 1940

Dobie, Armistead Mason, 1881- Cases on federal jurisdiction and procedure, Published/Created: St. Paul, West publishing co., 1935. Related Authors: United States. Supreme court. United States. District courts. United States. Circuit courts of appeals. Description: xxxix, 803 p. illus. (map) 26 cm. Subjects: Jurisdiction--United States--Cases. Courts--United States. Law reports, digests, etc.--United States. LC Classification: KF8839 .D6

Dobie, Armistead Mason, 1881- editor. Cases and materials on Federal jurisdication and procedure. Edition Information: 2d ed. of Dobie and Ladd, by Ray Forrester. Published/Created: St. Paul, West Pub. Co., 1950. Related Authors: Ladd, Mason, 1898- joint editor. Forrester, Ray, editor. United States. Supreme Court. Rules of civil procedure. United States. Laws, statutes, etc. Judicial code, 1948. Description: xxxii, 968, 283, 969-990 p. map. 27 cm. Notes: First ed., by A. M. Dobie, published in 1935 under title: Cases on Federal jurisdiction and procedure. "Sources": p. x. Appendix (283 p., 3d group): Federal rules of civil procedure.--Title 28, United States code, Judiciary and judicial procedure, with amendments to January 1, 1950. Bibliographical footnotes. Subjects: Jurisdiction--United States--Cases. Civil procedure--United States--Cases. Courts--United States. Court rules--United States. Series: American casebook series LC Classification: KF8858.A7 D6 1950 Dewey Class No.: 347.9

Dobie, Armistead Mason, 1881- Handbook of federal jurisdiction and procedure, by Armistead M. Dobie. Published/Created: St. Paul, Minn., West Publishing Co., 1928. Related Authors: United States. Judicial code. 1928. United States. Supreme Court. Description: xiii, 1151 p.

24 cm. Notes: Spine title: Dobie on federal procedure. Appendix (p. 951-1098): Judicial code.--Equity rules.--Supreme Court rules. Lacks Table of Cases which is included in another ed. published the same year. Subjects: Courts--United States. Jurisdiction--United States. Court rules--United States. Series: Hornbook series LC Classification: KF8858 .D6 1928

Dodd, Walter Fairleigh. The growth of judicial power. Published/Created: Boston, Ginn & company, 1909. Description: 1 p.l., p. [193]-207. 23 cm. Subjects: Courts--United States. LC Classification: JH1541 .D7

Doernberg, Donald L., 1945- Federal courts, federalism, and separation of powers: cases and materials / by Donald L. Doernberg, C. Keith Wingate. Edition Information: 2nd ed. Published/Created: St. Paul, Minn.: West Group, 2000. Related Authors: Wingate, C. Keith, 1953- Description: xxx, 1130 p.; 26 cm. + teacher's manual. ISBN: 031423280X Notes: Includes index. Kept up to date by supplements. Subjects: Courts--United States--Cases. Jurisdiction--United States--Cases. Federal government--United States--Cases. Separation of powers--United States--Cases. Series: American casebook series LC Classification: KF8735.A7 D64 2000 Dewey Class No.: 347.73/2 21

Doernberg, Donald L., 1945- Federal courts, federalism, and separation of powers: cases and materials / by Donald L. Doernberg, C. Keith Wingate. Published/Created: St. Paul, Minn.: West Pub. Co., 1994. Related Authors: Wingate, C. Keith, 1953- Description: xxi, xxxi, 935 p.; 26 cm. ISBN: 0314029966 Notes: Includes index. Kept up to date by supplements. Subjects: Courts--United States--Cases. Jurisdiction--United States--Cases. Federal government--United States--Cases. Separation of powers--United States--Cases. Series: American casebook series LC Classification: KF8735.A7 D64 1994 Dewey Class No.: 347.73/2 347.3072 20

Doernberg, Donald L., 1945- Identity crisis: federal courts in a psychological wilderness / Donald L. Doernberg. Published/Created: Durham, N.C.: Carolina Academic Press, c2001. Description: xii, 264 p.; 23 cm. ISBN: 0890897417 Notes: Includes bibliographical references and index. Subjects: Judicial power--United States--Psychological aspects. Courts--United States--Psychological aspects. Judicial process--United States--Psychological aspects. Jurisdiction--United States--Psychological aspects. LC Classification: KF5130 .D64 2001 Dewey Class No.: 347.73/2 21

Domestic relations practice. Published/Created: [Eau Claire, Wis.] (P.O. Box 1208, Eau Claire 54701): Professional Education Systems, [c1985- Related Authors: Professional Education Systems. Description: v.: ill.; 28 cm. Notes: Volume lacks name of state in title. LC holdings recorded in Shelflist only. Subjects: Domestic relations Courts--United States--States. LC Classification: KF505.5.Z95 D66 1985 Dewey Class No.: 346.7301/5 347.30615 19

Downie, Leonard. Justice denied; the case for reform of the courts [by] Leonard Downie, Jr. Published/Created: New York, Praeger [1971] Description: 224 p. 22 cm. Notes: Bibliography: p. 219-221. Subjects: Justice, Administration of--United States. Courts--United States. LC Classification: KF8700 .D65 Dewey Class No.: 347/.731

Drafting history of the Federal rules of criminal procedure including comments, recommendations, and suggestions on published drafts of the rules ... / compiled and edited by Madeleine J. Wilken and Nicholas Triffin. Published/Created: Buffalo, N.Y.: William S. Hein, 1991. Related Authors: Wilken, Madeleine J. Triffin, Nicholas. Description: 7 v. in 5; 26 cm. ISBN: 089941754X (alk. paper) Notes: Includes bibliographical references (v. 7, p. 295-302) and indexes. Subjects: United States. Supreme Court. Rules of criminal procedure for the United States District Courts. Criminal procedure--United States--History--Sources. Court rules--United States--History--Sources. LC Classification: KF9606.515 .A15 1991 Dewey Class No.: 345.73/05 347.3055 20

Du Ponceau, Peter Stephen, 1760-1844. A dissertation on the nature and extent of the jurisdiction of the courts of the United States, being a valedictory address delivered to the students of the Law Academy of Philadelphia, at the close of the academical year on 22d April, 1824. Published/Created: New York, Arno Press, 1972. Description: xxxiii, 254 p. 23 cm. ISBN: 0405040075 Notes: Reprint of the 1824 ed. Subjects: Courts--United States. Jurisdiction--United States. Law--Study and teaching. Series: American law: the formative years LC Classification: KF8858 .D8 1972 Dewey Class No.: 347/.73/12

Du Ponceau, Peter Stephen, 1760-1844. A dissertation on the nature and extent of the jurisdiction of the courts of the United States: being a valedictory address delivered to the students of the Law Academy of Philadelphia, at the close of the academical year, on the 22d April, 1824 / by Peter S. Du Ponceau. To which are added, a brief sketch of the national judiciary powers exercised in the United States prior to the adoption of the present federal Constitution, by Thomas Sergeant ... and the author's discourse on legal education, delivered at the opening of the Law Academy, in February, 1821: with an appendix and notes. Published/Created: Littleton, Colo.: F.B. Rothman, 1993. Related Authors: Sergeant, Thomas, 1782-1860. Description: xxxiii, 254 p.; 21 cm. ISBN: 0837720389 Notes: Spine title: Du Ponceau on jurisdiction. Originally published: Philadelphia: A. Small, 1824. Subjects: Courts--United States. Jurisdiction--United States. Law--Study and teaching. LC Classification: KF8858 .D8 1993 Dewey Class No.: 347.73/12 347.30712 20

Du Ponceau, Peter Stephen, 1760-1844. A dissertation on the nature and extent of the jurisdiction of the courts of the United States: being a valedictory address delivered to the students of the Law Academy of Philadelphia ... on the 22d April, 1824 / by Peter S. Du Ponceau; to which are added, A brief sketch of the national judiciary powers exercised in the United States prior to the adoption of the present federal Constitution, by Thomas Sergeant; and the author's Discourse on legal education, delivered at the opening of the Law Academy, in February, 1821. Published/Created: Philadelphia: Published by Abraham Small, 1824. Related Authors: Sergeant, Thomas, 1782-1860. Brief sketch of the national judiciary powers exercised in the United States, from the first settlement of the colonies to the time of the adoption of the present federal Constitution. Du Ponceau, Peter Stephen, 1760-1844. Address delivered at the opening of the Law Academy in Philadelphia. Law Academy of Philadelphia. Description: xxxiii, 254 p.; 22 cm. Notes: "With an appendix and notes." Includes index of cases. References: Shoemaker 16014 Subjects: Courts--United States. Jurisdiction--United States. Law--Study and teaching. LC Classification: KF8858 .D8

Dust, George. Evils of judicial despotism and the remedy, Published/Created: [Des Moines, Iowa, American lithographing and printing company, c1913] Description: cover-title, 62 p. port. 18 cm. Subjects: Courts--United States. Justice, Administration of--United States. LC Classification: JK1544 .D8

Duty of courts to refuse to execute statutes in contravention of law. Published/Created: Washington, Govt. print. off., 1916. Description: 31 p. 24 cm. Subjects: Courts--United States. United States--Constitutional law. LC Classification: JK1541 .N7

Dwyer, John William, 1865- The law and procedure of United States courts, Published/Created: Ann Arbor, Mich., G. Wahr, 1901. Description: xxi, 339 p. 24 cm. Subjects: Courts--United States. LC Classification: KF8858 .D9

Dyer-Smith, P. S. (Philip Sidney), b. 1881. Federal examinations before trial and depositions practice at home and abroad, by P. S. Dyer-Smith with a foreword by Professor Edson R. Sunderland. Published/Created: New York, Baker, Voorhis & co., 1939. Related Authors: United States. District Courts. United States. Laws, statutes, etc. Description: lxxix, 1076 p. 24 cm. Contents: pt. 1.Examinations before trial.--pt. 2 Discovery and depositions.--pt. 3.Foreign depositions. Notes: "Tables of cases": p. liii-lxxix. Subjects: Pre-trial procedure--United States Discovery (Law)--United States Depositions--United States Judicial assistance--United States LC Classification: KF8900 .D9

Early, Stephen Tyree, 1923- Constitutional Courts of the United States: the formal and informal relationships between the District Courts, the Courts of Appeals, and the Supreme Court of the U.S. / Stephen T. Early, Jr. Published/Created: Totowa, N.J.: Littlefield, Adams, 1977. Description: xii, 184 p.; 21 cm. ISBN: 0822603209 Notes: Includes bibliographical references and index. Subjects: United States. Supreme Court. United States. Courts of Appeals. United States. District Courts. LC Classification: KF8700 .E2 Dewey Class No.: 347/.73/1

Edelman, Daniel B. EEO in the judicial branch: an outline of policy and law / Daniel B. Edelman. Published/Created: Williamsburg, VA: National Center for State Courts, c1981. Related Authors: National Center for State Courts. Description: 22 p.; 28 cm. ISBN: 0896560546 (pbk.) Notes: Cover title. Subjects: Courts--United States--Officials and employees. Discrimination in employment--Law and legislation--United States. LC Classification: KF8770.Z9 E3 Dewey Class No.: 344.73/01133 347.3041133 19

Edgerton, Henry White, 1888- The incidence of judicial control over Congress, Published/Created: Ithaca, N.Y., 1937. Description: p. 299-348. 26 cm. Subjects: United States. Supreme court. United States. Congress. Courts--United States. Legislation--United States. United States--Constitutional law--Cases. LC Classification: KF4575.Z9 E3

Eichner, James A. Courts of law, by James A. Eichner. Illustrated by Marvin Besunder. Published/Created: New York, F. Watts [1969] Related Authors: Besunder, Marvin, illus. Description: 66 p. illus. 23 cm. Summary: Explains the functions of many courts from the lowest to the highest. Also illustrates a typical court case from its inception to the jury trial. Subjects: Courts--United States--Juvenile literature. Courts. LC Classification: KF8700 .Z9E5 Dewey Class No.: 347.99/73

Eldridge, William Butler. The district court executive pilot program: a report on the preliminary experience in five federal courts / by William B. Eldridge. Published/Created: Washington, D.C.: Federal Judicial Center, [1984] Related Authors: Federal Judicial Center. Description: 28 p.; 28 cm. Notes: "June 1984." Item 743-C-3 Subjects: Court administration--United States. District Courts--United States. Series: FJC staff paper; FJC-SP-84-6 LC Classification: KF8732 .E43 1984 Dewey Class No.: 347.73/22 347.3072 19 Govt. Doc. No.: J 13.10/2:84-6

Ellingwood, Albert R. (Albert Russell), b. 1887. Departmental coöperation in state government, by Albert R. Ellingwood. Published/Created: Menasha, Wis., George Banta Pub. Co., 1918. Description: 6 p., 300 p. 20 cm. Notes: Thesis (Ph. D.)--University of Pennsylvania, 1918. Published also without thesis note. Discussion of advisory opinion. Bibliography: p. [295]-296. Subjects: Legislation--United States. Courts--United States--States. LC Classification: JK2525 .F53

Elliott, Shelden Douglass, 1906- Improving our courts; collected studies on judicial administration. Published/Created: New York, Published for the Institute of Judicial

Administration by Oceana Publications [1959] Description: 190 p. 22 cm. Subjects: Courts--United States. Justice, Administration of--United States. LC Classification: KF213 .E5 1959 Dewey Class No.: 347.9973

Elliott, Ward E. Y. The rise of guardian democracy; the Supreme Court's role in voting rights disputes, 1845-1969, [by] Ward E. Y. Elliott. Published/Created: Cambridge, Harvard University Press, 1974. Description: xiv, 391 p. 25 cm. ISBN: 0674771567 Notes: Bibliography: p. 281-299. Subjects: United States. Supreme Court. Suffrage--United States--History. Series: Harvard political studies LC Classification: KF4891 .E43 Dewey Class No.: 342/.73/07

Emerging trends in courthouse planning, design, administration and funding: transcript of the proceedings: a conference / sponsored by the American Bar Association, the American Institute of Architects, National Center for State Courts. Published/Created: Ann Arbor, Mich.: Institute of Continuing Legal Education, c1975. Related Authors: American Bar Association. American Institute of Architects. National Center for State Courts. Institute of Continuing Legal Education (Mich.) Description: 227 p.: ill.; 28 cm. Subjects: Court administration--United States--Congresses. Courthouses--United States--Designs and plans--Congresses. LC Classification: KF8732.A75 E5 Dewey Class No.: 725/.15

Emery, Lucilius A. (Lucilius Alonzo), 1840-1920. Concerning justice / by Lucilius A. Emery. Published/Created: Union, NJ: Lawbrook Exchange, 2002. Description: p. cm. ISBN: 1584772344 (cloth: alk. paper) Notes: Originally published: New Haven: Yale University Press, 1914. Subjects: Justice. Justice, Administration of. Courts--United States. LC Classification: JC578 .E6 2002 Dewey Class No.: 340/.11 21

Emery, Lucilius A. (Lucilius Alonzo), 1840-1920. Concerning justice, by Lucilius A. Emery. Published/Created: New Haven, Yale university press; [etc., etc.] 1914. Description: 170 p. 20 cm. Notes: "The addresses contained in this book were delivered in the William L. Storrs lecture series, 1914, before the Law school of Yale university." Subjects: Justice. Justice, Administration of. Courts--United States. LC Classification: JC578 .E6

Empirical theories about Courts / edited by Keith O. Boyum and Lynn Mather. Published/Created: New York: Longman, c1983. Related Authors: Boyum, Keith O. Mather, Lynn M. Description: xi, 284 p.; 24 cm. ISBN: 0582282179 Notes: Includes index. Bibliography: p. 250-277. Subjects: Courts--Research--United States. Courts--Research. Series: Longman professional studies in law and public policy LC Classification: KF8719.A2 E46 1983 Dewey Class No.: 347.73/1/0724 347.30710724 19

England, George Allan. Socialism and the law; the basis and practice of modern legal procedure and its relation to the working class, Published/Created: [Fort Scott, Kan., Monitor bdg. & ptg. co., c1913] Description: 1 p.l., 62 p. 22 cm. Subjects: Socialism. Courts--United States. LC Classification: HX530 .E6

Equal employment opportunity and affirmative action: a sourcebook for court managers / Cynthia G. Sulton ... [et al.]; [Carolyn McMurran, editor]. Published/Created: [Williamsburg, Va.]: National Center for State Courts, c1982. Related Authors: Sulton, Cynthia G. McMurran, Carolyn. Description: vi, 57 p.; 28 cm. ISBN: 0896560570 Notes: Cover title. Includes bibliographical references. Subjects: Courts--United States--States--Officials and employees. Discrimination in employment--Law and legislation--United States--States. Affirmative action programs--Law and legislation--United States--States. Series: Publication (National Center for State Courts); R0063. LC Classification: KF8770.Z95 E65 1982 Dewey Class No.: 344.73/01133/0269 347.30411330269 19

Equal employment opportunity in the federal Courts / Administrative Office of the United States Courts. Published/Created: [Washington]: The Office, [1981?- Related Authors: United States. Administrative Office of the United States Courts. Description: v.; 28 cm. 1981- ISSN: 0735-9187 Notes: Vols. for 1981- accompanied by narrative statements of federal Courts in separately published appendices. SERBIB/SERLOC merged record Subjects: Courts--United States--Officials and employees Periodicals. Affirmative action programs--United States--Periodicals. Courts--United States--Officials and employees--Statistics Periodicals. Affirmative action programs--United States--Statistics Periodicals. LC Classification: KF8770 .A83 Dewey Class No.: 347.73/1 347.3071 19 Govt. Doc. No.: Ju 10.22:

Erwin, James S. Law and practice in the District Courts of New Jersey containing...forms... Published/Created: Newark, N.J. Soney & Sage Company, 1931. Description: p. cm. LC Classification: LAW

Evaluating performance of criminal justice agencies / Gordon P. Whitaker, Charles David Phillips, editors. Published/Created: Beverly Hills: Sage Publications, c1983. Related Authors: Whitaker, Gordon P. Phillips, Charles David. Description: 303 p.; 23 cm. ISBN: 0803920482 0803920490 (pbk. Notes: Includes bibliographies. Subjects: Police--United States. Courts--United States. Correctional institutions--United States. Series: Sage criminal justice system annuals; v. 19 LC Classification: HV8141 .E92 1983 Dewey Class No.: 350.74/0973 19

Everett, Pamela I. Legal secretary bankruptcy / Pamela I. Everett; edited by Shary Smith. Published/Created: Santa Ana, CA: James Pub., c1987- Related Authors: Smith, Shary. Description: 1 v. (loose-leaf); 23 cm. ISBN: 0938065254 (loose-leaf) Subjects: Legal secretaries--United States--Handbooks, manuals, etc. Bankruptcy--United States. Courts--United States--Directories. LC Classification: KF319 .E92 1987 Dewey Class No.: 346.73/078 347.30678 19

Explaining the Courts: materials and sources. Published/Created: Chicago, Ill.: American Bar Association: Additional copies, ABA/JAD Lawyers Conference Office, c1983. Related Authors: American Bar Association. JAD Lawyers Conference. Description: x, 102 p.; 28 cm. ISBN: 0897071085 (pbk.) Notes: Includes index. Subjects: Courts--United States--Bibliography. LC Classification: KF8700.A1 E95 1983 Dewey Class No.: 016.34773/1 016.3473071 19

Facts about the American judicial system. Published/Created: [Chicago, Ill.]: American Bar Association, Division for Media Relations and Public Affairs, c1999. Related Authors: American Bar Association. Division for Media Relations and Public Affairs. Description: 35 p.; 27 cm. Notes: Cover title. Includes bibliographical references (p. 35). Subjects: Courts--United States--Miscellanea. Judges--United States--Miscellanea. Justice, Administration of--United States--Miscellanea. LC Classification: KF8700.Z9 F33 1999

Fahy, Charles, 1892-1979. Papers of Charles Fahy, 1857-1985 (bulk 1942-1975) Description: 35,000 items. 103 containers. 40.2 linear feet. Summary: Diaries (1918-1949), family and general correspondence, legal case files, subject files, speeches and writings, and other papers. The bulk of the collection consists of Fahy's case files while serving on the U.S. Court of Appeals for the District of Columbia Circuit, documenting a number of notable decisions in civil and criminal law, 1949-1976, Other papers relate to Fahy's role as an advisor to and representative of the presidential administrations of Franklin D. Roosevelt, Harry S. Truman, Dwight D. Eisenhower, John F. Kennedy, and Lyndon B. Johnson, including his negotiations on lend-lease operations with Great Britain in 1941, his work on the Committee Appointed to Review the Decartelization

Program in Germany (Ferguson Commission) that oversaw the disolution of industrial production there following World War II, and his chairmanship of the President's Committee on Equality of Treatment and Opportunity in the Armed Services (1948-1950). Also documented are Fahy's affiliations with the American Bar Association, Bar Association of the District of Columbia, Georgetown University, and the University of Notre Dame; his practice of law in Washington, D.C., and Santa Fe, N.M.; and his World War I experience as a naval aviator. Fahy (Fahey) family papers include correspondence, naturalization papers of his father, Thomas Fahy, and reminiscences and photograph relating to the death of Ellen Axson Wilson. Principal correspondents include Felix Frankfurter, Theodore Martin Hesburgh, Philip Levy, Joseph O'Meara, Simon E. Sobeloff, and Harry S. Truman. Notes: Sound recording transferred to Library of Congress Motion Picture, Broadcasting and Recorded Sound Division. MSS20164 Subjects: Eisenhower, Dwight D. (Dwight David), 1890-1969. Fahey family. Fahy, Thomas, 1844-1917. Frankfurter, Felix, 1882-1965 --Correspondence. Hesburgh, Theodore Martin, 1917- --Correspondence. Johnson, Lyndon B. (Lyndon Baines), 1908-1973. Kennedy, John F. (John Fitzgerald), 1917-1963. Levy, Philip, d. 1970 --Correspondence. O'Meara, Joseph, 1898- --Correspondence. Roosevelt, Franklin D. (Franklin Delano), 1882-1945. Sobeloff, Simon Ernest, 1894-1973 --Correspondence. Truman, Harry S., 1884-1972 --Correspondence. Wilson, Ellen Axson. Committee Appointed to Review the Decartelization Program in Germany (U.S.) United Nations. United States. Court of Appeals (District of Columbia Circuit) United States. President's Committee on Equality of Treatment and Opportunity in the Armed Services. American Bar Association. Bar Association of the District of Columbia. Georgetown University. University of Notre Dame. Cartels--Germany. Civil law--United States. Courts--Washington (D.C.) Criminal law--United States. Industries--Germany. Lend-lease operations (1941-1945) Practice of law--New Mexico--Santa Fe. Practice of law--Washington (D.C.) World War, 1914-1918--Aerial operations, American. Germany--History--1945-1955. Great Britain--Foreign relations--United States. United States--Foreign relations--Great Britain. United States--Politics and government--1945- United States--Politics and government--1933-1945. Jurists. Lawyers. Public officials. Local Call/Shelving: 0619GG

Fallon, Richard H., 1952- Hart and Wechsler's The federal courts and the federal system. Edition Information: 4th ed. / by Richard H. Fallon, Jr., Daniel J. Meltzer, David L. Shapiro. Published/Created: Westbury, N.Y.: Foundation Press, 1996. Related Authors: Hart, Henry Melvin. Wechsler, Herbert, 1909- Meltzer, Daniel J., 1951- Shapiro, David L., 1932- Description: xcix, 1733 p.; 26 cm. ISBN: 1566623359 (hardcover) Notes: Includes index. Kept up to date by supplements. Subjects: Courts--United States--Cases. Jurisdiction--United States--Cases. Judicial power--United States--Cases. Series: University casebook series LC Classification: KF8718 .H32 1996 Dewey Class No.: 347.73/2 347.3071 20

Family and conciliation Courts review. Published/Created: [Los Angeles?]: Association of Family and Conciliation Courts, 1989-c2000. Related Authors: Association of Family and Conciliation Courts. Description: 12 v.; 28 cm. Vol. 27, no. 1 (July 1989)-v. 38, no. 4 (Oct. 2000). ISSN: 1047-5699 Notes: Published: Newbury Park, CA: Sage Publications, 1991-July 1993; Thousand Oaks, CA: Sage Publications, Oct. 1993-2000. Title from cover. Includes bibliographies. Journal of the Association of Family and Conciliation Courts. SERBIB/SERLOC merged record Subjects: Domestic relations Courts--United States--Periodicals. LC Classification: K3 .A43 Dewey Class No.: 346.01/66/05 342/616605 20

Family court review. Published/Created: Thousand Oaks, CA: Sage Publications,

Inc., c2001- Related Authors: Hofstra University. School of Law. Description: v.; 26 cm. Some issues devoted to special topics. Vol. 39, no. 1 (Jan. 2001)- ISSN: 1531-2445 Notes: Title from cover. Sponsored by: AFCC--an Association of Family, Court and Community Professionals, and published in cooperation with Hofstra University School of Law. Subjects: Domestic relations Courts--United States--Periodicals. LC Classification: K3 .A43 Dewey Class No.: 346.01/66/05 342/616605 20

Farmer, Larry C. Appeals expediting systems: an evaluation of second and eighth circuit procedures / Larry C. Farmer. Published/Created: Washington, D.C.: The Federal Judicial Center, [1981] escription: v, 87 p.: ill.; 28 cm. Notes: "September, 1981." Item 743-C-1 Includes bibliographical references. Subjects: United States. Court of Appeals (8th Circuit) United States. Court of Appeals (2nd Circuit) Court congestion and delay--United States. Appellate Courts--United States. Series: FJC-R; 81-7 LC Classification: KF8727 .F37 1981 Dewey Class No.: 347.73/24 347.30733 19 Govt. Doc. No.: Ju 3.2:Ap 2

Farnum, George Rossiter, 1885- The spirit of adjudication and the changing times, Published/Created: [n.p., 1934] Description: 6 p. 26 cm. Subjects: Law--United States--Addresses, essays, lectures. Courts--United States. LC Classification: KF389 .F3

Faust, Frederic L., comp. Juvenile justice philosophy: readings, cases, and comments. Edited by Frederic L. Faust and Paul J. Brantingham. Published/Created: St. Paul, West Pub. Co., 1974. Related Authors: Brantingham, Paul J., joint comp. Description: xv, 600 p. 23 cm. Notes: Includes bibliographical references. Subjects: Juvenile Courts--Juvenile justice, Administration of--United States. Series: Criminal justice series LC Classification: KF9709 .F38 Dewey Class No.: 345/.73/08

Federal class action digests, 1976 / edited by Joseph T. McLaughlin. Published/Created: New York: Practising Law Institute, c1976. Related Authors: McLaughlin, Joseph T. Practising Law Institute. Description: v, 855 p.; 24 cm. Notes: "H3-2933." Digest of cases involving rule 23 of the Rules of civil procedure for the United States District Courts. Subjects: Class actions (Civil procedure)--United States--Digests. LC Classification: KF8896.A59 F433 1976 Dewey Class No.: 347/.73/5

Federal class action digests. Published/Created: New York, Practising Law Institute [1971] Related Authors: Practising Law Institute. Description: viii, 141 p. 23 cm. Notes: "H3-2870." Digest of cases involving rule 23 of the Rules of civil procedure for the United States District Courts. Subjects: Class actions (Civil procedure)--United States--Digests. Series: Litigation sourcebook series, no. 3 LC Classification: KF8896 .A59F43 Dewey Class No.: 347/.73/5

Federal court civil practice and procedure / presented by Committee on Continuing Legal Education of the Virginia Law Foundation. Published/Created: [Virginia]: The Foundation, c1988. Related Authors: Virginia Law Foundation. Committee on Continuing Legal Education. Description: 221 p. in various pagings: forms; 28 cm. Subjects: Civil procedure--United States. Courts--United States. Civil procedure--Virginia. Courts--Virginia. LC Classification: KF8841 .F457 1988 Dewey Class No.: 347.73/05 347.3075 19

Federal court civil practice: recent developments and local quirks / presented by Committee on Continuing Legal Education of the Virginia Law Foundation; in cooperation with Roanoke Bar Association ... [et al.]. Published/Created: [Norfolk?]: The Foundation, c1984. Related Authors: Virginia Law Foundation. Committee on Continuing Legal Education. Roanoke Bar Association. Description: 1 v. (various pagings): forms; 28 cm. Notes: Includes bibliography. Subjects: Civil procedure--

United States. Courts--United States. Civil procedure--Virginia. Courts--Virginia. LC Classification: KF8841 .F46 1984 Dewey Class No.: 347.73/5 347.3075 19

Federal court directory. Published/Created: Washington, D.C.: WANT Pub. Co., Related Authors: Grannan, K. C. Description: v.; 26 cm. ISSN: 0277-0199 Notes: "Including judiciary and bankruptcy judges, clerks, U.S. Attorneys, U.S. magistrates, probation officers, counties in districts and places where court sits." Editor: K.C. Grannan. Description based on: 1981 ed. Vols. for <1979- published also by Lawyers Diary & Manual, Newark, N.J. SERBIB/SERLOC merged record Subjects: Judges--United States--Directories. Courts--United States--Directories. Series: Lawyer's telephone directory series LC Classification: KF8700.A19 F42 Dewey Class No.: 347.73/14/025 347.30714025

Federal Court of Appeals manual: local rules. Published/Created: St. Paul, MN: West Group, 2000- Related Authors: West Group. Description: v.; 25 cm. Issue designated 2000-2001 published as special issue. 2000- ISSN: 1536-4496 Subjects: Appellate procedure--United States. Appellate Courts--United States--Rules and practice. Court rules--United States. LC Classification: KF9052.A39 F43 Dewey Class No.: 347 13

Federal Courts and law enforcement [Filmstrip] Published/Created: [n.p.] McGraw-Hill Book Co., 1950. Related Authors: Ferguson, John Henry, 1907- McGraw-Hill Book Company. Description: p. 44 fr. b&w. 35 mm. Notes: American government series, set 2, no. 2. Political science series. A Pathescope production. Correlated with the books The American system of government, the American Federal Government, and Elements of America Government, by Ferguson and McHenry. SUMMARY: Uses captioned drawings to explain the distinction between the two types of Federal Courts: constitutional Courts, including the Supreme Court, and legislative Courts. Describes the five types of cases which reach Federal Courts. Discusses the distribution of responsibility for Federal judicial administration and law enforcement. Subjects: Courts--United States. Justice, Administration of--United States. Series: American government series [Filmstrip] set 2, no. 2. Political science series [Filmstrip]

Federal Courts and the first amendment: resolved that one or more presently existing restrictions on the first amendment of press and/or speech established in one or more federal court decisions should be curtailed or prohibited?: intercollegiate debate topic, 1986-1987, pursuant to Public Law 88-246 / compiled by the Congressional Research Service, Library of Congress. Published/Created: Washington: U.S. G.P.O., 1986. Related Authors: Library of Congress. Congressional Research Service. Description: v, 101 p.; 24 cm. Notes: Distributed to some depository libraries in microfiche. Shipping list no.: 86-767-P. Item 996-A, 996-B (microfiche) Subjects: Freedom of speech--United States--Bibliography. Freedom of the press--United States--Bibliography. Series: House document (United States. Congress. House); 99-252. LC Classification: KF4772.A1 F43 1986 Dewey Class No.: 016.34273/0853 016.347302853 19 Govt. Doc. No.: Y 1.1/7:99-252

Federal Courts in the 21st century: cases and materials / Howard P. Fink ... [et al.]. Edition Information: 2nd ed. Published/Created: Newark, NJ: LexisNexis, c2002. Related Authors: Fink, Howard P. Description: xxx, 1084, 8, 12 p.; 27 cm. ISBN: 082055362X (hardbound) Notes: Includes index. Subjects: Courts--United States. Jurisdiction--United States. Judicial power--United States. LC Classification: KF8719 .F425 2002 Dewey Class No.: 347.73/2 21

Federal Courts. Published/Created: Manchaca, Tex.: Sterling Swift Pub. Co., c1976. Related Authors: Sterling Swift Publishing Company. Description: 44 p.; 28 cm.

ISBN: 0884080765 Subjects: Courts--United States--Outlines, syllabi, etc. LC Classification: KF8720 .F39 Dewey Class No.: 347/.73/2

Federal Courts: [comprehensive digest and analysis of legislation and jurisprudence]. Edition Information: 1976 ed. Published/Created: Baton Rouge, La.: Highland Pub. Co., c1976. Related Authors: Highland Publishing Company. Description: 57 p.; 28 cm. Subjects: Courts--United States. LC Classification: KF8720 .F4 1976 Dewey Class No.: 347/.73/2

Federal Courts: adaptable to courses utilizing materials by McCormick / editorial advisors, David H. Barber, Jon Neville, Robert A. Wyler; authors, Richard I. Aaron ... [et al.]. Edition Information: 1st ed. Published/Created: New York: Harcourt Brace Jovanovich Legal and Professional Publications; Gardena, CA: Distributed by Law Distributors, 1984, c1985. Related Authors: Barber, David H. Aaron, Richard I. (Richard Irving), 1936- McCormick, Charles Tilford, 1889-1963. Cases and materials on Federal Courts. Description: xiii, 234 p.; 28 cm. Notes: Includes index. Subjects: Civil procedure--United States--Outlines, syllabi, etc. Jurisdiction--United States--Outlines, syllabi, etc. Series: Legalines LC Classification: KF8841 .F47 1985 Dewey Class No.: 347.73/05 347.3075 19

Federal digest. Published/Created: St. Paul, West Pub. Co. [1940-60 Related Authors: United States. Courts. West Publishing Company, St. Paul. Description: 82 v. in 113. 27 cm. Subjects: Law reports, digests, etc.--United States. LC Classification: KF105.1 .F4

Federal District Courts' implementation of the 1982 Pretrial Services Act: report / by the U.S. General Accounting Office. Published/Created: Washington, D.C.: The Office, 1985. Related Authors: United States. General Accounting Office. Description: 3, 22 p.; 28 cm. Notes: Cover title. Shipping list no.: 85-1131-P. "September 26, 1985." "GAO/GGD-85-84." "B-220114"--P. [1]. Item 546-D Subjects: Pre-trial service agencies--United States. Pre-trial release--United States. District Courts--United States. LC Classification: KF9632 .A82 1985 Dewey Class No.: 353.008/8 19 Govt. Doc. No.: GA 1.13:GGD-85-84

Federal Judicial Code Revision Project: Council draft / the American Law Institute. Published/Created: Philadelphia, PA (4025 Chestnut St., Philadelphia 19104-3099): Executive Office, American Law Institute, c1996- Related Authors: American Law Institute. Description: v. <1-4; 28 cm. Notes: Submitted to the meeting of the Council of the American Law Institute. Subjects: Jurisdiction--United States. District Courts--United States. Venue--United States. Removal of causes. LC Classification: KF8858 .F43 1996

Federal judicial code revision project: preliminary draft / the American Law Institute. Published/Created: Philadelphia, PA (4025 Chestnut St., Philadelphia 19104-3099): Executive Office, American Law Institute, c1996- Related Authors: American Law Institute. Description: v. <1-4; 28 cm. Notes: Includes bibliographical references. Subjects: Courts--United States. Jurisdiction--United States. LC Classification: KF8720 .F44 1996 Dewey Class No.: 347.73/1 21

Federal judiciary almanac / W. Stuart Dornette and Robert R. Cross. Published/Created: New York: Wiley Law Publications, c1984- Related Authors: Dornette, W. Stuart. Cross, Robert R. Description: 4 v.: maps; 26 cm. 1984-1987. ISSN: 0749-4963 Notes: Supplements accompany some issues. SERBIB/SERLOC merged record Subjects: Courts--United States--Directories. Judges--United States--Directories. Courts--United States--Officials and employees Directories. Series: Federal practice library LC Classification: KF8700.A19 F43 Dewey Class No.: 347.73/1/025 347.3071025 19

Federal law on disc. District Courts, Eighth Circuit [electronic resource]: decisions of the United States District Courts, Eighth Circuit. Published/Created: Charlottesville, Va.: Lexis Law Pub., Description: computer optical discs; 4 3/4 in. Issues are cumulative. ISSN: 1528-0055 Notes: Description based on: Sept. 1998; title on disc. System requirements: IBM PC compatible computer with an Intel-compatible 486 (or greater) processor; Microsoft Windows 3.1 or higher; minimum of 4 MB (8 or more MB is recommended) of RAM; at least one fixed disk drive (hard drive) with 14 or more MB of free space; Windows-supported monitor and mouse; CD-ROM drive (ISO 9660/High Sierra); a modem, network, or Internet connection for use with Online Connection. Subjects: Law reports, digests, etc.--United States. LC Classification: KF120 8th.1 Dewey Class No.: 348 13

Federal law on disc. District Courts, Eleventh Circuit [electronic resource]: decisions of the United States District Courts, Eleventh Circuit. Published/Created: Charlottesville, Va.: Lexis Law Pub., Description: computer optical discs; 4 3/4 in. Issues are cumulative. ISSN: 1528-0047 Notes: Description based on: Oct. 1998; title on disc. System requirements: IBM PC compatible computer with an Intel-compatible 486 (or greater) processor; Microsoft Windows 3.1 or higher; minimum of 4 MB (8 or more MB is recommended) of RAM; at least one fixed disk drive (hard drive) with 14 or more MB of free space; Windows-supported monitor and mouse; CD-ROM drive (ISO 9660/High Sierra); a modem, network, or Internet connection for use with Online Connection. Subjects: Law reports, digests, etc.--United States. LC Classification: KF120 11th.1 Dewey Class No.: 348 13

Federal law on disc. District Courts, Fifth Circuit [electronic resource]: decisions of the United States District Courts, Fifth Circuit. Published/Created: Charlottesville, Va.: Lexis Law Pub., Description: computer optical discs; 4 3/4 in. Issues are cumulative. ISSN: 1528-0101 Notes: Description based on: Sept. 1998; title on disc. System requirements: IBM PC compatible computer with an Intel-compatible 486 (or greater) processor; Microsoft Windows 3.1 or higher; minimum of 4 MB (8 or more MB is recommended) of RAM; at least one fixed disk drive (hard drive) with 14 or more MB of free space; Windows-supported monitor and mouse; CD-ROM drive (ISO 9660/High Sierra); a modem, network, or Internet connection for use with Online Connection. Subjects: Law reports, digests, etc.--United States. LC Classification: KF120 5th.1 Dewey Class No.: 348 13

Federal law on disc. District Courts, First Circuit [electronic resource]: decisions of the United States District Courts, First Circuit. Published/Created: Charlottesville, Va.: Lexis Law Pub., Description: computer optical discs; 4 3/4 in. Issues are cumulative. ISSN: 1528-0136 Notes: Description based on: Oct. 1998; title on disc. System requirements: IBM PC compatible computer with an Intel-compatible 486 (or greater) processor; Microsoft Windows 3.1 or higher; minimum of 4 MB (8 or more MB is recommended) of RAM; at least one fixed disk drive (hard drive) with 14 or more MB of free space; Windows-supported monitor and mouse; CD-ROM drive (ISO 9660/High Sierra); a modem, network, or Internet connection for use with Online Connection. Subjects: Law reports, digests, etc.--United States. LC Classification: KF120 1st.1 Dewey Class No.: 348 13

Federal law on disc. District Courts, Fourth Circuit [electronic resource]: decisions of the United States District Courts, Fourth Circuit. Published/Created: Charlottesville, Va.: Lexis Law Pub., Description: computer optical discs; 4 3/4 in. Issues are cumulative. ISSN: 1528-011X Notes: Description based on: Oct. 1998; title on disc. System requirements: IBM PC compatible computer with an Intel-compatible 486 (or greater) processor; Microsoft Windows 3.1 or higher; minimum of 4 MB (8 or more MB is recommended) of RAM; at least one fixed disk drive (hard drive) with 14 or more MB of free space; Windows-supported monitor and mouse; CD-ROM drive (ISO 9660/High Sierra); a modem, network, or Internet connection for use with Online Connection. Subjects: Law reports, digests, etc.--United States. LC Classification: KF120 4th.1 Dewey Class No.: 348 13

Federal law on disc. District Courts, Ninth Circuit [electronic resource]: decisions of the United States District Courts, Ninth Circuit. Published/Created: Charlottesville, Va.: Lexis Law Pub., Description: computer optical discs; 4 3/4 in. Issues are cumulative. ISSN: 1528-0063 Notes: Description based on: Oct. 1998; title on disc. System requirements: IBM PC compatible computer with an Intel-compatible 486 (or greater) processor; Microsoft Windows 3.1 or higher; minimum of 4 MB (8 or more MB is recommended) of RAM; at least one fixed disk drive (hard drive) with 14 or more MB of free space; Windows-supported monitor and mouse; CD-ROM drive (ISO 9660/High Sierra); a modem, network, or Internet connection for use with Online Connection. Subjects: Law reports, digests, etc.--United States. LC Classification: KF120 9th.1 Dewey Class No.: 348 13

Federal law on disc. District Courts, Second Circuit [electronic resource]: decisions of the United States District Courts, Second Circuit. Published/Created: Charlottesville, Va.: Lexis Law Pub., Description: computer optical discs; 4 3/4 in. Issues are cumulative. Issued in multiple discs: disc 1, since 1992; disc 2, 1979-1991; disc 3, 1808-1978. ISSN: 1528-0144 Notes: Description based on: Oct. 1998; title on disc. System requirements: IBM PC compatible computer with an Intel-compatible 486 (or greater) processor; Microsoft Windows 3.1 or higher; minimum of 4 MB (8 or more MB is recommended) of RAM; at least one fixed disk drive (hard drive) with 14 or more MB of free space; Windows-supported monitor and mouse; CD-ROM drive (ISO 9660/High Sierra); a modem, network, or Internet connection for use with Online Connection. Subjects: Law reports, digests, etc.--United States. LC Classification: KF120 2nd.1 Dewey Class No.: 348 13

Federal law on disc. District Courts, Seventh Circuit [electronic resource]: decisions of the United States District Courts, Seventh Circuit. Published/Created: Charlottesville, Va.: Lexis Law Pub., Description: computer optical discs; 4 3/4 in. Issues are cumulative. Issued in multiple discs. ISSN: 1533-9181 Notes: Description based on: Feb. 1999; title on disc. System requirements: IBM PC compatible computer with an Intel-compatible 486 (or greater) processor; Microsoft Windows 3.1 or higher; minimum of 4 MB (8 or more MB is recommended) of RAM; at least one fixed disk drive (hard drive) with 14 or more MB of free space; Windows-supported monitor and mouse; CD-ROM drive (ISO 9660/High Sierra); a modem, network, or Internet connection for use with Online Connection. Subjects: Law reports, digests, etc.--United States. LC Classification: KF120 7th.1 Dewey Class No.: 348 13

Federal law on disc. District Courts, Sixth Circuit [electronic resource]: decisions of the United States District Courts, Sixth Circuit. Published/Created: Charlottesville, Va.: Lexis Law Pub., Description: computer optical discs; 4 3/4 in. Issues are cumulative. ISSN: 1528-0071 Notes: Description based on: Sept. 1998; title on disc. System requirements: IBM PC compatible computer with an Intel-compatible 486 (or greater) processor; Microsoft Windows 3.1 or higher; minimum of 4 MB (8 or more MB is recommended) of RAM; at least one fixed disk drive (hard drive) with 14 or more MB of free space; Windows-supported monitor and mouse; CD-ROM drive (ISO 9660/High Sierra); a modem, network, or Internet connection for use with Online Connection. Subjects: Law reports, digests, etc.--United States. LC Classification: KF120 6th.1 Dewey Class No.: 348 13

Federal law on disc. District Courts, Tenth Circuit [electronic resource]: decisions of the United States District Courts, Tenth Circuit. Published/Created: Charlottesville, Va.: Lexis Law Pub., Description: computer optical discs; 4 3/4 in. Issues are cumulative. ISSN: 1528-0152 Notes: Description based on: Oct. 1998; title on disc. System requirements: IBM PC compatible computer with an Intel-compatible 486 (or greater) processor; Microsoft Windows 3.1 or higher; minimum of 4 MB (8 or more MB is recommended) of RAM; at least one fixed disk drive (hard drive) with 14 or more MB of free space; Windows-supported monitor and mouse; CD-ROM drive (ISO 9660/High Sierra); a modem, network, or Internet connection for use with Online Connection. Subjects: Law reports, digests, etc.--United States. LC Classification: KF120 10th.1 Dewey Class No.: 348 13

Federal law on disc. District Courts, Third Circuit [electronic resource]: decisions of the United States District Courts, Third Circuit. Published/Created: Charlottesville, Va.: Lexis Law Pub., Description: computer optical discs; 4 3/4 in. Issues are cumulative. Issued in multiple discs: disc 1, since 1987; disc 2, 1785-1986. ISSN: 1528-0128 Notes: Description based on: Oct. 1998; title on disc. System requirements: IBM PC compatible computer with an Intel-compatible 486 (or greater) processor; Microsoft Windows 3.1 or higher; minimum of 4 MB (8 or more MB is recommended) of RAM; at least one fixed disk drive (hard drive) with 14 or more MB of free space; Windows-supported monitor and mouse; CD-ROM drive (ISO 9660/High Sierra); a modem, network, or Internet connection for use with Online Connection. Subjects: Law reports, digests, etc.--United States. LC Classification: KF120 3rd.1 Dewey Class No.: 348 13

Federal local court forms / [managing editor, George L. Bounds; editor, Joel E. Smith; index editor, J.W. Thomey; support staff, Jeannine Sims]. Edition Information: 2nd ed. Published/Created: Rochester, N.Y. (Aqueduct Bldg., Rochester 14694): Lawyers Cooperative Pub., 1994- Related Authors: Bounds, George L. Smith, Joel E. Hollins, Royanne R. Federal local court forms. Description: 3 v. (loose-leaf): forms; 30 cm. Contents: binder 1. General forms. District Court forms: Alabama to Idaho -- binder 2. District Court forms: Illinois to North Carolina -- binder 3. District Court forms: North Dakota to Wyoming. Courts of Appeals forms. Index. Notes: Statement of responsibility from unnumbered prelim. leaf. Rev. ed. of: Federal local court forms / by Royanne R. Hollins. Includes index. Subjects: Civil procedure--United States--Forms. LC Classification: KF8836 .H582 Dewey Class No.: 347.73/05/0269 347.30750269 20

Federal offenders in the United States District Courts / Administrative Office of the U.S. Courts. Published/Created: [Washington]: The Office, Related Authors: United States. Administrative Office of the United States Courts. Description: v.; 28 cm. Report year ends June 30. None published in 1975-1978, 1986-1989; combined issue published in 1990, covers 1986 through 1990. Began with 1962/63 issue; ceased with 1986 through 1990. ISSN: 0503-471X Summary: Report for 1979 includes summary data for 1975-1978. Notes: Some issues have title: Federal offenders in the United States Courts. Description based on: 1964. SERBIB/SERLOC merged record Subjects: Criminal statistics--United States--Periodicals. District Courts--United States--Periodicals. LC Classification: KF183 .F43 Dewey Class No.: 345.73/02 347.3052 Govt. Doc. No.: JU 10.11:

Federal reporter. Second series. Cases argued and determined in the Circuit Courts of Appeals and District Courts of the United States and the Court of Appeals of the District of Columiba, with key-number annotations. Published/Created: St. Paul, Minn., West Pub. Co. Related Authors: United States. Court of Appeals (8th Circuit) United States. Court of Appeals (District of Columbia Circuit) West Publishing Company. Description: v. ill. 26 cm. v. 1 (2d)- Nov. 1924- Supersedes: Federal reporter Notes: Title varies slightly. Ultrafiche. St. Paul, Minn., West Pub. Co. [1977?- sheets. 11 x 15 cm. SERBIB/SERLOC merged record Subjects: Law reports, digests, etc.--United States. LC Classification: Ultrafiche LL-F-50 KF105

Federal rules digest / edited by Pike and Fischer, Inc. Edition Information: 3rd ed. Published/Created: [St. Paul, Minn.]: West Group, [1973- Description: v. <3; 26 cm. Notes: "Decisions since April 1954." Published: Wilmette, Ill.: Callaghan (1973-1991); Rochester, N.Y.: Lawyers Cooperative Pub. (1991-1997). Includes Finding aids volume and separately numbered FRAP (Federal rules of Appellate procedure) volume. Companion publication to Federal rules service. Description based on: t.p., rev. v., 1998. Kept up to date by pocket supplements and revised volumes. LC holdings recorded in Shelflist only. Subjects: Court rules--Civil procedure--United States--Digests. LC Classification: KF8830.1 .F43 1973 Dewey Class No.: 347.73/5 347.3075 19

Federal rules of criminal procedure for the United States District Courts: effective March 21, 1946, as amended through December 1, 2000. Published/Created: Notre Dame, Ind.: National Institute for Trial Advocacy, c2000. Description: 127 p.; 16 cm. ISBN: 1556817010 LC Classification: *

Federal social security laws: selected statutes and regulations. Edition Information: 2000 ed. Published/Created: St. Paul, MN: West Group, c2000. Related Authors: West Group. Description: ix, 1103 p.; 26 cm. ISBN: 0314246649 Notes: Includes indexes. "Includes the Laws of the 106th Congress, First Session (1999)". Subjects: United States. Social Security Administration.--Rules and practice. Social security--Law and legislation--United States. Social security Courts--United States.

Feeley, Malcolm. Court reform on trial: why simple solutions fail / Malcolm M. Feeley. Published/Created: New York: Basic Books, c1983. Related Authors: Twentieth Century Fund. Description: xvii, 251 p.; 22 cm. ISBN: 0465014372 : Notes: "A Twentieth Century Fund report." Includes bibliographical references and index. Subjects: Courts--United States. LC Classification: KF8719 .F43 1983 Dewey Class No.: 347.73/1 347.3071 19

Fersch, Ellsworth A. Law, psychology, and the courts: rethinking treatment of the young and the disturbed / by Ellsworth A. Fersch, Jr. Published/Created: Springfield, Ill.: Thomas, c1979. Description: ix, 172 p.; 24 cm. ISBN: 0398038740 Notes: Includes bibliographies and indexes. Subjects: Law--Psychological aspects. Psychology, Forensic. Insanity--Jurisprudence. Courts--United States. LC Classification: K487.P75 F47 Dewey Class No.: 347.01/019

Field, George W. (George Washington), 1826-1889. A treatise on the Constitution and jurisdiction of the courts of the United States, on pleading, practice and procedure therein, and on the powers and duties of commissioners of the circuit courts, with forms for said courts and commissioners. By George W. Field. Published/Created: Philadelphia, T. & J.W. Johnson, 1883. Description: xxvi, 918 p. 24 cm. Subjects: Courts--United States. Court rules--United States. LC Classification: KF8719 .F57

Field, Richard H. The Richard H. Field papers [microform]. Published/Created: Frederick, MD: University Publications of America, [1987], c1986. Related Authors: University Publications of America, Inc. Description: 28 microfilm reels; 35 mm. ISBN: 0890938059 (microfilm) : Notes: Accompanied by a printed reel guide. MSS83242 Subjects: Field, Richard H.--Archives. Harvard Law School--Archives. Civil procedure--Courts--United States--History--Sources. Series: American legal manuscripts from the Harvard Law School Library LC Classification: KF373 Microfilm 21,162 Dewey Class No.: 016.34773/1 016.3473071 19

Final amended report of the Michigan procedure commission, prepared and submitted to the Supreme court of Michigan pursuant to Act no. 377, P. A. 1927, constituting a consolidation of the original report and the amendments subsequently submitted ... Published/Created: [Ann Arbor, The Lawyers club of the University of Michigan, 1929] Related Authors: Cummins, Alva Marvin, 1869- Description: 1 p. l., 120 p. 23 cm. Notes: Alva M. Cummins, chairman. "The Lawyers club of the University of Michigan has published this edition ... for free distribution to the members of the Michigan state bar association. Subjects: Court rules--Appellate procedure--Equity pleading and procedure--Michigan. LC Classification: LAW

Fink, Howard P. Federal jurisdiction: policy and practice: case and materials / Howard P. Fink, Mark V. Tushnet. Edition Information: 2nd ed. Published/Created: Charlottesville, Va.: Michie Co., c1987. Related Authors: Tushnet, Mark V., 1945- Description: xxiii, 1073 p.; 27 cm. Notes: Kept up to date by supplements. Includes index. Subjects: Jurisdiction--Courts--United States--Cases. Series: Contemporary legal education series LC Classification: KF8858.A7 F56 1987 Dewey Class No.: 347.73/1 347.3071 19

First, kill all the lawyers: legal proverbs, epitaphs, jokes, and anecdotes / compiled by Bill Adler; illustrations by Richard Zorn. Edition Information: 1st Carol Publishing Group ed. Published/Created: New York, N.Y.: Carol Pub. Group, 1994. Related Authors: Adler, Bill, 1929- Adler, Bill, 1929- Great lawyer stories. Description: viii, 147 p.: ill.; 16 cm. ISBN: 0806515872 Notes: Rev. ed. of: Great lawyer stories / by Bill Adler. Carol Publishing Group ed. 1993. "A Citadel Press book." Subjects: Lawyers--Law--Courts--United States--Humor. Lawyers--Law--Courts--United States--Anecdotes. LC Classification: K184 .G735 1994 Dewey Class No.: 818/.5402 20

Fish, Peter Graham. Federal justice in the Mid-Atlantic South: United States courts from Maryland to the Carolinas, 1789-1835 / by Peter Graham Fish. Published/Created: [Washington, DC: Administrative Office of the United States Courts, 2002?] Related Authors: United States. Administrative Office of the United States Courts. Description: xiv, 338 p.: ill.; 29 cm. Notes: Shipping list no.: 2002-0204-P. Include bibliographical references and index. Subjects: United States. Court of Appeals (4th Circuit)--History. Appellate courts--Maryland--History. Appellate courts--Virginia--History. Appellate courts--West Virginia--History. Appellate courts--North Carolina--History. Appellate courts--South Carolina--History. Govt. Doc. No.: JU 10.2:C 83/6

Fitzpatrick, Anne, 1978- The judiciary / by Anne Fitzpatrick. Published/Created: [Mankato, Minn.]: Creative Education, 2003. Description: p. cm. ISBN: 1583412638 (alk. paper) Summary: Introduces the Judicial Branch of the United States government and how it works. Subjects: Justice, Administration of--United States--Juvenile literature. Courts--United States--Juvenile literature. Judicial power--United States--Juvenile literature. Justice, Administration of. Courts. Judicial power. Series: Let's investigate LC Classification: KF8700.Z9 F58 2003 Dewey Class No.: 347.73/1 21

Flanders, Steven. Case management and court management in United States district courts / by Steven Flanders. Published/Created: [Washington]: Federal Judicial Center, 1977. Description: xi, 153 p.; 27 cm. Notes: On spine: Case and court management. Includes bibliographical references. Subjects: Court administration--United States. Series: District court study series FJC-R; 77-6-1 LC Classification: KF8732 .F6 Dewey Class No.: 347/.73/13

Flanders, Steven. The 1979 Federal District Court time study / Steven Flanders. Published/Created: Washington, D.C.: Federal Judicial Center, 1980. Related Authors: Federal Judicial Center. Description: v, 111 p.: 2 forms; 28 cm. Notes: "October, 1980." Includes bibliographical references. Subjects: District Courts--United States. Court administration--United States. Time study. Series: FJC-R; 80-8 LC Classification: KF8754 .F6 Dewey Class No.: 347.73/223 347.30723 19 Govt. Doc. No.: Ju 13.2:F 31/979

Flango, Victor E., 1942- Assessing the need for judges and court support staff / by Victor E. Flango, Brian J. Ostrom. Published/Created: [Williamsburg, Va.]: National Center for State Courts, c1996. Related Authors: Ostrom, Brian J. Description: ix, 124 p.: ill.; 28 cm. ISBN: 0896561623 Notes: Includes bibliographical references. Subjects: Courts--United States--States--Officials and employees. Judges--United States--States. Court administration--United States--States. Series: Publication (National Center for State Courts); R-182. LC Classification: KF8770.Z95 F57 1996 Dewey Class No.: 347.73/1 21

Flango, Victor E., 1942- Implementing the model annual report: National Court Statistics Project / Victor E. Flango, Mary E. Elsner. Published/Created: Williamsburg, Va.: National Center for State Courts, c1982. Related Authors: Oram, Mary Elsner, 1948- National Court Statistics Project (U.S.) National Center for State Courts. Description: vi, 141 p.: forms; 29 cm. ISBN: 0896560619 (pbk.) Notes: Includes bibliographical references. Subjects: Court administration--United States--States. Courts--United States--States--Statistical methods. Report writing. LC Classification: KF8732.Z95 F42 1982 Dewey Class No.: 347.73/13 347.30713 19

Florida digest, 1846 to date, Published/Created: St. Paul. West Pub. Co. [1936- Related Authors: Florida. Courts. United States. Courts. West Publishing Company, St. Paul. Description: 22 v. in 27 cm. Subjects: Law reports, digests, etc.--Florida. Law reports, digests, etc.--Southern States. LC Classification: KFF57 .F56

Forer, Lois G., 1914- Money and justice: who owns the courts? / Lois G. Forer. Edition Information: 1st ed. Published/Created: New York: Norton, c1984. Description: 244 p.; 22 cm. ISBN: 0393018695 Notes: Includes index. Bibliography: p. [221]-236. Subjects: Equality before the law--United States. Courts--United States. Legal assistance to the poor--United States. Justice, Administration of--United States. LC Classification: KF4764 .F67 1984 Dewey Class No.: 347.73 347.307 19

Foster, Roger, 1857- A treatise on federal practice, civil and criminal, including practice in bankruptcy, admiralty, patent cases, foreclosure of railway mortgages, suits upon claims against the United States, equity pleading and practice, receivers and injunctions in the state courts, by Roger Foster. Edition Information: 5th ed., rev. and enl. Published/Created: Chicago, Callaghan & company, 1913. Description: 3 v. 26cm. Notes: Paged continuously. Subjects: Courts--United States. Equity pleading and procedure--United States. LC Classification: KF8840 .F6 1913

Foster, Roger, 1857-1924 A treatise on federal practice, civil and criminal, including practice in bankruptcy, admiralty, patent cases, foreclosure of railway mortgages, suits upon claims against the United States, proceedings before the Interstate commerce commission and the Federal trade commission, equity pleading and practice, receivers and injunctions in the state courts, by Roger Foster. Edition Information: 6th ed., rev. and enl. Published/Created: Chicago, Callaghan & company, 1920-22. Description: 4 v. 26 cm. Notes: Paged continuously. Subjects: Courts--United States Equity pleading and procedure--United States LC Classification: KF8855 .F6

Foster, Roger, 1857-1924. A treatise on federal practice, civil and criminal; including practice in bankruptcy, admiralty, patent cases, foreclosure of railway mortgages, suits upon claims against the United States, equity pleading and practice, receivers and injunctions in the state courts, Edition

Information: 4th ed. Published/Created: Chicago, Callaghan and company, 1909. Description: 3 v. 25 cm. Subjects: Courts--United States. Equity pleading and procedure--United States. LC Classification: KF8840 .F6 1909

Foster, Roger, 1857-1924. A treatise on pleading and practice in equity in the courts of the United States; with chapters on jurisdiction of the federal courts, practice at common law, removal of causes from state to federal courts, and writs of error and appeals, with special reference to patent causes and the foreclosure of railway mortgages. Published/Created: Boston, The Boston book company, 1890. Description: lxxx, 822 p. 24 cm. Subjects: Courts--United States. Equity pleading and procedure--United States. LC Classification: KF8840 .F6 1890 Microfilm LL 766 KF

Foster, Roger, 1857-1924. The federal judiciary acts of 1875 and 1887. Published/Created: New York, L. K. Strouse & co., 1887. Description: viii, 109 p. 22 cm. Subjects: Courts--United States. LC Classification: KF8714 1887 Microfilm LL 1290 KF

Foster, Roger, 1857-1924. A treatise on federal practice in civil causes: with special reference to patent cases and the foreclosure of railway mortgages / by Roger Foster. Edition Information: 2nd ed. Published/Created: Boston: Boston Book Co., 1892. Description: 2 v.; 24 cm. Subjects: Courts--United States. Equity pleading and procedure--United States. LC Classification: KF8840 .F6 1892

Foster, Roger, 1857-1924. A treatise on federal practice, including practice in bankruptcy, admiralty, patent cases, foreclosure of railway mortgages, suits upon claims against the United States, equity pleading and practice, receiver and injunctions in the state court, by Roger Foster... Edition Information: 3d ed., rev. and enl. ... Published/Created: Chicago, Callaghan and company, 1901. Description: 2 v. 25 cm. Subjects: Courts--United States. Equity pleading and procedure--United States. LC Classification: KF8840 .F6 1901

Franck, Thomas M. Political questions/judicial answers: does the rule of law apply to foreign affairs? / Thomas M. Franck. Published/Created: Princeton, N.J.: Princeton University Press, c1992. Description: 198 p.; 25 cm. ISBN: 0691092419 (alk. paper) : Notes: Includes bibliographical references and index. Subjects: Political questions and judicial power--United States. Judicial review--United States. Courts--Separation of powers--National security--Law and legislation--United States. United States--Foreign relations. LC Classification: KF4651 .F73 1992 Dewey Class No.: 342.73/044 347.30244 20

Frank, Jerome, 1889-1957. Courts on trial; myth and reality in American justice. Published/Created: Princeton, Princeton University Press, 1949. Description: xii, 441 p. 25 cm. Notes: Includes bibliographical footnotes. Subjects: Courts--United States. Justice, Administration of--United States. Law--Psychological aspects. LC Classification: KF8700 .F7 1949

Frank, John Paul, 1917- Papers of John Paul Frank, 1951-1987. Description: 14 items. Summary: Correspondence (1983-1987) together with a legislative bill and a statement by Frank before the U.S. House of Representatives Committee on the Judiciary regarding the creation of an intermediate court of appeals to assist in reducing the work of the Supreme Court of the United States. Additional correspondence relates to attempts to desegregate American law schools in 1951 while Frank was a professor at Yale Law School. Notes: MSS6409 Forms part of: Miscellaneous Manuscripts collection. Subjects: United States. Congress. House. Committee on the Judiciary. United States. Supreme Court. Yale Law School--Faculty. Appellate Courts--United States. Segregation in higher education. Authors. Lawyers. Local Call/Shelving: MMC 0438 (Unprocessed ac. 22,317)

Frankfurter, Felix, 1882- ed. Cases and other authorities on federal jurisdiction and procedure, Published/Created: Chicago, Callaghan and company, 1931. Related Authors: Katz, Wilber Griffith, joint ed. 1902. Description: xix, 769 p. front. (map) 26 cm. Subjects: Jurisdiction. United States--Cases. Courts--United States Appellate procedure--United States--Cases. LC Classification: KF8858 .F7

Frankfurter, Felix, 1882-1965 ed. Cases and other authorities on federal jurisdiction and procedure. Edition Information: Rev. ed. Published/Created: Chicago, Callaghan and company, 1937. Related Authors: Shulman, Harry, 1903- joint ed. Description: xxiii, 835 p. front. (map) 26 cm. Subjects: Courts--United States--Cases. Jurisdiction--United States--Cases. Appellate procedure--United States--Cases. LC Classification: KF8858 .F7 1937

Frankfurter, Felix, 1882-1965. Power of Congress over procedure in criminal contempts in "inferior" Federal courts--a study in separation of powers, Published/Created: Cambridge, Mass., The Harvard law review association, 1924. Related Authors: Landis, James McCauley, 1899-1964, joint author. Description: 1010-1113 p. 26 cm. Subjects: United States. Congress--Powers and duties. Contempt of court--United States. Courts--United States. LC Classification: KF9415 .F72

Frankfurter, Felix, 1882-1965. The business of the Supreme court; Published/Created: New York, The Macmillan company, 1928. Related Authors: Landis, James McCauley, joint author. Description: viii p., 1 l., 349 p. 24 cm. Subjects: United States. Supreme court. Courts--United States. United States--Constitutional law. LC Classification: KF8748 .F66 1928

Frankfurter, Felix, 1882-1965. The business of the Supreme court; Published/Created: New York, The Macmillan company, 1927. Related Authors: Landis, James McCauley, 1899- joint author. Description: viii p., 1 l., 349 p. 24 cm. Subjects: United States. Supreme court. Courts--United States. United States--Constitutional law. LC Classification: KF8748 .F66 1927 Microfilm LL 1174 KF

Frankfurter, Felix, 1882-1965. The business of the Supreme Court; a study in the Federal judicial system, by Felix Frankfurter and James M. Landis. New York, Macmillan, 1928. Published/Created: [New York, Johnson Reprint Corp., 1972] Related Authors: Landis, James McCauley, 1899-1964, joint author. Description: viii, 349 p. 23 cm. Notes: Includes bibliographical references. Subjects: United States. Supreme Court. Courts--United States. Constitutional law--United States. LC Classification: KF8748 .F66 1972 Dewey Class No.: 347/.73/2609

Franklin, Marc A. The dynamics of American law; courts, the legal process, and freedom of expression, by Marc A. Franklin. Published/Created: Mineola, N.Y., Foundation Press, 1968. Description: xxi, 803 p. 27 cm. Notes: Bibliography: p. 761-769. Subjects: Justice, Administration of--United States. Freedom of speech--United States. Courts--United States. LC Classification: KF8719 .F7 Dewey Class No.: 347.99/73

Frantz, Albert T., 1903- How courts decide, by Albert T. Frantz. Published/Created: Buffalo, N.Y., W. S. Hein [c1968] Description: iii, 111 p. 24 cm. Notes: Includes bibliographies. Subjects: Courts--United States. Judicial process--United States. LC Classification: KF8720 .F7 Dewey Class No.: 347.99/73

Freedom under law: the legal process in a free society. Published/Created: St. Louis, 1963. Related Authors: Kohn, Alan C., 1932- Description: 3 v. 28 cm. Subjects: Courts--United States. Procedure (Law)--United States. LC Classification: KF8719.A2 B3

Fremlin, Ronald H. Modern judicial administration; a selected and annotated bibliography. Edited by Ronald H. Fremlin. Published/Created: [Reno, Nev.,

Court Studies Division, National College of the State Judiciary, 1973] Related Authors: National College of the State Judiciary (U.S.). Court Studies Division. Description: vii, 359 p. 24 cm. Subjects: Courts--United States--Bibliography. Justice, Administration of--United States--Bibliography. Court administration--United States--Bibliography. LC Classification: KF8700.A1 F7 Dewey Class No.: 016.347/73/13

Fretz, Donald R. Courts and the public / text prepared by Donald R. Fretz. Published/Created: Reno: National College of the State Judiciary, University of Nevada, c1977. Related Authors: National College of the State Judiciary. Description: xi, 115 p.: ill.; 26 cm. Notes: "820." Includes index. Bibliography: p. [108]-112. Subjects: Judges--United States. Courts--Public relations. Court administration--United States. LC Classification: KF8775 .F7 Dewey Class No.: 347/.73/1

Freyer, Tony Allan. Democracy and judicial independence: a history of the federal courts of Alabama, 1820-1994 / Tony Freyer & Timothy Dixon. Published/Created: Brooklyn, N.Y.: Carlson Pub., 1995. Related Authors: Dixon, Timothy, 1950- Description: xiii, 384 p.: ill.; 24 cm. ISBN: 0926019864 (hardback: alk. paper) Notes: Includes bibliographical references (p. 325-352) and index. Subjects: District courts--Alabama--History. District Courts--United States--History. LC Classification: KFA515 .F74 1995 Dewey Class No.: 347.761/02 347.61072 20

Fried, Charles, 1935- Order and law: arguing the Reagan revolution: a firsthand account / Charles Fried. Published/Created: New York: Simon & Schuster, c1991. Description: 256 p.; 25 cm. ISBN: 0671725750 : Notes: Includes bibliographical references (p. 207-245) and index. Subjects: Reagan, Ronald. Fried, Charles, 1935- Political questions and judicial power--United States. Courts--United States. Conservatism--United States. United States--Politics and government--1981-1989. LC Classification: KF8700 .F75 1991 Dewey Class No.: 347.73/1 347.3071 20

Friendly, Henry J. Federal jurisdiction: a general view [by] Henry J. Friendly. Published/Created: New York, Columbia University Press, 1973. Description: 199 p. 24 cm. ISBN: 0231037414 Notes: Includes bibliographical references. Subjects: Jurisdiction--United States. Courts--United States. Series: James S. Carpentier lectures, 1972. LC Classification: KF8858 .F75 Dewey Class No.: 347/.73/12

Friesen, Ernest C., 1928- Managing the courts, by Ernest C. Friesen, Edward C. Gallas [and] Nesta M. Gallas. Published/Created: Indianapolis, Bobbs-Merrill [1971] Related Authors: Gallas, Edward C., joint author. Gallas, Nesta M., joint author. Description: xvi, 341 p. 24 cm. Notes: Includes bibliographical references. Subjects: Court administration--United States. LC Classification: KF8732 .F7 Dewey Class No.: 347/.73/13

Fulton County daily report. Published/Created: [Atlanta, Ga.]: George M. Luttrell, Description: v.: ill.; 45 cm. Began in 1889; ceased in 1992. Notes: Description based on: Feb. 1, 1889. "Official organ of the United States District Court ... and of the Superior Courts of Fulton County as the official court newspaper." Decisions appearing in the Fulton County daily report are indexed in Fulton County daily report opinions. Fulton County daily report opinions (OCoLC)17627231 Related Item: Fulton County daily report opinions (OCoLC)17627231 Subjects: Courts--Georgia--Fulton County. United States Georgia Fulton Atlanta. LC Classification: CURRENT ISSUES ONLY

Garland, Augustus Hill, 1832-1899. A treatise on the constitution and jurisdiction of the United States courts, on pleading, practice and procedure therein and on the powers and duties of United States commissioners, with rules of court and forms, Published/Created: Philadelphia, T. & J.W. Johnson & co., 1898. Related Authors:

Ralston, Robert, 1863-1916, joint author. Ingham, John Hall, 1860- Description: 2 v. 24 cm. Subjects: Courts--United States. Jurisdiction--United States. Court rules--United States. Forms (Law)--United States. LC Classification: KF8719 .G3

Gavit, Bernard Campbell, 1893-1954. Cases and materials on an introduction to law and the judical process, Published/Created: Chicago, Callaghan and company, 1936. Description: xxiii, 633 p. 26 cm. Subjects: Common law. Common law--United States. Law. Jurisprudence. Law--Philosophy. Courts--United States. Courts--Great Britain. Briefs--United States. Briefs--Great Britain. Law--Bibliography. Law reports, digests, etc.--United States. Law reports, digests, etc.--Great Britain. LC Classification: KF385.A4 G3 1936

Gazell, James A. State trial courts as bureaucracies: a study in judicial management / James A. Gazell. Published/Created: New York: Dunellen Pub. Co.; Port Washington, N.Y.: distributed by Kennikat Press, c1975. Description: 168 p.: ill.; 23 cm. ISBN: 080467101X : Notes: "This book rests mainly on adaptions from a trilogy of articles ... State trial courts: an odyssey into faltering bureaucracies, which appeared in the San Diego law review 8 (March, 1971) ... Developmental syndromes in judicial management, which was published by the Brooklyn law review 38 (Winter, 1972) ... Indicators of managerial consciousness in an urban judicial bureaucracy ... printed by the Denver law journal 49 (1973)" Includes index. Bibliography: p. 165-168. Subjects: Courts--United States--States. Court administration--United States--States. LC Classification: KF8736 .G39 Dewey Class No.: 347/.73/3

Gazell, James A. The future of state court management / James A. Gazell. Published/Created: Port Washington, N.Y.: Kennikat Press, 1978. Description: 90 p.; 22 cm. ISBN: 0804691959 : Notes: Includes bibliographical references and indexes. Subjects: Court administration--United States--States. Courts--United States--States. Series: Multi-disciplinary studies in the law LC Classification: KF8732.Z95 G39 Dewey Class No.: 347/.73/3

Gehr, Marilyn. Structure of the judiciary court organization and judicial administration in New York and other states: a selected annotated bibliography / compiled by Marilyn Gehr and Katherine Storms. Published/Created: Albany: University of the State of New York, State Education Dept., New York State Library, Legislative Service, 1977. Related Authors: Storms, Katherine, joint author. Description: 25 p.; 28 cm. Subjects: Courts--United States--States--Bibliography. Court administration--United States--States--Bibliography. Courts--New York (State)--Bibliography. Court administration--New York (State)--Bibliography. LC Classification: KF8736.A1 G4 Dewey Class No.: 016.347/73/12

General digest of the decisions of the principal Courts in the United States, England and Canada. Published/Created: Rochester, N.Y., The Lawyers' co-operative publishing company, 1896-1907. Related Authors: United States. Courts. Great Britain. Courts. Canada. Courts. Description: 22 v. 25-27 cm. Subjects: Law reports, digests, etc.--United States. Law reports, digests, etc.--Great Britain. Law reports, digests, etc.--Canada. LC Classification: LAW

General digest of the decisions of the principal Courts in the United States, England and Canada. Includes all officially reported cases and all cases not to be officially reported which were first published between Sept. l, 1895, and [Oct.l, 1906] ... Refers to all reports, official and unofficial. v. 1-22. Edition Information: New series. Published/Created: Rochester, N.Y., The Lawyers' Co-operative publishing company, 1896-1907. Related Authors: United States. Courts. Great Britain. Courts. Canada. Courts. Description: 22 v. 25-27 cm. Notes: Title varies: v. l, General digest of the decisions of the principal Courts in the United States, England and

Canada; v. 2, General digest, American and English; v. 3-22, General digest, American and English, annotated. Subtitle varies. No more published. Subjects: Law reports, digests, etc.--United States. Law reports, digests, etc.--Great Britain. Law reports, digests, etc.--Canada. LC Classification: LAW

Geographical boundaries of U.S. courts of appeals and U.S. district courts, as set forth by 28 U.S.C. [Section] 41, 81-131 / Federal Judicial Center. Published/Created: [Washington, D.C.]: The Center, 1992. Description: 1 map: col.; 22 x 28 cm. Scale Information: Scale not given. Notes: Word section in the title represented by symbols. Includes ancillary maps of Alaska, Hawaii, Northern Mariana Islands, Guam, Puerto Rico and the Virgin Islands. Subjects: Appellate Courts--United States--Maps. District Courts--United States--Maps. LC Classification: G3701.F85 1992 .F4 Geographic Class No.: 3701

George, Jody. Handbook on jury use in the federal district courts / Jody George, Deirdre Golash, and Russell Wheeler. Published/Created: Washington, D.C.: Federal Judicial Center, 1989. Related Authors: Golash, Deirdre. Wheeler, Russell R., 1943- Federal Judicial Center. Description: xiii, 93 p.; 24 cm. Notes: Shipping list no.: 89-357-P. Item 743-C-3 Includes bibliographical references. Subjects: Jury--United States. District Courts--United States. Series: FJC-M; 89-1 LC Classification: KF8972 .G46 1989 Dewey Class No.: 347.73/0752 347.307752 20 Govt. Doc. No.: Ju 13.10/3:89-1

Gerber, Rudolph Joseph, 1938- Lawyers, courts, and professionalism: the agenda for reform / Rudolph J. Gerber; forewords by Sandra Day O'Connor, Daniel J. Meador. Published/Created: New York: Greenwood Press, 1989. Description: xiv, 156 p.; 24 cm. ISBN: 0313265674 (lib. bdg.: alk. paper) Notes: Includes index. Bibliography: p. [151]-152. Subjects: Lawyers--United States. Justice, Administration of--United States. Courts--United States. Series: Contributions in legal studies, 0147-1074; no. 50 LC Classification: KF297 .G47 1989 Dewey Class No.: 349.73/092/2 347.300922 19

Gilbert law summaries. Federal Courts. Published/Created: Chicago, IL: Harcourt Brace Jovanovich Legal and Professional Publications; Gardena, CA: Distributed by Law Distributors, c1987- Description: v.; 28 cm. 1st ed. (1987-88)- ISSN: 1051-5585 Notes: Some issues have also supplements included in pages preceding t.p. SERBIB/SERLOC merged record Subjects: Courts--United States--Outlines, syllabi, etc. Jurisdiction--United States--Outlines, syllabi, etc. LC Classification: KF8720 .G55 Dewey Class No.: 347.73/2 347.3072 20

Giles, William Branch, 1762-1830. Speech of Mr. Giles. Published/Created: [Washington? 1802] Description: 20 p. 23 cm. Subjects: Courts--United States. LC Classification: JK1551 .G45

Giles, William Branch, 1762-1830. The speeches of Mr. Giles and Mr. Bayard, the House of representatives of the United States, February, 1802. Published/Created: Boston: Printed by Munroe & Francis, Half-court square, opposite the south-east corner of the Mercury-office. Sold by them, and at the several book-stores, 1802. Related Authors: Bayard, James Asheton, 1767-1815. Description: 56 p. 21 cm. Subjects: Courts--United States. LC Classification: JK1551 .G5

Gillespie, George Benjamin, 1863- The judicial power; its content, source and adaptation to modern society. Published/Created: [Springfield, Ill., Phillips brothers, 1933] Description: cover-title, 2 p. l., 3-119 p. 24 cm. Notes: Foreword signed: George B. Gillespie. Subjects: Courts--United States. United States--Constitutional law. LC Classification: JK1551 .G54

Gillespie, Robert W. Judicial productivity and court delay: an exploratory analysis of the Federal District Courts / Robert W. Gillespie. Published/Created:

[Washington]: National Institute of Law Enforcement and Criminal Justice, Law Enforcement Assistance Administration, United States Dept. of Justice: for sale by Supt. of Docs., U.S. Govt. Print. Off., 1977. Related Authors: National Institute of Law Enforcement and Criminal Justice. Description: xxi, 90 p.: graphs; 26 cm. Notes: At head of title: Visiting fellowship program report. Includes bibliographical references. Subjects: Court congestion and delay--United States. District Courts--United States. Judicial statistics--United States. LC Classification: KF8727 .G5 Dewey Class No.: 347/.73/223

Gisnet, Morris, 1880- A lawyer tells the truth, by Morris Gisnet, introduction by Norman Thomas ... Published/Created: New York, J.P. Kahn, 1931. Description: 160 p. 20 cm. Subjects: Lawyers--United States. Justice, Administration of--United States. Courts--United States. Legal ethics--United States. LC Classification: KF306.Z9 G5

Givler, David Byers. Illinois civil practice desk book, Edition Information: 1st ed. Published/Created: Springfield, Ill., Western law book company, inc. [c1939] Related Authors: United States. Supreme court. United States. District courts. Description: 3 p.l., 380 p. 24 cm. Subjects: Civil procedure--Illinois. Courts--Illinois. Court rules--Illinois. Court rules--United States. LC Classification: KFI1729 .A2 1939

Glick, Henry Robert, 1942- Courts, politics, and justice / Henry R. Glick. Edition Information: 3rd ed. Published/Created: New York: McGraw-Hill, c1993. Description: xiv, 465 p.: ill., maps; 24 cm. ISBN: 0070235538 Notes: Cover title: Courts, politics & justice. Includes bibliographical references and index. Subjects: Courts--United States. Judicial process--United States. Political questions and judicial power--United States. LC Classification: KF8700 .G55 1993 Dewey Class No.: 347.73/1 347.3071 20

Glick, Henry Robert, 1942- Courts, politics, and justice / Henry R. Glick. Edition Information: 2nd ed. Published/Created: New York: McGraw-Hill, c1988. Description: xiv, 378 p.: maps; 24 cm. ISBN: 0070234930 (pbk.) : Notes: Includes bibliographies and index. Subjects: Courts--United States. Judicial process--United States. LC Classification: KF8700 .G55 1988 Dewey Class No.: 347.73/1 347.3071 19

Glick, Henry Robert, 1942- Courts, politics, and justice / Henry R. Glick. Published/Created: New York: McGraw-Hill, c1983. Description: x, 355 p.; 23 cm. ISBN: 0070234906 (pbk.) : Notes: Includes bibliographical references and index. Subjects: Courts--United States. Judicial process--United States. LC Classification: KF8700 .G55 1983 Dewey Class No.: 347.73/1 347.3071 19

Glick, Henry Robert, 1942- State court systems [by] Henry Robert Glick [and] Kenneth N. Vines. Published/Created: Englewood Cliffs, N.J., Prentice-Hall [1973] Related Authors: Vines, Kenneth Nelson, 1924- joint author. Description: xiv, 111 p. 23 cm. ISBN: 0138429979 Notes: Includes bibliographical references. Subjects: Courts--United States--States. Judges--United States--States. LC Classification: KF8736 .G54 Dewey Class No.: 347/.73/1

Glover, Denise Marie. A total approach to diversity: an assessment and curriculum guide for state courts / [Denise M. Glover and John G. Richardson] Published/Created: [Williamsburg, Va.]: National Center for State Courts, c1997. Related Authors: Richardson, John G. (John Gregory), 1958- National Center for State Courts. Description: 1 v. (various pagings); 28 cm. ISBN: 0896561755 Contents: Introduction and overview -- Getting started -- Assessing the diversity-training needs of your court -- Working with diversity consultants -- Designing the program -- Evaluating the program -- Appendices. Notes: This title is based on Denise Glover's Diversity in the courts: a guide for assessment and training. Includes bibliographical references. Funded by a grant from the Bureau of Justice Assistance

95-DD-BX-0010 Subjects: Courts--United States--Officials and employees. Court administration--United States. Diversity in the workplace--United States. Series: Access to justice for persons of color; model guide 1 Publication (National Center for State Courts); R-194. LC Classification: KF8770 .G5 1997 Dewey Class No.: 347.73/13 21

Goldberg, Louis Palatnik, 1888- Lawless judges Published/Created: New York, The Rand school press, 1935. Related Authors: Levenson, Eleanore, 1905- joint author. Description: 3 p.l., x, 303 p. 22 cm. Subjects: Justice, Administration of--United States. Courts--United States. Judges--United States. Law reports, digests, etc.--United States. LC Classification: KF8700 .G6 1935

Goldberg, Louis Palatnik, 1888- Lawless judges [by] Louis P. Goldberg and Eleanore Levenson. With an introd. by Morris R. Cohen. Published/Created: New York, Da Capo Press, 1970 [c1935] Related Authors: Levenson, Eleanore, 1905- joint author. Description: x, 303 p. 24 cm. ISBN: 0306700700 Notes: Includes bibliographical references. Subjects: Justice, Administration of--United States. Courts--United States. Judges--United States. Civil rights--United States. Series: Civil liberties in American history LC Classification: KF8700 .Z9G6 1970 Dewey Class No.: 347.99/73

Goldberg, Louis Palatnik, 1888- Lawless judges [by] Louis P. Goldberg and Eleanore Levenson. With an introd. by Morris R. Cohen. Published/Created: New York, Negro Universities Press [1969] Related Authors: Levenson, Eleanore, 1905- joint author. Description: x, 303 p. 23 cm. ISBN: 0837126967 Notes: Reprint of the 1935 ed. Subjects: Justice, Administration of--United States. Courts--United States. Judges--United States. Civil rights--United States. LC Classification: KF8700 .Z9G6 1969 Dewey Class No.: 347.99/73

Goldman, Jerry. Attitudes of United States judges toward limitation of oral argument and opinion-writing in the United States Courts of Appeals / Jerry Goldman. Published/Created: Washington: Federal Judicial Center, 1975. Related Authors: Federal Judicial Center. Description: 25, 29, 13 p.; 27 cm. Notes: "(FJC no. 75-3)" Subjects: United States. Courts of Appeals. Oral pleading--United States. Judicial opinions--United States. Judges--United States--Attitudes. LC Classification: KF9052 .G6 Dewey Class No.: 347/.73/2405

Goldman, Sheldon. Picking federal judges: lower court selection from Roosevelt through Reagan / Sheldon Goldman. Published/Created: New Haven: Yale University Press, c1997. Description: xv, 428 p.; 25 cm. ISBN: 0300069626 (cl: alk. paper) Notes: Includes bibliographical references (p. 370-411) and index. Subjects: Judges--Selection and appointment--United States--History. District courts--Officials and employees--Selection and appointment--United States--History. LC Classification: KF8776 .G65 1997 Dewey Class No.: 347.73/234 21

Goldman, Sheldon. The federal courts as a political system / Sheldon Goldman, Thomas P. Jahnige. Edition Information: 3rd ed. Published/Created: New York: Harper & Row, c1985. Related Authors: Jahnige, Thomas P. Description: viii, 263 p.: ill.; 24 cm. ISBN: 0060423765 (pbk.) Notes: Includes bibliographies and index. Subjects: Courts--United States. Law and politics. LC Classification: KF8700.Z9 G63 1985 Dewey Class No.: 347.73/202 347.30712 19

Goldman, Sheldon. The Federal courts as a political system / Sheldon Goldman, Thomas P. Jahnige. Edition Information: 2d ed. Published/Created: New York: Harper & Row, c1976. Related Authors: Jahnige, Thomas P., joint author. Description: xii, 305 p.; 21 cm. ISBN: 006042382X Notes: Includes bibliographical references and index. Subjects: Courts--United States. Law and politics. LC Classification: KF8700.Z9 G63 1976 Dewey Class No.: 347.73/202 347.30712 19

Goldman, Sheldon. The Federal courts as a political system [by] Sheldon Goldman [and] Thomas P. Jahnige. Published/Created: New York, Harper & Row [1971] Related Authors: Jahnige, Thomas P., joint author. Description: x, 292 p. illus., map. 21 cm. ISBN: 0060423854 Notes: Includes bibliographical references. Subjects: Courts--United States. Law and politics. LC Classification: KF8700 .Z9G63 Dewey Class No.: 347/.732/02

Goodloe, Daniel Reaves, 1814- Federalism unmasked; or, The rights of the states, the Congress, the executive, and the people vindicated against the encroachments of the judiciary, prompted by the modern apostate democracy. Being a compilation from the writings and speeches of the leaders of the old Jeffersonian Republican party. By Daniel R. Goodloe. Published/Created: [Washington, Buell & Blanchard, 1860] Description: 15, [1] p. 24 cm. Notes: Caption title. Advertisement of the Republican Executive Congressional Committee on p. [16]. Subjects: Courts--United States. LC Classification: JK1541 .G6

Governing through Courts / edited by Richard A.L. Gambitta, Marlynn L. May, James C. Foster. Published/Created: Beverly Hills: Sage Publications, c1981. Related Authors: Gambitta, Richard A. L. May, Marlynn L. Foster, James C. (James Carl) Description: 319 p.; 23 cm. ISBN: 0803917198 0803917201 (pbk.) Notes: Includes bibliographies. Subjects: Judge-made law--United States. Law--United States--Interpretation and construction. LC Classification: KF8700 .G66 1981 Dewey Class No.: 349.73 347.3 19

Government: a book for all civil service examinations, open competitive and promotion, in which a knowledge of civil government, the courts and their functions, etc., is required. Published/Created: New York, The N.Y. civil service employees, pub. co., inc. [c1922] Description: 156 p. 17 cm. Subjects: Courts--New York (City) Civil service--United States--Examinations. New York (City)--Politics and government--Handbooks, manuals, etc. New York (State)--Politics and government--Handbooks, manuals, etc. LC Classification: JS1228 .N4

Grand and petit juror service in United States District Courts / prepared by Statistical Analysis and Reports Division, Administrative Office of the United States Courts. Published/Created: Washington, D.C.: The Division, 1983- Related Authors: United States. Administrative Office of the United States Courts. Statistical Analysis and Reports Division. Description: v.: ill. (some col.); 28 cm. Discontinued. 1982- ISSN: 0737-3309 Notes: SERBIB/SERLOC merged record Subjects: Jury--United States--Statistics--Periodicals. District Courts--United States--Statistics--Periodicals. LC Classification: KF8971.A152 A46 Dewey Class No.: 347.73/225 347.30725 19 Govt. Doc. No.: Ju 10.13:

Graves, W. Brooke (William Brooke), 1899- Uniform state action; a possible substitute for centralization. Published/Created: Chapel Hill, The University of North Carolina Press, 1934. Description: xii, 368 p. illus. (maps.) 24 cm. Notes: "Classified list of national and sectional organizations of state administrative officers": p.[307]-325. Includes bibliographical references. Subjects: Cooperation--United States. Uniform state laws. State governments. Administrative law--United States. Courts--United States--States. LC Classification: JK2441 .G7 1934 Dewey Class No.: 353.9

Gray, Cynthia. When judges speak up: ethics, the public, & the media: instructor's manual / by Cynthia Gray. Published/Created: Chicago: American Judicature Society; [Washington, D.C.]: State Justice Intstitute, c1998. Description: 2 v.; 28 cm. ISBN: 0938870823 0938870831 Contents: [v. 1.] Instructor's manual -- [v. 2.] Self study guide. Notes:

LC copy lacks accompanying videotape. Subjects: Judges--Education (Continuing education)--United States. Judicial ethics--Study and teaching--United States. Public relations--Courts--United States. LC Classification: KF276 .G73 1998 Dewey Class No.: 174/.3/0711 21

Great lawyer stories: from courthouse to jailhouse, tall tales, jokes, and anecdotes / by Bill Adler. Edition Information: Carol Publishing Group ed. Published/Created: New York, NY: Carol Pub. Group, 1993. Related Authors: Adler, Bill, 1929- Description: 141 p.; 21 cm. ISBN: 080651373X Notes: "A Citadel Press book." Subjects: Lawyers--United States--Humor. Law--United States--Humor. Courts--United States--Humor. Lawyers--United States--Anecdotes. Law--United States--Anecdotes. Courts--United States--Anecdotes. LC Classification: K184 .G735 1993 Dewey Class No.: 349.73/0207 347.300207 20

Green, Carl R. The judiciary / Carl R. Green and William R. Sanford. Published/Created: Vero Beach, FL: Rourke Corp., c1990. Related Authors: Sanford, William R. (William Reynolds), 1927- Description: 96 p.: ill.; 24 cm. ISBN: 0865930864 Summary: Examines the working of American courts and judicial systems through the eyes of a fictional federal district judge, Duncan Reilly. Notes: Includes biibliographical references (p. 94) and index. Subjects: Justice, Administration of--United States--Juvenile literature. Courts--United States--Juvenile literature. Judicial process--United States--Juvenile literature. Justice. Courts. Judicial process. Series: American government LC Classification: KF8700.Z9 G74 1990 Dewey Class No.: 347.73/1 347.3071 20

Greenwood, J. Michael. The impact of word processing and electronic mail on United States Courts of Appeals / by J. Michael Greenwood and Larry Farmer. Published/Created: Washington: Federal Judicial Center, 1979. Related Authors: Farmer, Larry C., joint author. Federal Judicial Center. Description: ix, 91 p.; 27 cm. Notes: Includes bibliographical references. Subjects: United States. Courts of Appeals. Court administration--United States--Data processing. Series: Courtran II series LC Classification: KF8750 .G73 Dewey Class No.: 347.73/24 347.3073 19

Gresham, Otto, 1859- What shall the salvage be? Published/Created: Chicago, Printed by Alger-Reichel-Barrett, 1932. Description: 180 p. incl. front. (port.) 23 cm. Subjects: Corruption (in politics) Courts--United States. United States--Politics and government. LC Classification: E743 .G74

Gresham, Otto, 1859- A petition to the Congress. Published/Created: [Chicago: s.n., 1932] Description: 3 p. leaf, 9-180 p.; 23 cm. Notes: Preface signed: Otto Gresham. Issued also under title: What shall the salvage be? Subjects: Political corruption. Courts--United States. United States--Politics and government. LC Classification: E743 .G742

Gresham, Otto, 1859- The petition of Otto Gresham: submitting amendments to the Judiciary and Civil rights acts, and a complaint against the Indianapolis bar association. Published/Created: Williamsport, Ind: The Review-Republican, 1949. Description: 88 p.; 23 cm. Notes: At head of title: To the committee of the American Bar Association on the bills of rights. Subjects: Indianapolis Bar Association. Civil rights--United States. Courts--United States. LC Classification: KF4750 .G73

Griffin, Patrick. Trying juveniles as adults in criminal court: an analysis of state transfer provisions: report / Patrick Griffin, Patricia Torbet, Linda Szymanski. Published/Created: Washington, DC: U.S. Dept. of Justice, Office of Justice Programs, Office of Juvenile Justice and Delinquency Prevention, [1998] Related Authors: Torbet, Patricia M. Szymanski, Linda A. National Center for Juvenile Justice. Description: viii, 17, 85 p.; 28 cm. Notes: "December 1998." Subjects: Juvenile Courts--United States--States.

Criminal Courts--United States--States. Juvenile delinquents--United States--States--Transfer. Prosecution--United States--States--Decision making. Series: OJJDP report LC Classification: KF9795.Z95 G75 1998

Groat, George Gorham, 1871- Attitude of American courts in labor cases; Published/Created: New York, Longmans, Green & co., agents; [etc., etc.] 1911. Description: p. cm. Subjects: Labor laws and legislation--United States. Labor and laboring classes--United States. Labor unions--United States. Courts--United States. LC Classification: H31 .C7 vol. 42

Guam reports: current cases. Published/Created: Orford, N.H.: Equity Pub. Corp., c1976- Related Authors: United States. District Court (Guam) Guam. Superior Court. Guam. Supreme Court. Description: v. (loose-leaf); 25 cm. Notes: Containing opinions of the District, Superior, and Supreme Courts. Bound volumes periodically replace current material. L.C. holdings recorded in shelflist only. Subjects: Law reports, digests, etc.--Guam. LC Classification: KVQ2.2 .A3 1976 Dewey Class No.: 348.96/7043 349.670843 19

Guide to educating the public about the Courts. Published/Created: Chicago, IL: American Bar Association, Division for Public Education, c1994. Related Authors: American Bar Association. Public Education Division. Description: 96 p.: ill.; 28 cm. ISBN: 1570730482 Notes: Includes bibliographical references (p. 93-95). Subjects: Courts--Study and teaching--United States. Procedure (Law)--Study and teaching--United States. LC Classification: KF8720 .G79 1994

Guide to the federal Courts: an introduction to the federal Courts and their operation: includes explanation of how a case is litigated. Published/Created: Washington, DC: WANT Pub. Co., c1982. Description: ii, 97 p.: ill.; 28 cm. ISBN: 0942008022 (pbk.) : Subjects: Courts--United States--Popular works. Civil procedure--United States--Popular works. Series: Know your government series LC Classification: KF8720 .G795 1982 Dewey Class No.: 347.73/2 347.3072 19

Guidelines for the use of lawyers to supplement judicial resources / Advisory Board on the Use of Volunteer Lawyers as Supplemental Judicial Resources. Published/Created: [Williamsburg, Va.]: National Center for State Courts, c1984. Related Authors: Advisory Board on the Use of Volunteer Lawyers as Supplemental Judicial Resources (U.S.) National Center for State Courts. Description: viii, 45 p.; 23 cm. ISBN: 0896560767 (pbk.) Notes: Includes bibliographical references. Subjects: Courts--United States--States--Officials and employees. Court administration--United States--States. Lawyers--United States--States. LC Classification: KF8795.Z95 G84 1984 Dewey Class No.: 347.73/1 347.3071 19

Haar, Charles Monroe, 1920- Fairness and justice: law in the service of equality / by Charles M. Haar and Daniel Wm. Fessler. Edition Information: 1st Touchstone ed. Published/Created: New York: Simon & Schuster, 1987, c1986. Related Authors: Fessler, Daniel William. Description: 335 p.: ill.; 24 cm. ISBN: 0671633112 (pbk.) Notes: Originally published under title: The wrong side of the tracks. Includes index. Bibliography: p. 257-323. Subjects: Discrimination in municipal services--Law and legislation United States. Equality before the law--United States. Courts--United States. Common law--United States. LC Classification: KF5305 .H3 1987 Dewey Class No.: 342.73/085 347.30285 19

Haar, Charles Monroe, 1920- Suburbs under siege: race, space, and audacious judges / Charles M. Haar. Published/Created: Princeton, N.J.: Princeton University Press, c1996. Description: xiv, 266 p.: ill.; 25 cm. ISBN: 0691044449 (acid-free paper) Notes: Includes bibliographical references (p. [209]-252) and index. Subjects: Discrimination in housing--Law and legislation--United States. Land use--Law and legislation--United States. Courts--United States. Social justice--United States. United States--Race relations. LC Classification: KF5740.Z9 H3 1996 Dewey Class No.: 344.73/0636351 347.304636351 20

Haar, Charles Monroe, 1920- The wrong side of the tracks: a revolutionary rediscovery of the common law tradition of fairness in the struggle against inequality / by Charles M. Haar and Daniel Wm. Fessler. Published/Created: New York: Simon and Schuster, c1986. Related Authors: Fessler, Daniel William. Description: 335 p.: ill.; 24 cm. ISBN: 0671601873 : Notes: Includes index. Bibliography: p. 257-323. Subjects: Discrimination in municipal services--Law and legislation United States. Equality before the law--United States. Courts--United States. Common law--United States. LC Classification: KF5305 .H3 1986 Dewey Class No.: 342.73/085 347.30285 19

Haines, Charles Grove, 1879-1948 The American doctrine of judicial supremacy, by Charles Grove Haines... Published/Created: New York, The macmillan company, [c1914] Description: xviii p., 1 1.,365 p. 20 1/2 Notes: Reprinted in part from Political science review and Michigan law review. Subjects: Courts--United States. United States--Constitutional law. LC Classification: JK1541 .H18

Haines, Charles Grove, 1879-1948. The conflict over judicial powers in the United States to 1870, by Charles Grove Haines. Published/Created: New York, Columbia University, 1909. Description: 180 p. 23 cm. Notes: Issued also as thesis (Ph. D.) Columbia University. Subjects: Courts--United States. Series: Columbia University. Studies in history, economics and public law, v. 35, no. 1 LC Classification: JK1541 .H2

Halemba, Gregg. Hall, John E. (John Elihu), 1783-1829. The practice and jurisdiction of the Court of Admiralty: in three parts ... / by John E. Hall. Published/Created: Baltimore: Printed by Geo. Dobbin and Murphy, 1809. Related Authors: Clerke, Francis, fl. 1594. Praxis curiae admiralitatis anglia. English. Description: xxviii, iv, [3], 211, [5] p.; 22 cm. Contents: I. An historical examination of the civil jurisdiction of the Court of Admiralty -- II. A translation of Clerke's Praxis, with notes on the jurisdiction and practice of the district courts -- III. A collection of precedents. Notes: Includes bibliographical references. References: Shaw & Shoemaker 17697 Subjects: Great Britain. High Court of Admiralty. Admiralty--Great Britain. District Courts--United States. LC Classification: KF1112 .H3

Hall, Kermit. From local courts to national tribunals: the federal district courts of Florida, 1821-1990 / Kermit L. Hall & Eric W. Rise. Published/Created: Brooklyn, N.Y.: Carlson Pub., 1991. Related Authors: Rise, Eric W. Description: x, 252 p.: ill.; 24 cm. ISBN: 0926019597 Notes: Includes bibliographical references (p. 227-238) and index. Subjects: District courts--Florida--History. District Courts--United States--History. LC Classification: KFF515 .H35 1991 Dewey Class No.: 347.759/02 347.59072 20

Hand, Learned, 1872-1961. Papers of Learned Hand, 1909-1924. Description: 30 items. 7 containers. Summary: Concise summaries of trials in civil, criminal, and admiralty courts presided over by Hand as U.S. judge of the Southern District of New York. Notes: MSS24760 Subjects: United States. District Court (New York: Southern District) Trials--New York (State) Courts--New York (State) Jurists. Local Call/Shelving: MMC-3555

Handbook of court administration and management / edited by Steven W. Hays, Cole Blease Graham, Jr. Published/Created: New York: M. Dekker, c1993. Related Authors: Hays, Steven W. Graham, Cole Blease. Description: vii, 533 p.; 24 cm. ISBN: 0824787692 (acid-free paper) Notes: Includes bibliographical references and index. Subjects: Court administration--United States. Courts--

United States. Series: Public administration and public policy; 49 LC Classification: KF8732 .H36 1993 Dewey Class No.: 347.73/1 347.3071 20

Hanford, Cornelius Holgate, 1849- Conflicting decisions of federal and state courts; Published/Created: [n. p., 1902] Description: cover-title, 16 p. 24 cm. Subjects: Conflict of judicial decisions. Courts--United States. LC Classification: KF8735.Z9 H35

Hanford, Cornelius Holgate, 1849- National progression and the increasing responsibilities of our national judiciary; Published/Created: [n.p., 1908?] Description: 20 p. 23 cm. Subjects: Courts--United States. Industry and state--United States. LC Classification: KF1600.Z9 H3

Hanson, Roger A. Handbook for appellate judges: management information and court performance / Roger A. Hanson. Published/Created: Williamsburg, VA.: National Center for State Courts, c1995. Description: viii, 133 p.: ill., forms; 22 cm. ISBN: 0896561569 Notes: "Submitted to the State Justice Institute by National Center for State Courts and the ABA/JAD Lawyers Conference Task Force on Reduction of Litigation Cost and Delay." Includes bibliographic references. "This report was developed under a grant from the State Justice Institute, grant number SJI-92-06F-B-138"--T.p. verso. Subjects: Appellate Courts--United States--Administration. Court congestion and delay--United States. Series: Publication (National Center for State Courts); R176. LC Classification: KF8750 .H36 1995 Dewey Class No.: 347.73/24 347.3073 20

Harley, Herbert Lincoln, 1871- A unified state court system; address before the Nebraska state bar association [December 29, 1914] Published/Created: [Chicago, Chicago legal-news co., 1915?] Description: 1 p.l., 25 p. 25 cm. Subjects: Courts--United States. LC Classification: KF8736 .H3

Harman, S. W. Hell on the border; he hanged eighty-eight men. A history of the great United States criminal court at Fort Smith, Arkansas, and of crime and criminals in the Indian Territory, and the trial and punishment thereof before ... Judge Isaac C. Parker ... and by the courts of said territory, embracing the leading sentences and charges to grand and petit juries delivered by the world famous jurist--his acknowledged masterpieces, besides much other legal lore ... illustrated with over fifty fine half-tones. By S. W. Harman, compiled by C. P. Sterns. Published/Created: Fort Smith, Ark., The Phoenix publishing company [c1898] Related Authors: Sterns, C. P., comp. Description: xiii, 720 p. front., illus. (incl. ports.) 22 cm. Subjects: Parker, Isaac Charles, 1838-1896. United States. District Court (Arkansas: Western District) United States. Circuit Court (8th Circuit) Crime--Indian Territory. LC Classification: KF213.P27 H37 1898

Harrington, Christine B. Shadow justice: the ideology and institutionalization of alternatives to court / Christine B. Harrington. Published/Created: Westport, Conn.: Greenwood Press, 1985. Description: x, 216 p.; 22 cm. ISBN: 0313243328 (lib. bdg.) Notes: Includes index. Bibliography: p. [179]-203. Subjects: Neighborhood justice centers--United States. Dispute resolution (Law)--United States. Courts--United States. Series: Contributions in political science, 0147-1066; no. 133 LC Classification: KF9084 .H37 1985 Dewey Class No.: 347.73 347.307 19

Harris, Silas Adelbert, 1888- The rule-making power, by Silas A. Harris ... Prepared under the auspices of the Special committee on improving the administration of justice of the American bar association. Published/Created: [Chicago? 194-] Related Authors: American Bar Association. Description: 23, [1] p. illus. (maps) 22 cm. Notes: "Selected bibliography": p. 23. Subjects: Court rules--United States. Courts--United States. LC Classification: KF8816 .H35

Hart and Wechsler's The federal Courts and the federal system. Edition Information: 3rd ed. / by Paul M. Bator ... [et al.]. Published/Created: Westbury, N.Y.: Foundation Press, 1988. Related Authors: Hart, Henry Melvin. Wechsler, Herbert, 1909- Bator, Paul. Description: ci, 1898 p.; 26 cm. ISBN: 0882776479 Notes: Kept up to date by supplements. Includes index. Subjects: Courts--United States--Cases. Jurisdiction--United States--Cases. Series: University casebook series LC Classification: KF8718 .H32 1988 Dewey Class No.: 347.73/2 347.3071 19

Hart and Wechsler's The federal Courts and the federal system. Edition Information: 2d ed. by Paul M. Bator, Paul J. Mishkin, David L. Shapiro [and] Herbert Wechsler. Published/Created: Mineola, N.Y., Foundation Press, 1973. Related Authors: Bator, Paul M. Wechsler, Herbert, 1909- Hart, Henry Melvin. Federal Courts and the federal system. Description: lxxxviii, 1657 p. 27 cm. Notes: Accompanied by supplement (446 p.) issued in 1981. Rev. ed. of The federal Courts and the federal system, by Henry M. Hart, Jr., and Herbert Wechsler. Subjects: Courts--United States--Cases. Jurisdiction--United States--Cases. Series: University casebook series LC Classification: KF8718 .H32 1973 Dewey Class No.: 347/.73/2

Hart, Henry Melvin. The Federal courts and the Federal system, by Henry M. Hart, Jr., and Herbert Wechsler. Published/Created: Brooklyn, Foundation Press, 1953. Related Authors: Wechsler, Herbert, 1909- Description: lvii, 1445 p. 27 cm. Subjects: Courts--United States--Cases. Jurisdiction--United States--Cases. Series: University casebook series LC Classification: KF8718 .H3 Dewey Class No.: 347.97

Haynsworth, Clement F. (Clement Furman), 1912- Papers of Clement F. Haynsworth, 1886-1989 (bulk 1957-1989) Description: 71,575 items. 205 containers. 81.8 linear feet. Summary: Correspondence, memoranda, reports, opinions, orders, briefs, writs, petitions, notes, agenda and minutes of meetings, and genealogical and printed material chiefly from Haynsworth's career (1957-1989) as a federal judge on the U.S. Court of Appeals, 4th Circuit. Case topics include civil rights, constitutional law, industrial relations, antitrust matters, maritime law, government regulation, and prisoners' rights. Correspondents include Jacques Barzun, William J. Brennan, Warren E. Burger, Tom C. Clark, John Paul Frank, Ernest F. Hollings, Edward Moore Kennedy, J. Woodrow Lewis, Daniel John Meador, Arthur Raphael Miller, Richard M. Nixon, Lewis F. Powell, Strom Thurmond, Johnnie McKeiver Walters, Bernard J. Ward, and Charles Alan Wright. Notes: Audio casettes transferred to Library of Congress Motion Picture, Broadcasting and Recorded Sound Division. MSS79781 Subjects: Barzun, Jacques, 1907- Brennan, William J. (William Joseph), 1906- Burger, Warren E., 1907- Clark, Tom C. (Tom Campbell), 1899-1977. Frank, John Paul, 1917- Hollings, Ernest F., 1922- Kennedy, Edward Moore, 1932- Lewis, J. Woodrow. Meador, Daniel John. Miller, Arthur Raphael, 1934- Nixon, Richard M. (Richard Milhous), 1913- Powell, Lewis F., 1907- Thurmond, Strom, 1902- Walters, Johnnie McKeiver. Ward, Bernard J. Wright, Charles Alan. United States. Court of Appeals (4th Circuit) Administrative law--Antitrust law--United States. Appellate courts. Civil rights--Industrial relations--Judges--Judicial opinions--Maritime law--United States. Prisoners--Legal status, laws, etc. United States--Constitutional law. Jurists. Local Call/Shelving: 0623Q

Hays, Steven W. Court reform: ideal or illusion? / Steven W. Hays. Published/Created: Lexington, Mass.: Lexington Books, c1978. Description: xiii, 151 p.: ill.; 24 cm. ISBN: 0669018414 Notes: Includes bibliographical references and index. Subjects: Courts--Florida. Courts--United States. LC Classification: KFF508 .H38 Dewey Class No.: 347/.759/01

Hazard, Geoffrey C. Court finance and unitary budgeting [by] Geoffrey C. Hazard, Jr., Martin B. McNamara [and] Irwin F. Sentilles, III. Published/Created: [Chicago, American Bar Association, 1973] Related Authors: McNamara, Martin B., joint author. Sentilles, Irvin F., joint author. American Bar Association. Commission on Standards of Judicial Administration. Description: 16 p. 23 cm. Notes: "Prepared ... for the information of the commission." "Originally published in 81 Yale law journal 1286 (1972)" Includes bibliographical references. Subjects: Courts--United States--Finance. Series: Supporting studies, 1. LC Classification: KF8732.5.Z9 H38 Dewey Class No.: 347/.73/1

Heidepriem, Nikki. "There is no liberty-- ": a report on congressional efforts to curb the federal courts and to undermine the Brown Decision. Published/Created: Washington, D.C.: Citizens Commission on Civil Rights, [1982] Related Authors: Citizens' Commission on Civil Rights (U.S.) Description: xxi, 114 p.; 28 cm. Notes: Cover title. "October 1982." Includes bibliographical references. Subjects: Busing for school integration--Law and legislation--United States. Discrimination in education--Law and legislation--United States. Courts--United States. LC Classification: KF4155 .H43 1982 Dewey Class No.: 344.73/0798 347.304798 19

Heim, Fred J. The proposed reorganization of the United States judicial system. Published/Created: [n.p., 1937] Description: 32 p. 23 cm. Subjects: United States. Supreme court. Courts--United States. LC Classification: KF8720 .H4

Helm, Lynn, 1857-1921. A progressive judiciary. President's annual address by Lynn Helm, Published/Created: [n.p., 1911?] Related Authors: California bar association. Description: 21 p. 23 cm. Subjects: Courts--United States. LC Classification: KF8700.Z9 H44

Henderson, Dwight F., 1937- Congress, courts, and criminals: the development of federal criminal law, 1801-1829 / Dwight F. Henderson. Published/Created: Westport, Conn.: Greenwood Press, c1985. Description: x, 257 p.; 25 cm. ISBN: 0313246009 (alk. paper) Notes: Includes index. Bibliography: p. [221]-233. Subjects: Criminal law--United States--History. Courts--United States--History. Series: Contributions in American history, 0084-9219; no. 113 LC Classification: KF9219 .H39 1985 Dewey Class No.: 345.73 347.305 19

Henderson, Dwight F., 1937- Courts for a new nation [by] Dwight F. Henderson. Foreword by Tom C. Clark. Published/Created: Washington, Public Affairs Press [1971] Description: viii, 166 p. 24 cm. Notes: Bibliography: p. 136-158. Subjects: Courts--United States--History. LC Classification: KF8754 .H4 Dewey Class No.: 347/.73/109

Henry, Morton Pearson, 1826-1901. The jurisdiction and procedure of the admiralty courts of the United States in civil causes. (On the instance side.) By Morton P. Henry. Published/Created: Philadelphia, Kay & brother, 1885. Description: xi, p., 1 l., 496 p. 25 cm. Subjects: Admiralty--United States. Courts--United States LC Classification: KF11O4 .H45

Heydebrand, Wolf V., 1930- Rationalizing justice: the political economy of federal district courts / Wolf Heydebrand and Carroll Seron. Published/Created: Albany: State University of New York Press, c1990. Related Authors: Seron, Carroll. Description: xxii, 308 p.; 24 cm. ISBN: 0791402959 0791402967 (pbk.) Notes: Includes bibliographical references (p. 261-293) and index. Subjects: District Courts--United States--History. Court administration--United States--History. Courts--Economic aspects--United States--History. Series: SUNY series in the sociology of work LC Classification: KF8754 .H45 1990 Dewey Class No.: 347.73/2 347.3072 20

Hicks, Frederick Charles, 1875- Organization and ethics of the bench and bar, cases and other materials, Published/Created: Rochester, N.Y., The Lawyers co-operative publishing company, 1932. Description: v, 606 p. diagrs. 26 cm. Subjects: Admission to the bar--United States. Legal ethics--United States. Courts--United States. Courts--Great Britain. Judges--United States. Lawyers--United States. LC Classification: KF306.A4 H5

Hill, Walter B. (Walter Barnard), 1851-1905. Relief of suitors in the federal courts. Argument of Walter B. Hill, before the U. S. Senate and House judiciary subcommittees, February 13th, 1890 ... Published/Created: Macon, Ga., J.W. Burke & co., printers, 1890. Description: 31 p. 23 cm. Subjects: Law reform. Courts--United States. Appellate procedure--United States. LC Classification: KF9050 .A25 1890

Histoire d'un Pierrot = Pierrot the prodigal / Celio Film; director, Baldassarre Negroni. Published/Created: Italy: Italica Ars, 1913. Related Authors: Negroni, Baldassarre, 1877-1948, direction. Bertini, Francesca, 1892- , cast. Gys, Leda, 1892-1957, cast. Ghione, Emilio, cast. Ciaffi, Amedeo, cast. Redaelli, Elvira, cast. Beissier, Fernand. Costa, Pasquale Mario, 1858-1933. Description: 4 reels of 4 (inc.) (1437 ft.): si., b&w; 16 mm. ref print. 4 reels of 4 (inc.) (3500 ft.): si., b&w; 35 mm. dupe neg. Summary: Pierrot Courts and marries Louisette; she deserts him when a former rival for her affections pushes Pierrot into a life of dissipation. After six years and with the aid of his fatherly good friend, Pochinet, Pierrot is reunited with his wife and young son. Notes: Minor change version: [English language version] -- United States: George Kleine, 1914. Copyright for minor change version: George Kleine (Società Italiana Celio, author); 8Jun14; LU2821. Original title, release, credit and cast information from Maria Prolo's Storia del cinema muto italiano, p. 162. Production company credit from Filmlexicon degli autori e delle opere, v. 4, p. 1247. All copies lack main titles and some introductory sequences. Based on the French musical pantomime, Histoire d'un Pierrot / pantomime by Fernand Beissier; music by Pasquale Mario Costa. References: Moving picture world, v. 20, p. 1703. Subjects: Husband and wife--Drama. Courtship--Drama. Family--Drama. Friendship--Drama. Feature films. Silent films. LC Classification: FLA 0705-0708 (ref print) FPA 2600-2603 (dupe neg)

Hoffecker, Carol E. Federal justice in the first state: a history of the United States District Court for the District of Delaware / Carol Hoffecker; with an introduction by Joseph J. Longobardi. Published/Created: Wilmington, Del.: The Historical Society for the United States District Court for the District of Delaware, c1992. Description: xvi, 252 p.: ill.; 26 cm. Notes: Includes bibliographical references (p. 221-232). Subjects: United States. District Court (Delaware)--History. District courts--Delaware--History. LC Classification: KFD529.5.D57 H64 1992 Dewey Class No.: 347.751/02 347.51072 20

Holding Courts accountable: counting what counts / National Association for Court Management, Comprehensive Public Information Programs Subcommittee. Published/Created: Williamsburg, VA (300 Newport Ave., Williamsburg 23187-8798): The Association, [1999] Description: 39 p.: ill., forms; 28 cm. Notes: "NACM mini-guide, Spring 1999"--Cover. Includes bibliographical references (p. 24-25). Subjects: Court administration--United States--Evaluation. Courts--United States--Evaluation. LC Classification: KF8732 .H65 1999

Holmes, Oliver Wendell, jr., 1841- Speech of Mr. Justice Holmes, at a dinner of the Harvard law association of New York, on February 15, 1913 ... Published/Created: Washington, Govt. print. off., 1913. Description: 5 p. 24 cm. Subjects: Courts--United States. United States--Politics and government--1909- LC Classification: KF389 .H65

Holt, George Chandler, 1843-1931. The concurrent jurisdiction of the federal and state courts / by George C. Holt.

Published/Created: Littleton, Colo.: F.B. Rothman, 1980, c1888. Description: xxvi, 237 p.; 19 cm. ISBN: 0837706300 Notes: Reprint. Originally published: New York: Baker, Voorhis, 1888. Includes index. Subjects: Jurisdiction--United States. Courts--United States. LC Classification: KF8735 .H6 1980 Dewey Class No.: 347.73/202 347.30712 19

Holt, George Chandler, 1843-1931. The concurrent jurisdiction of the federal and state courts. By George C. Holt. Published/Created: New York, Baker, Voorhis, 1888. Description: xxvi p., 1 l., 237 p. 24 cm. Subjects: Jurisdiction--United States. Courts--United States. LC Classification: KF8735 .H6

Holtzoff, Alexander, 1886- Federal procedural forms for use in civil and criminal actions, bankruptcy proceedings, Published/Created: Indianapolis, The Bobbs-Merrill company [c1940] Related Authors: Cozier, Allen Randall, 1898- joint author. United States. Supreme court. United States. District courts. United States. District court. District of Columbia. United States. Court of claims. Description: xxiii, 1010 p. 26 cm. Subjects: Civil procedure--United States--Forms. Criminal procedure--United States--Forms. Equity pleading and procedure--United States--Forms. Court rules--United States. Forms (Law)--United States. LC Classification: KF8836 .H6

Holtzoff, Alexander, 1886- Two years' experience under the Federal rules of civil procedure; Published/Created: [Boston, 1940] Related Authors: United States. Supreme court. United States. District courts. Description: 1 p.l., 16 numb. l. 26 cm. Subjects: Civil procedure--United States. LC Classification: KF8841 .H625

Holtzoff, Alexander, 1886-1969. New federal procedure and the courts / by Alexander Holtzoff. Published/Created: Chicago, Ill.: American Bar Association, c1940. Related Authors: United States. Supreme Court. United States. District Court (District of Columbia) Description: viii, 208 p.; 23 cm. Notes: Includes index. Subjects: Civil procedure--United States. Equity pleading and procedure--United States. Court rules--United States. LC Classification: KF8841 .H58

Hood, Jack B. Appellate brief writing and moot court competition guide / Jack B. Hood with William S. Lockett, Jr., and Douglas J. Centeno and the assistance of the Henry Upson Sims Moot Court Board. Published/Created: [Birmingham, Ala.]: The Board: J.B. Hood, c1982. Related Authors: Lockett, William S. Centeno, Douglas J. Cumberland School of Law. Henry Upson Sims Moot Court Board. Description: v leaves, 174 p.: ill.; 26 cm. Notes: Includes bibliographical references. Subjects: Moot courts. Briefs--United States. Appellate procedure--United States. LC Classification: KF281.A2 H66 1982 Dewey Class No.: 340/.07/1173 19

Hooper, Laural L. Neutral science panels: two examples of panels of court-appointed experts in the breast implants product liability litigation / Laural L. Hooper, Joe S. Cecil, Thomas E. Willging. Published/Created: Washington, DC (One Columbus Circle, N.E., Washington 20002-8003): Federal Judicial Center, 2001. Related Authors: Cecil, Joe S. Willging, Thomas E. Federal Judicial Center. Description: v, 104 p.; 23 cm. Notes: Shipping list no.: 2001-0238-P. Includes bibliographical references. Subjects: Evidence, Expert--United States. Courts--United States. Products liability--Breast implants. Govt. Doc. No.: JU 13.2:N 39

Hornblower, William Butler, 1851- The independence of the judiciary, the safeguard of free institutions. Published/Created: Washington, Govt. print. off., 1913. Description: 15 p. 25 cm. Subjects: Recall. Courts--United States. United States--Politics and government--Addresses, essays, lectures. LC Classification: JK1553 .H7 Microfilm 33528 JK

Horowitz, Donald L. The courts and social policy / Donald L. Horowitz. Published/Created: Washington: Brookings Institution, c1977. Description: 309 p.; 24 cm. ISBN: 0815737343: 0815737335 Notes: Includes bibliographical references and indexes. Subjects: Judicial process--United States. Sociological jurisprudence. LC Classification: KF8700 .H57 Dewey Class No.: 347/.73/1

Houghteling, James Lawrence, 1920- The dynamics of law [by] James L. Houghteling. Published/Created: New York, Harcourt, Brace & World [1968] Description: ix, 237 p. 23 cm. Notes: "Adapted from part 1 of ... The legal environment of business [by J. L. Houghteling and G. G. Pierce]" Bibliographical references included in "Notes" (p. 225-227) Subjects: Justice, Administration of--United States. Courts--United States. Law--United States. LC Classification: KF8700 .H6 Dewey Class No.: 340/.0973

Houghton, George Lampton. Appealed cases. A history of certain court corruptions, in the U. S. and state courts of Dakota, with ramifications and connections, etc. Published/Created: [Woodstock? Minn., c1900], Description: p. cm. Subjects: Courts--United States. Courts--Dakota. Law reform. LC Classification: KFS3508.Z9 H68 1895

Houghton, George Lampton. Appealed cases. Edition Information: 2d ed. Published/Created: [Seattle, The Metropolitan press printing company, c1913] Description: p. cm. Subjects: Courts--United States. Courts--South Dakota. Law reform. LC Classification: KF8779.Z9 H6 1913

Houston, Sam, 1793-1863. Speech of Hon. Sam Houston, of Texas, exposing the malfeasance and corruption of John Charles Watrous, judge of the federal court in Texas, and of his confederates: delivered in the Senate of the United States, Feb. 3, 1859. Published/Created: New-York: Pudney & Russell, printers, 1860. Related Authors: Joseph Meredith Toner Collection (Library of Congress) Description: 100 p., [1] leaf of plates: ill.; 19 cm. References: Cohen, M. Bib. of early Amer. law, 14544 Subjects: Watrous, John C. (John Charles), 1806-1874. Judges--United States--Discipline. Courts--United States. Land grants--Texas. LC Classification: KF8782.W37 H68 1860

How the public views the state Courts: a 1999 national survey / by the National Center for State Courts; funded by the Hearst Corporation. Published/Created: Williamsburg, VA (300 Newport Ave., Williamsburg 23187): National Center for State Courts; New York (959 Eighth Ave., New York 10019): The Hearst Corporation, c1999. Related Authors: National Center for State Courts. Hearst Corporation. Description: 43 p.: ill.; 25 cm. Notes: "Interviews conducted by Indiana University Public Opinion Laboratory; Survey designed and analyzed in collaboration with the University of Nebraska Public Policy Center and Scientific Resources for the Law, Inc.; Presented at the National Conference on Public Trust and Confidence in the Justice System, May 14, 1999, Washington, DC." Subjects: Courts--United States--States--Public opinion. Public opinion--United States. LC Classification: KF8736 .H65 1999 Dewey Class No.: 347.73/3 21

How to practice before the new Court of Appeals for the Federal Circuit: patents, international trade & customs / chairman, Donald R. Dunner. Published/Created: New York, N.Y.: Law & Business, inc./Harcourt Brace Jovanovich, c1982. Related Authors: Dunner, Donald R., 1931- Law & Business, inc. United States. Federal Courts Improvement Act of 1982. Description: iv, 277 p.: ill.; 22 cm. Notes: "Federal Courts Improvement Act of 1982"--P. 1-36. Subjects: United States. Court of Appeals (Federal Circuit) United States. Claims Court. LC Classification: KF9053 .H68 1982 Dewey Class No.: 347.73/24 347.30733 19

Howard, J. Woodford. Courts of appeals in the Federal judicial system: a study of the Second, Fifth, and District of Columbia Circuits / J. Woodford Howard, Jr. Published/Created: Princeton, N.J.: Princeton University Press, c1981. Description: xxvi, 415 p.; 25 cm. ISBN: 0691076235: 0691101000 (pbk.) : Notes: Includes bibliographical references and index. Subjects: United States. Court of Appeals (2nd Circuit) United States. Court of Appeals (5th Circuit) United States. Court of Appeals (District of Columbia Circuit) Appellate Courts--United States. Judicial process--United States. LC Classification: KF8750 .H68 Dewey Class No.: 347.73/24

Hubbell's legal directory for the service of the lawyer and business executive. Published/Created: New York, N.Y. [etc.] Hubbell Pub. Co. [etc.] Related Authors: Hubbell, John Henry, 1837-1906, ed. Lynch, Joseph A., ed. Description: 60 v. 17-25 cm. Notes: PREMARC/SERLOC merged record Subjects: Lawyers--United States--Directories. Lawyers--Canada--Directories. Law--United States--Digests. Law--Canada--Digests. Courts--United States--Directories. Court calendars--United States. LC Classification: KF190 .H8

Hughes, Charles Evans, 1862-1948. Remarks of Chief Justice Hughes before the meeting of the American Law Institute, held at the Hotel Mayflower, Washington, D.C., on Thursday morning, May 7, 1936, at 10 o'clock. Published/Created: [Washington, D.C.?: s.n., 1936] Description: 6 numb. leaves; 24 cm. Notes: Caption title. Printed on one side of leaf only. "To be released for publication on delivery, and not to be previously published, quoted from, or used in any way." Subjects: Wickersham, George W. (George Woodward), 1858-1936. United States. Supreme Court. Advisory Committee on Rules for Civil Procedure. Law--United States. District Courts--United States. LC Classification: KF389 .H8

Hughes, Graham, 1928- The conscience of the courts: law and morals in American life / by Graham Hughes. Edition Information: 1st ed. Published/Created: Garden City, N.Y.: Anchor Press, 1975. Description: 324 p.; 22 cm. ISBN: 0385089430 Notes: Includes bibliographical references and index. Subjects: Judicial process--United States. Law and ethics. Sociological jurisprudence. LC Classification: KF380 .H8 Dewey Class No.: 340.1/12

Hughes, Robert M. (Robert Morton), 1855-1940. Handbook of jurisdiction and procedure in United States courts / by Robert M. Hughes. Edition Information: 2nd ed. Published/Created: St. Paul, Minn.: West, 1913. Description: xviii, 766 p.; 24 cm. Subjects: Courts--United States. Jurisdiction--United States. Civil procedure--United States. Series: Hornbook series; no. 30 LC Classification: KF8858 .H83 1913

Hughes, Robert M. (Robert Morton), 1855-1940. Handbook of jurisdiction and procedure in United States courts / by Robert M. Hughes. Published/Created: St. Paul, Minn.: West Pub. Co., 1904. Description: xviii, 634 p.; 24 cm. Subjects: Courts--United States. Jurisdiction--United States. Civil procedure--United States. Series: Hornbook series; no. 30 LC Classification: KF8719 .H8 1904

Hughes, William Joseph, 1863-1938. Federal practice, Published/Created: St. Paul, Minn., West publishing co. [c1931-40] Related Authors: Thorpe, George Cyrus, 1875-1936, joint author. Darnieder, Francis Andrae, 1893- ed. Wheaton, Carl, 1889- joint ed. Viesselman, Percival William, 1890- ed. Description: 19 v. fold. diagr. (in pocket) 24 cm. Subjects: Courts--United States. Jurisdiction--United STates. Civil procedure--United States. Criminal procedure--United States. Court rules--United States. Forms (Law)--United States. LC Classification: KF8858 .H82

Human rights in the states: new directions in constitutional policymaking / edited by Stanley H. Friedelbaum.

Published/Created: New York: Greenwood Press, c1988. Related Authors: Friedelbaum, Stanley H. (Stanley Herman), 1927- Description: xxi, 200 p.; 24 cm. ISBN: 0313254516 (lib. bdg.: alk. paper) Notes: Includes index. Bibliography: p. [185]-188. Subjects: Civil rights--United States--States. Courts--United States--States. Federal government--United States. Series: Contributions in legal studies, 0147-1074; no. 43 LC Classification: KF4750.Z95 H86 1988 Dewey Class No.: 342.73/085 347.30285 19

Hurme, Sally Balch. Steps to enhance guardianship monitoring / by Sally Balch Hurme; American Bar Association, Commission on the Mentally Disabled and Commission on Legal Problems of the Elderly. Published/Created: Washington, DC: American Bar Association, Commission on the Mentally Disabled, c1991. Related Authors: American Bar Association. Commission on the Mentally Disabled. ABA Commission on Legal Problems of the Elderly. Description: 101, [98] p.; 28 cm. ISBN: 0897076540 Notes: Includes bibliographical references. Subjects: Guardian and ward--United States--States--State supervision. Courts--United States--States. LC Classification: KF553.Z95 H86 1991 Dewey Class No.: 346.7301/8 347.30618 20

Hurst, James Willard, 1910- ed. Some problems in the relationship of the legislative and judicial processes, materials selected by Willard Hurst ... Published/Created: Madison, Wis., The College Typing Company, c1938. Description: 2 p. l., 287 numb. l. 29 cm. Subjects: Legislation--United States. Courts--United States. Law--United States--Interpretation and construction. United States--Constitutional law--Cases. LC Classification: KF4930.A7 H87

Hurst, James Willard, 1910- A history of the principal agencies of law in the United States / by Willard Hurst. Published/Created: Madison, Wis.: Law School, University of Wisconsin, c1948. Description: 2 v. (664, 17 leaves); 29 cm. Notes: Spine title: Law agencies in U.S. Bibliography: v. 2, leaves 1-17. Subjects: Law--United States--History. Courts--United States--History. Constitutional history--United States. LC Classification: KF352 .H8145 1948 Dewey Class No.: 349.73 347.3 19

Hutchinson, William Easton. Judicial innovations of 1911; Published/Created: [Topeka? 1912?] Description: 12 p. 24 cm. Subjects: Courts--United States. LC Classification: JK1544 .H8

Illinois code of civil procedure and court rules. Published/Created: St. Paul, Minn.: West Pub. Co., c1983-c1996. Related Authors: West Publishing Company. United States. Court of Appeals (7th Circuit) Description: 14 v.; 25 cm. 1983-1996. ISSN: 8756-8969 Notes: "Smith-Hurd Illinois annotated statutes, chapter 110, Practice, chapter 110A, Practice rules, Federal court rules, U.S. Court of Appeals for the Seventh Circuit, U.S. District Courts." "Desk copy"--Cover. Vols. for 1986-1996 have title: Illinois code of civil procedure and rules of court. State and federal. SERBIB/SERLOC merged record Complements information found in the companion publication: Illinois local court rules. Merged with: Illinois local court rules, to form: Illinois court rules and procedure. Illinois local court rules (DLC) 96644755 (OCoLC)34992803 Related Item: Illinois local court rules (DLC) 96644755 (OCoLC)34992803 Subjects: Court rules--Illinois. Civil procedure--Illinois. LC Classification: KFI1729 .A195 Dewey Class No.: 347.773/05 347.73075 19

Illinois digest, 1818 to date, covering Illinois Supreme and Appellate Court reports and North eastern reporter, as well as Illinois cases decided in Supreme Court of the United States, Circuit Court of Appeals and Federal Circuit and District Courts. Published/Created: St. Paul, West Pub. Co. [1939- v.1, 1940] Related Authors: Illinois. Courts United States. Courts West Publishing Company Description: v. 26 cm. Notes: "West key number system."

Some vols. have title: West's Illinois digest. Subtitle varies. Kept up to date by regular cumulative supplementary services and replacement vols., including numbered and lettered vols., e.g. 1, 1A, 1B. Subjects: Law reports, digests, etc.--Illinois. LC Classification: KFI1257 .I4

Illinois practice act and rules. With amendments to December 1, 1973. Published/Created: St. Paul, Minn., West Pub. Co. [1974] Related Authors: Illinois. Laws, statutes, etc. Civil practice act. 1974. Illinois. Supreme Court. Rules. 1974. United States. Court of Appeals (7th Circuit) United States. District Courts. West Publishing Company. Description: v, 604 p. 24 cm. Notes: "Smith-Hurd Illinois annotated statutes. Chapter 110: Practice; chapter 110A: Practice rules. Federal court rules, U.S. Court of Appeals for the Seventh Circuit, U.S. District Courts." "Provides ... the text of the Civil practice act and related laws found in chapter 110 of the Illinois revised statutes, the text of the practice rules found in chapter 110A, and the text of Federal court rules essential to Federal practice in Illinois." Subjects: Civil procedure--Illinois. Court rules--Illinois. LC Classification: KFI1729 .A2 1974 Dewey Class No.: 347/.773/05

Illinois practice act and rules. With amendments to January 1, 1970. Published/Created: St. Paul, West Pub. Co. [1970] Related Authors: Illinois. Laws, statutes, etc. Civil practice act. 1970. Illinois. Supreme Court. Rules. 1970. United States. Court of Appeals (7th Circuit) United States. District Courts. West Publishing Company. Description: v, 490 p. 24 cm. Notes: "Smith-Hurd Illinois annotated statutes. Chapter 110: Practice; chapter 110A: Practice rules. Federal court rules, U.S. Court of Appeals for the Seventh Circuit, U.S. District Courts." "Provides ... the text of the Civil practice act and related laws found in chapter 110 of the Illinois revised statutes, the text of the practice rules found in chapter 110A, and the text of Federal court rules essential to Federal practice in Illinois." Subjects: Civil procedure--Illinois. Court rules--Illinois. LC Classification: KFI1729 .A2 1970 Dewey Class No.: 347.99/773

Illinois practice act and rules. With amendments to January 10, 1973. Published/Created: St. Paul, West Pub. Co. [1973] Related Authors: Illinois. Laws, statutes, etc. Civil practice act. 1973. Illinois. Supreme Court. Rules. 1973. United States. Court of Appeals (7th Circuit) United States. District Courts. West Publishing Company. Description: v, 584 p. 24 cm. Notes: "Smith-Hurd Illinois annotated statutes. Chapter 110: Practice; chapter 110A: Practice rules. Federal court rules, U.S. Court of Appeals for the Seventh Circuit, U.S. District Courts." "Provides ... the text of the Civil practice act and related laws found in chapter 110 of the Illinois revised statutes, the text of the practice rules found in chapter 110A, and the text of Federal court rules essential to Federal practice in Illinois." Subjects: Civil procedure--Illinois. Court rules--Illinois. LC Classification: KFI1729 .A2 1973 Dewey Class No.: 347/.773/05

Illinois practice act and rules. With amendments to November 1, 1971. Published/Created: St. Paul, West Pub. Co. [1972] Related Authors: Illinois. Laws, statutes, etc. Civil practice act. 1972. Illinois. Supreme Court. Rules. 1972. United States. Court of Appeals (7th Circuit) United States. District Courts. West Publishing Company. Description: v, 532 p. 24 cm. Notes: "Smith-Hurd Illinois annotated statutes: chapter 110, Practice; chapter 110A, Practice rules. Federal court rules; U.S. Court of Appeals for the Seventh Circuit; U.S. District Courts." "Provides ... the text of the Civil practice act and related laws found in chapter 110 of the Illinois revised statutes, the text of the practice rules found in chapter 110A, and the text of Federal court rules essential to Federal practice in Illinois." Subjects: Civil procedure--Illinois. Court rules--Illinois. LC Classification: KFI1729 .A2 1972 Dewey Class No.: 347/.773/05

Illinois practice act and rules. Published/Created: St. Paul, Minn.: West

Pub. Co., -c1982. Related Authors: West Publishing Company. United States. Court of Appeals (7th Circuit) Description: v.; 25 cm. -1982. Notes: "Smith-Hurd Illinois annotated statutes, chapter 110, practice, chapter 110A, practice rules, Federal court rules, U.S. Court of Appeals for the Seventh Circuit, U.S. District Courts." "Desk copy"--Cover. Description based on: Jan. 10, 1973. SERBIB/SERLOC merged record Subjects: Court rules--Illinois. Civil procedure--Illinois. LC Classification: KFI1729 .A195 Dewey Class No.: 347.773/05 347.73075 19

Illinois practice act and rules: Smith-Hurd Illinois annotated statutes--chapter 110, Practice, chapter 110A, Practice rules, Federal court rules--U.S. Court of Appeals for the Seventh Circuit, U.S. District Courts, with amendments received to March 1, 1976. Published/Created: St. Paul: West Pub. Co., 1976. Related Authors: Illinois. Laws, statutes, etc. Civil practice act. 1976. Illinois. Supreme Court. Rules. 1976. United States. Court of Appeals (7th Circuit) United States. District Courts. West Publishing Company. Description: v, 635 p.: forms; 24 cm. Notes: "Supersedes 1975 pamphlet." "Illinois Supreme Court rules": p. 69-257. "Including consolidated index convering chapters 110 and 110A." Subjects: Civil procedure--Illinois. Court rules--Illinois. LC Classification: KFI1729 .A2 1976 Dewey Class No.: 347/.773/05

Illinois practice act and rules: Smith-Hurd Illinois annotated statutes, chapter 110, practice, chapter 110A, practice rules, Federal court rules, U.S. Court of Appeals for the Seventh Circuit, U.S. District Courts, with amendments received to November 24, 1976. Published/Created: St. Paul: West Pub. Co., c1977. Related Authors: Illinois. Laws, statutes, etc. Civil practice act. 1977. Illinois. Supreme Court. Rules. 1977. United States. Court of Appeals (7th Circuit) United States. District Courts. West Publishing Company. Description: v, 690 p.; 24 cm. Notes: "Supersedes 1976 pamphlet." "Illinois Supreme Court rules": p. 81-272. "Including consolidated index covering chapters 110 and 110A." Subjects: Civil procedure--Illinois. Court rules--Illinois. LC Classification: KFI1729 .A2 1977 Dewey Class No.: 347/.773/05

Illinois practice act and rules: with amendments received to April 1, 1975. Published/Created: St. Paul: West Pub. Co., c1975. Related Authors: Illinois. Laws, statutes, etc. Civil practice act. 1975. Illinois. Supreme Court. Rules. 1975. United States. Court of Appeals (7th Circuit) United States. District Courts. West Publishing Company. Description: v, 584 p.; 24 cm. Notes: "Smith-Hurd Illinois annotated statutes: Chapter 110, Practice; Chapter 110A, Practice rules. Federal court rules: U.S. Court of Appeals for the Seventh Circuit, U.S. District Courts." "Provides ... the text of the Civil practice act and related laws found in Chapter 110 of the Illinois revised statutes, the text of the practice rules found in Chapter 110A, and the text of Federal court rules essential to Federal practice in Illinois." "Illinois Supreme Court rules": p. 63-248. Subjects: Civil procedure--Illinois. Court rules--Illinois. LC Classification: KFI1729 .A2 1975 Dewey Class No.: 347/.773/05

Illinois practice act and rules: with amendments received to January 3, 1978: including cnsolidated index, covering chapters 110 and 110A. Published/Created: St. Paul: West Pub. Co., 1978. Related Authors: Illinois. Laws, statutes, etc. Civil practice act. 1978. Illinois. Supreme Court. Rules. 1978. United States. Court of Appeals (7th Circuit) United States. District Courts. West Publishing Company. Description: v, 699 p.; 24 cm. Notes: "Supersedes 1977 pamphlet." "Smith-Hurd Illinois annotated statutes, chapter 110, Practice, chapter 110A, Practice rules; Federal court rules, U.S. Court of Appeals for the Seventh Circuit, U.S. District Courts." "Illinois Supreme Court rules": p. 109-282. Subjects: Civil procedure--Illinois. Court rules--Illinois. LC Classification: KFI1729 .A2 1978 Dewey Class No.: 347/.773/05

Illustrative rules governing complaints of judicial misconduct and disability: with commentary / prepared by a special committee of the Conference of Chief Judges of the United States Courts of Appeals. Published/Created: Washington, D.C. (1520 H St., N.W., Washington 20005): Federal Judicial Center, 1986. Related Authors: Conference of Chief Judges of the United States Courts of Appeals. Description: ix, 68 p.: ill.; 24 cm. Subjects: Judges--United States--Discipline. Judges--Retirement--United States. Judicial ethics--United States. LC Classification: KF8779 .I38 1986 Dewey Class No.: 347.73/14 347.30714 19

Implementation of the Civil Justice Reform Act in pilot and comparison districts / James S. Kakalik ... [et al.]. Published/Created: Santa Monica, CA: RAND, 1996. Related Authors: Kakalik, James S. Institute for Civil Justice (U.S.) Judicial Conference of the United States. Description: xxiii, 263 p.: ill.; 28 cm. ISBN: 0833024558 Notes: "The Institute for Civil Justice." "Prepared for the Judicial Conference of the United States"--Cover p. [2]. "MR-801-ICJ"--Cover p. [4]. Includes bibliographical references (p. 239-246). Subjects: District Courts--United States--Administration. Justice, Administration of--United States. Court congestion and delay--United States. LC Classification: KF8754 .I46 1996

In the Courts / Criminal Justice Coordinating Council. Published/Created: [Atlanta, GA]: The Council, Related Authors: Criminal Justice Coordinating Council (Ga.) Description: v.; 29 cm. Notes: Description based on: Summer 1989; title from cover. SERBIB/SERLOC merged record Subjects: Criminal law--United States--Digests. LC Classification: KF9210.3 .I5 Dewey Class No.: 345.73/002648 347.30502648 20

Index and legislative history, Uniform Code of Military Justice, 1950 (1985). Published/Created: [Falls Church, Va.]: U.S. Army Legal Services Agency, 1985. Related Authors: United States. Army. Court of Military Review. Description: 3 v. (3070 p.); 28 cm. Notes: Originally published: Washington: U.S. Govt. Print. Off., 1950. Vols. 2-3: Indexed and compiled by the U.S. Army Court of Military Review. Spine title: An authoritative index and legislative history of the Uniform Code of Military Justice, 1950 (1985) Subjects: United States. Uniform Code of Military Justice. Courts-martial and Courts of inquiry--United States. LC Classification: KF7604.553 .A15 1985 Dewey Class No.: 343.73/0143/0262 347.3031430262 19

Index and legislative history, Uniform Code of Military Justice. Edition Information: UCMJ 50th anniversary ed., 1950-2000. Published/Created: Buffalo, N.Y.: W.S. Hein, 2000. Related Authors: United States. Navy. Office of the Judge Advocate General. Description: 1 v. (various pagings); 23 cm. ISBN: 1575886219 (alk. paper) Notes: Originally published: Washington: U.S. G.P.O, 1950. Subjects: United States. Uniform Code of Military Justice Legislative history. Courts-martial and Courts of inquiry--United States Indexes. LC Classification: KF7604.553 .A15 2000 Dewey Class No.: 343.73/0143/0262 21

Indiana and North eastern digest, 1817 to date ... covering all cases reported in Indiana reports, Indiana Appellate court reports and North eastern reporter. Published/Created: St. Paul, Minn., West publishing co. [c1940-] Related Authors: Indiana. Courts. Indiana. Appellate court. West publishing co., St. Paul. Description: 1 v. 27 cm. Subjects: Law reports, digests, etc.--Indiana. Law reports, digests, etc.--United States. LC Classification: LAW

Indiana and North eastern digest, covering all cases reported in Indiana reports, Indiana Appellate court reports and North eastern reporter, with current cumulative pocket service keeping the digest always to date. Published/Created: St. Paul, Minn., West publishing co. [c1933-] Related Authors: Indiana. Courts. Indiana. Appellate court. West publishing co., St. Paul. Description: v. 26 cm. Subjects: Law reports, digests, etc.--Indiana. Law reports, digests, etc.--United States. LC Classification: KFI3057 .I5

Indiana rehearing and transfer table covering all cases of the Supreme and Appellate Courts reported in North eastern reporter in which there has been a subsequent opinion by the state Courts or by the Supreme Court of the United States. Published/Created: St. Paul, Minn.: West Pub. Co., Description: v.; 26 cm. Began: 1979. ISSN: 1044-3282 Notes: Description based on: 1987. Kept up to date by a cumulative table in Indiana cases advance sheets. SERBIB/SERLOC merged record Supplement to: West's north eastern reporter (DLC) 88648614 (OCoLC)17624552 Subjects: Annotations and citations (Law)--Indiana. LC Classification: KFI3047.2 .I53 Dewey Class No.: 348.772/048 347.720848 20

Individual judges' rules, procedures, and forms in United States District Courts for the Southern, Eastern, Northern, and Western Districts of New York. Edition Information: 2nd ed. Published/Created: [S.l.]: New York State Bar Association, Committee on Federal Courts, 1986- Related Authors: New York State Bar Association. Committee on Federal Courts. Description: 1 v. (loose-leaf): ill.; 30 cm. Subjects: Court rules--New York (State) District Courts--New York (State) LC Classification: KF8820 .A2 1986 Dewey Class No.: 347.73/22 347.3072 19

Inside the marble palace: the internal operations of the Supreme Court / edited with a preface by Kermit L. Hall. Published/Created: New York: Carlson Publishing, 1996. Related Authors: Hall, Kermit. Description: p. cm. ISBN: 0926019945 (alk. paper) Notes: Includes bibliographical references and index. Subjects: United States. Supreme Courts--Judicial process--Court administration--United States--History. Series: Equal justice under law; 2 LC Classification: KF8742.A45 E68 1996 vol. 2 KF8742 Dewey Class No.: 347.73/26 s 347.73/26 347.30735 s 347.30735 20

Intermediate appellate courts. Published/Created: Frankfort, 1956. Description: iv, 24 p. tables. 27 cm. Notes: Bibliography: p. 23-24. Subjects: Appellate courts--Kentucky. Appellate Courts--United States. Series: Informational bulletin, no. 12 LC Classification: KFK1227 .A154 no. 12

Intermediate Appellate Courts: improving case processing: final report / submitted to the State Justice Institute by National Center for State Courts; Joy A. Chapper, co-project director, Roger A. Hanson, co-project director. Published/Created: Williamsburg, VA: The Center, 1990. Related Authors: Chapper, Joy A. Hanson, Roger A. State Justice Institute (U.S.) National Center for State Courts. Description: xv, 107 p.; 23 cm. ISBN: 0896561003 (pbk.) Notes: "April 1990." Includes bibliographical references (p. 67-69). Includes bibliographical references. Subjects: Appellate Courts--United States--States. Court congestion and delay--United States--States. LC Classification: KF8736 .I59 1990 Dewey Class No.: 347.73/24 347.3073 20

Internal operating procedures of Appellate Courts; a report by a committee. Published/Created: [Los Angeles? 1961] Description: x, 68 p. 23 cm. Notes: Cover title. Subjects: Appellate Courts--United States. LC Classification: KF8750 .A97 Dewey Class No.: 347.95

Iowa, Minnesota, North Dakota, South Dakota, and Wisconsin. Published/Created: Minneapolis [P. M. Woodman] 18 Related Authors: Woodman, Prentiss M., ed. Description: v. 22 x 18 cm. Subjects: Courts--United States. United States--Directories. LC Classification: JK1597 .C7 1900

Jacob, Herbert, 1933- Justice in America: courts, lawyers, and the judicial process / Herbert Jacob. Edition Information: 4th ed. Published/Created: Boston: Little, Brown, c1984. Description: xiv, 273 p.: ill.; 21 cm. ISBN: 0316455326 (pbk.) Notes: Includes bibliographical references and indexes.

Subjects: Courts--United States. Justice, Administration of--United States. Law and politics. LC Classification: KF8700.Z9 J3 1984 Dewey Class No.: 347.73 347.307 19

Jacob, Herbert, 1933- Justice in America: courts, lawyers, and the judicial process / Herbert Jacob. Edition Information: 3d ed. Published/Created: Boston: Little, Brown, c1978. Description: xii, 247 p.; 21 cm. Notes: Includes bibliographical references and index. Subjects: Courts--United States. Justice, Administration of--United States. Law and politics. LC Classification: KF8700.Z9 J3 1978 Dewey Class No.: 347/.73

Jacob, Herbert, 1933- Justice in America; courts, lawyers, and the judicial process. Edition Information: 2d ed. Published/Created: Boston, Little, Brown [1972] Description: xii, 237 p. 21 cm. Notes: Includes bibliographical references. Subjects: Courts--United States. Justice, Administration of--United States. Law and politics. LC Classification: KF8700.Z9 J3 1972 Dewey Class No.: 347/.73

Jacob, Herbert, 1933- Justice in America; courts, lawyers, and the judicial process. Published/Created: Boston, Little, Brown [1965] Description: viii, 215 p. 22 cm. Notes: Bibliographical footnotes. Subjects: Courts--United States. Justice, Administration of--United States. Law and politics. LC Classification: KF8700 .Z9J3 Dewey Class No.: 347.9973

Jacob, Herbert, 1933- Law and politics in the United States / Herbert Jacob. Published/Created: Boston: Little, Brown, c1986. Description: xi, 302 p.; 24 cm. ISBN: 0316455520 Notes: Includes bibliographical references and index. Subjects: Law--United States. Law and politics. Courts--United States. LC Classification: KF380 .J33 1986 Dewey Class No.: 347.73 347.307 19

Jacobson, Charles, 1874- Arkansas chancery practice and procedure, with forms; containing rules of Federal civil procedure. Published/Created: St. Louis, Thomas law book company, 1940. Related Authors: Reeder, Lyman F., joint author. United States. Circuit court (8th circuit), United States. Supreme court. United States. District courts. Description: p. cm. Subjects: Equity pleading and procedure--Arkansas. Equity pleading and procedure--United States. Probate law and practice--Arkansas. Civil procedure--Arkansas. Civil procedure--United States. Court rules--Arkansas. Court rules--United States. Forms (Law)--Arkansas. Forms (Law)--United States. LC Classification: KFA4131 .J3

Jacoby, Sidney B. (Sidney Bernhard), 1908- Ohio civil practice; a guide to civil practice in Ohio under the rules of civil procedure, by Sidney B. Jacoby. Published/Created: Cleveland, Banks-Baldwin Law Pub. Co. [1970- Related Authors: Ohio. Courts. Rules of civil procedure. 1970. United States. District Courts. Rules of civil procedure. 1970. Description: 2 v. (loose-leaf) forms. 27 cm. Notes: At head of title: Jacoby. Includes the texts of the (Ohio) Rules of civil procedure and of the Rules of civil procedure for the U.S. District Courts. Subjects: Court rules--Ohio. Civil procedure--Ohio. LC Classification: KFO529 .A2 1970 Dewey Class No.: 347/.771/05

Jamieson, Richard Watson, 1861- Our courts; the truth about them plainly and impartially told by one who knows ... Published/Created: Tacoma, Wash., The Truth publishing co., c1916. Description: 48 p. 20 cm. Subjects: Courts--United States. LC Classification: JK1544 .J3

Jellett, J. H. (Jonathan Henry) Pacific coast collection laws; a summary of the laws of California, Nevada, Oregon, Washington Territory, Idaho, Montana, Utah, Wyoming, Arizona, and British Columbia, including insolvency laws, also the jurisdiction of U.S. courts with the names of reliable attorneys in the principal cities and towns throughout the Pacific coast, and a notary public for San Francisco, by J.H. Jellett ... Edition Information: [Rev. ed.] Published/Created: San Francisco,

Pettit & Russ, Printers, 1880. Description: 385 p. 22 cm. Subjects: Collecting of accounts. Bankruptcy--Pacific Coast. Courts--United States. LC Classification: HF5559.U5 J4 1880

Jellett, Jonathan Henry. Pacific coast collection laws; Edition Information: [Rev. ed.] Published/Created: San Francisco, W. C. Brown, 1890. Description: xxii, 399 p. 23 cm. Subjects: Collecting of accounts. Bankruptcy--Pacific coast. Courts--United States. LC Classification: HF5559.U5 J4 1890 Microfilm 68833 HF

Jellett, Jonathan Henry. Pacific coast collection laws; Published/Created: San Francisco, Bacon & company, printers, 1876. Description: 318 p. 23 cm. Subjects: Collecting of accounts. Bankruptcy--Pacific coast. Courts--United States. LC Classification: HF5559.U5 J4 1876

Johnson, Frank Minis, 1918- Papers of Frank Minis Johnson, 1945-1989 (bulk 1955-1986) Description: 116,000 items. 332 containers. 133.6 linear feet. Summary: Correspondence, memoranda, agendas and minutes of meetings, reports, opinions, orders, briefs, writs, motions, petitions, depositions, transcripts, notes, clippings, and printed materials documenting Johnson's career as a judge on the U.S. District Court for the Middle District of Alabama (1955-1979), the Temporary Emergency Court of Appeals of the U.S. (1972-1982), the U.S. Court of Appeals, 5th Circuit (1979-1981) and 11th Circuit (1981-), and his involvement in professional activities including membership on the Advisory Committee on Criminal Rules for the Judicial Conference of the United States. Johnson's cases as district court judge pertain primarily to civil rights for African Americans, the mentally ill, and prison inmates. Significant cases include those relating to the Montgomery, Ala., bus boycott (Browder v. Gayle), the Selma-Montgomery march (Williams v. Wallace), school desegregation (Lee v. Macon County Board of Education), and living conditions in Alabama prisons (Pugh v. Locke and James v. Wallace) and in the state's psychiatric hospitals (Wyatt v. Stickney). Papers from his service on the Temporary Emergency Court of Appeals focus on energy regulations relating to the Emergency Petroleum Allocation Act of 1973. Johnson's files as appellate judge include cases relating to civil rights, constitutional law including search and seizure and constitutional challenges to state statutes, antitrust issues, prisoners' rights, and tax and bankruptcy issues. Also documents his work on the Judicial Council of the 11th Circuit leading to the impeachment of U.S. District Court judge Alcee L. Hastings. Correspondents include Griffin B. Bell, Harry Blackmun, John Robert Brown, Paul W. (Bear) Bryant, Warren E. Burger, Emanuel Celler, Morris Dees, Ira DeMent, John Doar, John C. Godbold, William B. Harvey, Fob James, Vernon E. Jordan, William C. Keady, Clarence M. Kelley, Robert F. Kennedy, Seybourne H. Lynne, Burke Marshall, Walter F. Mondale, Huey P. Newton, Richard T. Rives, Hugh Scott, Edward A. Tamm, Elbert P. Tuttle, Robert E. Varner, and Earl Warren. Notes: MSS80675 Subjects: Bell, Griffin B., 1918- Blackmun, Harry A. (Harry Andrew), 1908- Browder, Aurelia S.--Trials, litigation, etc. Brown, John Robert, 1909- Bryant, Paul W. Burger, Warren E., 1907- Celler, Emanuel, 1888-1981. Dees, Morris. DeMent, Ira, 1931- Doar, John, 1921- Gayle, W. A.--Trials, litigation, etc. Godbold, John C. (John Cooper), 1920- Harvey, William Burnett, 1922- Hastings, Alcee L. James, Fob, 1934- James, Worley--Trials, litigation, etc. Jordan, Vernon E. (Vernon Eulion), 1935- Keady, William C., 1913- Kelley, Clarence M. Kennedy, Robert F., 1925-1968. Lee, Anthony T.--Trials, litigation, etc. Locke, Judson C.--Trials, litigation, etc. Lynne, Seabourn H. (Seabourn Harris), 1907- Marshall, Burke, 1922- Mondale, Walter F., 1928- Newton, Huey P. Pugh, Jerry Lee--Trials, litigation, etc. Rives, Richard T. (Richard Taylor), 1895-1992. Scott, Hugh, 1900- Stickney, Stonewall B.--Trials, litigation, etc. Tamm, Edward A. (Edward Allen), 1906- Tuttle, Elbert P.

(Elbert Parr), 1897- Varner, Robert E. (Robert Edward), 1921- Wallace, George C. (George Corley), 1919- --Trials, litigation, etc. Warren, Earl, 1891-1974. Williams, Hosea, 1926- --Trials, litigation, etc. Wyatt, Ricky--Trials, litigation, etc. Macon County (Ala.) Board of Education--Trials, litigation, etc. United States Law, statutes, etc. Emergency petroleum allocation act of 1973. United States. Court of Appeals (5th Circuit) United States. Court of Appeals (11th Circuit) United States. Court of Appeals (11th Circuit). Judicial Council. United States. District Court (Alabama: Middle District) United States. Temporary Emergency Court of Appeals. Judicial Conference of the United States. Advisory Committee on Criminal Rules. African Americans--Civil rights. Antitrust law. Appellate courts. Bankruptcy. Civil rights demonstrations--Alabama. Civil rights. Constitutional law. District courts--Alabama. Energy policy--United States. Federal-state controversies. Mentally ill--Civil rights--Alabama. Petroleum law and legislation--United States. Prisoners--Civil rights. Searches and seizures. Selma-Montgomery Rights March, 1965. Taxation. Trials. Jurists. Lawyers. Local Call/Shelving: 0469A LCA Bay 3 (Unprocessed ac. 22,160) 0438 (Unprocessed ac. 22,310)

Journal of the Center for Families, Children & the Courts. Published/Created: San Francisco, Calif.: Judicial Council of California, c2000- Related Authors: Center for Families, Children & the Courts. California. Judicial Council. Description: v.: ill.; 28 cm. Vol. 2 (2000)- ISSN: 1532-0685 Subjects: Domestic relations Courts--California--Periodicals. Domestic relations--California--Periodicals. Domestic relations Courts--United States--Periodicals. Domestic relations--United States--Periodicals. LC Classification: K10 .O89576 Dewey Class No.: 347 13

Judicial and statutory definitions of words and phrases. 3d series. Collected, edited, and compiled by the editorial staff of the National reporter system. Published/Created: St. Paul, West publishing co., 1928-29. Related Authors: West Publishing Company. Description: 7 v. 26 cm. Notes: "Contains the judicial interpretation and construction of words and phrases found in the reported decisions of the American Appellate Courts from January 1, 1913... down to January 1, 1928." --Pref. v. 1. Subjects: Law--United States--Dictionaries. Law--United States--Terminology. LC Classification: KF156 .J813

Judicial articles; selected recent proposals, with explanatory comments. Published/Created: New York, 1958. Description: 104 l. 29 cm. Subjects: Courts--United States--States. Judges--United States--States. LC Classification: KF8736 .I58

Judicial cases concerning American slavery and the Negro / edited by Helen Tunnicliff Catterall. Published/Created: Buffalo, N.Y.: W.S. Hein, 1998. Related Authors: Catterall, Helen Tunnicliff, 1870-1933. Hayden, James J. (James John), 1894- Description: 5 v.; 24 cm. ISBN: 1575884119 (set: alk. paper) Contents: v. 1. Cases from the Courts of England, Virginia, West Virginia, and Kentucky -- v. 2. Cases from the Courts of North Carolina, South Carolina, and Tennessee -- v. 3. Cases from the Courts of Georgia, Florida, Alabama, Mississippi, and Louisiana -- v. 4. Cases from the Courts of New England, the middle states, and the District of Columbia -- v. 5. Cases from the Courts of states north of the Ohio and west of the Mississippi rivers, Canada, and Jamaica. Notes: "With additions by James J. Hayden"--T.p., vols. 4 and 5. Originally published: Washington, D.C.: Carnegie Institution of Washington, 1926-1937. Includes indexes. Subjects: Slavery--Law and legislation--United States--Cases. African Americans--Legal status, laws, etc.--Cases. Slavery--Law and legislation--Cases. LC Classification: KF4545.S5 J83 1998 Dewey Class No.: 342.73/087 21

Judicial cases concerning American slavery and the Negro / edited by Helen Tunnicliff Catterall. Published/Created: New York: Negro Universities Press, [1968] Related

Authors: Catterall, Helen Tunnicliff, 1870-1933. Hayden, James J. (James John), 1894- Description: 5 v.; 27 cm. Contents: v. 1. Cases from the Courts of England, Virginia, West Virginia, and Kentucky -- v. 2. Cases from the Courts of North Carolina, South Carolina, and Tennessee -- v. 3. Cases from the Courts of Georgia, Florida, Alabama, Mississippi, and Louisiana -- v. 4. Cases from the Courts of New England, the middle states, and the District of Columbia -- v. 5. Cases from the Courts of states north of the Ohio and west of the Mississippi rivers, Canada and Jamaica. Notes: Vols. 4-5: with additions by James J. Hayden. Reprint. Originally published: Carnegie Institution of Washington, 1926-1937. Includes indexes. Subjects: Slavery--United States--Canada--Great Britain--Jamaica--Cases. Afro-Americans--Legal status, laws, etc. LC Classification: KF4545.S5 J83 1968 Dewey Class No.: 342/.7/085

Judicial Conference report to the Supreme Court containing the amendments [to the Rules of civil procedure for the United States District Courts] and the notes of the Advisory Committee. Published/Created: Washington, U.S. Govt. Print. Off., 1963. Related Authors: United States. Supreme Court. Description: iii, 66 p. 24cm. Subjects: United States. District Courts. Rules of civil procedure. Civil procedure--Court rules--United States. Series: House document (United States. Congress. House); 88th Congress, 1st session, no. 67. LC Classification: KF8820 .A25 1963

Judicial conflict and consensus: behavioral studies of American Appellate Courts / edited by Sheldon Goldman and Charles M. Lamb. Published/Created: Lexington, KY: University Press of Kentucky, c1986. Related Authors: Goldman, Sheldon. Lamb, Charles M. Description: 305 p.: ill.; 24 cm. ISBN: 081311554X : Notes: Includes bibliographies and index. Subjects: Judicial process--United States. Appellate Courts--United States. LC Classification: KF8775 .J82 1986 Dewey Class No.: 347.73/242 347.3073 19

Judicial discretion, does sex make a difference? / the National Judicial Education Program to Promote Equality for Women and Men in the Courts. Published/Created: New York: NOW Legal Defense and Education Fund, 1981. Related Authors: Wikler, Norma. National Judicial Education Program to Promote Equality for Women and Men in the Courts. NOW Legal Defense & Education Fund. Description: 2 v.: ill.; 28 cm. Contents: Instructor's manual -- Participant's binder. Notes: "Materials for this course were prepared by Dr. Norma J. Wikler ... [et al.]" "California Continuing Judicial Studies Program, January 18-24, 1981, Berkeley, California"--Cover, Participant's binder. Includes bibliographies. Subjects: Judicial discretion--California. Sex discrimination--California. Judicial discretion--United States. Sex discrimination--United States. LC Classification: KFC995 .J83 1981 Dewey Class No.: 347.794/075 347.940775 19

Judicial Division record / Judicial Division, American Bar Association. Published/Created: Chicago, IL: American Bar Association, Judicial Division, Description: v.: ill.; 28 cm. Has an occasional special issue. Began with spring 1998 issue. ISSN: 1528-7254 Contents: Appellate judges news -- Lawyers letter -- Administrative judiciary news and journal -- Federal trial news -- Special court news -- Trial judges news. Notes: Description based on: Vol. 1, no. 2 (fall 1998); title from caption. Beginning with the special issue designated summer 1998, the newsletter for the Judicial Division and all the Conference newsletters, previously published separately, are available only in the continuously paged publication: Judicial Division record, with each title retaining its own vol. numbering, but sharing the chronological designation. Subjects: American Bar Association. Judicial Division--Periodicals. Judges--Courts--United States--Periodicals. LC Classification: KF8775.A15 J83 Dewey Class No.: 347 13

Judicial independence at the crossroads: an interdisciplinary approach / Stephen B. Burbank, Barry Friedman, editors. Published/Created: Thousand Oaks, Calif.: Sage Publications, c2002. Related Authors: Burbank, Stephen B. Friedman, Barry. Description: [4], 298 p.: ill.; 25 cm. ISBN: 0761926569 (cloth: alk. paper) 0761926577 (pbk.) Contents: Reconsidering judicial independence -- The meaning of judicial independence: theoretical dimensions -- Theory and evidence -- Comparative dimensions. Notes: "With special thanks to: American Judicature Society Brennan Center for Justice." Includes bibliographical references and index. Subjects: Judicial process--United States. Judicial power--United States. Judges--United States. Courts--United States. LC Classification: KF8775 .J825 2002 Dewey Class No.: 347.73/12 21

Judicial politics: readings from Judicature / Elliot E. Slotnick, editor. Edition Information: 2nd ed. Published/Created: Chicago, IL: American Judicature Society, c1999. Related Authors: Slotnick, Elliot E. American Judicature Society. Description: viii, 648 p.: ill.; 26 cm. ISBN: 0938870912 (pbk.) Notes: Includes bibliographical references. Subjects: Judicial process--United States. Political questions and judicial power--United States. Courts--United States. Justice, Administration of--United States. LC Classification: KF8775.A7 J8 1999 Dewey Class No.: 347.73/1 21

Judicial politics: readings from Judicature / Elliot E. Slotnick, editor. Published/Created: Chicago, IL: American Judicature Society, c1992. Related Authors: Slotnick, Elliot E. Description: viii, 663 p.: ill.; 26 cm. ISBN: 0938870564 Notes: Includes bibliographical references. Subjects: Judicial process--United States. Political questions and judicial power--United States. Courts--United States. Justice, Administration of--United States. LC Classification: KF8775.A7 J8 1992 Dewey Class No.: 347.73/1 347.3071 20

Judicial rulemaking: a compendium / Donna J. Pugh ... [et al.]. Published/Created: Chicago: American Judicature Society; Frederick, Md.: University Publications of America, c1984. Related Authors: Pugh, Donna J. Korbakes, Chris A. Judicial rulemaking in the state Courts. American Judicature Society. Description: vi, 308 p.; 24 cm. ISBN: 0890935602 : Notes: Updated ed. of: Judicial rulemaking in the state Courts / Chris A. Korbakes, James J. Alfini, Charles W. Grau. 1978. Bibliography: p. [293]-306. Subjects: Court rules--United States--States. LC Classification: KF8734.Z95 J8 1984 Dewey Class No.: 347.73/51 347.30751 19

Judicial staff directory. Published/Created: Mt. Vernon, Va.: Congressional Staff Directory, Ltd., 1986- Related Authors: Brownson, Charles Bruce, 1914- ed. Brownson, Anna L. Congressional Staff Directory (Firm) Description: v.: ill.; 24 cm. 1986- ISSN: 1091-3742 Notes: Publisher: Staff Directories, Ltd., <1996- Containing, in convenient arrangement, useful, accurate and timely information concerning the Federal Judiciary, with emphasis on the staffs of the judges and the Federal Courts, together with ... biographies. Editors: 1986- C. B. Brownson and Anna L. Brownson. SERBIB/SERLOC merged record Also issued as part of: Staff directories on CD-ROM, <1993- Staff directories on CD-ROM 1080-9546 (DLC) 95645648 (OCoLC)31944525 Subjects: Judges--United States--Directories. Courts--United States--Directories. Courts--United States--Officials and employees Directories. Judges--United States--Biography. LC Classification: KF8700.A19 J83 NAL Class No.: KF8700.A19J83 Dewey Class No.: 347.73/1/025 347.3071025 19

Judicial yellow book: who's who in federal and state Courts. Published/Created: New York, N.Y.: Leadership Directories, Inc., c1995- Related Authors: Leadership Directories, Inc. Description: v.; 29 cm. Vol. 1, no. 1 (fall 1995)- ISSN: 1082-3298 Notes: SERBIB/SERLOC merged record Subjects: Courts--United States--

Directories. Judges--United States--Directories. State Courts--United States--Directories. LC Classification: KF8700.A19 J835 Dewey Class No.: 347.73/1/025 21

Judiciary automation fund annual report. Published/Created: [Washington, D.C.?]: Administrative Office of the United States Courts, [1990?- Related Authors: United States. Administrative Office of the United States Courts. Description: v.: ill.; 28 cm. Fiscal year 1990- Notes: Title from cover. SERBIB/SERLOC merged record Subjects: Court administration--United States--Data processing Periodicals. Courts--United States--Finance--Periodicals. LC Classification: KF8733.A15 J83 Dewey Class No.: 347.73/13/0285 347.307130285 20 Govt. Doc. No.: JU 13.1:

Judson, Frederick Newton, 1845-1919. The judiciary and the people, Published/Created: New Haven, Yale university press; [etc., etc.] 1913. Description: 3 p.l., 270 p. 19 cm. Subjects: Courts--United States. LC Classification: KF8700.Z9 J8

Judson, Frederick Newton, 1845-1919. The judiciary and the people / by Frederick N. Judson. Published/Created: Littleton, Colo.: F.B. Rothman, 1982, c1913. Description: 270 p.; 19 cm. ISBN: 0837703301 : Notes: Reprint. Originally published: New Haven: Yale University Press, 1913. Includes bibliographical references and index. Subjects: Courts--United States. Courts--Great Britain. LC Classification: K2100 .J82 1982 Dewey Class No.: 347.73/1 347.3071 19

Juries and Courts of law. Published/Created: [Boston, D. Clapp & son, prs., 189-?] Description: 22 p. 23 cm. Subjects: Jury. Courts--United States. Law reform. LC Classification: KF8972.Z9 J8

Juris '96: handbook for federal judicial law clerks / [the 1996 Federal Law Clerk Training Committee, U.S. District Court, Southern District of Florida]. Published/Created: [Miami]: The Committee, 1996. Related Authors: United States. District Court (Florida: Southern District). Federal Law Clerk Training Committee. Description: 1 v. (various pagings): forms; 28 cm. Subjects: Law clerks--United States--Handbooks, manuals, etc. District Courts--United States--Handbooks, manuals, etc. LC Classification: KF8807 .J87 1996 Dewey Class No.: 347.73/22 21

Juror utilization in United States District Courts / prepared by Operations Branch, Division of Information Systems, Administrative Office of the United States Courts. Published/Created: Washington, D.C.: The Branch, 1974- Related Authors: United States. Administrative Office of the United States Courts. Division of Information Systems. Operations Branch. United States. Administrative Office of the United States Courts. Division of Information Systems. Statistical Analysis and Reports Branch. United States. Administrative Office of the United States Courts. Statistical Analysis and Reports Division. Description: v.: ill., maps; 28 cm. 1974- ISSN: 0098-3950 Notes: Prepared by: Operations Branch, Division of Information Systems, Administrative Office of the United States Courts, 1974; by: Statistical Analysis and Reports Branch, Division of Information Systems, Administrative Office of the United States Courts, 1975-1976; by: Statistical Analysis and Reports Division, Administrative Office of the United States Courts, 1977-<1978 SERBIB/SERLOC merged record Continued in 1982 by: Grand and petit juror service in United States District Courts. Subjects: Jury--United States--Statistics--Periodicals. District Courts--United States--Statistics--Periodicals. LC Classification: KF8971.A152 A46 Dewey Class No.: 347.73/225 347.307225 19 Govt. Doc. No.: Ju 10.13:

Jury instructions in criminal antitrust cases, 1976-1980: a compilation of instructions given by United States District Courts. Published/Created: [Chicago, Ill.]: American Bar Association, Section of

Antitrust Law, c1982. Related Authors: United States. District Courts. American Bar Association. Section of Antitrust Law. Description: xv, 408 p.; 28 cm. ISBN: 0897070542 (pbk.) Notes: Includes index. Subjects: Instructions to juries--United States. Antitrust law--United States. LC Classification: KF1657.C7 J87 1982 Dewey Class No.: 343.73/072/0269 347.303720269 19

Just, speedy, and inexpensive?: an evaluation of judicial case management under the Civil Justice Reform Act / James S. Kakalik ... [et al.]. Published/Created: Santa Monica, Calif.: RAND, The Institute for Civil Justice, 1996. Related Authors: Kakalik, James S. Institute for Civil Justice (U.S.) Judicial Conference of the United States. Description: ix, 44 p.: ill.; 28 cm. ISBN: 0833024728 Notes: " ... prepared for the Judicial Conference of the United States ..."--P. 2 of cover. "MR-800-ICJ"--P. 4 of cover. Includes bibliographical references. Subjects: District Courts--United States--Administration. Court congestion and delay--United States. Justice, Administration of--United States. LC Classification: KF8754 .J87 1996

Justice calling, 1958; a definitive program devoted to improvements in the administration of justice. Edition Information: 4th ed. Published/Created: [Washington] 1958. Description: 83 p. illus. 23 cm. Notes: "A restatement of objectives" first published in a handbook in 1949 under title: The improvement of the administration of justice. Subjects: Courts--United States. Procedure (Law)--United States. LC Classification: KF8700.Z95 A45 1958 Dewey Class No.: 347.90973

Justice denied: underfunding of the Courts: report of a roundtable discussion / [edited] by Barbara Wolfson. Published/Created: Washington, DC (1050 31st St., NW, Washington 20007): Roscoe Pound Foundation, c1994. Related Authors: Wolfson, Barbara. Roscoe Pound Foundation. Description: vi, 26 p.; 28 cm. Subjects: Courts--United States--Finance. Justice, Administration of--United States. Series: Papers of the Roscoe Pound Foundation LC Classification: KF8732.5.Z9 J87 1994

Justice for the child; the juvenile court in transition. Edited by Margaret Keeney Rosenheim. Published/Created: New York, Free Press of Glencoe [1962] Related Authors: Rosenheim, Margaret K. (Margaret Keeney), 1926- ed. Description: 240 p. 22 cm. Notes: Includes bibliography. Subjects: Juvenile Courts--United States. LC Classification: KF9709 .J86 Dewey Class No.: 364.52

Justice for women: first report / of the Nevada Supreme Court Task Force on Gender Bias in the Courts; Charles E. Springer, chairperson; Deborah A. Agosti, member ... [et al.]. Published/Created: [Carson City, Nev.]: The Task Force, [1988] Description: ii leaves, 89 p.; 28 cm. Notes: Includes bibliographical references. Subjects: Courts--Nevada. Judicial process--Nevada. Sex discrimination against women--Law and legislation Nevada. Courts--United States--Officials and employees. LC Classification: KFN1108 .A845 1988 Dewey Class No.: 347.793/01/082 347.93071082 20

Justice through simplified legal procedure / editors in charge of this volume, Carl Kelsey and Henry W. Jessup. Published/Created: Philadelphia: American Academy of Political and Social Sicence, 1917. Related Authors: Kelsey, Carl, 1870-1953. Jessup, Henry Wynans, 1864-1934. American Academy of Political and Social Science. Description: vii, 251 p.; 24 cm. Notes: Includes index. "Bibliography of procedural reform, including organization of Courts": p. 90-103. Subjects: Justice, Administration of--United States. Courts--United States. Series: Annals of the American Academy of Political and Social Science; v. 73. LC Classification: H1 .A4 vol. 73

Justice without law: a reconsideration of the "Broad Equitable Powers" of the Federal Courts. Published/Created: [Washington, D.C.?]: U.S. Dept. of Justice, Office of

Legal Policy, [1988] Related Authors: United States. Dept. of Justice. Office of Legal Policy. Description: viii, 169 p.; 23 cm. Notes: Cover title: Report to the Attorney General. Shipping list no.: 89-153-P. "August 31, 1988." Item 718-A-22 Includes bibliographical references. Subjects: Equitable remedies--United States. Injunctions--United States. Equity--United States. LC Classification: KF9010 .A85 1988 Dewey Class No.: 347.73/077 347.30777 20 Govt. Doc. No.: J 1.96:L 41

Justices and juries in colonial America; two accounts, 1680-1722. Published/Created: New York, Arno Press, 1972. Related Authors: Hawles, John, Sir, 1645-1716. English-mans right. 1972. Description: xii, 299, 40 p. 24 cm. ISBN: 0405039956 Contents: Conductor generalis. 1722.--The English-mans right, by Sir J. Hawles. 1680. Subjects: Courts--United States--Officials and employees. Courts--Great Britain--Officials and employees. Jury--United States. Jury--Great Britain. Inheritance and succession--United States. Inheritance and succession--Great Britain. Series: American law: the formative years LC Classification: KF8770 .J76 1972 Dewey Class No.: 347/.73/1

Juvenile & family court journal. Published/Created: Reno, Nev., National Council of Juvenile and Family Court Judges. Related Authors: National Council of Juvenile and Family Court Judges. Description: v. 26 cm. v. 29, no. 2- May 1978- ISSN: 0161-7109 Notes: "The journal of the National Council of Juvenile and Family Court Judges. SERBIB/SERLOC merged record Indexed entirely by: Legal resource index 1980- Subjects: Juvenile justice, Administration of--United States Periodicals. Juvenile Courts--United States--Periodicals. Domestic relations Courts--United States--Periodicals. LC Classification: K10 .U84

Juvenile and family court newsletter. Published/Created: Reno, Nev., National Council of Juvenile and Family Court Judges. Related Authors: National Council of Juvenile and Family Court Judges. Description: v. ill. 28 cm. v. 8- Feb. 1978- ISSN: 0162-9859 Notes: SERBIB/SERLOC merged record Subjects: National Council of Juvenile and Family Court Judges Periodicals. Juvenile justice, Administration of--United States Periodicals. Juvenile Courts--United States--Periodicals. Domestic relations Courts--United States--Periodicals. LC Classification: KF9772 .J88 Dewey Class No.: 347/.73/08

Kakalik, James S. Costs of the civil justice system: court expenditures for processing tort cases / James S. Kakalik, Abby Eisenshtat Robyn. Published/Created: Santa Monica, CA: Rand Corp.: Institute for Civil Justice, 1982. Related Authors: Robyn, Abby Eisenshtat, 1943- Institute for Civil Justice (U.S.) Rand Corporation. Description: xxviii, 91 p.; 23 cm. ISBN: 0833004646 (pbk.) Notes: "R-2888-ICJ." Bibliography: p. 87-91. Subjects: Court administration--United States. Courts--United States--Finance. Torts--United States. LC Classification: KF8732.5 .K34 1982 Dewey Class No.: 346.7303/0269 347.30630269 19

Kakalik, James S. Costs of the civil justice system: court expenditures for various types of civil cases / J.S. Kakalik, R.L. Ross. Published/Created: Santa Monica, CA: Rand Corp., 1983. Related Authors: Ross, Randy L., 1951- Description: xxix, 125 p.; 23 cm. ISBN: 0833005170 Notes: "This research is supported by the Institute for Civil Justice." "R-2985-ICJ." Includes bibliographical references. Subjects: Court administration--United States. Courts--United States--Finance. LC Classification: KF8732.5 .K343 1983 Dewey Class No.: 338.4/3347731 19

Karlen, Delmar. Address, prepared for delivery before the Attorney General's National Conference on Congestion in the Courts. Published/Created: [New York, Institute of Judicial Administration] 1958. Description: p. cm. Subjects: Justice, Administration of--United States. Courts--United States. LC Classification: KF8727.Z9 K36

Karlen, Delmar. Appellate courts in the United States and England / Delmar Karlen; forewords by Lord Evershed and William J. Brennan, Jr. Published/Created: Westport, Conn.: Greenwood Press, 1984, c1963. Description: x, 180 p.; 24 cm. ISBN: 0313242917 (lib. bdg.) Notes: Reprint. Originally published: New York: New York University Press, c1963. Includes bibliographical references and index. Subjects: Appellate Courts--United States. Appellate courts--Great Britain. LC Classification: KF8750.Z9 K3 1984 Dewey Class No.: 347.73/24 347.3073 19

Karlen, Delmar. Appellate courts in the United States and England. Forewords by Lord Evershed and William J. Brennan, Jr. Published/Created: [New York] New York University Press, 1963. Description: x, 180 p. 25cm. Subjects: Appellate Courts--United States. Appellate courts--Great Britain. Series: The Judicial administration series LC Classification: KF8750.Z9 K3 Dewey Class No.: 347.73/24 347.3073 19

Karlen, Delmar. Law in action. Published/Created: New York, Holt, Rinehart and Winston [1964] Description: 94 p. illus. 21cm. Notes: Bibliography: p. 93-94. Subjects: Courts--United States--Popular works. Procedure (Law)--United States--Popular works. LC Classification: KF8720 .K35 Dewey Class No.: 347.90973

Karlen, Delmar. The citizen in court: litigant, witness, juror, judge. Published/Created: New York, Da Capo Press, 1974 [c1964] Description: viii, 211 p. 22 cm. ISBN: 0306706148 Notes: Reprint of the ed. published by Holt, Rinehart and Winston, New York. Bibliography: p. 203-205. Subjects: Courts--United States--Popular works. Procedure (Law)--United States--Popular works. LC Classification: KF8720 .K3 1974 Dewey Class No.: 347/.73/5

Karlen, Delmar. The citizen in court: litigant, witness, juror, judge / Delmar Karlen. Published/Created: New York: Holt, Rinehart and Winston, c1964. Description: viii, 211 p.; 21 cm. Notes: Includes index. Bibliography: p. 203-205. Subjects: Courts--United States--Popular works. Procedure (Law)--United States--Popular works. LC Classification: KF8720 .K3 Dewey Class No.: 347.90973

Katz, Roberta R. Justice matters: rescuing the legal system for the twenty-first century / Roberta R. Katz; with Philip Gold. Edition Information: Limited 1st ed. Published/Created: Seattle, Wash.: Discovery Institute, c1997. Related Authors: Gold, Philip, 1944- Description: 160 p.; 21 cm. ISBN: 0963865412 Notes: Includes bibliographical references. Subjects: Justice, Administration of--United States. Courts--United States. Law reform--United States. LC Classification: KF8700 .K368 1997 Dewey Class No.: 347.73 21

Katzmann, Robert A. Courts and Congress / Robert A. Katzmann. Published/Created: Washington, D.C.: Brookings Institution Press/Governance Institute, c1997. Description: xvi, 163 p.; 24 cm. ISBN: 0815748655 (pbk.: alk. paper) 0815748663 (cloth: alk. paper) Contents: Courts, Congress, and the challenges of governance -- Advice and consent -- Approaching statutes: theory and practice -- An experiment in statutory communication -- Building bridges across the communications gulf -- What lies ahead. Notes: Includes bibliographical references (p. 115-153) and index. Subjects: United States. Supreme Court--History. Courts--United States. Political questions and judicial power--United States. Law--United States--Interpretation and construction. United States--Politics and government. LC Classification: KF8700 .K37 1997 Dewey Class No.: 347.73/2 21

Kaufman, Irving R. (Irving Robert), 1910-1992. Papers of Irving R. Kaufman, 1934-1992 (bulk 1949-1992) Description: 43,000 items. 143 containers plus 3 OVSD. 58.7 linear feet. Summary: Court papers, office and subject files, speeches and writings, and scrapbooks chiefly documenting Kaufman's judicial career (1949-1992) on the U.S. District Court, Southern District of New York (1949-1961) and U.S. Court of Appeals, Second Circuit (1961-1992). Court papers include affirmances, appeals, case files, dockets, opinions, and sentences. Includes material on the espionage trial of Ethel and Julius Rosenberg (1953), the trial of reputed underworld figure Joseph Bonanno (1959), and the New Rochelle, N.Y., school desegregation case, Taylor v. Board of Education (1961). Other papers relate to the Juvenile Justice Standards Program and other American Bar Association committees on which he served. Correspondents include Warren E. Burger, Tom C. Clark, and Simon H. Rifkind. Notes: MSS81576 Subjects: Bonanno, Joseph, 1905- Burger, Warren E., 1907- Clark, Tom C. (Tom Campbell), 1899-1977. Rifkind, Simon H. (Simon Hirsch), 1901- Rosenberg, Ethel, 1915-1953. Rosenberg, Julius, 1918-1953. American Bar Association. Juvenile Justice Standards Project. United States. Court of Appeals (2nd Circuit) United States. District Court (New York: Southern District) Appellate courts. Discrimination in education--New York (State)--New Rochelle. District courts--New York (State) Judicial opinions--United States. Juvenile justice, Administration of--United States. Racketeering. Trials (Espionage)--United States. Jurists. Local Call/Shelving: 0531M OVSD 0115M

Keigwin, Charles Albert, 1862- Cases in equity pleading, Published/Created: Rocehster, N.Y., The Lawyers co-operative publishing company, 1924. Related Authors: United States. District courts. Description: xxvi, 698 p. 24 cm. Subjects: Equity pleading and procedure--Cases. Equity pleading and procedure--United States. Court rules--United States. LC Classification: KF8854 .K44 1924b

Kelly, Zachary A., 1970- Our court system / Zachary A. Kelly. Published/Created: Vero Beach, Fla.: Rourke Corp., c1999. Description: 48 p.: col. ill.; 27 cm. ISBN: 0865935750 Summary: Explains elements of the justice system including the kinds of courts; the roles of attorneys, judges, and jurors; pretrial arraignments; preliminary hearings; and trials. Notes: Includes bibliographical references (p. 47) and index. Subjects: Courts--United States--Juvenile literature. Procedure (Law)--United States--Juvenile literature. Courts. Law. Series: Law and order. LC Classification: KF8720 .K43 1999 Dewey Class No.: 347.73/1 21

Kelly, Zachary A., 1970- The court system / by Zachary A. Kelly. Published/Created: Vero Beach, FL: Rourke Publications, 1998. Description: p. cm. ISBN: 0866256628 Summary: Explains the procedures which criminal and civil courts follow in performing their functions and defines terminology associated with the system. Subjects: Courts--United States--Juvenile literature. Procedure (Law)--United States--Juvenile literature. Courts. Series: Law and order LC Classification: KF8720 .K4 1998 Dewey Class No.: 347.73/1 21

Kerr, Michael C. (Michael Crawford), 1827-1876. United States courts in Indiana. Published/Created: [Washington, Printed at the Congressional globe office, 1869] Description: 4 p. 24 cm. Subjects: Courts--United States. Courts--Indiana. LC Classification: JK1598.I6 K4

Kirby, James Patrick, 1892- comp. Selected articles on criminal justice. Published/Created: New York, Wilson, 1926. Description: liii,314p. 20cm. Subjects: Justice, Administration of--Crime and criminals--United States. Courts--United States. Series: The handbook series LC Classification: JK1544 .K5

Kirshbaum, Jerome M. Outline of federal practice and procedure, Published/Created: Brooklyn, N.Y., Academy publications [c1941] Related Authors: United States. Supreme Court. United States. Supreme Court. Description: 13 p.l., 111 numb. l. 28 x 22 cm. Subjects: Courts--United States. Jurisdiction--Civil procedure--Appellate procedure--United States. LC Classification: KF8720 .K5

Klein, David E., 1970- Making law in the United States Courts of Appeals / David E. Klein. Published/Created: New York: Cambridge University Press, 2002. Description: p. cm. ISBN: 052181023X (hbk.) 0521891450 (pbk.) Notes: Includes bibliographical references and index. Subjects: Appellate Courts--United States. Judicial process--United States. Federal courts LC Classification: KF8750 .K59 2002 Dewey Class No.: 347.73/24 21

Klein, Fannie J. Survey of the United States District Court, Western District of Pennsylvania. Published/Created: [n.p.] 1960. Related Authors: United States. Administrative Office of the United States Courts. Description: v, 124 l. tables. 27 cm. Subjects: United States. District Court. Pennsylvania (Western District) LC Classification: KF8755.P4 K6

Klein, Fannie J. Federal and State court systems: a guide / by Fannie J. Klein, with contributions by Edward J. Bander and John P. Richert. Published/Created: Cambridge, Mass.: Published for the Institute of Judicial Administration by Ballinger Pub. Co., c1977. Related Authors: Bander, Edward J., joint author. Richert, John P., joint author. Institute of Judicial Administration. Description: xxii, 303 p.: diagrs.; 24 cm. ISBN: 088410219X Notes: Includes bibliographies and index. Subjects: Courts--United States. Court congestion and delay--United States. Justice, Administration of--United States. LC Classification: KF8700 .K6 Dewey Class No.: 347/.73/1

Klein, Fannie J. How much do you know about the American courts systems? By Fannie J. Klein. With a special pref. by Harold R. Medina. Published/Created: [n.p., Alumni Offset, 1953] Description: 23 p. illus. 17 cm. Notes: Cover title. Subjects: Courts--United States--Popular works. LC Classification: KF8720 .K58 Dewey Class No.: 347/.73/1

Klein, Fannie J. Judicial administration and the legal profession; a bibliography compiled and annotated by Fannie J. Klein. Published/Created: Dobbs Ferry, N.Y., Published for the American Judicature Society and the Inst. of Judicial Administration by Oceana Publications, 1963. Description: xxxii, 650 p. 24 cm. Subjects: Justice, Administration of--Courts--Lawyers--United States--Bibliography. LC Classification: KF8700.A1 K4 Dewey Class No.: 016.3400973

Klein, Fannie J. The administration of justice in the courts: a selected annotated bibliography / compiled and annotated by Fannie J. Klein. Published/Created: Dobbs Ferry, N.Y.: Published for the Institute of Judicial Administration and National Center for State Courts by Oceana Publications, 1976. Description: 2 v. (lx, 1152 p.); 24 cm. ISBN: 0379101378 (v. 1) : Contents: book 1. The courts.--book 2. The administration of criminal justice in the courts. Notes: Updates and expands the author's Judicial administration and the legal profession. Includes indexes. Subjects: Justice, Administration of--Courts--United States--Bibliography. LC Classification: KF8700.A1 K39 Dewey Class No.: 016.347/73/1

Klein, Mitchell S. G. Law, courts, and policy / Mitchell S.G. Klein. Published/Created: Englewood Cliffs, N.J.: Prentice-Hall, c1984. Description: viii, 327 p.; 23 cm. ISBN: 0135260795 (pbk.) Notes: Includes index. Bibliography: p. 294-315. Subjects: Justice, Administration of--Courts--Law--United States. Sociological jurisprudence. LC Classification: KF8700 .K63 1984 Dewey Class No.: 347.73 347.307 19

Knibb, David G. Federal Court of Appeals manual: a manual on practice in the United States Court of Appeals / by David G. Knibb. Edition Information: 2nd ed. Published/Created: St. Paul, Minn.: West Pub. Co., 1990. Description: xvii, 595 p.; 26 cm. ISBN: 0314702490 Notes: Includes index. Subjects: Appellate procedure--Appellate Courts--United States. LC Classification: KF9052 .K63 1990 Dewey Class No.: 347.73/24 347.3073 20

Knibb, David G. Federal Court of Appeals manual: a manual on practice in the United States Court of Appeals / by David G. Knibb. Published/Created: St. Paul, Minn.: West Pub. Co., 1981. Description: xii, 542 p.; 26 cm. Notes: Kept up to date by cumulative pocket parts, the last of which was published in 1989. Includes index. Subjects: Appellate procedure--United States. Appellate Courts--United States. LC Classification: KF9052 .K63 Dewey Class No.: 347.73/24 347.3073 19

Knibb, David G. Federal Court of Appeals manual: a manual on practice in the United States Courts of Appeals / by David G. Knibb. Edition Information: 4th ed. Published/Created: St. Paul, Minn: West Group, 2000. Description: xxv, 956 p.: forms; 26 cm. ISBN: 0314244468 Notes: Includes index. Subjects: Appellate procedure--United States. Appellate Courts--United States. LC Classification: KF9052 .K63 2000

Knibb, David G. Federal Court of Appeals manual: a manual on practice in the United States Courts of Appeals / by David G. Knibb. Edition Information: 3rd ed. Published/Created: St. Paul, Minn: West Pub., 1997. Description: xxxi, 861 p.: forms; 26 cm. ISBN: 0314216561 (hardcover: alk. paper) Notes: Pocket parts published: St. Paul, Minn.: West Group (1998-). Includes index. Kept up to date by pocket parts. Subjects: Appellate procedure--United States. Appellate Courts--United States. LC Classification: KF9052 .K63 1997 Dewey Class No.: 347.73/8 21

Know the law: a compilation of selected articles on various phases of law applicable to traffic police and traffic court activities / by Robert L. Donigan and Edward C. Fisher, compilers. Published/Created: Evanston, IL: Traffic Institute of Northwestern University, c1958 Related Authors: Donigan, Robert L. Fisher, Edward C. (Edward Cole), 1900- Description: xi, 442 p.; 24 cm. Notes: "These articles have appeared in the 'Know the Law' section of the Traffic digest & review and (before consolidation with TD&R) the Traffic digest and the Traffic review." Subjects: Traffic violations--United States. Traffic police--United States. Traffic Courts--United States. LC Classification: KF2231 .D4 Dewey Class No.: 614.862

Koenig, Susan R. Model court rules for the use of facsimile technology by state courts / Susan R. Koenig, Frederick G. Miller, Frederick M. Russillo. Published/Created: Williamsburg, VA: National Center for State Courts; [Washington, D.C.]: State Justice Institute, c1992. Related Authors: Miller, Frederick G. Russillo, Frederick M. Description: v, 27 p.; 23 cm. ISBN: 0896561194 Notes: "Submitted to the State Justice Institute by the National Center for State Courts." Subjects: Court records--United States--States. Courts--United States--States--Technological innovations. Facsimile transmission--Law and legislation--United States States. Series: Publication (National Center for State Courts); R142. LC Classification: KF8733.Z95 K63 1992 Dewey Class No.: 347.73/013 347.30713 20

Kooman, Harold Albert. Federal civil practice, by Harold A. Kooman. Published/Created: Atlanta, Harrison Co. [1967- Related Authors: United States District Courts. Federal Rules of civil procedure. 1967- Description: v. (loose-leaf) 26 cm. Notes: Commentary on the Federal rules of civil procedure. Bound with the author's Florida treatment to Federal civil practice. Atlanta [1967-; the author's Georgia treatment to Federal civil practice. Atlanta [1967-; and Burns, R. H., 1912- North Carolina treatment to Federal civil practice. Atlanta [1969- Subjects: Court rules--United States. Civil procedure--United States. LC Classification: KF8820.A313 K6 Dewey Class No.: 347/.73/1

Kowalski, Kathiann M., 1955- Order in the court: a look at the judicial branch / by Kathiann M. Kowalski. Published/Created: Minneapolis: Lerner Publications Company, 2004. Description: p. cm. ISBN: 0822546981 (lib. bdg.: : alk. paper)

Contents: Real-life courtroom dramas -- The courts from top to bottom -- All the way to the Supreme Court -- Crime and punishment: criminal law -- Let's be civil: civil law -- Your role in the court system. Notes: Includes bibliographical references and index. Subjects: Courts--United States--Juvenile literature. Judicial power--United States--Juvenile literature. Series: How government works LC Classification: KF8700.Z9 K69 2004

Kozlowski, Mark, 1958- The myth of the imperial judiciary: why the right is wrong about the courts / Mark Kozlowski. Published/Created: New York: New York University Press, 2002. Description: p. cm. ISBN: 0814747752 (cloth: alk. paper) Contents: The imperial judiciary and its malcontents -- The constitution and the judiciary -- The judiciary in history -- The judiciary and the extent of rights -- The judiciary and the politics of rights -- The judiciary and the polity. Notes: Includes bibliographical references and index. Subjects: Justice, Administration of--United States. Courts--United States. Political questions and judicial power--United States. Conservatism--United States. United States--Politics and government--1989- . LC Classification: KF8700 .K69 2002 Dewey Class No.: 347.73 21

Krafka, Carol. Stalking the increase in the rate of federal civil appeals / Carol Krafka, Joe S. Cecil, and Patricia A. Lombard. Published/Created: Washington, D.C.: Federal Judicial Center, 1995. Related Authors: Cecil, Joe S. Lombard, Patricia A. Federal Judicial Center. Description: 29 p: ill.; 23 cm. Notes: Shipping list no.: 95-0277-P. Includes bibliographical references. Subjects: Appellate Courts--United States. District Courts--United States. LC Classification: KF9050.Z9 K73 1995 Dewey Class No.: 347.73/24 347.3073 20 Govt. Doc. No.: JU 13.2:ST 1

Kramer, Daniel C., 1934- The courts, the welfare state, and civil liberties / Daniel C. Kramer. Published/Created: New York: P. Lang, 2003. Description: p. cm. Notes: Includes bibliographical references and index. Subjects: Civil rights--United States. Public welfare--Economic assistance, Domestic--Subsidies--Law and legislation--United States. Series: Teaching texts in law and politics; vol. 30 LC Classification: KF4749 .K73 2003 Dewey Class No.: 342.73/085 21

Krislov, Samuel. The rise of consumerism in the U.S. courts / Samuel Krislov. Published/Created: [Tel Aviv]: Tel Aviv University, Aranne School of History, [198-] Description: 24 p.; 23 cm. Notes: "Edition Aranne Foundation, 1978"--Cover. Subjects: Courts--Justice, Administration of--United States. Series: The Kenneth Keating memorial lecture; 1979/80 LC Classification: KF8700 .K75 1980z Dewey Class No.: 347.73/1 347.3071 19

Kuersten, Ashlyn K. Decisions on the U.S. Courts of Appeals / Ashlyn K. Kuersten and Donald R. Songer. Published/Created: New York: Garland Pub., 2001. Related Authors: Songer, Donald R. Description: xvi, 332 p.: ill., 1 map; 24 cm. ISBN: 0815335725 (hardbound: acid-free paper) Notes: Includes bibliographical references (p. [265]-286) and index. Subjects: United States. Courts of Appeals. Appellate Courts--Appellate procedure--United States. LC Classification: KF8750 .K84 2001 Dewey Class No.: 347.73/24 21

Landis, James McCauley, 1899-1964. The administrative process, by James M. Landis. Published/Created: New Haven, Yale University Press; London, H. Milford, Oxford University Press, 1938. Related Authors: Ganson Goodyear Depew Memorial Fund. Description: 4 p. l., 160 p. 21 cm. Notes: "Published on the fund established in memory of Ganson Goodyear Depew." Subjects: Administrative law--United States. Courts--United States. Executive departments--United States. Federal government. Series: Storrs lectures on jurisprudence, Yale School of law ... 1938 LC Classification: KF5407.Z9 L35 1938

Langner, James E. Comparative report on internal operating procedures of U.S. Courts of Appeals / prepared by James E. Langner, Steven Flanders. Published/Created: Washington: Federal Judicial Center, 1973. Related Authors: Flanders, Steven, joint author. Description: 91 p.; 27 cm. Subjects: United States. Courts of Appeals. Court administration--United States. LC Classification: KF8750 .L35 Dewey Class No.: 347/.73/2403

Larsen, Lawrence Harold, 1931- Federal justice in western Missouri: the judges, the cases, the times / Lawrence H. Larsen; with a foreword by Harry A. Blackmun. Published/Created: Columbia: University of Missouri Press, c1994. Description: xiii, 285 p.: ill.; 24 cm. ISBN: 0826209734 (acid-free paper) Notes: Includes bibliographical references and index. Subjects: United States. District Court (Missouri: Western District)--History. Judges--Missouri--History. Judges--United States--History. Courts--Missouri--History. Courts--United States--History. Justice, Administration of--Missouri--History. LC Classification: KF8821.M59 A2 1994 Dewey Class No.: 347.778/01 347.78071 20

Law & the Courts. Published/Created: Chicago, IL: Division for Public Education, American Bar Association, c1998. Related Authors: American Bar Association. Public Education Division. Description: 2 v.: ill.; 23 cm. ISBN: 1570736197 (v. 1) 1570736464 (v. 2) 1590310136 (v. 3) Contents: v. 1. The role of Courts -- v. 2. Court procedures -- v. 3. Juries. Notes: Includes bibliographical references. Subjects: Justice, Administration of--United States--Popular works. Courts--United States--Popular works. Judges--United States--Popular works. LC Classification: KF8700.Z9 .L38 1998 Dewey Class No.: 347.73/1 21

Law and tactics in juvenile cases / Paul Piersma ... [et al.]. Edition Information: 3d ed. Published/Created: Philadelphia: American Law Institute-American Bar Association Committee on Continuing Professional Education, c1977. Related Authors: Piersma, Paul. American Law Institute-American Bar Association Committee on Continuing Professional Education. National Juvenile Law Center. Description: xx, 801 p.; 26 cm. Notes: "A project of the National Juvenile Law Center." Includes bibliographies and index. Subjects: Juvenile Courts--United States. Juvenile justice, Administration of--United States. Trial practice--United States. LC Classification: KF9794 .L38 1977 Dewey Class No.: 345.73/08

Law and the Courts: a handbook about United States law and court procedures: with a glossary of legal terms. Edition Information: New ed. Published/Created: [Chicago, Ill.]: American Bar Association, Division for Public Education, c1995. Related Authors: American Bar Association. Public Education Division. Description: 80 p.: ill.; 23 cm. ISBN: 1570730490 Notes: Includes bibliographical references. Subjects: Procedure (Law)--United States--Popular works. Series: You and the law series LC Classification: KF8841 .L33 1995 Dewey Class No.: 347.73/5 347.3075 20

Law and the Courts: a handbook about United States law and court procedures: with a glossary of legal terms. Published/Created: Chicago, Ill.: American Bar Association, Public Education Division, c1987. Related Authors: American Bar Association. Public Education Division. Description: 80 p.: ill.; 23 cm. ISBN: 0897073312 (pbk.) : Notes: "Revised and expanded edition"--P. 7. Subjects: Procedure (Law)--United States--Popular works. Series: You and the law series LC Classification: KF8841 .L33 1987 Dewey Class No.: 347.73/5 347.3075 19

Law and the legal process / edited by Victoria L. Swigert. Published/Created: Beverly Hills, Calif.: Published in cooperation with the American Society of Criminology [by] Sage Publications, c1982. Related Authors: Swigert, Victoria Lynn. American Society of Criminology. Description: 160 p.; 23 cm. ISBN: 080391900X 0803919018 (pbk.) Contents: "Seize the time": Justice Tom Clark's role in Mapp v. Ohio / Dennis D. Dorin --Corporate criminal liability: the role of the Appellate Courts / Victoria L. Swigert, Ronald A. Farrell -- Building a case: state and defense in felony jury trials / Marianne Hopper -- Factors in juvenile intake decisions / Jean Scherz Huryn -- The impact of delinquency on adolescent attitudes and self-image / Susan K. Datesman -- Conflict and boundaries between political and criminal prisoners / Stanley K. Shernock. Notes: Includes bibliographies. Subjects: Criminal justice, Administration of--United States. Judicial process--United States. Series: Sage research progress series in criminology; v. 25 LC Classification: KF9223.A75 L38 1982 Dewey Class No.: 345.73/05 347.3055 19

Law bulletin / Treasury Department, United States Coast Guard. Published/Created: Washington, D.C.: The Coast Guard, 1933- Related Authors: United States. Coast Guard. Description: v.; 26 cm. Some nos. issued combined. No. 1 (Jan. 15, 1933)- Subjects: United States. Coast Guard--Regulations--Periodicals. Admiralty--United States--Periodicals. Naval law--United States--Periodicals. Courts-martial and Courts of inquiry--United States Periodicals. LC Classification: KF7445.A15 L39

Law for the junior officer, NL-400. Edition Information: 1987 rev. ed. Published/Created: Annapolis, Md.: U.S. Naval Academy; Dubuque, Iowa: Kendall/Hunt Pub. Co., c1990. Related Authors: United States Naval Academy. Description: 1 v. (various pagings): ill.; 28 cm. ISBN: 0840362706 Subjects: Military law--United States. Courts-martial and Courts of inquiry--United States. Midshipmen--Handbooks, manuals, etc. LC Classification: KF7650 .L39 1990 Dewey Class No.: 343.73/01 347.3031 20

Law, Stephen Dodd. The jurisdiction and powers of the United States courts and the rules of practice of the Supreme court of the United States and of the Circuit and District courts in equity and admiralty, with notes and references, and an appendix containing the orders of the High court of chancery of England, Published/Created: Albany, Little & company, 1852. Related Authors: United States. Supreme court. United States. Circuit courts. United States. District courts. Description: xiii, 845 p., 1 l. 24 cm. Subjects: Courts--United States. Court rules--United States. Jurisdiction--United States. LC Classification: KF8719 .L3

Lawson, Harry O. Fiscal administration in state-funded courts / Harry O. Lawson, Barbara J. Gletne. Published/Created: Williamsburg, Va.: National Center for State Courts, c1981. Related Authors: Gletne, Barbara J. Description: x, 154 p. 23 cm. ISBN: 0896560538 : Notes: Bibliography: p. 106-113. Subjects: Courts--United States--States--Finance. Court administration--United States--States. LC Classification: KF8732.5.Z95 L38 Dewey Class No.: 347.73/3/0681 347.30710681 19

Lawson, Harry O. Personnel administration in the courts / Harry O. Lawson, H. R. Ackerman and Donald E. Fuller. Published/Created: Boulder, Colo.: Westview Press, 1979. Related Authors: Ackerman, H. R. (Howard R.), joint author. Fuller, Donald E., joint author. Description: xvii, 397 p.; 24 cm. ISBN: 0891585885 : Notes: Includes bibliographical references. Subjects: Courts--United States--Officials and employees. Courts--United States--Personnel management. LC Classification: KF8770 .L38 Dewey Class No.: 658/.91/347731

Lawson, Harry O. Workload measures in the court / Harry O. Lawson and Barbara J. Gletne. Published/Created: Williamsburg, Va.: National Center for State Courts, Publications Dept., 1980. Related Authors: Gletne, Barbara J., joint author. State Court Financing Project (U.S.) Description: xi, 188 p.: graphs; 23 cm. ISBN: 0896560430 (pbk.) Notes: "A monograph of the State Court Financing Project, National Center for State Courts." Bibliography: p. 171-186. Subjects: Court administration--United States--States. Courts--United States--States--Personnel management. Courts--United States--States--Finance. Series: Publication (National Center for State Courts); R0051. LC Classification: KF8732.Z95 L38 Dewey Class No.: 347.73/13 347.30713 19

Lawyers' guide to the Courts and judges in greater New York. Published/Created: [New York] American surety company of New York, c1932. Related Authors: New York (State) Supreme court. New York (City) City court. New York (City) Municipal court. Description: 19 p. 23 x 19 cm. fold. to 23 x 10 cm. Subjects: Court calendars--New York (State) Court calendars--New York (State)--New York. Courts--New York (State) Courts--New York (State)--New York. Judges--New York (State) Judges--New York (State)--New York. LC Classification: LAW

Lawyers letter / Judicial Administration Division, American Bar Association, Lawyers Conference. Published/Created: [Chicago, Ill.]: The Conference, c1983- Related Authors: JAD Lawyers Conference. Description: v.; 28 cm. Vol. 1, no. 1 (July 1983)- Ceased in 1996. ISSN: 0740-0519 Notes: Title from caption. SERBIB/SERLOC merged record Beginning in summer 1998, resumed publication as a section of: Judicial Division record. Subjects: Courts--United States--Periodicals. LC Classification: KF8700.A15 L38 Dewey Class No.: 347.73/1 347.3071 19

Lee, Katherine J. Courts & judges: how they work. Edition Information: [1st ed.]. Published/Created: [Washington, D.C.]: HALT, Inc., 1987. Description: 205 p.; 22 cm. ISBN: 0910073023 (pbk.) Notes: "Katherine J. Lee"--P. [1]. Subjects: Courts--Judges--United States--Popular works. Series: Citizens legal manual LC Classification: KF8700.Z9 L4 1987

Leflar, Robert Allen, 1901- comp. Appellate judicial opinions / edited by Robert A. Leflar; sponsored by the Institute of Judicial Administration, New York University School of Law. Published/Created: St. Paul, Minn.: West Pub. Co., 1974. Description: xix, 343 p.; 26 cm. Notes: Includes index. Bibliography: p. 327-338. Subjects: Judicial opinions--United States. Appellate Courts--United States. LC Classification: KF9050.A75 L4 Dewey Class No.: 347/.73/245

Leflar, Robert Allen, 1901- Internal operating procedures of appellate courts / Robert A. Leflar; prepared under the auspices of the American Bar Foundation, in collaboration with the Appellate Judges' Conference. Published/Created: Chicago: ABF, 1976. Related Authors: American Bar Foundation. Appellate Judges Conference (U.S.) Description: xiv, 142 p.; 24 cm. ISBN: 0910058792. 0910058776 Notes: Includes bibliographical references and index. Subjects: Appellate Courts--United States. Court administration--United States. LC Classification: KF8750 .L4 Dewey Class No.: 347.73/245 347.3073 19

Legal aspects of Christian Science; decisions of Courts, opinions of lawyers, etc. Published/Created: Boston, The Christian Science Publishing Society, 1899. Description: 83 p. 20 cm. Subjects: Christian Scientists--Legal status, laws, etc. United States--Courts. LC Classification: KF2913.C45 A5 1899

Legal issues in criminal justice: the Courts / edited by Sloan T. Letman, Dan W. Edwards, Daniel J. Bell. Published/Created: Cincinnati, Ohio: Pilgrimage, c1984. Related Authors: Letman, Sloan T. Edwards, Dan W. Bell, Daniel J. Description: viii, 249 p.; 21 cm. ISBN: 093293059X (pbk.) Notes: Includes bibliographical references. Subjects: Criminal procedure--Criminal Courts--Criminal justice, Administration of--United States. Series: Criminal justice studies LC Classification: KF9619.A2 L44 1984 Dewey Class No.: 345.73/01 347.3051 19

Legal rights of children: status, progress, and proposals; a symposium edited by the staff of Columbia human rights law review. Introd. by Rena K. Uviller. Published/Created: Fair Lawn, N.J., R. E. Burdick [1973] Description: 212 p. 24 cm. ISBN: 0913638048 Notes: "Original text published as pages 303-500 of the Columbia human rights law review, volume 4, number 2." Includes bibliographical references. Subjects: Juvenile Courts--United States. Children--Legal status, laws, etc.--United States. LC Classification: KF9709.A2 L4 Dewey Class No.: 345/.73/08

Legislative history of the Military Justice Act of 1983 / indexed by the U.S. Army Court of Military Review; compiled by the U.S. Army Legal Services Agency, Law Library and the Government Appellate Division. Published/Created: Falls Church, Va. (5611 Columbia Pike, Falls Church 22041): The Agency, 1985. Related Authors: United States. Army. Court of Military Review. U.S. Army Legal Services Agency. Law Library. U.S. Army Legal Services Agency. Government Appellate Division. Description: ix, 783 p.: ill.; 29 cm. Notes: Spine title: Index and legislative history--Uniform Code of Military Justice. Subjects: United States. Military Justice Act of 1983. Courts-martial and Courts of inquiry--United States. LC Classification: KF7604.56 .A15 1985 Dewey Class No.: 343.73/0143 347.303143 19

Legislative history of Title 28, United States code, "Judiciary and Judicial Procedure." Act of June 25, 1948, Public Law 773 (H.R. 3214) 80th Congress, 2d session, approved June 25, 1948, effective September 1, 1948. Published/Created: Holmes Beach, Fla., W. W. Gaunt, 1971. Related Authors: Mersky, Roy M. Jacobstein, J. Myron. United States. Congress. House. Committee on the Judiciary. Subcommittee No. 1. Revision of titles 18 and 28 of the United States code. 1971. United States. Congress. House. Committee on the Judiciary. Revision of Title 28, United States code. 1971. United States. Congress. Senate. Committee on the Judiciary. Description: 1 v. (various pagings) 25 cm. ISBN: 0912004002 Contents: Congressional record citations.--U.S. Congress. House. Committee on the Judiciary. Subcommittee No. 1. Revision of titles 18 and 28 of the United States code. Hearings, 80th Congress, 1st session on H.R. 1600 and H.R. 2055.--U.S. Congress. House. Committee on the Judiciary. Revision of Title 28, United States code; report to accompany H.R. 3214.--U.S. Congress. Senate. Committee on the Judiciary. Judicial code and judiciary. Hearings, 80th Congress, 2d session on H.R. 3214.--U.S. Congress. Senate. Committee on the Judiciary. Revising, codifying, and enacting into law Title 28 of the United States code, entitled "Judicial code and judiciary; report to accompany H.R. 3214. Notes: Compiled by Roy M. Mersky and J. Myron Jacobstein. Subjects: United States. Judiciary and Judicial Procedure. Courts--United States. Series: United States Government documents, v. 1 LC Classification: KF8714 .548.A15 1971 Dewey Class No.: 347/.73/2

Legislative resource manual for implementation of the Juvenile Justice and Delinquency Prevention Act. Published/Created: Washington, D.C.: U.S. Dept. of Justice, Office of Juvenile Justice and Delinquency Prevention: For sale by the Supt. of Docs., U.S. G.P.O., 1980, c1979. Description: ii, 285 p.; 28 cm. Notes: "Materials ... for parts I, II, and appendix were developed by staff of the National Juvenile Law Center, Inc., Youth Legal Assistance Project, St. Louis, Missouri; materials for part III were developed by staff of the Youth Law Center, Juvenile Justice Legal Advocacy Project, San Francisco, California." Includes bibliographical references. Subjects: Juvenile justice, Administration of--United States. Juvenile Courts--United States. LC Classification: KF9779 .L43 1980 Dewey Class No.: 345.73/08 347.3058 19

Leland, John, 1754-1841. An elective judiciary, Published/Created: Pittsfield:

Printed by Phinehas Allen, 1805. Description: 23 p. 22 cm. Subjects: Fourth of July orations. Courts--United States. LC Classification: E286 .C513 1805

Letter from the Chief Justice of the United States, transmitting a copy of the report of the proceedings of a special meeting of the Judicial Conference of the United States, held at Washington, D.C., January 13, 1965, pursuant to title 28, U.S. Code, section 331. Published/Created: Washington, U.S. Govt. Print. Off., 1965. Description: ix, 97 p. forms. 24 cm. Subjects: Criminal justice, Administration of--United States. Courts--United States. Series: House document (United States. Congress. House); 89th Congress, 1st session, no. 62. LC Classification: KF9223 .A84 Dewey Class No.: 347/.73/0061

Letter from the Chief Justice, Supreme Court of the United States transmitting the Report of the proceedings of the Annual meeting of the Judicial Conference of the United States, held in Washington, D.C., September 22-23, 1966, pursuant to the provisions of title 28, United States Code, section 331. Published/Created: Washington, U.S. Govt. Print. Off., 1967. Description: vi, 29-70 p. 24 cm. Notes: "January 10, 1967.--Referred to the Committee on the Judiciary." The Report of the Judicial Conference was originally issued in the 1966 Report of the director of the Administrative Office of the United States Courts. Subjects: Courts--Justice, Administration of--United States. Series: House document (United States. Congress. House); 90th Congress, 1st session, no. 37. LC Classification: KF8700 .A84 Dewey Class No.: 347/.73/5

Leveraging the law: using the Courts to achieve social change / David A. Schultz, editor. Published/Created: New York: P. Lang, c1998. Related Authors: Schultz, David A. (David Andrew), 1958- Description: x, 354 p.; 23 cm. ISBN: 0820434922 (alk. paper) Notes: Includes bibliographical references. Subjects: Judge-made law--United States. Social change--United States. Series: Teaching texts in law and politics, 1083-3447; vol. 3 LC Classification: KF8700 .L47 1998 Dewey Class No.: 340/.115/0973 21

Levi, Edward Hirsch, 1911- The sovereignty of the courts / Edward H. Levi. Published/Created: Chicago, Ill. (1111 E. 60th St., Chicago 60637): Law School, University of Chicago, c1981. Description: 23 p.; 23 x 10 cm. Notes: Includes bibliographical references. Subjects: Courts--United States--History. Judicial power--United States--History. Series: Occasional papers from the Law School, the University of Chicago; no. 17 LC Classification: KF352.Z9 L48 Dewey Class No.: 347.73/12 347.30712 19

Levy, Herbert Monte, 1923- How to handle an appeal. Published/Created: New York, Practising law Institute [1968] Related Authors: United States. Courts of Appeals. Federal rules of appellate procedure. 1968. United States. Supreme Court. Rules of the Supreme Court of the United States. 1968. Description: 1 v. (various pagings) forms. 25 cm. Notes: Includes Federal rules of appellate procedure and Rules of the Supreme Court of the United States. Bibliographical footnotes. Subjects: Appellate procedure--United States. Trial practice--United States. Series: Personal injury law and technique practice handbook series, no. 1 LC Classification: KF9050 .L4 Dewey Class No.: 347.99/73

Lewis, David John, 1869- Nullification of acts of Congress ... Published/Created: Washington, U. S. Govt. print. off., 1935. Description: 39 p. 24 cm. Subjects: United States. Supreme court. Courts--United States. United States--Constitutional law. LC Classification: JK1541 .L4

Lieberman, Jethro Koller. Court in session. Introd. by Kenneth B. Keating. Published/Created: New York, Sterling Pub. Co. [1966] Description: 112 p. illus. 22 cm. Subjects: Courts--United States--Popular works. Law--United States--Popular works. LC Classification: KF8720 .L5 Dewey Class No.: 347.9973

List of bankrupts in the district of Massachusetts. Compiled under the direction of the clerk of the U. S. District court, Mass. district. From Aug. 1, 1898, to July 31, 1905 (nos. 1 to 10476, law of 1898), giving status of each case at the last date. Published/Created: Boston, Hooper, Lewis & co. (incorporated) 1905. Related Authors: United States. District Courts. Massachusetts. Description: 271 p. 28 cm. Subjects: Bankruptcy--Massachusetts. LC Classification: HG3767.M42 L7 Microfilm 82/6346 HG

Livingston, Edward, 1764-1836. Mr. Livingston's motion: 13th February, 1800, ordered to lie on the table. Published/Created: [Philadelphia]: Published by order of the House of Representatives, [1800] Related Authors: Marian S. Carson Collection (Library of Congress) Description: [4] p.; 22 cm. Notes: A motion proposing an amendment to the United States Constitution barring judges from simultaneously holding more than one judicial post. References: Evans 38790 Subjects: Judges--Selection and appointment--Selection and appointment--United States--Early works to 1800. Courts--United States--Early works to 1800. LC Classification: KF8776 .A25 1800

Llewellyn, Karl N. (Karl Nickerson), 1893-1962. The common law tradition: deciding appeals / Karl N. Llewellyn. Published/Created: Buffalo, N.Y.: W.S. Hein, 1996. Description: xii, 565 p.: ill.; 26 cm. ISBN: 1575880768 Notes: Originally published: Boston: Little, Brown, 1960. Includes index. Subjects: Common law--United States. Judicial process--United States. Appellate Courts--United States. Stare decisis--United States. LC Classification: KF394 .L58 1996 Dewey Class No.: 347.73/24 21

Local rules of the District Courts in Texas / [compiled by] Sterling W. Steves. Edition Information: 3rd ed. Published/Created: [United States]: Lexis Pub., c2000- Related Authors: Steves, Sterling W., 1925- Description: 2 v. (loose-leaf): forms, maps; 30 cm. ISBN: 0327155426 (v. 1) 0327001984 (v. 2) Subjects: Court rules--Texas. District Courts--Texas. LC Classification: KFT1729 .A2 2000

Long, Joseph R. (Joseph Ragland), 1870-1932. Outline of the jurisdiction and procedure of the federal courts, by Joseph R. Long. Edition Information: 3d ed. Published/Created: Chicago, Callghan and company, 1917. Related Authors: United States. Laws, statutes, etc. Description: xxi, 406 p. 24 cm. Subjects: Courts--United States. Jurisdiction--United States. LC Classification: KF8720 .L65 1917

Long, Joseph R. (Joseph Ragland), 1870-1932. Outline of the jurisdiction and procedure of the federal courts, by Joseph R. Long. Edition Information: 2d ed., containing the judicial code of 1911. Published/Created: Charlottesville, Va., The Michie Company, 1911. Related Authors: United States. Laws, statutes, etc. Description: xxii p., 2 l., [3]-278 p. 24 cm. Subjects: Courts--United States. Jurisdiction--United States. LC Classification: KF8720 .L65 1911

Longsdorf, George Foster. Cyclopedia of federal procedure, civil and criminal, by George Foster Longsdorf and complete forms by Clark A. Nichols. Published/Created: Chicago, Callaghan and company, 1928-30. Related Authors: Nichols, Clark Asahel, 1875- Greenfield, John Mabry, 1878- editor. Description: 8 v. 26 cm. Notes: Vol. 8 has title: Cyclopedia of federal procedure; forms, civil and criminal, by Clark A. Nichols. Subjects: Civil procedure--United States. Criminal procedure--United States. Courts--United States. LC Classification: KF8835 .L65

Loughran, Patrick Henry. Judical review of federal executive action: a compilation of cases that exhibit the extent of the power in the federal judiciary to review the acts of executive officers, boards, bureaus and commissions of the United States in proceedings for injunction and mandamus under the law in the District of Columbia, Published/Created: Charlottesville, Va., The Michie company, c1930- Related

Authors: United States. Congress. United States. District courts. Description: v. 26 cm. Subjects: Executive departments--United States. Executive power--United States. Administrative law--United States. Courts--United States. Injunctions--Washington (D.C.) Mandamus--Washington (D.C.) Remedies (Law)--United States. United States--Officials and employees. LC Classification: KF5425.A7 L67

Louisiana court rules. Published/Created: St. Paul, Minn.: West Pub. Co., -c1977. Related Authors: West Publishing Company. Description: v.; 25 cm. -1977. Notes: On cover: Desk copy. Includes rules from the State Supreme Court, Courts of Appeals, and District Courts, as well as pertinent Federal rules. Description based on: 1956. Supplemented by weekly advance sheets for Louisiana cases. SERBIB/SERLOC merged record Subjects: Court rules--Louisiana. Court rules--United States. LC Classification: KFL529 .A198 Dewey Class No.: 347.763/051 347.630751 19

Love, John, 1857- The annotations of the Missouri Supreme Court reports, vol. 1 to 129 inclusive, embracing Missouri appeal reports, vol. 1 to 63 inclusive and United States Supreme Court to date. Published/Created: Saint Louis, Mo., Love Annotating Co., 1896. Related Authors: Missouri. Supreme Court. Missouri. Courts of Appeal. Description: 260, 126 p. 24 cm. Subjects: Annotations and citations (Law)--Missouri. LC Classification: LAW

Loveland, Frank O. (Frank Olds), 1861-1915. The appellate jurisdiction of the federal courts / by Frank O. Loveland. Published/Created: Cincinnati: W.H. Anderson, 1911, c1910. Description: xviii, 1216 p.; 24 cm. Notes: Spine title: Loveland's appellate jurisdiction of federal courts, with forms. Includes index. Subjects: Appellate procedure--United States. Courts--United States. LC Classification: KF9050 .L67

Loveland, Franklin Olds, 1861-1915. Forms of federal procedure in the courts of the United States, Published/Created: Cincinnati, Ohio, W. H. Anderson & co., 1898. Description: 772 p. 24 cm. Subjects: Forms (Law)--United States. Courts--United States. LC Classification: KF8836 .L65 1898

Low, Peter W., 1937- Federal courts and the law of federal-state relations / by Peter W. Low and John C. Jeffries, Jr. Edition Information: 3rd ed. Published/Created: Westbury, N.Y.: Foundation Press, 1994. Related Authors: Jeffries, John Calvin, 1948- Description: lxv, 1341 p.; 26 cm. ISBN: 1566621607 Notes: Kept up to date by supplements. Subjects: Courts--United States--Cases. Jurisdiction--United States--Cases. Federal government--United States--Cases. State action (Civil rights)--United States--Cases. Series: University casebook series LC Classification: KF8735.A7 L69 1994 Dewey Class No.: 347.73/2 347.3072 20

Low, Peter W., 1937- Federal courts and the law of federal-state relations / by Peter W. Low and John Calvin Jeffries, Jr. Edition Information: 2nd ed. Published/Created: Westbury, N.Y.: Foundation Press, 1989. Related Authors: Jeffries, John Calvin, 1948- Description: lxxvii, 1243, [52] p.; 26 cm. ISBN: 0882777084 (alk. paper) Notes: Kept up to date by supplements. Includes index. Subjects: Courts--United States--Cases. Jurisdiction--United States--Cases. Federal government--United States--Cases. State action (Civil rights)--United States--Cases. Series: University casebook series LC Classification: KF8735.A7 L69 1989 Dewey Class No.: 342.73/042 347.30242 19

Low, Peter W., 1937- Federal courts and the law of federal-state relations / by Peter W. Low and John Calvin Jeffries, Jr. Published/Created: Mineola, N.Y.: Foundation Press, 1987. Related Authors: Jeffries, John Calvin, 1948- Description: lxxvii, 1177, [66] p.; 26 cm. ISBN: 0882775464 Notes: Kept up to date by supplements. Includes index. Subjects:

Courts--Jurisdiction--Federal government--State action (Civil rights)--United States--Cases. Series: University casebook series LC Classification: KF8735.A7 L69 1987 Dewey Class No.: 347.73/2 347.3071 19

Low, Peter W., 1937- Federal courts and the law of federal-state relations / by Peter W. Low, John C. Jeffries, Jr. Edition Information: 4th ed. Published/Created: New York: Foundation Press, 1998. Related Authors: Jeffries, John Calvin, 1948- Description: lxv, 1206, 16, 37, 11 p.; 27 cm. ISBN: 1566626188 (hc.: alk. paper) Notes: Includes bibliographical references (p. xlv-lxiv). Kept up to date by supplements. Subjects: Courts--United States--Cases. Jurisdiction--United States--Cases. Federal government--United States--Cases. State action (Civil rights)--United States--Cases. Series: University casebook series LC Classification: KF8735.A7 L69 1998 Dewey Class No.: 347.73/2 21

Lowe, Isidore Jacob, 1890- Key to the year of decisions of cases in the United States Supreme Court, Federal and State reports and other legal reports. Published/Created: Washington, U.S. Govt. Print. Off., 1952. Related Authors: United States. Supreme Court. United States. Courts. Description: vii, 153 p. 24 cm. Subjects: Law reports, digests, etc.--United States--Indexes. LC Classification: KF127 .L68

Lowell, John, 1824-1897. Judgements delivered in the courts of the United States for the district of Massachusetts. Published/Created: Boston, Little, Brown, and company, 1872-77. Related Authors: United States. Circuit court (1st circuit) United States. District courts. Massachusetts. Description: 2 v. 24 cm. Subjects: Law reports, digests, etc.--Massachusetts. LC Classification: LAW

Lucie, Patricia Allan, 1946- Freedom and federalism: Congress and courts, 1861-1866 / Patricia Allan Lucie. Published/Created: New York: Garland Pub., 1986. Description: iv, 270 p.; 24 cm. ISBN: 0824082850 (alk. paper) : Notes: Written originally as a dissertation in 1972. Bibliography: p. [258]-270. Subjects: Courts--Federal government--United States--History. Afro-Americans--Civil rights--History. Reconstruction. United States--Politics and government--1861-1865. Series: American legal and constitutional history LC Classification: KF8719 .L83 1986 Dewey Class No.: 347.73/1 347.3071 19

Lurie, Jonathan, 1939- Arming military justice: the origins of the United States Court of Military Appeals, 1775-1950 / Jonathan Lurie. Published/Created: Princeton, N.J.: Princeton University Press, c1992. Description: xix, 274 p.: ill.; 25 cm. ISBN: 0691069441 (acid-free paper) : Subjects: United States. Court of Military Appeals--History. Courts-martial and courts of inquiry--United States History. Appellate Courts--United States--History. LC Classification: KF7667 .L87 1992 Dewey Class No.: 343.73/0143 347.303143 20

Lyles, Kevin L., 1959- The gatekeepers: federal district courts in the political process / Kevin L. Lyles. Published/Created: Westport, Conn.: Praeger, 1997. Description: x, 316 p.: ill.; 24 cm. ISBN: 027596082X (alk. paper) Notes: Includes bibliographical references (p. [291]-303) and index. Subjects: District Courts--Political questions and judicial power--Judges--Selection and appointment--United States. LC Classification: KF8754 .L95 1997 Dewey Class No.: 347.73/22 21

Lyman, John Grant. Am I insane? Published/Created: [Los Angeles, Segnogram press, 1913] Description: p. cm. Subjects: Courts--United States. LC Classification: JK1544 .L8

Maberry, John O. Take your traffic ticket to court and win, by John O. Maberry. Published/Created: North Hollywood, Calif. [Brandon House, 1967] Description: 48 p. 20 cm. Subjects: Traffic Courts--United States--Popular works. Traffic violations--United States--Popular works. LC Classification: KF2232.Z9 M3 Dewey Class No.: 340

Mabie, Edward Charles, ed. The courts and social reform, Published/Created: Minneapolis, The H. W. Wilson company, 1913. Related Authors: White, Leonard Dupee, 1891-1958, joint ed. New England triangular league. Brown University. Dartmouth College. Williams College. Description: 67 p. 23 cm. Subjects: Recall. Courts--United States. Debating. LC Classification: JK1533 .M2

MacChesney, Nathan William, 1878- A plan for modern unified courts, An address delivered at the annual meeting of the Bar association of Tennessee, held at Nashville, Tennessee June 11th and 12th, 1914. Published/Created: [n.p., 1914] Description: 20 p. 23 cm. Subjects: Courts--United States. LC Classification: KF8720 .M3

Macomber, William, 1857-1920. The fixed law of patents as established by the Supreme Court of the United States and the nine circuit courts of appeals, by William Macomber. Published/Created: Boston, Little, Brown and Company, 1909. Related Authors: United States. Supreme Court. United States. Courts of Appeals. Description: cxlv, 925 p. 27 cm. Subjects: Patent laws and legislation--United States. LC Classification: KF3105.5 .M3 1909

Managing appeals in federal Courts. Published/Created: Washington, D.C.: Federal Judicial Center, 1988. Related Authors: Federal Judicial Center. Description: vi, 825 p.: ill.; 25 cm. Notes: Shipping list no.: 88-689-P. Item 743-C-3 Includes bibliographical references. Subjects: Appellate Courts--United States. Appellate procedure--United States. Court administration--United States. Court congestion and delay--United States. Series: FJC-R; 88-1. LC Classification: KF8750 .A86 1988 Dewey Class No.: 347.73/24 347.3073 20 Govt. Doc. No.: JU 13.10:88-1

Managing the State Courts: text and readings / [edited] by Larry C. Berkson, Steven W. Hays, Susan J. Carbon. Published/Created: St. Paul: West Pub. Co., 1977. Related Authors: Berkson, Larry Charles. Hays, Steven W. Carbon, Susan B. Description: xiii, 366 p.; 25 cm. Notes: Includes index. Bibliography: p. 357. Subjects: Courts--United States--States. Court administration--United States--States. LC Classification: KF8736.A7 M36 Dewey Class No.: 347/.73/3

Manier, W. H. (Wesley H.), 1829-1897, comp. Law of eminent domain, and of railroads and warehouses, comprising the constitutional and statutory provisions, in the state of Illinois, together with the decisions relating thereto, of the Supreme court and Appelate court of the state of Illinois, and the courts of last resort in other states, and of the Supreme court of the United States. / Compiled and annotated by W. H. Manier. Published/Created: Springfield, Ill., D. W. Lusk, 1888. Related Authors: Illinois. Law, statutes, etc. Illinois. Supreme Court. Illinois. Appellate Court. United States. Supreme Court. Description: vi, 467 p. 23 cm. Subjects: Eminent domain--Illinois. Railroad law--Illinois. Warehouses--Illinois. LC Classification: KFI1650.A59 M3

Manual for Courts-martial, United States. Published/Created: [Washington, D.C.]: U.S. G.P.O., 1984- Related Authors: United States. Dept. of Defense. United States. Joint Service Committee on Military Justice. Description: v.: ill.; 25-28 cm. Starting in 1994, issues designated as 1994 ed.- 1984- Notes: Vol. for 1984 published in looseleaf format. Vols. for 1984-1994 issued by: the Secretary of Defense; 1995-<1998 by: Joint Service Committee on Military Justice. SERBIB/SERLOC merged record Continues a monograph with the same title. Subjects: Courts-martial and Courts of inquiry--United States Handbooks, manuals, etc. LC Classification: KF7625 .M36 Govt. Doc. No.: D 1.15:

Mariano, John Horace, 1896-1972. The Italian immigrant and our courts / by John H. Mariano. Published/Created: Boston, U.S.A.: Christopher Pub. House, c1925.

Description: 87 p.; 21 cm. Subjects: Italian Americans--Legal status, laws, etc. Courts--United States. Lawyers--United States. Attorneys--United States. LC Classification: KF390.I5 I74

Mariano, John Horace, 1896-1972. The Italian immigrant and our courts / John Horace Mariano. Published/Created: New York: Arno Press, 1975 [c1925] Description: 83 p.; 21 cm. ISBN: 0405064101 Notes: Reprint of the ed. published by Christopher Pub. House, Boston. Subjects: Italian Americans--Legal status, laws, etc. Courts--United States. Lawyers--United States. Series: The Italian American experience LC Classification: KF390.I5 I74 1975 Dewey Class No.: 347/.73/5

Marker, Roy Baron, 1885- Federal appellate jurisdiction and proceedure, Published/Created: Chicago, Callaghan and company, 1935. Related Authors: United States. District courts. United States. Courts of appeal. Description: xiii, 400 p. 26 cm. Subjects: Appellate procedure--United States. Jurisdiction--United States. Court rules--United States. Forms (Law)--United States. LC Classification: KF9052 .M37

Marsh, Jennifer Evans. The use of visiting judges in the federal district courts: a guide for judges & court personnel / Jennifer Evans Marsh. Published/Created: Washington, D.C. (1 Columbus Circle, N.E., Washington 20002): Federal Judicial Center, 2001. Description: xi, 67 p.: forms; 23 cm. Subjects: District Courts--United States--Officials and employees. Judges--United States. LC Classification: KF8754 .M37 2001 Dewey Class No.: 347.73/2234 21

Martin, Fenton S. The U.S. Supreme Court: a bibliography / Fenton S. Martin, Robert U. Goehlert. Published/Created: Washington, D.C.: Congressional Quarterly, c1990. Related Authors: Goehlert, Robert, 1948- Description: xv, 594 p.; 27 cm. ISBN: 0871875543 : Notes: Includes indexes. Subjects: United States. Supreme Court--Bibliography. Courts of last resort--United States--Bibliography. LC Classification: KF8741.A1 M37 1990 Dewey Class No.: 016.34773/26 016.34730735 20

Martin, John A. Appellate court delay: structural responses to the problems of volume and delay / John A. Martin, Elizabeth A. Prescott; edited, and with a foreword by Michael J. Hudson. Published/Created: Williamsburg, Va.: National Center for State Courts, c1981. Related Authors: Prescott, Elizabeth A. Hudson, Michael J. National Center for State Courts. Description: xxi, 162 p.: ill.; 23 cm. ISBN: 0896560481 (pbk.) Notes: Includes bibliographical references. Subjects: Court congestion and delay--United States--States. Appellate Courts--United States--States. LC Classification: KF8727 .M37 Dewey Class No.: 347.73/8 347.3078 19

Martindale's American law directory. Published/Created: Chicago: J.B. Martindale, Related Authors: Martindale, James B. (James Boyd), 1836-1904. Description: v.; 26 cm. Ceased in 1930. Notes: Vols. for <1917-1930 published: New York: Martindale's American Law Directory, Inc. Description based on: 27th year (1894-95). Merged with: Hubbell's legal directory, to form: Martindale-Hubbell law directory, ISSN 0191-0221. Subjects: Lawyers--United States--Canada--Directories. Patent lawyers--Courts--United States--Directories. Law--United States--Digests. Law--Canada--Digests. LC Classification: KF190 .H813

Marvell, Thomas B., 1939- Appellate courts and lawyers: information gathering in the adversary system / Thomas B. Marvell. Published/Created: Westport, Conn.: Greenwood Press, 1978. Description: x, 391 p.; 24 cm. ISBN: 0313203121 : Notes: Includes index. Bibliography: p. [257]-285. Subjects: Appellate Courts--United States. Adversary system (Law)--United States. Judicial process--United States. Series: Contributions in legal studies; no. 4 0147-1074 LC Classification: KF8750 .M37 Dewey Class No.: 347/.73/24

Massachusetts court rules, Published/Created: Boston, Boston Law Book Co., 1950. Related Authors: Crane, Joseph Gerard, 1902- Boston. Municipal Court. Rules of the Municipal Court of the City of Boston. United States. District Courts. United States District Court. Massachusetts. United States. Circuit Court of Appeals (1st Circuit. Description: vi, 859 p. 27 cm. Subjects: Court rules--Massachusetts. LC Classification: KFM2480 .M3 vol. 8 1950

Mathews, Stanley, 1824-1889. The judicial power of the United States in some of its aspects, Published/Created: New Haven, Conn., Hoggson & Robinson, printers, 1888. Related Authors: Yale university. School of law. Description: 39 p. 22 cm. Subjects: Courts--United States. LC Classification: KF5130 .M3

Maurer, Robert Adam, 1879- Jurisdiction of federal courts copyright ... Published/Created: [Washington, D.C.] 1940. Description: 1 p.l., 7a (i.e. 9) numb. l. 28 cm. Subjects: United States. Supreme court. Jurisdiction--United States. Courts--United States. LC Classification: KF8858.Z9 M38

Maury, William A. (William Arden), d. 1918, comp. Federal jurisdiction and procedure, as modified by the Act of Congress of March 3, 1891, and March 3, 1887, corrected by the Act of August 13, 1888. Edition Information: 2d ed. Published/Created: Washington, W. H. Lowdermilk, 1901. Related Authors: United States. Laws, statutes, etc. Act to establish Circuit Courts of Appeals. 1901. United States. Laws, statutes, etc. Act to determine the jurisdiction of Circuit Courts of the United States. 1901. Description: 70 p. forms. 18 cm. Notes: "Prepared for use in the Law School of Columbia University." Subjects: Courts--United States. Jurisdiction--United States. LC Classification: KF8700 .A3 1901 Dewey Class No.: 347/.73/1

Maury, William Arden, comp. Federal jurisdiction and procedure, as modified by the acts of Congress of March 3, 1891, and March 3, 1887, Published/Created: Washington, D.C., W. H. Lowdermilk & co., 1896. Related Authors: United States. Laws, statutes, etc. Description: 54, [7] p. 18 cm. Subjects: Courts--United States. Jurisdiction. LC Classification: KF8700 .A3 1896

May it please the court: Courts, kids, and the constitution / edited by Peter Irons. Published/Created: New York: New Press, c2000. Related Authors: Irons, Peter H., 1940- Description: xiii, 348 p.; 23 cm. + 4 sound cassettes (90 min. each) ISBN: 1565846133 (hc) Notes: Includes bibliographical references. Subjects: United States. Supreme Court. Educational law and legislation--United States--Cases. Constitutional law--United States--Cases. Series: May it please the court series LC Classification: KF4118 .M39 2000 Dewey Class No.: 344.73/071 21

Mayers, Lewis, 1890- The American legal system: the administration of justice in the United States by judicial, administrative, military, and arbitral tribunals / by Lewis Mayers. Published/Created: Littleton, Colo.: Rothman, 1981, c1964. Description: xi, 594 p.; 21 cm. ISBN: 0837708397 : Notes: Reprint. Originally published: Rev. ed. New York: Harper & Row, 1964. Includes indexes. Bibliography: 568-573. Subjects: Justice, Administration of--United States. Courts--United States. Administrative Courts--United States. Courts-martial and courts of inquiry--United States. Arbitration and award--United States. LC Classification: KF8700 .M36 1981 Dewey Class No.: 347.73 347.307 19

Mayers, Lewis, 1890- The American legal system; the administration of justice in the United States by Judicial, administrative, military, and arbitral tribunals. Edition Information: Rev. ed. Published/Created: New York, Harper & Row [1964] Description: xi, 594 p. 24 cm. Notes: Bibliography: p. 568-573. Bibliographical footnotes. Subjects: Justice, Administration of--United States. Courts--United States. Administrative Courts--United States.

Courts-martial and courts of inquiry--United States. Arbitration and award--United States. LC Classification: KF8700 .M36 1964 Dewey Class No.: 347.90973

Mayers, Lewis, 1890- The American legal system; the administration of justice in the United States by judicial, administrative, military and arbitral tribunals. Edition Information: [1st ed.] Published/Created: New York, Harper [1955] Description: ix, 589 p. 24 cm. Notes: Bibliography: p. 559-562. Subjects: Justice, Administration of--United States. Courts--United States. Administrative Courts--United States. Courts-martial and courts of inquiry--United States. Arbitration and award--United States. LC Classification: KF8700 .M36 1955 Dewey Class No.: 347.9

Mayers, Lewis, 1890- The machinery of justice; an introduction to legal structure and process. Edition Information: [Rev. ed.] Published/Created: Totowa, N.J., Littlefield, Adams, 1973. Description: xi, 115 p. 23 cm. Notes: Bibliography: p. 108-110. Subjects: Procedure (Law)--United States. Judicial review--United States. Courts--United States. LC Classification: KF8841 .M38 1973 Dewey Class No.: 347/.73

Mayers, Lewis, 1890- The machinery of justice; an introduction to legal structure and process. Published/Created: Englewood Cliffs, N.J., Prentice-Hall [1963] Description: xi, 115 p. 23 cm. Notes: "Suggested readings": p. 108-110. Subjects: Procedure (Law)--United States. Judicial review--United States. Courts--United States. LC Classification: KF8841 .M38 Dewey Class No.: 347.9

McDowell, Gary L., 1949- Curbing the courts: the Constitution and the limits of judicial power / Gary L. McDowell. Published/Created: Baton Rouge: Louisiana State University Press, c1988. Description: xiv, 214 p.; 24 cm. ISBN: 0807113395 Notes: Includes bibliographies and indexes. Subjects: Courts--United States. Political questions and judicial power--United States. Constitutional law--United States. Legislative power--United States. LC Classification: KF8700 .M37 1988 Dewey Class No.: 347.73/1 347.3071 19

McGowan, Carl, 1911-1987. The organization of judicial power in the United States. Published/Created: Evanston, Ill., Northwestern University Press [1969] Description: vii, 133 p. 22 cm. ISBN: 081010007X Notes: Bibliographical references included in "Notes" (p. 107-128) Subjects: Courts--United States. Series: Rosenthal lectures, 1967 LC Classification: KF8735.Z9 M3 Dewey Class No.: 347.99/73

McGowan, Jonas Hartzell, 1837-1909. The lawyer's hand book of federal practice; Published/Created: Washington, D.C., The Brodix publishing company, 1891. Description: ix p. 1 l., 7-232 p. maps (part fold.) 24 cm. Subjects: Courts--Civil procedure--Criminal procedure--Equity pleading and procedure--Forms (Law)--United States. United States--Executive departments. LC Classification: KF8841 .M35

McKenna, Judith A. Case management procedures in the Federal Courts of Appeals / Judith A. McKenna, Laural L. Hooper, Mary Clark. Published/Created: Washington, DC (One Columbus Circle, N.E., Washington, 20002-8003): Federal Judicial Center, 2000. Related Authors: Hooper, Laural L. Clark, Mary. Federal Judicial Center. Description: xiii, 210 p.; 23 cm. Subjects: Appellate Courts--Court administration--United States. LC Classification: KF8750 .M39 2000 Dewey Class No.: 347.73/24 21

McLauchlan, William P. American legal processes / William P. McLauchlan. Published/Created: New York: Wiley, c1977. Description: xv, 218 p.; 22 cm. ISBN: 0471585602. 0471585610 Notes: Includes index. Subjects: Courts--Procedure (Law)--United States. LC Classification: KF8700 .M3 Dewey Class No.: 347/.73/1

McLaughlin, Andrew Cunningham, 1861- The courts, Published/Created: Chicago, Ill., The University of Chicago press [1912] Description: vii, 299 p. 20 cm. Subjects: Courts--United States. United States--Constitutional history--Politics and government. LC Classification: JK1541 .M3

McLaughlin, Andrew Cunningham, 1861-1947. The courts, the Constitution, and parties; studies in constitutional history and politics. Published/Created: New York, Da Capo Press, 1972 [c1912] Description: vii, 299 p. 22 cm. ISBN: 030671549X Subjects: Courts--Constitutional history--United States. United States--Politics and government. LC Classification: JK1541 .M3 1972 Dewey Class No.: 320.9/73

McLaughlin, Andrew Cunningham, 1861-1947. The courts, the constitution, and parties: studies in constitutional history and politics / by Andrew C. McLaughlin. Published/Created: Union, N.J.: Lawbook Exchange, 2001. Description: vii, 299 p.; 23 cm. ISBN: 1584771550 (acid-free paper) Notes: Originally published: Chicago: University of Chicago Press, 1912. Includes bibliographical references and index. Subjects: Courts--Constitutional history--United States--Politics and government. LC Classification: KF8700 .M38 2001 Dewey Class No.: 347.73/1 21

McMillin, Benton, 1845-1933. Encroachments of the United States courts. Speech of Hon. Benton McMillin, of Tennessee, in the House of Representatives, U. S., February 11, 1880 ... Published/Created: Washington [Govt. Print. Off.] 1880. Description: 14 p. 23 cm. LC Classification: JK1591 .M2

Meador, Daniel John. American courts / Daniel John Meador. Edition Information: 2nd ed. Published/Created: St. Paul, Minn.: West Group, 2000. Description: vii, 103 p.: map; 23 cm. ISBN: 0314251332 (alk. paper) Notes: Includes bibliographical references (p. 99-101) Subjects: Courts--United States. LC Classification: KF8720 .M43 2001

Meador, Daniel John. American courts / Daniel John Meador. Published/Created: St. Paul, Minn.: West Pub. Co., 1991. Description: vi, 113 p.: map; 23 cm. ISBN: 0314867171 (alk. paper) Notes: Includes bibliographical references (p. 104-106) and index. Subjects: Courts--United States. LC Classification: KF8720 .M43 1991 Dewey Class No.: 347.73/1 347.3071 20

Meador, Daniel John. Appellate courts in the United States / Daniel John Meador, Jordana Simone Bernstein. Published/Created: St. Paul, Minn.: West Pub. Co., 1994. Related Authors: Bernstein, Jordana Simone. Description: vi, 151 p.; 23 cm. ISBN: 0314037489 (alk. paper) Notes: Includes bibliographical references (p. 148-149) and index. Subjects: Appellate Courts--United States. LC Classification: KF8750 .M4 1994 Dewey Class No.: 347.73/24 347.30724 20

Meador, Daniel John. Appellate courts: staff and process in the crisis of volume: an appellate justice project of the National Center for State Courts / by Daniel J. Meador. Published/Created: St. Paul: West Pub. Co., 1974. Related Authors: National Center for State Courts. Description: xiv, 248 p.; 27 cm. Notes: "A report on the second year of the appellate justice project of the National Center for State Courts" issued as 1975 suppl. (vi, 29 p.) and inserted at end. Includes bibliographical references and index. Subjects: Appellate Courts--United States--States. Appellate Courts--United States. LC Classification: KF8750.Z95 M4 Dewey Class No.: 347/.73/24

Meador, Daniel John. Appellate courts: structures, functions, processes, and personnel / Daniel J. Meador, Maurice Rosenberg, Paul D. Carrington. Published/Created: Charlottesville, Va.: Michie Co., c1994. Related Authors: Rosenberg, Maurice, 1919- Carrington, Paul D., 1931- Description: xl, 1193 p.: ill., forms; 27 cm. + teacher's manual. ISBN: 1558341927 Notes: Includes bibliographical references and index. Subjects: Appellate Courts--United States.

Appellate procedure--United States. Series: Contemporary legal education series LC Classification: KF8750 .M43 1994 Dewey Class No.: 347.73/24 347.3073 20

Mecartney, Harry S., 1860-1927. Some work for the American bar association, by a member. Published/Created: [Chicago? 1907?] Description: 2 p.l., 43 p. 26 cm. Subjects: American bar association. Law reform--United States. Courts--United States. LC Classification: KF326 .M43 1907

Medina, Harold R. (Harold Raymond), 1888- ed. Cases and materials on jurisdiction of courts, by Harold R. Medina. Published/Created: [New York, 1931] Description: xv, 302 p. 26 cm. Notes: Bibliography: p. 295-302. Subjects: Courts--United States. Courts--New York (State). Jurisdiction--United States. Jurisdiction--New York (State). Law reports, digests, etc.--United States. Law reports, digests, etc.--New York (State) LC Classification: KF8858.A7 M4

Medina, Harold Raymond, 1888- ed. Cases on federal jurisdiction and procedure, selected from the decisions of the federal courts, Published/Created: St. Paul, West publishing company, 1926. Related Authors: Kuhn, Bernard Edwin, joint ed. Description: x, 674 p. 26 cm. Subjects: Courts--United States. Jurisdiction--United States. Appellate procedure--United States. Law reports, digests, etc.--United States. LC Classification: KF8718 .M4 Microfilm LL 1463 KF

Meeting criticism of bench and Courts / by the American Bar Association Task Force on Courts and the Public. Published/Created: [Chicago: ABA], c1975. Description: 9 p.; 23 cm. Subjects: Judges--United States--Public opinion. Courts--United States--Public opinion. LC Classification: KF8775.Z9 A55 Dewey Class No.: 347/.73/1

Meierhoefer, Barbara Stone. The caseload experiences of the district courts from 1972 to 1983: a preliminary analysis / by Barbara Stone Meierhoefer and Eric V. Armen. Published/Created: Washington, D.C.: Federal Judicial Center, 1985. Related Authors: Armen, Eric V. Federal Judicial Center. Description: iii, 20 p.: ill.; 28 cm. Notes: Item 743-C-3 Includes bibliographical references. Subjects: Court congestion and delay--United States. District Courts--United States. Series: FJC staff paper; FJC-SP-85-1 LC Classification: KF8727 .M45 1985 Dewey Class No.: 347.73/13 347.30713 19 Govt. Doc. No.: Ju 13.10/2:85-1

Meigs, William Montgomery, 1852-1929. The relation of the judiciary to the Constitution. Published/Created: New York, Da Capo Press, 1971 [c1919] Description: 248 p. 23 cm. ISBN: 0306719886 Notes: Includes bibliographical references. Subjects: Judicial power--United States. Courts--United States. LC Classification: KF5130 .M4 1971 Dewey Class No.: 347/.73/12

Meigs, William Montgomery, 1852-1929. The relation of the judiciary to the Constitution / by William M. Meigs. Published/Created: New York: Neale Pub. Co., 1919. Description: 248 p.; 20 cm. Notes: Includes bibliographical references and index. Subjects: Judicial power--United States. Courts--United States. United States--Constitutional law. LC Classification: JK1541 .M4

Melone, Albert P. The American legal system: an introduction / Albert P. Melone, Allan Karnes. Published/Created: Los Angeles, CA: Roxbury Pub., 2003. Related Authors: Karnes, Allan, 1953- Description: p. cm. ISBN: 1891487922 Notes: Includes bibliographical references and index. Subjects: Law--United States. Courts--United States. Justice, Administration of--United States. LC Classification: KF386 .M45 2003 Dewey Class No.: 349.73 21

Members of State courts of last resort and their terms of office. Published/Created: Lexington, Ky., 1971. Related Authors: Conference of Chief Justices. Description: 20 l. 29 cm. Notes: "A compilation prepared for the Conference of Chief

Justices." Subjects: Courts of last resort--United States--States. Judges--United States--States. Series: RM; 461. LC Classification: JS308 .C6 no. 461 KF8736.Z9 Dewey Class No.: 347/.73/3634

Members of State courts of last resort and their terms of office. Published/Created: Chicago, 1965. Related Authors: Conference of Chief Justices. Description: 20 l. 28 cm. Subjects: Courts of last resort--United States. Judges--United States. Series: Its MS-43. LC Classification: JS308 .C58 no. 43

Members of state courts of last resort and their terms of office: a compilation prepared for the Conference of Chief Justices. Edition Information: Rev. Published/Created: Lexington, Ky.: Council of State Governments, 1974. Related Authors: Conference of Chief Justices. Description: 20 p.; 28 cm. Subjects: Courts of last resort--United States--States. Judges--United States--States. Series: RM; 537. LC Classification: JS308 .C6 no.537 KF8736 Dewey Class No.: 353.9/08 s 347/.73/3634

Members of State courts of last resort, and their terms of office. Published/Created: Chicago, 1959. Description: 18 l. 28 cm. Subjects: Courts of last resort--United States. Judges--United States. LC Classification: JS308 .C6 no. 326

Mennel, Robert M. Thorns & thistles; juvenile delinquents in the United States, 1825-1940 [by] Robert M. Mennel. Published/Created: Hanover, Published for the University of New Hampshire by the University Press of New England, 1973. Description: xxvii, 231 p. 24 cm. ISBN: 0874510708 Notes: Bibliography: p. 202-211. Subjects: Juvenile delinquency--United States--History. Juvenile delinquents--Rehabilitation--United States History. Juvenile Courts--United States--History. LC Classification: HV9104 .M45 Dewey Class No.: 364.36/0973

Merrill, Fredric R., 1937- Federal courts, problems and materials / by Dominick Vetri, Fredric R. Merrill. Edition Information: 2nd ed. Published/Created: St. Paul, Minn.: West Pub. Co., 1984. Related Authors: Vetri, Dominick R. Merrill, Fredric R., 1937- Problems and materials on Federal courts and civil procedure. Description: xxxvii, 232 p.; 25 cm. ISBN: 0314823786 (pbk.) Notes: Rev. ed. of: Problems and materials on Federal courts and civil procedure / by Fredric R. Merrill and Dominick R. Vetri. 1974. Includes index. Subjects: Civil procedure--United States--Cases. Courts--United States--Cases. Series: American casebook series LC Classification: KF8839 .M47 1984 Dewey Class No.: 347.73/5 347.3075 19

Merrill, Fredric R., 1937- Problems and materials on Federal courts and civil procedure, by Fredric R. Merrill and Dominick R. Vetri. Published/Created: St. Paul, West Pub. Co., 1974. Related Authors: Vetri, Dominick R., joint author. Description: xxxviii, 460 p. illus. 25 cm. Notes: On spine: Problems in Federal courts. Includes bibliographical references. Subjects: Civil procedure--United States--Cases. Courts--United States--Cases. Series: American casebook series LC Classification: KF8839 .M47 Dewey Class No.: 347.73/5 347.3075 19

Mershon, Jerry L. Juvenile justice, the adjudicatory process / by Jerry L. Mershon. Published/Created: Reno, Nev. (Box 8978, Reno 89507): National Council of Juvenile and Family Court Judges, c1982. Description: 73 p.; 26 cm. Notes: Includes index. Subjects: Juvenile Courts--United States--Outlines, syllabi, etc. Juvenile justice, Administration of--United States Outlines, syllabi, etc. Series: Juvenile justice textbook series; 501 LC Classification: KF9795 .M47 1982 Dewey Class No.: 345.73/081 347.30581 19

Messinger, I. Scott. Order in the courts: a history of the federal court clerk's office / I. Scott Messinger. Published/Created: Washington, DC: Federal Judicial Center, 2002. Related Authors: Federal Judicial Center. Description: v, 79 p.; 23 cm. Contents: Federal court clerks in the new nation and the early republic, 1789-1839 -- Pure and honest beyond suspicion: the clerks and the emergence of Executive Branch supervision of the federal courts, 1839-1869 -- The clerks and court reform, 1870-1919 -- Toward a more efficient and independent judiciary: the Federal Court Clerks Association, the Judicial Conference, and the Administrative Office of the U.S. Courts, 1919-1969 -- The emergence of the court executive, 1970-1981 -- Court administration in the information age: the automated clerk's office -- Chronology -- A note on sources for additional research at the National Archives. Notes: Includes bibliographical references. Subjects: Courts--Officials and employees--History. Clerks of court--United States--History.

Metcalf, Theron, 1784-1875. Digest of the decisions of the courts of common law and admiralty in the United States. Published/Created: Boston, Hilliard, Gray, and company, 1840-46. Related Authors: Perkins, J. C. (Jonathan Cogswell), 1809-1877. joint author. Curtis, George Ticknor, 1812-1894. joint author. United States. Courts. Description: 8 v. 27 cm. Subjects: Law reports, digests, etc.--United States. LC Classification: KF148 .M48

Mezey, Susan Gluck, 1944- In pursuit of equality: women, public policy, and the federal courts / Susan Gluck Mezey. Published/Created: New York: St. Martin's Press, c1992. Description: xiii, 295 p.; 23 cm. ISBN: 0312065205 0312049056 (pbk.) Notes: Includes bibliographical references (p. 270-280) and index. Subjects: Women--Legal status, laws, etc.--United States. Sex discrimination against women--Law and legislation United States. Women's rights--United States. Courts--United States. LC Classification: KF478 .M49 1992 Dewey Class No.: 346.7301/34 347.306134 20

Michigan court rules, 1973; the manual of Michigan rules. As amended to May 1, 1973. Published/Created: St. Paul, West Pub. Co., 1973. Related Authors: Michigan. Courts. Michigan court rules, annotated. United States. Court of Appeals (6th Circuit). Rules. United States. District Court. Michigan (Western District). Rules. United States. District Court. Michigan (Eastern District). Rules. Description: v, 944 p. 25 cm. Notes: Includes Rules of United States Court of Appeals for the Sixth Circuit, and local rules of the United States District Courts for the Western and Eastern Districts. "For use with Honigman and Hawkins: Michigan court rules annotated." Subjects: Court rules--Michigan. LC Classification: KFM4729 .A2 1973 Dewey Class No.: 347/.774/05

Michigan court rules, 1974: the manual of Michigan rules, as amended to May 1, 1974, for use with Honigman and Hawkins. Michigan court rules annotated. Published/Created: St. Paul: West Pub. Co., 1974. Related Authors: Michigan. Courts. Michigan court rules, annotated. United States. Court of Appeals (6th Circuit). Rules. United States. District court. Michigan (Western District. Rules. United States. District court. Michigan (Eastern District). Rules. Description: iv, 972 p.; 26 cm. Notes: Includes Rules of the United States Court of Appeals for the Sixth Circuit, local rules of the United States District Courts for the Western and Eastern Districts, and indexes. Subjects: Court rules--Michigan. LC Classification: KFM4729 .A2 1974 Dewey Class No.: 347/.774/05

Miller, Leonard G., 1937- Double jeopardy and the federal system. Published/Created: [n.p., n.d.] Description: ii, 206 l. Notes: Thesis (Ph. D.)--University of Chicago, 1964. Bibliography: leaves 194-206. Microfilm. Chicago [Library, Dept. of Photographic Reproduction, University of Chicago] 1964. Subjects: Judicial process--United States. Courts--United States. LC Classification: Microfilm 10226

Miller, Samuel Freeman, 1816-1890. Papers of Samuel Freeman Miller, 1854-1887. Related Authors: Ballinger, William Pitt, 1825-1888. Diaries (1871-1886) Description: 185 items. 2 containers. 3 microfilm reels. 0.8 linear feet. Summary: Letters from Miller to his brother-in-law,

William Pitt Ballinger, an attorney of Galveston, Texas, concerning the status of cases before the U.S. Supreme Court, nomination of John Marshall Harlan to the Court, judicial appointments, Republican Party politics, Abraham Lincoln's election in 1860, Reconstruction and relations between North and South, and Miller's membership in the Electoral Commission appointed to decide the disputed 1876 presidential election between Rutherford B. Hayes and Samuel J. Tilden. Also includes microfilm edition of Ballinger's diaries (1871-1876). Notes: Microfilm edition of typewritten typescripts of the diaries of William Pitt Ballinger held by the University of Texas Library (Austin, Tex.). University of Texas Library, Austin, TX MSS65919 Subjects: Ballinger, William Pitt, 1825-1888 --Correspondence. Harlan, John Marshall, 1833-1911. Hayes, Rutherford Birchard, 1822-1893. Lincoln, Abraham, 1809-1865. Tilden, Samuel J. (Samuel Jones), 1814-1886. United States. Electoral Commission (1877) United States. Supreme Court. Republican Party (U.S.: 1854-) Courts--United States--Officials and employees. Justice, Administration of. Practice of law--Texas--Galveston. Presidents--United States--Election--1860. Presidents--United States--Election--1876. Reconstruction. United States--History--1865-1898. United States--Politics and government--19th century. Jurists. Lawyers. Local Call/Shelving: MMC-3615 Microfilm 19,814-3P (Microfilm 19,814-2N & 19,884-2N)

Mills, George, 1906- No one is above the law: the story of southern Iowa's federal court / George Mills, Richard W. Peterson. Published/Created: [United States?: s.n., 1994?] Related Authors: Peterson, Richard W. (Richard William), 1925- Description: 177 p.: ill.; 25 cm. Notes: Cover title. Includes bibliographical references. Subjects: United States. District Court (Iowa: Southern District) History. Courts--Iowa--History. Judges--Iowa--Biography. LC Classification: KF8755.I8 M55 1994 Dewey Class No.: 347.777/02 347.77072 20

Minnesota digest, 1851 to date. Covering Minnesota reports and North Western reporter as well as Minnesota cases decided in Supreme Court of the United States, circuit Courts of Appeals, and Federal circuit and District Courts. Published/Created: St. Paul, West Pub. Co., [1942- Related Authors: West Publishing Company. Description: v. 27 cm. Notes: Kept up to date by replacement volumes, cumulative supplements, supplementary pamphlets, and pocket parts with title: West's Minnesota digest. Later supplements also update: West's Minnesota digest 2d. LC holdings recorded in Shelflist only. LC copy of later supplements shelved with: West's Minnesota digest 2d (KFM5457.W47 1988). Subjects: Law reports, digests, etc.--Minnesota. LC Classification: KFM5457 .M5

Misdemeanor Courts. Published/Created: [Washington, D.C.]: U.S. Dept. of Justice, National Institute of Justice, 1981. Related Authors: Alfini, James J. Rubin, H. Ted, 1926- American Judicature Society. Institute for Court Management. National Institute of Justice (U.S.) Description: 2 v.: ill.; 28 cm. Contents: [v. 1]. Designs for change / [H. Ted Rubin, editor] -- [v. 2]. Policy concerns and research perspectives / James J. Alfini, editor. Notes: "A joint project of American Judicature Society and Institute for Court Management." "July 1981." "Grant number 76-NI-99-0114 and grant number 78-NI-AX-8072"--Verso of t.p. S/N 027-000-01118-7 (v. 1) S/N 027-000-01119-5 (v. 2) Includes bibliographies. Subjects: Criminal Courts--United States. Municipal Courts--United States. Criminal justice, Administration of--United States. LC Classification: KF9223 .M57 1981 Dewey Class No.: 347.73/4 347.3072 19 Govt. Doc. No.: J 28.2:M 68/v. 1-2

Missouri blue book; tables of cases reported in Missouri reports ... and Missouri appeal reports ... showing volume and page of South western reporter ... Published/Created: St. Paul, Minn., West publishing co. [1937] Related Authors: Missouri. Courts. Missouri. Courts of

Appeals. West publishing co., St. Paul. Description: v. 26 cm. Subjects: Law reports, digests, etc.--Missouri. Annotations and citations (Law)--Missouri. LC Classification: LAW

Missouri. Courts of Appeals Reports. Published/Created: [n.p., n.d.] Description: p. cm. LC Classification: LAW

Model judicial article / Judicial Administration Division, Committee on Standards of Judicial Administration. Published/Created: [Washington, D.C.?]: State Justice Institute, 1995. Related Authors: State Justice Institute (U.S.) Description: vi, 12 p.; 23 cm. ISBN: 1570731675 Notes: Publication developed under grant SJI-90-04X-E-001-P92 from the State Justice Institute. Subjects: Courts--United States. LC Classification: KF8700 .A952 1995 Dewey Class No.: 347.73/1 347.3071 20

Modern criminal procedure; cases, comments, and questions, by Livingston Hall [and others] Edition Information: 3d ed. Published/Created: St. Paul, Minn., West Pub. Co., 1969. Related Authors: Hall, Livingston, 1903- Description: lxxiii, 1456 p. 26 cm. Notes: Previous editions by Hall, Kamisar, and LaFave are entered under Hall, Livingston. "Federal rules of criminal procedure for the United States Districts Courts. (As amended effective July 1, 1968)": p. 1426-1446. Bibliography: p. xxxix-liv. Subjects: Criminal procedure--United States--Cases. Series: American casebook series LC Classification: KF9618 .M6 1969 Dewey Class No.: 343/.0973/03

Moley, Raymond, 1886- Our criminal courts, by Raymond Moley. Published/Created: New York, Minton, Balch & company, 1930. Description: xxiii, 271 p. 23 cm. Subjects: Justice, Administration of--United States. Criminal procedure--United States. Trial practice--United States. Jury. Courts--United States. LC Classification: KF9223 .M635 Dewey Class No.: 345/.73/05

Montgomery, Charles Carroll, 1876- A manual of federal jurisdiction and procedure, with statutes, rules and forms, by Charles C. Montgomery. Edition Information: 3d ed., by Berkeley Reynolds Davids. Published/Created: San Francisco, Brancroft-Whitney company, 1927. Related Authors: Davids, Berkeley Reynolds, 1879- ed. United States. Laws, statutes, etc. Description: xlix, 1511 p. 23 cm. Notes: Map on front lining-paper. Subjects: Courts--United States. Jurisdiction--United States. Court rules--United States. Forms (Law)--United States. LC Classification: KF8840 .M6 1927

Montgomery, Charles Carroll, 1876- Montgomery's manual of federal procedure, by Charles C. Montgomery. Published/Created: San Francisco, Bancroft-Whitney company, 1914. Description: viii, 1057 p. 21 cm. Subjects: Courts--United States. LC Classification: KF8840 .M6 1914

Montgomery, Charles Carroll, 1876- Montgomery's manual of federal procedure, practice and forms. Edition Information: 2d ed. By Charles C. Montgomery. Published/Created: San Francisco, Bancroft-Whitney company, 1918. Description: xliv, 1222 p. 21cm. Subjects: Courts--United States. Civil procedure--United States. Equity pleading and procedure--United States. Criminal procedure--United States. Forms (Law)--United States. LC Classification: KF8840 .M6 1918

Montgomery, Charles Carroll, 1876- Montgomery's Manual. Edition Information: 4th ed. Federal jurisdiction and procedure, with statutes, rules and forms, by Charles C. Montgomery. Published/Created: San Francisco, Bancroft-Whitney company, 1942. Description: lxviii, 1560 p. 24cm. Notes: Map on front lining-paper. Pocket on inside of back cover. First and second editions have title: Montgomery's Manual of federal procedure; 3d ed., A manual of federal jurisdiction and procedure. Subjects: Courts--United States. Civil procedure--United States. Equity pleading and procedure--United States. Criminal procedure--United States. Jurisdiction--United States. Court rules--United States. LC Classification: KF8840 .M6

Moon, Reuben Osborne, 1847- Revision of the laws--The judiciary. Published/Created: Washington [Govt. print. off.] 1911. Related Authors: Heyburn, Weldon Brinton, 1852- United States. Laws, statutes, etc. The judiciary. Description: 21 p. 25 cm. Subjects: Courts--United States. LC Classification: JK1507.1910 .M7

Moon, Reuben Osborne, 1847-1919. Revision and codification of the laws relating to the judiciary; speech of Hon. Reuben O. Moon of Pennsylvania ... in the House of representatives, Wednesday, December 7, 1910. Published/Created: Washington, 1910. Description: 22 p. 23 cm. Subjects: Courts--United States. LC Classification: JK1507.1910 .M72

Moore, James William, 1905- Judicial code; commentary. Published/Created: Albany, Bender, 1949. Related Authors: United States. Laws, statutes, etc. Judicial code, 1948. Description: viii, 684 p. 24 cm. Notes: Cover title: Commentary on the U.S. Judicial code. Subjects: Courts--United States. LC Classification: LAW

Moore, James William, 1905- Moore's Federal practice: a treatise on the Federal rules of civil procedure, by James Wm. Moore [and] Joseph Friedman with foreword by Hon. Martin T. Manton. Published/Created: Albany, N.Y., M. Bender, 1938-42. Related Authors: Friedman, Joseph, joint author. Greenfield, John Mabry, 1878- , joint author. Pike, James A. (James Albert), 1913-1969, joint author. Fischer, Henry G. (Henry Gold), 1911- joint author. Willis, John William, 1913- , ed. United States. Supreme Court. United States. District Courts. United States. District Court (District of Columbia) United States. Courts. Description: 4 v. mounted fold. diagr. 25 cm. Notes: Paged continuously. Map on front lining paper of v. 1. Supplements to be inserted in pocket at end of each volume. Appendix. v. 3. p. 3589-4017: Forms. Supreme court rules. April 1937 draft of Federal rules. Bibliography. Tables of equity rules. Tables of statutes. Tables of selected cases. Index. Vol 4: Forms, by J. A. Pike and H. G. Fischer under the immediate direction of J. W. Willis. Subjects: Court rules--Civil procedure--Equity pleading and procedure--United States. Appellate procedure--United States. Forms (Law)--United States. LC Classification: KFP26.A313 M62

More humor in the court / edited by Mary Louise Gilman. Published/Created: Vienna, Va.: National Shorthand Reporters Association, c1984. Related Authors: Gilman, Mary Louise. Description: 64 p.: chiefly ill.; 22 cm. Subjects: Law--United States--Anecdotes. Courts--United States--Anecdotes. LC Classification: K184 .M67 1984 Dewey Class No.: 347.73/1/0207 347.30710207 19

Moreland, Carroll C. (Carroll Collier), 1903- Equal justice under law: the American legal system / by Carroll C. Moreland; introduction by David F. Maxwell; epilogue by Jefferson B. Fordham. Published/Created: New York: Oceana Publications, c1957. Description: 128 p.; 22 cm. Notes: Includes bibliographical references (p. 121-127) and index. Subjects: Courts--Justice, Administration of--United States. LC Classification: KF8700.Z9 M65 Dewey Class No.: 347.9

Morris, Leigh. National Center for State Courts: an annotated bibliography, 1971-1977 / compiled and annotated by Leigh Morris. Published/Created: [Williamsburg, Va.]: The Center, 1978. Related Authors: National Center for State Courts. Description: 82 p.; 23 cm. Subjects: Courts--Court administration--United States--States--Bibliography. Series: Publication (National Center for State Courts); F0001. LC Classification: KF8736.A1 M67 Dewey Class No.: 016.347/73/1

Most-cited U.S. Courts of Appeals cases from 1932 until the late 1980s / compiled by Robert Schriek. Published/Created: Buffalo, N.Y.: W.S. Hein & Co., 1994. Related Authors: Schriek, Robert. Description: xix, 454 p.; 26 cm. ISBN: 0899418619 (acid-free paper) Subjects: Law reports, digests, etc.--United States. Law--United States--Cases. LC Classification: KF110 .M67 1994 Dewey Class No.: 348.73/48 347.30848 20

Murphy, Walter F., 1929- ed. Courts, judges, and politics: an introduction to the judicial process. [Edited by] Walter F. Murphy [and] C. Herman Pritchett. Edition Information: 2d ed. Published/Created: New York, Random House [1974] Related Authors: Pritchett, C. Herman (Charles Herman), 1907- joint ed. Description: xvi, 719 p. 24 cm. ISBN: 0394318099 Notes: Includes bibliographies. Subjects: Judicial process--United States. Law and politics. LC Classification: KF8700.A7 M8 1974 Dewey Class No.: 347/.73/1

Murphy, Walter F., 1929- ed. Courts, judges, and politics: an introduction to the judicial process / [edited by] Walter F. Murphy, C. Herman Pritchett. Edition Information: 3d ed. Published/Created: New York: Random House, 1979. Related Authors: Pritchett, C. Herman (Charles Herman), 1907- Description: xiii, 769 p.; 24 cm. ISBN: 0394321170 Notes: Includes bibliographical references and indexes. Subjects: Judicial process--United States. Law and politics. LC Classification: KF8700.A7 M8 1979 Dewey Class No.: 347.73/1 347.3071 19

Murphy, Walter F., 1929- ed. Courts, judges, and politics; an introduction to the judicial process [edited by] Walter F. Murphy [and] C. Herman Pritchett. Published/Created: New York, Random House [1961] Related Authors: Pritchett, C. Herman (Charles Herman), 1907- joint ed. Description: 707 p. 24 cm. Subjects: Judicial process--United States. Law and politics. LC Classification: KF8700.A7 M8 Dewey Class No.: 347.90973

Murray, Daniel H. Outline of Federal courts / by Daniel H. Murray; edited by Grace Powers Monaco and Lawrence A. Monaco, Jr. Published/Created: Irvington-on Hudson, N.Y.: [American Legal Publications], c1975. Description: vii, 93 leaves; 28 cm. Notes: Cover title: Federal courts (practice & procedure) Subjects: Courts--United States--Compends. Procedure (Law)--United States--Compends. LC Classification: KF8700.Z9 M87 Dewey Class No.: 347/.73/2

Murray, James Andrew. A treatise on proceedings in the United States courts, designed for the use of attorneys and counselors practicing therein, and also for the duputies of the United States marshals, and other officers of the United States, with practical forms and an appendix. By James Andrew Murray. Published/Created: Albany, Weed, Parsons and company, 1869. Description: 188 p. 23 cm. Subjects: Courts--United States Civil procedure--United States Criminal procedure--United States Forms (Law)--United States LC Classification: KF8841 .M8

National Center for State Courts publications list [microform]: alphabetical list. Published/Created: Buffalo, N.Y.: W.S. Hein, 1987- Related Authors: National Center for State Courts. Description: Jan. (1987)- Notes: Microfiche. Buffalo, N.Y.: William S. Hein, [198-?] microfiches: negative. Subjects: National Center for State Courts--Collected works. Courts--United States--States. LC Classification: Microfiche (o) 95/10012

National legal register ... Published/Created: Chicago, Ill., National credit corporation [c1933-] Description: v. 20 cm. Notes: PREMARC/SERLOC merged record Subjects: Lawyers--United States--Directories. Courts--United States--Directories. LC Classification: KF190 .N357

Navigating through the New York State & federal Courts. Published/Created: New York, N.Y.: Practising Law Institute, c1999-c2000. Related Authors: Practising

Law Institute. Description: 2 v.: forms; 23 cm. 1999-2000. Notes: "Understanding the practical application of civil procedure." Prepared for distribution at a program of the same name. Subjects: Court rules--New York (State). Civil procedure--New York (State). Court rules--United States. Civil procedure--United States. Series: Litigation and administrative practice series Litigation course handbook series LC Classification: KFN5995.Z9 N38

Needles, Alfred P., comp. Rules to regulate the practice of the federal, state, and city and county courts of the city and county of San Francisco, as it appears from the minutes of said courts, with other matters of practice in said courts. Published/Created: San Francisco, Law journal print. 1877. Related Authors: United States. Circuit court (9th circuit) United States. District court. California. California. Courts. San Francisco. Courts. Description: 219 p. 23 cm. Subjects: Court rules--San Francisco. Court rules--California. Court rules--United States. LC Classification: KFC992 .A2 1877

Neely, Richard, 1941- How courts govern America / Richard Neely. Published/Created: New Haven, Conn.: Yale University Press, c1981. Description: xvii, 233 p.; 24 cm. ISBN: 0300025890 (jacket) Notes: Includes index. Subjects: Judicial power--United States. Political questions and judicial power--United States. Judge-made law--United States. LC Classification: KF5130 .N43 1981 Dewey Class No.: 347.73/1 347.3071 19

Neely, Richard, 1941- Judicial jeopardy: when business collides with the courts / Richard Neely. Published/Created: Reading, Mass.: Addison-Wesley, c1986. Description: xviii, 189 p.; 25 cm. ISBN: 0201057360 : Notes: Includes bibliographical references and index. Subjects: Courts--United States. Judicial process--United States. Political questions and judicial power--United States. Industrial policy--United States. LC Classification: KF8700 .N44 1986 Dewey Class No.: 347.73/1 347.3071 19

Neely, Richard, 1941- The product liability mess: how business can be rescued from the politics of state courts / Richard Neely. Published/Created: New York: Free Press; London: Collier Macmillan, c1988. Description: ix, 181 p.; 24 cm. ISBN: 0029226805 Notes: Includes bibliographical references and index. Subjects: United States. Supreme Court. Products liability--United States. Insurance, Products liability--United States. Damages--United States. Corporations, Foreign--United States--States. Courts--United States--States. LC Classification: KF1296 .N44 1988 Dewey Class No.: 346.7303/82 347.306382 19

Neff, Alan. The United States district judge nominating commissions: their members, procedures, and candidates / Alan Neff. Published/Created: Chicago, Ill. (200 W. Monroe St., Suite 1606, Chicago 60606): American Judicature Society, c1981. Description: x, 203 p.: forms; 23 cm. Notes: Includes bibliographical references and index. Subjects: Judges--Selection and appointment--United States. District Courts--United States. United States--Politics and government--1977-1981. Series: Federal judicial selection during the Carter administration; v. 2 LC Classification: KF8776 .F43 vol. 2 Dewey Class No.: 347.73/2034 s 347.73/2234 347.30714 s 347.307234 19

Neier, Aryeh, 1937- Only judgment, the limits of litigation in social change / Aryeh Neier. Edition Information: 1st ed. Published/Created: Middletown, Conn.: Wesleyan University Press, c1982. Description: 265 p.; 23 cm. ISBN: 0819550795 : Notes: Includes bibliographical references and index. Subjects: United States. Supreme Court. Courts--United States. Judicial power--United States. Public policy (Law)--United States. Sociological jurisprudence. LC Classification: KF8748 .N38 1982 Dewey Class No.: 347.73/26 347.30735 19

Nepos-Mowinckel: depositions, briefs in District Courts, and law notes. Published/Created: [S.l.]: R.J.M. Bullowa,

[1915?] Description: 1 v. (various pagings); 28 cm. Notes: Binder's title. Subjects: Mowinckel, Johan Ludwig, 1870- --Trials, litigation, etc. Nepos (Steamer) Mowinckel (Steamer) Breach of contract--United States. Charter-parties--United States. Contraband of war. LC Classification: KF228.M69 N46 1915 Dewey Class No.: 346.73/022 347.30622 20

Neubauer, David W. Judicial process: law, courts, and politics in the United States / David W. Neubauer. Edition Information: 2nd ed. Published/Created: Fort Worth: Harcourt Brace College Publishers, c1997. Description: xvi, 544 p.: ill., maps; 24 cm. ISBN: 0030193842 Notes: Includes bibliographical references and index. Subjects: Procedure (Law)--United States. Courts--United States. Judicial process--United States. Law and politics. LC Classification: KF8719 .N48 1997 Dewey Class No.: 347.73/5 21

Neubauer, David W. Judicial process: law, courts, and politics in the United States / David W. Neubauer. Published/Created: Pacific Grove, Calif.: Brooks/Cole Pub., c1991. Description: xix, 452 p.; 25 cm. ISBN: 0534153844 Notes: Includes bibliographical references and index. Subjects: Procedure (Law)--United States. Courts--United States. Judicial process--United States. Law and politics. LC Classification: KF8719 .N48 1991 Dewey Class No.: 347.73/5 347.3075 20

New Hampshire court rules annotated / edited and published by Equity Publishing Corporation. Published/Created: Orford, N.H.: The Corporation, c1979- Related Authors: Equity Publishing Corporation. New Hampshire. Supreme Court. Description: 2 v. (loose-leaf): forms; 24 cm. Notes: Previously published under title: New Hampshire court rules, 1979. Other title information: Including the rules of court governing practice in the Supreme Court, Superior Court, District and Municipal Courts, Probate Courts, United States District Court for the District of New Hampshire (1979-). State court rules promulgated by the Supreme Court. Accompanied by regular updates of: Directory of attorneys in good standing. Imprint of directory varies. Includes indexes. Description based on: v. 1, 1986 t.p. Subjects: Court rules--New Hampshire. LC Classification: KFN1729 .A2 1979 Dewey Class No.: 347.742/051 347.420751 19

New Jersey digest, annotated, covering all cases reported in New Jersey reports and Atlantic reporter, 1790-1931, Published/Created: Newark, Soney & Sage co.; St. Paul, West publishing co., 1932. Related Authors: New Jersey. Courts. Soney & Sage co., Newark, N.J. West publishing co., St. Paul. Description: 12 v. 26 cm. Subjects: Law reports, digests, etc.--New Jersey. LC Classification: LAW

New Jersey rules of court. Published/Created: St. Paul, Minn.: West Pub. Co., 1992- Related Authors: New Jersey. Supreme Court. United States. Supreme Court. West Publishing Company. West Group. Description: v.; 25 cm. Vols. for 2001- issued in 2 pts.: State, Federal. 1993- ISSN: 1070-6364 Notes: Vols. for <2001- published by West Group. SERBIB/SERLOC merged record Subjects: Court rules--New Jersey. Court rules--United States. LC Classification: KFN2329 .A196 Dewey Class No.: 347/.749/05

New York federal cases [electronic resource]. Notes: New York federal case law library Published/Created: Conklin, NY: Matthew Bender, Related Authors: Matthew Bender (Firm) United States. Court of Appeals (2nd Circuit) Description: computer laser optical discs; 4 3/4 in. Issues for issued on three discs: disc 1, 1990-present; disc 2, 1984-1989; and disc 3, Prior to 1984. Each issue is cumulative. Summary: Contains decisions of the U.S. Court of Appeals for the Second Circuit and the U.S. District Courts for New York. Notes: "Folio infobase." At head of disc: Authority from Matthew Bender. Description based on: Release 2 (7/96); title from disc label. System requirements: 386 or higher IBM compatible; Microsoft Windows 3.1 or higher; DOS 3.1 or higher; 4MB RAM; 10MB hard drive space available; CD-ROM drive; mouse; color monitor. Quick install; How to use the Authority case law update feature; Using the LEXIS-NEXIS online connection. Subjects: Law reports, digests, etc.--United States--Databases. Law reports, digests, etc.--New York (State)--Databases.

New York practice notes; a comprehensive compilation containing notes of decisions handed down prior to the enactment of, and applicable to, the Civil practice act, the rules of civil practice, the Surrogate's court act, the Justice court act, the Court of claims act, the Municipal court code and the New York city court act ... Published/Created: New York, Chicago, Callaghan and company, 1927- Related Authors: Cahill, James Christopher, 1885- ed. Description: v. 27 cm. Subjects: Civil procedure--New York (State) Probate law and practice--New York (State) Court rules--New York (State) Courts--New York (State) Courts--New York (City) Law reports, digests, etc.--New York (State) LC Classification: LAW

Nicholson, Joseph Hopper, 1770-1817. Speech of Mr. Nicholson, on the bill received from the Senate, Published/Created: [Washington? 1802] Description: 36 p. 22 cm. Subjects: Courts--United States. LC Classification: JK1551 .N5

Niemic, Robert J., 1950- Guide to judicial management of cases in ADR / Robert J. Niemic, Donna Stienstra, Randall E. Ravitz. Published/Created: Washington, D.C.: Federal Judicial Center, 2001. Related Authors: Stienstra, Donna. Ravitz, Randall E. Federal Judicial Center. Description: xi, 193 p.; 25 cm. Notes: Includes bibliographical references and index. Subjects: Dispute resolution (Law)--United States. Mediation--United States. District Courts--United States. LC Classification: KF9084 .N54 2001 Govt. Doc. No.: JU 13.8:

Niemic, Robert J., 1950- Mediation & conference programs in the federal courts of appeals: a sourcebook for judges and lawyers / Robert J. Niemic. Published/Created: Washington, D.C. (One Columbus Cir., N.E., Washington 20002-8003): Federal Judicial Center, 1997. Related Authors: Federal Judicial Center. Description: v, 107 p.; 23 cm. Notes: Includes bibliographical references (p. 104-107). Subjects: Appellate Courts--United States. Mediation--United States. LC Classification: KF8750 .N54 1997 Dewey Class No.: 347.73/24 21

Noel, Francis Regis, 1891- Vestiges of a Supreme court among the colonies and under the Articles of confederation, Published/Created: Washington, 1937. Description: p. 123-143. 24 cm. Subjects: United States. Supreme court. Courts--United States--History. LC Classification: F191 .C72 vol. 37-38

Noel, Francis Regis, 1891- Vestiges of a Supreme court among the colonies and under the Articles of confederation, Published/Created: [Washington, D.C., W. F. Roberts co., 1935?] Description: 21 p. 23 cm. Subjects: United States. Supreme court. Courts--United States--History. LC Classification: KF8742.Z9 N6 1935

Norris, Loretta A. American colonial courts and lawyers: an annotated bibliography / prepared by Loretta A. Norris and Larry M. Boyer. Published/Created: Washington: Library of Congress, Law Library, 1976. Related Authors: Boyer, Larry M., joint author. Library of Congress. Law Library. Description: vi, 24 p.; 27 cm. Notes: "Bibliography of works found in the Law Library of Congress." Includes bibliographical references. Subjects: Courts--United States--History--Bibliography. Lawyers--United States--History--Bibliography. LC Classification: KF361 .N67 Dewey Class No.: 016.347/73/1

North Carolina reporter, covering cases reported in South eastern reporter, second series. Published/Created: St. Paul, West

Pub. Co., 1963- Related Authors: North Carolina. Courts. West Publishing Company, St. Paul. Description: v. 27 cm. Subjects: Law reports, digests, etc.--North Carolina. LC Classification: LAW

North Carolina rules of court, with amendments received to .... Published/Created: St. Paul, Minn.: West Pub. Co., Related Authors: North Carolina. Supreme Court. United States. District Court (North Carolina) United States. District Court (North Carolina: Eastern District) United States. Court of Appeals (4th Circuit) Description: v.; 25 cm. Began in 1973. ISSN: 0732-281X Summary: Includes local rules for the U.S. District Courts for North Carolina, District Court for the Eastern District, rules of the U.S. Court of Appeals for the Fourth Circuit, the Federal rules of evidence, and Federal rules of Appellate procedure. Notes: Rules for <1991-2000 published in 2 v.: North Carolina rules of court. State, and: North Carolina rules of court. Federal. Description based on: 1980. Supplements issued between eds. SERBIB/SERLOC merged record Subjects: Court rules--North Carolina. Court rules--United States. LC Classification: KFN7929 .A195 Dewey Class No.: 347.756/051 347.560751

North Carolina rules: including the annotated rules of the Courts and the rules of the commissions in North Carolina, the rules of the Federal Courts, and the rules of the Supreme Court of the United States. Edition Information: 1977 ed. Published/Created: Charlottesville, Va.: Michie Co., c1977. Related Authors: North Carolina. Courts. Michie Company. Description: 1220 p.; 26 cm. Notes: Includes index. Subjects: Court rules--North Carolina. LC Classification: KFN7929 .A2 1977 Dewey Class No.: 347/.756/05

North Dakota and North western digest, covering all cases reported in North Dakota reports, North western reporter and all of the north western states reports from the earliest times, with current cumulative pocket service keeping this digest always to date. Published/Created: St. Paul, West publishing co. [c1932-] Related Authors: North Dakota. Courts. West publishing co., St. Paul. Description: v. 26 cm. Subjects: Law reports, digests, etc.--North Dakota. Law reports, digests, etc.--United States. LC Classification: KF148 .N6

North Dakota blue & white book ... Published/Created: St. Paul, Minn., West publishing co. [19 -] Related Authors: West publishing co., St. Paul. North Dakota. Courts. North Dakota. Supreme court. North western reporter. North western reporter (2d ser.) Description: 1 v. 26 cm. Subjects: Law reports, digests, etc.--North Dakota. Annotations and citations (Law)--North Dakota. LC Classification: LAW

North eastern digest, 1936- annual, covering volumes 199-200, North eastern reporter, and 1- North eastern reporter, second series, with references to corresponding volumes of state reports as far as available ... Table of cases, table of statutes construed. Published/Created: St. Paul, Minn., West publishing co. [c1937-52] Related Authors: United States. Courts. West publishing co., St. Paul. Description: 17 v. 26 cm. Subjects: Law reports, digests, etc.--United States. LC Classification: KF135.N01 N63

North eastern reporter. Published/Created: St. Paul, West Pub. Co. Related Authors: Massachusetts. Supreme Judicial Court. Ohio. Supreme Court. Indiana. Supreme Court. Illinois. Supreme Court. New York (State). Court of Appeals. Indiana. Appellate Court. Ohio. Courts of Appeals. West Publishing Company. Description: 200 v. 23-27 cm. July/Sept. 1885-Mar./Apr. 1936. Superseded by: North eastern reporter. Second series Summary: Includes the decisions of the Supreme Courts of Massachusetts, Ohio, Indiana, and Illinois, and Court of Appeals of New York; May/July 1891-Mar./Apr. 1936, Appellate Court of Indiana; Dec. 1926/Feb. 1927-Mar./Apr. 1936, Courts of Appeals of Ohio. Notes: "Cases argued and determined in the Courts of Illinois, Indiana, Massachusetts, New York, Ohio."

Vols. for May/Aug. 1889-June/Sept. 1932 called "Permanent edition." At head of title, Apr./June 1887-Nov. 1931/Jan. 1932: National reporter system. State series. Title varies slightly. Ultra fiche. St. Paul, West Pub. Co. [1974?] 200 sheets. 11.5 x 15 cm. Subjects: Law reports, digests, etc.--United States. LC Classification: Ultrafiche LL-F-16 KF135.N6

Notebooks of course materials. Published/Created: Reno, Nev., 1969] Description: 11 v. 30 cm. Contents: 100. Court administration.--200. Civil proceedings before trial.--300. Judicial discretion.--400. Domestic relations.--500. Evidence.--600. Special problems in the judicial function.--700. Jury.--800. Community relations.--900. Sentencing and probation.--1000. Special problems in criminal law.--1100. Recent developments in the civil law. Notes: Each vol. has special t.p. only; some cover titles vary slightly. Subjects: Courts--United States. Procedure (Law)--United States. LC Classification: KF8719 .N32 Dewey Class No.: 347.99/73

Notebooks of course materials. Published/Created: Reno, Nev., 1968] Description: 10 v. 28 cm. Contents: [100] Court administration.--[200] Civil proceedings before trial.--[300] Judicial discretion.--[400] Domestic relations.--[500] Evidence.--[600] Special problems in the judicial function.--[700] Jury.--[800] Community relations.--[900] Sentencing and probation.--[1100] Recent developments in the civil law. Notes: No notebook was printed for course no. 1000. Subjects: Courts--United States. Procedure (Law)--United States. LC Classification: KF8719 .N3 Dewey Class No.: 347.99/73

Notes on practice in the Court of appeals of the District of Columbia, including the removal of cases from the Supreme court of the District of Columbia, the Municipal, Police, and Juvenile Courts; and removal of cases to the Supreme court of the United States, Published/Created: Washington, D. C., M Burke, c1924. Description: 92 p. 23 cm. Subjects: District of Columbia. Court of appeals. Appellate procedure--Washington (D.C.) Forms (Law)--Washington (D.C.) LC Classification: LAW

Notes on the Wyoming reports ... including the citations of each case as a precedent (1) by any court of last resort in any jurisdiction of this country; (2) by the extensive and thorough annotations of the leading annotated reports. Published/Created: Rochester, N.Y., The Lawyers cooperative publishing company, 1911- Related Authors: Wyoming. Courts. Description: 1-2 v. 23 cm. Subjects: Law reports, digests, etc.--Wyoming. LC Classification: LAW

Notes to the rules of criminal procedure for the District Courts of the United States / as prepared under the direction of the Advisory Committee on Rules of Criminal Procedure. Published/Created: Washington: U.S. G.P.O., 1945. Related Authors: United States. Supreme Court. Advisory Committee on Rules of Criminal Procedure. Description: xii, 58 p.; 23 cm. Notes: "March 1945." Includes bibliographical references: (p. 57-58). Subjects: Court rules--United States. Criminal procedure--United States. LC Classification: LAW Govt. Doc. No.: JU 6.11:C 86/3

Novak, Rita M. Delay on appeal: a process for identifying causes and cures / Rita M. Novak, Douglas K. Somerlot. Published/Created: Chicago, Ill.: American Bar Association, c1990. Related Authors: Somerlot, Douglas K. American Bar Association. Lawyers Conference Task Force on Reduction of Litigation Cost and Delay. Appellate Judges Conference (U.S.). Appellate Delay Reduction Committee. Standards relating to appellate delay reduction. Description: xviii, 220 p.; 23 cm. ISBN: 0897075110 (pbk.) Notes: "Based upon the American Bar Association's Standards relating to appellate delay reduction." "American Bar Association, Judicial Administration Division, Lawyers Conference Task Force on Reduction of Litigation Cost and

Delay." Includes bibliographical references (p. 217-220). Subjects: Court congestion and delay--Appellate Courts--United States. LC Classification: KF8727 .N68 1990 Dewey Class No.: 347.73/13 347.30713 20

Objections to the bill to remove the federal Courts from Keokuk to Burlington, Iowa. Published/Created: [S.l.: s.n., 1874?] Related Authors: Gillmore, Robert H. YA Pamphlet Collection (Library of Congress) Description: 11 p.; 23 cm. Notes: Caption title. Date derived from text, p. 9. Signed at end: Robert H. Gillmore [and 4 others]. Source: Source unknown. Subjects: Courts--United States. Iowa--Politics and government. United States--Politics and government--1869-1877. LC Classification: YA 8083

O'Brien, David M. What process is due?: courts and science-policy disputes / David M. O'Brien. Published/Created: New York: Russell Sage Foundation, c1987. Description: xviii, 242 p.; 24 cm. ISBN: 087154623X (alk. paper) : Notes: Includes index. Bibliography: p. [209]-223. Subjects: Toxic torts--Hazardous substances--Law and legislation--United States. Courts--Judge-made law--United States. Science and law. LC Classification: KF1299.H39 O27 1987 Dewey Class No.: 346.7303/0269 347.30630269 19

Ohlinger, Gustavus, 1877- Jurisdiction and procedure of the courts of the United States in civil actions under the constitution, United States code and the new federal rules of civil procedure, by Gustavus Ohlinger ... Published/Created: Cincinnati, The W.H. Anderson company, [c1938- Related Authors: Loveland, Frank O. (Frank Olds), 1861-1915 Description: v. 25 cm. Notes: On cover: Ohlinger's federal practice. Loveland's revised forms. Subjects: Courts--United States. Jurisdiction--United States. Civil procedure--United States. Court rules--United States. Forms (Law)--United States. LC Classification: KF8840 .O349

Oklahoma digest and statute service; a service which supplements the digest and statute annotations. Published/Created: Indianapolis, The Bobbs-Merrill company [c1931-] Related Authors: Crockett, Daniel Woolsey, 1862- ed. Oklahoma. Supreme court. Oklahoma. Criminal court of appeals. United States. Courts. Oklahoma. Constitution. United States. Constitution. Bobbs-Merrill company, Indianapolis. Description: v. 26 cm. Notes: Serial. Subjects: Law reports, digests, etc.--Oklahoma. Law--Oklahoma--Digests. LC Classification: KFO1257 .O38

Origins of the federal judiciary: essays on the Judiciary Act of 1789 / edited by Maeva Marcus. Published/Created: New York: Oxford University Press, 1992. Related Authors: Marcus, Maeva, 1941- Description: vi, 312 p.: ill.; 22 cm. ISBN: 0195067215 (acid-free paper) : Notes: Papers based on the Bicentennial Conference on the Judiciary Act of 1789. Includes bibliographical references and index. Subjects: Courts--United States--History. LC Classification: KF8719 .O75 1992 Dewey Class No.: 347.73/2 347.3072 20

Osthus, Marlin O. State intermediate appellate courts: a research project of the American Judicature Society / Marlin O. Osthus; revised by Mayo H. Stiegler. Published/Created: Chicago, Ill.: The Society, 1980. Related Authors: Stiegler, Mayo H. American Judicature Society. Description: v, 50 p.; 23 cm. Notes: Bibliography: p. 47-49. Subjects: Appellate Courts--United States--States. LC Classification: KF8736 .O78 Dewey Class No.: 347.73/34 19

Otis, Merrill E. (Merrill Edward), 1884-1944. A proposed tribunal: is it constitutional? Published/Created: Kansas City, Mo., The University of Kansas City press [1939?] Description: 53 p. 26 cm. Subjects: Impeachments--United States. Judges--United States. Courts--United States. LC Classification: KF8781.Z9 O8 1939 Microfilm LL 477 KF

Otis, Merrill E. (Merrill Edward), 1884-1944. A proposed tribunal: is it constitutional? Published/Created: [Kansas City? Mo., 1938?] Description: [3]-49 p. 25 cm. Subjects: Impeachments--United States. Judges--United States. Courts--United States. LC Classification: KF8781.Z9 O8 1938

Ott, James Cramer, 1793?-1867. Index to a plan for our courts / by James Cramer Ott. Published/Created: Albany, N.Y.: Printed for the author, 1846. Description: 16 p.: 1 ill.; 22 cm. Notes: "Book to be had at Jones' Depot, Albany, under the Museum." Subjects: Courts--United States. Justice, Administration of--United States. LC Classification: KF8700.Z9 O8

Outline of basic Appellate court structure in the United States (1975) / compiled on behalf of the National Conference of Appellate Court Clerks by Wilfried J. Kramer, with the assistance of the clerks of the various states. Published/Created: Denver: The Conference, c1976. Related Authors: Kramer, Wilfried J. National Conference of Appellate Court Clerks. Description: iii, 211 p.; 25 cm. Notes: On spine: Basic Appellate court structure--1975. Subjects: Appellate procedure--United States--States. Appellate Courts--United States--States. LC Classification: KF9050.Z95 O8 Dewey Class No.: 347/.73/24

Overholser, Winfred, 1892-1964. Psychiatric service in penal and reformatory institutions and criminal courts in the United States, Published/Created: New York city, The National committee for mental hygiene, inc., 1928. Description: 1 p.l., 38 p. incl. tables. 23 cm. Subjects: Insanity--Jurisprudence. Prisons--United States. Reformatories--United States. Courts--United States. LC Classification: HV8841 .O8 Microfilm 65999 HV

Owen, Robert Latham, 1856-1947. Withdrawing power from federal courts to declare acts of Congress void. An address delivered at the Auditorium in Oklahoma City, Okla., January 27, 1917, by Robert L. Owen ... Published/Created: Washington, Govt. Print. Off., 1917. Description: 24 p. 24 cm. Notes: Presented by Mr. Sheppard. Ordered printed February 27, 1917. Subjects: United States. Congress--Powers and duties. Courts--United States. LC Classification: JK1541 .O7 Govt. Doc. No.: Y 1.3:C 83

Pacific Coast law journal: containing all the decisions of the Supreme Court of California, and the important decisions of the U.S. Circuit and U.S. District Courts for the District of California, and of the U.S. Supreme Court and higher Courts of other states. Published/Created: San Francisco: W.T. Baggett and Co., 1878-1883. Description: 12 v.; 22-24 cm. Vol. 1, no. 1 (Mar. 2, 1878)-v. 12, no. 16-19 (Dec. 8, 15, 22, 29, 1883). Notes: Title from caption. Supplement to Apr. 3, 1880: Circuit Court of the United States, in and for the Ninth Judicial Circuit, District of California, in re Tiburcio Parrott on Habeas corpus (with Pacific Coast law journal, v. 5). Supplement to June 5, 1880: Superior Court, County of Alameda. [No. 202] J. W. Crowley vs. A.E. Davis (with Pacific Coast law journal, v. 5). Supplement: Review of the recent decisions of the Supreme Court of the United States affecting the Central Pacific and Union Pacific Railroads (with Pacific Coast law journal, v. 4). Holdings in 3x5 file. Subjects: Law reports, digests, etc.--California. Law reports, digests, etc.--United States. LC Classification: KFC47 .P33

Pagan, Oliver Elwood, 1858-1932. Precendents and forms of indictments, information, complaints ... adapted to practice in United States criminal and civil cases, together with forms and instructions pertaining to the accounts and fees of United-States attorneys and commissioners. Published/Created: Chicago, Callaghan and company, 1894. Description: xii, 570 p. 24 cm. Subjects: Forms (Law)--United States. Courts--United States. Costs (Law)--United States. LC Classification: KF8868.1 .P3 Microfilm LL 1185 KF

Papers of the Morris and Popham families, 1667-1892 (bulk 1750-1850) Description: 770 items. 4 containers. Summary: Correspondence, notebooks, account books, and legal papers. Includes the papers of Lewis Morris (1671-1746), owner of most of the land now known as the Bronx, chief justice of the Province of New York, and governor of the Province of New Jersey; Lewis Morris (1698-1762), judge of the Vice Admiralty Court of Connecticut, New York and New Jersey; Robert Hunter Morris (1700-1764), governor of Pennsylvania; Richard Morris (1730-1801), chief justice of New York State, and Major William Popham (1752-1849), Richard Morris' son-in-law, whose papers include a record of the court martial of Col. Moses Hazen in 1780, his correspondence as President-General of the Society of the Cincinnati, and letters from James Tilton, Peter Stephen Du Ponceau and John Taylor of Caroline. Most of the letters after 1849 are to Major Popham's son, William S. Popham, a leading member of the New York State Society of the Cincinnati. Notes: MSS33647 Subjects: Morris, Lewis, 1671-1746. Morris, Lewis, 1698-1762. Morris, Robert Hunter, ca. 1700-1764. Morris, Richard, 1730-1810. Popham, William. Hazen, Moses, 1733-1803. Tilton, James, 1745-1822. Du Ponceau, Peter Stephen, 1760-1844. Taylor, John, 1753-1824. Popham, William S. Morris family. Popham family. New York State Society of the Cincinnati. Practice of law--Connecticut. Practice of law--New Jersey. Practice of law--New York (State) Courts--New York (State) Courts-martial and Courts of inquiry. Bronx (New York, N.Y.) New Jersey--Politics and government. Pennsylvania--Politics and government. United States--History--Revolution, 1775-1783. New Jersey--History--Colonial period, ca. 1600-1775. Local Call/Shelving: MMC-3304

Parajudges, their role in today's court systems: prepared for the Wisconsin Judicial Council. Published/Created: Denver: Research and Information Service, National Center for State Courts, 1976. Related Authors: Wisconsin. Judicial Council. Description: v, 73 p.; 23 cm. Notes: Bibliography: p. 73. Subjects: Courts--United States--States--Officials and employees. Series: Publication (National Center for State Courts); R0027. LC Classification: KF8807 .N37 Dewey Class No.: 347/.73/16

Parascope: the quarterly publication of the National Committee of Appellate Court Staff Counsel. Published/Created: Chicago: National Committee of Appellate Court Staff Counsel, 1979- Related Authors: American Bar Association. National Committee of Appellate Court Staff Counsel. Description: v.; 28 cm. Vol. 1- ISSN: 0738-1247 Notes: Title from caption. SERBIB/SERLOC merged record Subjects: Appellate Courts--United States--Periodicals. Appellate Courts--United States--Officials and employees Periodicals. Appellate procedure--United States--Periodicals. LC Classification: KF8750.A15 P37 Dewey Class No.: 347.73/24/05 347.307305 19

Parker, Charles, 1916- The court reporting system in United States District Courts, 1960 [by Charles Parker, Jr. and Norman R. Tharp. Published/Created: Washington] Administrative Office of the U.S. Courts [1960] Related Authors: Tharp, Norman R., joint author. Description: 139 p. illus. 27 cm. Subjects: United States. District Courts. Law reporting--United States. LC Classification: KF255 .P37 Dewey Class No.: 347.9973

Part II, District of Columbia code, "Judiciary and judical procedure," effective January 1, 1964. Revision notes and distribution tables. Published/Created: Washington, U.S. Govt. Print. Off., 1964. Related Authors: United States. Congress. House. Committee on the Judiciary. Description: vi, 373 p. 24 cm. Notes: At head of title: Committee print. Subjects: Courts--Washington (D.C.) Procedure (Law)--Washington (D.C.) LC Classification: KFD1708.A333 A2 1964

Partridge, Anthony, 1929- A reevaluation of the Civil Appeals Management Plan / by

Anthony Partridge and Allan Lind. Published/Created: Washington, D.C.: Federal Judicial Center, [1983] Related Authors: Lind, E. Allan (Edgar Allan), 1948- Federal Judicial Center. Description: vii, 115 p.: forms; 24 cm. Notes: "August 1983." Item 743-C-3 Includes bibliographical references. Subjects: Appellate Courts--United States. Court administration--United States. Series: FJC-R; 83-2 LC Classification: KF8750 .P37 1983 Dewey Class No.: 347.73/24 347.3073 19 Govt. Doc. No.: Ju 13.10:83-2

Partridge, Anthony, 1929- The sentencing options of federal district judges / by Anthony Partridge. Edition Information: June 1985 revision. Published/Created: Washington, D.C.: Federal Judicial Center, 1985. Related Authors: Federal Judicial Center. Description: vii, 67 p.: forms; 24 cm. Notes: "FJC-ETS-85-4"--T.p. verso. Item 743-C-4 Subjects: United States Parole Commission. Sentences (Criminal procedure)--United States. Parole--United States. District Courts--United States. Series: Education and training series (Federal Judicial Center); 85-4. LC Classification: KF9685 .P373 1985 Dewey Class No.: 345.73/0772 347.305772 19 Govt. Doc. No.: Ju 13.9:85-4

Partridge, Anthony, 1929- The Sentencing options of federal district judges / by Anthony Partridge, Alan J. Chaset, and William B. Eldridge. Published/Created: Washington, D.C.: Federal Judicial Center: [Information Services Office, distributor], 1983. Related Authors: Chaset, Alan J. Eldridge, William B. Federal Judicial Center. Description: vii, 59 p.; 24 cm. Notes: "FJC-ETS-83-3"--T.p. verso. Subjects: United States Parole Commission. Sentences (Criminal procedure)--United States. Parole--United States. District Courts--United States. Series: Education and training series (Federal Judicial Center); 83-3. LC Classification: KF9685 .P373 1983 Dewey Class No.: 345.73/0772 347.305772 19

Partridge, Anthony, 1929- The sentencing options of federal district judges / by Anthony Partridge, Alan J. Chaset, and William B. Eldridge. Edition Information: Revision of Feb. 1981. Published/Created: Washington, D.C.: Federal Judicial Center, Research Division: Information Services Office [distributor], 1981. Related Authors: Chaset, Alan J. Eldridge, William B. Federal Judicial Center. Research Division. Description: 1 v. (various pagings); 28 cm. Notes: Nov. 1979. "ETS-79-2"--T.p. verso. Item 743-C-4 Includes bibliographical references. Subjects: United States Parole Commission. Sentences (Criminal procedure)--United States. Parole--United States. District Courts--United States. Series: Education and training series (Federal Judicial Center); 79-2. LC Classification: KF9685 .P373 1981 Dewey Class No.: 345.73/0772 347.305772 19 Govt. Doc. No.: Ju 13.9:79-2/2

Pascoe, Elaine. America's courts on trial: questioning our legal system / Elaine Pascoe. Published/Created: Brookfield, Conn.: Millbrook Press, c1997. Description: 112 p.: ill.; 24 cm. ISBN: 0761301046 (lib. bdg.) Summary: Examines controversial aspects of America's court system such as whether the concept of trial by jury is outmoded, the courts are racially biased, or media coverage of trials should be limited. Notes: Includes bibliographical references (p. 105-106) and index. Subjects: Courts--United States--Juvenile literature. Justice, Administration of--United States--Juvenile literature. Courts. Justice, Administration of. Series: Issue and debate LC Classification: KF8700.Z9 P37 1997 Dewey Class No.: 347.73/1 21

Paston, David George. Summary judgment in New York: including summary judgment rules in other States and in the U. S. District Courts. Published/Created: New York, Central Book Co., 1958. Description: xiii, 450 p. 24 cm. Subjects: Summary proceedings--New York (State) Summary proceedings--United States. LC Classification: KFN6052 .P3

Patterson, R. F. (Robert Foster) The Federal courts: a brief survey for high schools / by

R.F. Patterson. Published/Created: Vermillion, S.D.: Governmental Research Bureau, University of South Dakota, 1944. Description: 11 leaves: maps; 28 cm. Notes: Cover title. Bibliography: leaves 10-11. Subjects: Courts--United States--Popular works. Series: South Dakota. University. Governmental Research Bureau. Report; no. 12. LC Classification: KFS3421.Z9 S6 no. 12 KF8720 Dewey Class No.: 347.73/2 347.3071 19

Paulsen, Monrad G. Juvenile law and procedure / by Monrad G. Paulsen and Charles H. Whitebread. Published/Created: Reno, Nev.: National Council of Juvenile Court Judges, 1974. Related Authors: Whitebread, Charles H., joint author. Description: vii, 207 p.; 26 cm. Notes: Includes bibliographical references and index. Subjects: Juvenile Courts--United States. Juvenile justice, Administration of--United States. Series: Juvenile justice textbook series LC Classification: KF9709 .P34 Dewey Class No.: 345/.73/08

Paxson, Edward M., 1824-1905. Address delivered at the centennial banquet of the Supreme court of the United States, Published/Created: Philadelphia, J. M. P. Wallace, 1890. Description: p. cm. Subjects: Courts--United States. Judges--United States. LC Classification: KF8700.Z9 P38

Pearson, Enika H. Introduction to the American judicial system: a practical nuts-and-bolts handbook, written especially for Texas court professionals--probation officers, court reporters, and court clerks / by Enika H. Pearson, P. Michael Jung, Rebecca P. Adams. Edition Information: Texas ed. Published/Created: Dallas, Tex.: Pearson Publications Co., c1982. Related Authors: Jung, P. Michael. Adams, Rebecca P. Description: 107 p.; 22 cm. Notes: Includes bibliographical references and index. Subjects: Courts--United States. Criminal justice, Administration of--United States. Courts--Texas. LC Classification: KF8720 .P36 1982 Dewey Class No.: 347.73 347.307 19

Peltason, J. W. (Jack Walter), 1923- Federal courts in the political process. Published/Created: Garden City, N.Y., Doubleday, 1955. Description: 81 p. 24cm. Subjects: Courts--United States. Judges--United States. Judges, Administration of--United States. LC Classification: KF8775.Z9 P4 Dewey Class No.: 347.9

Pennsylvania blue & white book ... Published/Created: St. Paul, Minn., West publishing co. [c1941-] Related Authors: Pennsylvania. Courts. Pennsylvania. Superior court. Atlantic reporter. Atlantic reporter (2 d ser.) West publishing co., St. Paul. Description: v. 26 cm. Subjects: Law reports, digests, etc.--Pennsylvania. Annotations and citations (Law)--Pennsylvania. LC Classification: LAW

Pennsylvania justices' law reporter; containing cases decided in the Courts of the several counties of Pennsylvania, affecting justices of the peace, aldermen, magistrates, burgesses, and all other county and township officials. Published/Created: Lansdale, Pa., A. R. Place [etc., etc.] 1902-18. Related Authors: Pennsylvania. Courts. Description: 16 v. 23 cm. Notes: Serial. Subjects: Law reports, digests, etc.--Pennsylvania. Local government--Pennsylvania. Law--Periodicals. LC Classification: LAW

Pennsylvania Law Journal Reports, containing cases decided by the federal and state Courts of Pennsylvania ... 1842-1852 ... Published/Created: Philadelphia, J. Campbell & Son, 1872-73. Description: 5 v. cm. LC Classification: LAW

Pennsylvania law journal reports, containing cases decided by the federal and state Courts of Pennsylvania. Originally reported in the Pennsylavnai law journal and American law journal, from 1842 to 1852, inclusive. Published/Created: Philadelphia, J. Campbell & son, 1872-73. Related Authors: Clark, John Alexander, ed. Description: 5 v. 23 cm. Subjects: Law reports, digests, etc.--Pennsylvania. LC Classification: LAW

Pennsylvania reporter, covering cases reported in Atlantic reporter, second series. Published/Created: St. Paul, West Pub. Co., 1944- Related Authors: West Publishing Company Description: 27cm. 1A. 2d-2A. 2d- ISSN: 0745-8037 Subjects: Pennsylvania. Courts. Law reports, digests, etc.--Pennsylvania. LC Classification: LAW Dewey Class No.: 345.42

Peters, Richard, 1780-1848. A full and arranged digest of the decisions in common law, equity, and admiralty, of the courts of the United States, from the organization of the government in 1789 to 1847, in the Supreme, Circuit, District and admiralty courts: reported in Dallas, Cranch, Wheaton, Peters, and Howard's Supreme court reports: in Gallison, Mason, Paine, Peters, Washington, Wallace, Sumner, Story, Baldwin, Brockenborough, and McLean's Circuit court reports; and in Bees, Ware, Peters, and Gilpin's District and admiralty reports. Published/Created: Philadelphia, Sherman, printer, 1848. Related Authors: United States. Courts. United States. Supreme court. United States. Circuit courts. Description: 2 v. 27 cm. Subjects: Law reports, digests, etc.--United States. Common law--United States. Equity--United States. Admiralty--United States. Court rules--United States. LC Classification: LAW

Peters, Richard, 1780-1848. A full and arranged digest of cases, decided in the Supreme, Circuit and District courts of the United States, from the organization of the government of the United States. By Richard Peters. Published/Created: Philadelphia, Thomas, Cowperthwait & co., 1838-1839. Related Authors: United States. Courts. United States. Supreme Court. United States. Circuit Courts. Description: 3 v. 27 cm. Notes: Vol. 1 mutilated: t.-p. wanting. Subjects: Law reports, digests, etc.--United States. LC Classification: LAW

Phelps, Edith M. Selected articles on the recall including the recall of judges and judicial decisions, compiled by Edith M. Phelps Edition Information: 2d ed. rev. and enl Published/Created: White Plains, New York, H.W. Wilson Co., 1915 Description: xivii, 273 p map. 20 cm Notes: Bibliography: p. xxi-xiviii Subjects: Recall. Judges--United States. Courts--United States. LC Classification: JK448 .P5 1915

Phelps, Edith May, 1881- comp. Selected articles on the recall, including the recall of judges and judicial decisions, Published/Created: White Plains, N.Y., and New York city, The H. W. Wilson company, 1913. Description: xlv, [1] 228 p. incl. map. fold. tab. 21 cm. Subjects: Recall. Judges--United States. Courts--United States. LC Classification: JK448 .P5 Microfilm 34615 JK

Philadelphia reports; or, Legal intelligencer condensed. Containing the decisions published in the Legal intelligencer, from 1850 to [1891] ... Published/Created: Philadelphia, J.M.P. Wallace [c1856]-93. Related Authors: Wallace, Henry Edward, 1814-1879, ed. Brown, Henry C., comp. Pennsylvania. Courts (Philadelphia co.) Pennsylvania. Courts. United States. Courts. Description: 20 v. 24 cm. Subjects: Law reports, digests, etc.--Pennsylvania. Law reports, digests, etc.--Philadelphia. LC Classification: LAW

Phillips, Philip, 1807-1884. The statutory jurisdiction and practice of the Supreme court of the United States, together with forms of process and rules established for the Supreme court, the Court of claims, the courts of equity, the courts of admiralty, and the courts in bankruptcy. By P. Phillips ... Edition Information: Rev. ed., September, 1878. Published/Created: Washington, W.H. & O.H. Morrison, 1878. Description: 2 p.l., ix-xx, 9-612 p. 24 cm. Notes: Microfilm. Washington, D.C., Library of Congress. Subjects: United States. Supreme court. Appellate procedure--United States. Court rules--United States. LC Classification: KF9057 .P5 1878 Microfilm LL 1179 KF

Phillips, Philip, 1807-1884. The statutory jurisdiction and practice of the Supreme

Court of the United States: together with forms of process and rules established for the Supreme Court, the Court of Claims, the courts of equity, the courts of admiralty, and the courts in bankruptcy / by P. Phillips. Published/Created: Washington: W.H. & O.H. Morrison, 1872. Description: 438 p.; 24 cm. Notes: Includes index. Subjects: United States. Supreme Court. Appellate procedure--United States. Court rules--United States. LC Classification: KF9057 .P5 1872

Pike, James A. (James Albert), 1913-1969. Cases and other materials on new Federal and code procedure, by James A. Pike. Published/Created: Chicago, Callaghan and company, 1939. Related Authors: United States. Courts. United States. Supreme Court. United States. District Courts. Description: xviii, 857 p. 26 cm. Subjects: Civil procedure--United States--Cases. Code pleading--United States--Cases. Equity pleading and procedure--United States--Cases. Forms (Law)--United States. LC Classification: KF8839 .P5

Pilchen, Ira. The future and the courts: conducting state court futures activities / prepared by Ira Pilchen and Sandra Ratcliff. Published/Created: Chicago, Ill.: American Judicature Society, c1993. Related Authors: Ratcliff, Sandra. American Judicature Society. State Justice Institute (U.S.) Description: 59 p.; 28 cm. ISBN: 0938870637 Notes: "This guidebook is the culmination of a project made possible by a grant from the State Justice Institute"--T.p. verso. Includes bibliographical references. Subjects: Courts--United States--States. LC Classification: KF8936 .P55 1993 Dewey Class No.: 347.73/3 347.3071 20

Pinckney, Charles, 1757-1824. Speeches of Charles Pinckney, Esq. in Congress: on the subject of having impartial juries, by lot, in all the federal courts: on the independence of the judges in the same courts: on the exclusive right of the state legislatures, and under their direction, of the people, to the the election of the President and Vice-President of the United States: on the defined privileges of Congress, and the liberty of the press: and, on the intercourse bill with France. Published/Created: [Philadelphia? s.n.], printed in 1800. Related Authors: American Imprint Collection (Library of Congress) William Duane Pamphlet Collection (Library of Congress) Miscellaneous Pamphlet Collection (Library of Congress) Description: [4], iii, [1], 135, [1] p.; 24 cm. (8vo) Notes: Signatures: [A]4 B-S4. References: Evans 38270 Subjects: United States. Congress--Privileges and immunities Speeches in Congress. Courts--United States--Speeches in Congress. Presidents--United States--Election--Speeches in Congress. United States--Politics and government--1797-1801 Speeches in Congress. LC Classification: E302.1 .P64

Pirsig, Maynard E., 1902- Cases and materials on judicial administration / by Maynard E. Pirsig. Published/Created: St. Paul, Minn.: West Pub. Co., 1946. Description: xxvii, 1017 p.; 26 cm. Notes: "Table of articles": p. xix-xxvi. Subjects: Justice, Administration of--United States. Justice, Administration of--United States--Cases. Courts--United States. Series: American casebook series LC Classification: KF8700.A7 P57

Planning guide for using the trial court performance standards and measurement system. Published/Created: Washington, DC: Bureau of Justice Assistance, [1997] Related Authors: United States. Bureau of Justice Assistance. Description: xii, 162 p.: ill.; 28 cm. Notes: Shipping list no.: 97-0067-S. "July 1997." Includes bibliographical references (p. 23-25). Subjects: Court administration--United States. Justice, Administration of--United States. State Courts--Standards--United States. Series: Monograph (United States. Bureau of Justice Assistance) LC Classification: KF8732 .P583 1997 Govt. Doc. No.: J 26.30:P 69

Planning handbook for federal Courts / edited by William M. Lucianovic. Published/Created: Washington, DC:

Administrative Office of the U.S. Courts, Long Range Planning Office, [1994] Related Authors: Lucianovic, William M. (William Mark), 1942- United States. Administrative Office of the United States Courts. Long Range Planning Office. Description: 1 v. (various pagings): ill.; 28 cm. Notes: "March 1994"--Cover. Includes bibliographical references. Subjects: Court administration--United States--Planning--Handbooks, manuals, etc. Courts--United States--Planning--Handbooks, manuals, etc. Justice, Administration of--United States--Planning Handbooks, manuals, etc. LC Classification: KF8732 .P584 1994 Dewey Class No.: 347.73/2 347.3071 20

Plapinger, Elizabeth S. ADR and settlement in the federal district courts: a sourcebook for judges & lawyers / Elizabeth Plapinger, Donna Stienstra with the assistance of Laural Hooper & Melissa Pecherski. Published/Created: Washington, DC: Federal Judicial Center, 1996. Related Authors: Stienstra, Donna. Federal Judicial Center. CPR Institute for Dispute Resolution. Description: vii, 308 p.; 25 cm. Notes: "A joint project of the Federal Judicial Center and the CPR Institute for Dispute Resolution." Subjects: Dispute resolution (Law)--United States. Compromise (Law)--United States. District Courts--United States. LC Classification: KF9084 .P58 1996

Polansky, Larry P. A primer for the technologically challenged judge / Larry P. Polansky. Published/Created: United States: L.P. Polansky, 1995 (Ann Arbor, Mich.: Edwards Brothers) Related Authors: State Justice Institute (U.S.) Description: viii, 106 p.: ill.; 23 cm. Subjects: Courts--Court administration--United States--Data processing. Information storage and retrieval systems--Court administration--United States. LC Classification: KF276 .P65 1995 Dewey Class No.: 347.73/13/0285 347.307130285 20

Posner, Richard A. The federal courts: challenge and reform / Richard A. Posner. Published/Created: Cambridge, Mass.: Harvard University Press, 1996. Description: xvi,413 p.: ill.; 24 cm. ISBN: 0674296265 (cloth: alk. paper) Notes: Includes bibliographical references and index. Subjects: Courts--United States. Judicial process--United States. Judges--United States. Court congestion and delay--United States. Federal courts LC Classification: KF8700 .P67 1996 Dewey Class No.: 347.73/2 347.3072 20

Posner, Richard A. The federal courts: crisis and reform / Richard A. Posner. Published/Created: Cambridge, Mass.: Harvard University Press, 1985. Description: xvii, 365 p.; 25 cm. ISBN: 0674296257 Notes: Includes bibliographical references and index. Subjects: Courts--United States. Judicial process--United States. Judges--United States. Court congestion and delay--United States. LC Classification: KF8700 .P67 1985 Dewey Class No.: 347.73/2 347.3071 19

Potts, Charles Shirley, 1872- Cases on criminal procedure pselected from decisions of English and American courts, Published/Created: Austin, Tex., The author, 1921. Description: xii, 255 p. 26 cm. Subjects: Criminal procedure--Cases. Criminal procedure--Texas. Criminal procedure--Great Britain. Criminal procedure--United States. LC Classification: KFT1775.A7 P67

Pound, Roscoe, 1870-1964. Organization of courts / by Roscoe Pound. Published/Created: Westport, Conn.: Greenwood Press, 1979, c1940. Description: xiii, 322 p.; 22 cm. ISBN: 0313219982 Notes: Reprint of the ed. published by Little, Brown, Boston in Series: The Judicial administration series. Includes index. Bibliography: p. [295]-304. Subjects: Courts--Jurisdiction--Justice, Administration of--Judges--United States. Series: Judicial administration series. LC Classification: KF8700 .P68 1979 Dewey Class No.: 347/.73/12

Pound, Roscoe, 1870-1964. Organization of courts [by] Roscoe Pound; Methods of selecting and retiring judges [by] Albert M. Kales; Local courts of limited jurisdiction [by] Herbert Harley. Published/Created: Chicago, Barnard & Miller print [1914] Related Authors: Kales, Albert Martin, 1875-1922. Methods of selecting and retiring judges. Harley, Herbert Lincoln, 1871- Description: 68 p. 26 cm. Notes: The article by Mr. Pound was delivered as an address at the meeting of the Minnesota state bar association held at St. Paul, August 20, 1914. In substantially the same form this address was also delivered before the Law association of Philadelphia, January 31, 1913; the article by Mr. Kales was an address delivered at the meeting of the Minnesota state bar association held at St. Paul, August 20, 1914; Mr. Harley's article was a paper prepared for publication in the California law review. Subjects: Courts--United States. Judges--United States. LC Classification: KF8700.A75 Pl

Pound, Roscoe, 1870-1964. Organization of courts, by Roscoe Pound. Published/Created: Boston, Little, Brown and Company, 1940. Description: xiii, 322 p. 24 cm. Notes: Bibliography: p. [295]-304. Subjects: Courts--United States. Courts--Great Britain. Jurisdiction--United States. Justice, Administration of--United States. Judges--United States. Series: Judicial administration series LC Classification: KF8700 .P68

Powers, Stephen, 1961- The least dangerous branch?: consequences of judicial activism / Stephen P. Powers and Stanley Rothman. Published/Created: Westport, Conn.: Praeger, 2002. Related Authors: Rothman, Stanley, 1927- Description: p. cm. ISBN: 0275975363 (alk. paper) 0275975371 (pbk.: alk. paper) Notes: "Under the auspices of the Center for the Study of Social and Political Change, Smith College." Includes bibliographical references and index. Subjects: United States. Supreme Court. Courts--United States. Political questions and judicial power--United States. LC Classification: KF5130 .P69 2002 Dewey Class No.: 347.73/1 21

Practice commentaries-FRCrP / Louis M. Natali ... [et al.]. Edition Information: 2002/2003 ed. Published/Created: Notre Dame, Ind.: National Institute for Trial Advocacy, c2001. Related Authors: Natali, Louis M., 1942- Description: xix, 298 p.; 23 cm. ISBN: 1556817622 (pbk.: alk. paper) Subjects: United States. Supreme Court. Rules of criminal procedure for the United States District Courts. Criminal procedure--United States. Series: The practice commentaries series LC Classification: KF9606.515 .P73 2001 Dewey Class No.: 345.73/05 21

Preamble and resolutions of the legislature of Kentucky: in relation to the late decision of the Court of Appeals on the replevin and endorsement laws, and of the Supreme Court of the United States on the occupying claimant laws of said state. Published/Created: [Frankfort, Ky.: s.n., 1824] Description: 28 p.; 24 cm. Notes: Caption title. Text dated (p. 28): December 29th, 1823. References: Shoemaker 16784 Subjects: Kentucky. Court of Appeals. Legislation--Kentucky. Courts--United States. LC Classification: JK1541 .K4

Preliminary draft of proposed amendments to certain rules of civil procedure for the United States District Courts. Jan. 1961. Published/Created: Washington, U.S. Govt. Print. Off., 1961. Related Authors: United States. District Courts. Rules of civil procedure. Description: 11 p. 24 cm. Subjects: Civil procedure--United States Court rules--United States LC Classification: LAW

Preliminary draft of proposed rules of evidence for the United Stated District Courts and magistrates. Published/Created: [Washington] 1969. Related Authors: United States. District Courts. Description: xii, 254 p. 24 cm. Subjects: Evidence (Laws)--United States. Court rules--United States. LC Classification: KF8935 .A34 Dewey Class No.: 347.99/73

Preliminary report on efficiency in the administration of justice, prepared by Charles W. Eliot, Moorfield Storey, Louis

D. Brandeis, Adolph J. Rodenbeck, Roscoe Pound, for the National Economic League. Published/Created: Boston, [Caustis-Claflin Company, Printers, 1914?] Related Authors: Eliot, Charles William, 1834-1926. Storey, Moorfield, 1845-1929. Brandeis, Louis Dembitz, 1856-1941. Rodenbeck, Adolph Julius. Pound, Roscoe, 1870-1964, ed. Description: 32 p. 21 cm. Notes: Cover title. Subjects: Justice, Administration of--United States. Courts--United States. LC Classification: KF8700.7 .N3

Preserving access to justice: the impact on state courts of the proposed long range plan for the federal courts: report of the 1995 Forum for State Judges / cosponsored by the Roscoe Pound Foundation and Yale Law School; edited by James E. Rooks, Jr., and Barbara Wolfson. Published/Created: Washington, DC: The Foundation, c1996 Related Authors: Rooks, James E. Wolfson, Barbara. Roscoe Pound Foundation. Yale Law School. Description: xi, 71 p.: ill.; 28 cm. ISBN: 0933067178 Notes: Includes bibliographical references. Subjects: Courts--United States--States. Jurisdiction--United States. Federal government--United States. Federal-state controversies--United States. Justice, Administration of--United States. LC Classification: KF8736 .F67 1995 Dewey Class No.: 347.73/1 21

Procedure and evidence in the juvenile court: a guidebook for judges. Published/Created: New York: National Council on Crime and Delinquency, 1962. Related Authors: National Council on Crime and Delinquency. Advisory Council of Judges. Description: xii, 84 p.; 22 cm. Notes: Includes bibliographical references. Subjects: Juvenile Courts--United States. Juvenile justice, Administration of--United States. LC Classification: KF9710 .N3 Dewey Class No.: 364.520973

Proceedings of the National Conference on Gender Bias in the Courts / edited by Dixie K. Knoebel and Marilyn McCoy Roberts; sponsored by the National Association of Women Judges, the William Bingham Foundation, [and] the National Center for State Courts. Published/Created: [Williamsburg, Va.]: The Center, c1990. Related Authors: Knoebel, Dixie K. Roberts, Marilyn McCoy. National Association of Women Judges (U.S.) William Bingham Foundation. National Center for State Courts. Description: vii, 69 p., [2] p. of plates: ill.; 28 cm. ISBN: 0896560988 Notes: Conference held May 18-21, 1989 at the National Center for State Courts, Williamsburg, Va. Includes bibliographical references. Subjects: Courts--United States--Congresses. Judicial process--United States--Congresses. Sex discrimination against women--Law and legislation United States--Congresses. Courts--United States--Officials and employees Congresses. Series: Publication (National Center for State Courts); R116. LC Classification: KF8700 .A17 1989 Dewey Class No.: 347.73/1 347.3071 20

Progress in the law / editor in charge of this volume John S. Bradway. Published/Created: Phildelphia: American Academy of Political and Social Science, 1928. Related Authors: Bradway, John Saeger, 1890- American Academy of Political and Social Science Description: 187 p.; 24 cm. Subjects: Law--United States--History. Law reform--United States. Courts--United States. Civil procedure--United States. Criminal procedure--United States. Public defenders--United States. Lawyers--United States. Series: Annals of the American Academy of Political and Social Science; v. 136 LC Classification: H1 .A4 vol. 136

Proposed re-making of the federal judiciary; analysis of Logan-Hatch-Ashurst amendment regarding the federal Courts. Printed under the auspices of the Special committee on the Supreme court proposal of the American bar association in cooperation with the Junior bar conference of the American bar association. Published/Created: [Chicago?] 1937. Related Authors: American Bar Association. Junior Bar Conference. Description: 24 p. 25 cm. Notes: "Booklet no. 3." Subjects: United States. Supreme Court. Courts--United States. LC Classification: KF8700.Z9 A4

Proppèr, Albert Herschel, 1876- The brief; adventures in the courts of a new country and incidental studies in the morbid anatomy of government by organized corruption, Published/Created: Boston, The Four seas company [c1918] Description: 128 p. 1 l. 18 cm. Subjects: Courts--United States. LC Classification: KF373.P74 A32 1918

Proppèr, Albert Herschel, 1876- The brief; adventures in the courts of a new country and incidental studies in the morbid anatomy of government by organized corruption, by the Counselor [pseud.] Published/Created: Hyde Park, Mass., Hyde Park Pub. Co. [c1918] Description: 128 p., 1 l. 18 cm. Notes: Compiled by the Hyde Park Publishing Company from diary entries and other undisputable documents of Albert Herschel de Proppèr.--Pub. answer. Subjects: Courts--United States. LC Classification: JK1544 .B7

Proppèr, Albert Herschel, 1876- The pandect of Colonel X; adventures in the courts of a new country. Published/Created: [Philadelphia, Wissinoming publishing company, c1928] Description: 401 p. 18 cm. Notes: Part I published in 1918 under title: The brief; adventures in the courts of a new country and incidental studies in the morbid anatomy of government by organized corruption, by the Counselor. Subjects: Courts--United States. LC Classification: JK1544 .P72

Prosecutors in state Courts. Published/Created: Washington, D.C.: U.S. Dept. of Justice, Office of Justice Programs, Bureau of Justice Statistics, [1992- Related Authors: United States. Bureau of Justice Statistics. Description: v.; 28 cm. None published 2000. 1990- Notes: Title from caption. Distributed to depository libraries in print version, <1990-1996. SERBIB/SERLOC merged record Subjects: Criminal statistics--United States--Periodicals. Prosecution--United States--States--Statistics Periodicals. Series: Bulletin (United States. Bureau of Justice Statistics) LC Classification: KF183 .P77 Dewey Class No.: 345.73/01 21 Govt. Doc. No.: J 29.11/15:

Provine, Doris Marie. Settlement strategies for federal district judges / by D. Marie Provine. Published/Created: Washington, D.C. (1520 H St., N.W., Washington 20005): Federal Judicial Center, 1986. Related Authors: Federal Judicial Center. Description: vi, 103 p.; 23 cm. Notes: Includes bibliographical references. Subjects: Compromise (Law)--United States. Judges--United States. District Courts--United States. LC Classification: KF9084 .P76 1986 Dewey Class No.: 347.73/22 347.3072 19

Psychological evaluations for the Courts: a handbook for mental health professionals and lawyers / Gary B. Melton ... [et al.]. Edition Information: 2nd ed. Published/Created: New York: Guilford Press, [1997] Related Authors: Melton, Gary B. Description: xxix, 794 p.; 26 cm. ISBN: 1572302364 (hardcover: acid-free paper) Notes: Includes bibliographical references and index. Subjects: Psychology, Forensic. Forensic psychiatry. Evidence, Expert--Insanity--Jurisprudence--United States. LC Classification: KF8922 .P77 1997 Dewey Class No.: 347.73/67 21

Psychological evaluations for the Courts: a handbook for mental health professionals and lawyers / Gary B. Melton ... [et al.].; foreword by Richard J. Bonnie, Loren H. Roth, and John Monahan. Published/Created: New York: Guilford Press, c1987. Related Authors: Melton, Gary B. Description: xxviii, 511 p.; 26 cm. ISBN: 089862276X Notes: Includes bibliographies and index. Subjects: Psychology, Forensic. Forensic psychiatry--United States. Psychologists--Psychiatrists--Legal status, laws, etc.--United States. Series: The Guilford law and behavior series LC Classification: KF8922 .P77 1987 Dewey Class No.: 347.73/66 347.30766 19

Puerto Rico rules of court, federal. Published/Created: St. Paul, Minn.: West Group, Description: v.; 25 cm. Notes: Description based on: 2000. "Including amendments received through November 1, ..." Part of a 2 vol. set; the Commonwealth Courts' rules are published in Spanish with title: Manual de reglas para la práctica en Puerto Rico. Manual de reglas para la práctica en Puerto Rico (DLC) 2001206412 Subjects: Appellate Courts--Puerto Rico--Rules and practice. District Courts--Puerto Rico--Rules and practice. Court rules--Puerto Rico. Court rules--United States. LC Classification: KGV2569.A32 P84

Purcell, Edward A. Litigation and inequality: federal diversity jurisdiction in industrial America, 1870-1958 / Edward A. Purcell, Jr. Published/Created: New York: Oxford University Press, 1992. Description: x, 446 p.; 25 cm. ISBN: 0195073290 (acid-free paper) Notes: Includes bibliographical references and index. Subjects: Jurisdiction--Social aspects--United States--History. Civil procedure--Social aspects--United States--History. Courts--United States--History. Actions and defenses--United States--History. LC Classification: KF8858 .P87 1992 Dewey Class No.: 347.73/12 347.30712 20

Quarles, William Daniel, 1948- Summary adjudication: dispositive motions and summary trials / by William Daniel Quarles, Joseph C. Howard, and Roger Tehan Scully. Published/Created: New York: Wiley Law Publications, c1991. Related Authors: Howard, Joseph C. Scully, Roger Tehan. Description: xix, 343 p.; 26 cm. ISBN: 0471538175 (cloth) Notes: Includes index. Subjects: Summary judgments--United States. Civil procedure--United States. District Courts--United States. Series: Trial practice library LC Classification: KF8999 .Q37 1990 Dewey Class No.: 347.73/75 347.30775 20

Ralston, Jackson H. (Jackson Harvey), 1857-1945. Study and report for American federation of labor upon judicial control over legislatures as to constitutional questions, by Jackson H. Ralston. Edition Information: 2d ed., rev. and enl. to October, 1923. Published/Created: Washington, D.C., The Law reporter printing company, 1923. Related Authors: American Federation of Labor. Description: 92 p., 1 l. 23 cm. Notes: Cover-title. "Ordered prepared and printed in pamphlet form by St. Paul convention of the A. F. of L." Subjects: Courts--United States. United States--Constitutional law. LC Classification: JK1541 .R2 1923 Dewey Class No.: 347.99 [353.5]

Ralston, Jackson H. (Jackson Harvey), 1857-1945. Study and report for American Federation of Labor upon judicial control over legislatures as to constitutional questions / by Jackson H. Ralston. Published/Created: Washington, D.C.: Law Reporter Print. Co., 1919. Related Authors: American Federation of Labor. Description: 80 p.; 23 cm. Notes: Cover title. "Ordered prepared and printed in pamphlet form by St. Paul Convention of the A.F. of L." Subjects: Courts--United States. Judicial power--United States. Legislation--United States. United States--Constitutional law. LC Classification: JK1541 .R2

Ransom, William Lynn, 1883-1949. Majority rule and the judiciary: an examination of current proposals for constitutional change affecting the relation of courts to legislation, Published/Created: New York, C. Scribner's sons, 1912. Related Authors: Roosevelt, Theodore, President, U. S., 1858-1919. Description: xx, 183 p. 20 cm. Subjects: Courts--United States. Recall--United States. LC Classification: KF5130 .R3 1912

Records and briefs of the United States Circuit Court of Appeals for the Seventh Circuit] [microform] Published/Created: [S.l.: s.n., Related Authors: United States. Circuit Court of Appeals (7th Circuit) Description: v.; 28 cm. Notes: Title supplied. Beginning date of publication unknown. The Court had its first session on June 16, 1891. Description based on: no. 8350 (1943). Microfiche. Philadelphia, Pa.: Microform,

Inc. microfiches: negative. Briefs issued after Sept. 1, 1948 bear the Court's later name: United States Court of Appeals for the Seventh Circuit. SERBIB/SERLOC merged record Subjects: Briefs--United States. LC Classification: Microfiche (o) 93/10007

Records and briefs of the United States Court of Appeals for the Seventh Circuit] [microform] Published/Created: [s.l.: s.n., Related Authors: United States. Court of Appeals (7th Circuit) Description: v.; 28 cm. Notes: Description based on: 82-1025. Microfiche. Washington, D.C.: Microform, Inc. microfiches: negative. Briefs issued before Sept. 1, 1948 bear the Court's earlier name: United States Circuit Court of Appeals for the Seventh Circuit. SERBIB/SERLOC merged record Subjects: Briefs--United States. LC Classification: Microfiche (o) 93/10007

Records management in federal Courts: a NARA evaluation. Published/Created: Washington, DC: National Archives and Records Administration, [1992] Related Authors: United States. National Archives and Records Administration. Description: 131 p.; 28 cm. Notes: "August 1992." Subjects: Court records--United States. Court administration--United States. LC Classification: KF8733 .A87 1992 Dewey Class No.: 347.73/77 347.3077 20

Redish, Martin H. Federal courts: cases, comments, and questions / by Martin H. Redish. Published/Created: St. Paul, Minn.: West Pub. Co., 1983. Description: xli, 878 p.; 26 cm. ISBN: 0314711465 : Notes: Includes index. Subjects: Courts--United States--Cases. Series: American casebook series LC Classification: KF8718 .R33 1983 Dewey Class No.: 347.73/1 347.3071 19

Redish, Martin H. Federal courts: cases, comments, and questions / by Martin H. Redish, Gene R. Nichol. Edition Information: 3rd ed. Published/Created: St. Paul, Minn.: West Pub. Co., 1994. Related Authors: Nichol, Gene R., 1951- Description: xxix, 1000 p.; 27 cm. ISBN: 0314039902 (alk. paper) Notes: Includes index. Kept up to date by supplements. Subjects: Courts--United States--Cases. Series: American casebook series LC Classification: KF8718 .R33 1994 Dewey Class No.: 347.73/1 347.3071 20

Redish, Martin H. Federal courts: cases, comments, and questions / by Martin H. Redish, Suzanna Sherry. Edition Information: 5th ed. St. Paul, MN: West Group, c2002. Related Authors: Sherry, Suzanna. Description: xli, 1093 p.; 26 cm. ISBN: 0314260102 (alk. paper) Notes: Includes index. Subjects: Courts--Judicial power--Jurisdiction--United States--Cases. Series: American casebook series LC Classification: KF8718 .R33 2002 Dewey Class No.: 347.73/202 21

Redish, Martin H. Federal courts: cases, comments, and questions / by Martin H. Redish, Suzanna Sherry. Edition Information: 4th ed. Published/Created: St. Paul, Minn.: West Group, 1998. Related Authors: Sherry, Suzanna. Description: xxxi, 1026 p.; 26 cm. ISBN: 0314230475 (hardcover: alk. paper) Notes: Includes index. Kept up to date by supplements. Subjects: Courts--Judicial power--Jurisdiction--United States--Cases. Series: American casebook series LC Classification: KF8718 .R33 1998 Dewey Class No.: 347.73/202 21

Redish, Martin H. Federal courts: cases, comments, and questions / Martin H. Redish. Edition Information: 2nd ed. Published/Created: St. Paul, Minn.: West, 1989. Description: xxxix, 1122 p.; 26 cm. ISBN: 0314439196 Notes: Kept up to date by annual supplements. Includes index. Subjects: Courts--United States--Cases. Series: American casebook series LC Classification: KF8718 .R33 1989 Dewey Class No.: 347.73/1 347.3071 19

Redish, Martin H. The federal courts in the political order: judicial jurisdiction and American political theory / Martin H. Redish. Published/Created: Durham, N.C.: Carolina Academic Press, c1991. Description: viii, 192 p.; 24 cm. ISBN:

0890894116 Notes: Includes bibliographical references (p. [141]-188) and index. Subjects: Courts--United States. Judicial power--United States. Jurisdiction--United States. LC Classification: KF8700 .R42 1991 Dewey Class No.: 347.73/2 347.3072 20

Reed, Thomas Buck, 1787-1829. Speech of Mr. Reed, of Mississippi, in the Senate, on the bill further to amend the judicial system of the United States: delivered April, 1826. Published/Created: Washington: Printed by Davis & Force, 1826. Related Authors: Miscellaneous Pamphlet Collection (Library of Congress) Joseph Meredith Toner Collection (Library of Congress) Description: 31 p.; 23 cm. References: Shoemaker 25906 Subjects: Justice, Administration of--United States--Speeches in Congress. Courts--United States--Speeches in Congress. LC Classification: AC901 .M5 vol. 774, no. 13

Reforming the civil justice system / edited by Larry Kramer. Published/Created: New York: New York University Press, c1996. Related Authors: Kramer, Larry, 1958- Research Conference on Civil Justice Reform in the 1990s (1993: New York, N.Y.) Description: vii, 449 p.: ill.; 26 cm. ISBN: 0814746659 (alk. paper) Notes: Papers presented as part of the Institute of Judicial Administration's Research Conference on Civil Justice Reform in the 1990s, held in New York, October 15-16, 1993. Includes bibliographical references and index. Subjects: Justice, Administration of--Courts--Civil procedure--Law reform--United States. Series: Justice and judicial administration LC Classification: KF8700.A75 R44 1996 Dewey Class No.: 347.73 347.307 20

Reorganization of the federal judiciary. Lower federal court study with respect to congestion of calendars and assignment of judges and how the same will be affected by the proposed reform of the federal judiciary. Published/Created: [Chicago?] 1937. Description: 2 p.l., 64 p. 24 cm. Subjects: United States. Supreme court. Courts--United States. LC Classification: KF8720 .A45

Reorganization of the federal judiciary. Statement by Hon. Edward R. Burke ... on the business of the Supreme court. Research statement of the Junior Bar conference filed with the Judiciary committee of the United States Senate April 28, 1937, with supporting quotations, answering testimony in behalf of the proposals as to the federal Courts. Printed under the auspices of the Special Committee on the Supreme Court Proposal of the American Bar Association in cooperation with the Junior Bar Conference of the American Bar Association. Published/Created: [Chicago] 1937. Related Authors: Burke, Edward Raymond 1880- Description: 204 p. diagrs. 25 cm. Subjects: United States. Supreme Court. Courts--United States. LC Classification: KF8742 .A77

Report - National Center for State Courts. [Williamsburg, Va., etc.] National Center for State Courts. Description: 20 v. ill. 28 cm. v. 1- 1974- Ceased with Vol. 20, no. 11 (Nov. 1993). ISSN: 0195-5241 Notes: SERBIB/SERLOC merged record Merged with: Survey of judicial salaries, to become: State court report. Subjects: National Center for State Courts--Courts--Court administration--United States--States--Periodicals. LC Classification: KF8736.A15 N37 Dewey Class No.: 347.73/33 347.3013

Report ... to the Oregon bar association, November 18, 1913. Published/Created: [n.p., 1913] Description: [3]-29 p. 25 cm. Subjects: Costs (Law) Courts--United States. LC Classification: KF8995.Z9 O73

Report ... New York state bar association. Committee on the duty of courts to refuse to execute statutes in contravention of the fundamental law. Published/Created: [New York? 1915-] Description: v. 23 cm. Notes: Serial. PREMARC/SERLOC merged record Subjects: Courts--United States. United States--Constitutional law. LC Classification: JK1541 .N6

Report and tentative recommendations of the Committee to Consider Standards for Admission to Practice in the Federal Courts to the Judicial Conference of the United States, September 21, 22, 1978. Published/Created: [Washington, D.C.]: The Committee, [1978] Description: 167 p. in various pagings; 27 cm. Notes: Includes "Supplement A: Report of the Subcommittee on Remedies to the Committee of the Judicial Conference of the United States to Consider Standards for Admission to Practice in the Federal Courts, August 1978" (46 p.); "Supplement B: Tentative draft of proposed uniform rules governing admission to practice in United States district courts, September 21, 1978" (17 p.); and "Supplement C: Final report of the Subcommittee on Rules for Limited Admission to Practice of Law Students to Committee of the Judicial Conference of the United States to Consider Standards for Admission to Practice in the Federal Courts, February 1978" (67, [5]p.) Includes bibliographical references. Subjects: Admission to the bar--United States. District Courts--United States. LC Classification: KF302 .J8 Dewey Class No.: 347.73/504 19

Report of proposed amendments to certain Rules of civil procedure for the United States District Courts. Published/Created: Washington, U.S. Govt. Print. Off., 1961. Description: 11 p. 24 cm. Subjects: United States. District courts. Rules of civil procedure. Civil procedure--United States. Court rules--United States. LC Classification: LAW

Report of the Committee on federal legislation of the Association of the bar of the city of New York on the amendment (in the nature of a substitute) to Senate bill 1392 to reorganize the judicial branch of the government. Published/Created: [New York? 1937] Related Authors: Laporte, Cloyd, 1892- Description: 13 p. 23 cm. Subjects: Courts--United States. LC Classification: KF8720 .A8

Report of the Committee on rule-making power and judicial councils. Published/Created: [n.p., 1932?] Related Authors: Grinnell, Frank Washburn, 1873- Description: p. [33]-38. 23 cm. Subjects: Courts--United States. Judicial councils--United States. LC Classification: KF8705.Z9 C63

Report of the District of Columbia Court System Study Committee of the District of Columbia Bar / prepared for the Subcommittee on Governmental Efficiency and the District of Columbia of the Committee on Governmental Affairs, United States Senate. Published/Created: Washington: U.S. G.P.O., 1983. Related Authors: United States. Congress. Senate. Committee on Governmental Affairs. Subcommittee on Governmental Efficiency and the District of Columbia. Description: ix, 1090 p.; 24 cm. Notes: At head of title: 98th Congress, 1st session. Committee print. "April 1983." Item 1037-B, 1037-C (microfiche) Includes bibliographies. Subjects: Courts--Washington (D.C.) Court administration--Washington (D.C.) Series: S. prt.; 98-34 LC Classification: KFD1710 .A25 1983 Dewey Class No.: 347.753/01 347.53071 19 Govt. Doc. No.: Y 4.G 74/9:S.prt.98-34

Report of the federal Courts Study Committee. Published/Created: [Philadelphia, Pa.?: Federal Courts Study Committee, 1990] Description: xi, 203 p.; 25 cm. Notes: Shipping list no.: 90-426-P. "April 2, 1990." Item 729 Subjects: Courts--United States. Court congestion and delay--United States. Justice, Administration of--United States. LC Classification: KF8719 .A345 1990 Dewey Class No.: 347.73/1 347.3071 20 Govt. Doc. No.: Ju 10.2:F 31

Report of the Judicial Conference of the United States. Report of the director of the Administrative Office of the United States Courts. 1940- Published/Created: Washington, U. S. Govt. Print. Off. [n.d.] Related Authors: United States Administrative Office of the United States Courts. Report. Description: v. 24 cm. Subjects: Courts--United States. Justice, Administration of --United States. LC Classification: KF8700 .A843

Report of the proceedings of a special meeting of the Judicial Conference of the United States. Letter from Chief Justice, Supreme Court of the United States, transmitting copy of the Report of the proceedings of a special meeting of the Judicial Conference of the United States, held at Washington, D.C., March 18-19, 1965, pursuant to the provisions of title 28, United States code, section 331. Published/Created: Washington, U.S. Govt. Print. Off., 1965. Description: vi, 47-112 p. 24 cm. Subjects: Courts--United States. Series: House document (United States. Congress. House); 89th Congress, 1st session, no. 205. LC Classification: KF8700 .A845 1965

Report of the proceedings of a special session of the Judicial Conference of the United States, March 10-11, 1960, Washington, D.C. Published/Created: [Washington, D.C.]: U.S. G.P.O., 1960. Description: iv, 57 p.; 24 cm. Subjects: Courts--United States. LC Classification: KF8700 .A845 1960 Dewey Class No.: 347.73/1 347.3071 19

Report of the proceedings of the Judicial Conference of the United States. Published/Created: Washington, D.C.: [Administrative Office of the United States Courts]: U.S.G.P.O., 1965- Related Authors: United States. Administrative Office of the United States Courts. Description: v.; 24-28 cm. Some years include reports from special sessions. Vols. for Mar. 12-13, 1986 and special session June 30, 1986 issued together in single bound v. Sept. 22-23,1965- Current Frequency: Semiannual Notes: SERBIB/SERLOC merged record Annual publication also issued, 1963-1992: Judicial Conference of the United States. Reports of the proceedings of the Judicial Conference of the United States (1963); 1993: United States courts (Washington, D.C.: 1993); 1994-: Reports of the proceedings of the Judicial Conference of the United States (1994). Judicial Conference of the United States. Reports of the proceedings of the Judicial Conference of the United States (1963) 0892-9297 (DLC)sn 84043037 (OCoLC)8721524 United States courts (Washington, D.C.: 1993) (DLC)sn 94028450 (OCoLC)31091324 Reports of the proceedings of the Judicial Conference of the United States (1994) (DLC)sn 98017379 (OCoLC)33827021 Subjects: Judicial Conference of the United States--Periodicals. Judicial councils--Courts--Justice, Administration of--United States--Periodicals. Judges--United States--Periodicals. LC Classification: KF8705 .A828 Dewey Class No.: 347.73/1/05 347.307105 20 Govt. Doc. No.: JU 10.10:

Report of the proceedings. Published/Created: Washington, [U.S. Govt. Print. Off.] Description: 24 cm. 1927, 1931- Former Report 1927-47 Summary: Includes regular annual and special meetings. Notes: "First report appears only in the report of the Attorney General, U.S., in very brief form, in 1924. Reports for 1925, 1926, 1928, 1929 and 1930 appear only in the report of the Attorney General as: Report of Conference of Senior Circuit Judges."--Prefatory note bound with Reports, 1927-38. Issued 1927-47 by the conference under its earlier name: Judicial Conference of Senior Circuit Judges. Beginning in 1940 issued also with the Report of the director of the Administrative Office of the United States Courts. Subjects: Courts--United States. Justice, Administration of--United States. LC Classification: KF8700 .A844 Govt. Doc. No.: Ju 10.10:

Report of the Task Force on the Civil Justice Reform Act / co-chairs, Brad D. Brian, Richard McMillan, Jr.; members, John P. Driscoll [et al.]. Published/Created: [S.l.: American Bar Association?], 1992. Related Authors: Brian, Brad D. McMillan, Richard, Jr. Description: 1 v. (various pagings); 28 cm. Notes: At head of title: Section of Litigation, American Bar Association. Subjects: Court congestion and delay--District Courts--Dispute resolution (Law)--United States. LC Classification: KF8727 .R46 1992 Dewey Class No.: 347.73/13 347.30713 20

Report to the Judicial Conference of the Committee on Local District Court Rules. Published/Created: Washington, D.C.: Administrative Office of the United States Courts: [U.S. G.P.O., 1940] Related Authors: Judicial Conference of Senior Circuit Judges. United States. Administrative Office of the United States Courts. Description: iv, 54 p.; 24 cm. Subjects: District Courts--Court rules--United States. Civil procedure--United States. LC Classification: LAW

Reports of cases argued and determined in the District Courts of the United States within the Second Circuit: [1865-1879] / by Robert D. Benedict. Published/Created: New York: Baker, Voorhis, 1869-82. Related Authors: Benedict, Robert D. (Robert Dewey), 1828-1911, reporter. Benedict, Benj. Lincoln (Benjamin Lincoln), 1835- reporter. United States. District Court (New York) United States. District Court (Vermont) United States. District Court (Connecticut) Description: 10 v.; 24 cm. Notes: Vols 7-10, by Robert D. Benedict and B. Lincoln Benedict. Title from spine: Benedict's District Court reports. Subjects: Law reports, digests, etc.--United States. Law reports, digests, etc.--New York (State)--Connecticut--Vermont. LC Classification: LAW

Reports of cases at common law and in equity, argued and decided in the Court of Appeals of the commonwealth of Kentucky, by Thomas B. Monroe. Edition Information: 2d ed. Published/Created: Cincinnati, H. W. Derby, 1850. Related Authors: Monroe, Thomas Bell, 1795-1865, reporter. Description: 7 v. in 3. 25 cm. Notes: "Containing cases determined at the Fall term, 1824-Fall term 1828." Also numbered as v. 17-23 of Kentucky reports. Vol. 2 includes "The statute regulating the court, and its rules of practice; also an appendix of the rules of chancery practice in the federal courts, and their execution laws in Kentucky." Subjects: Law reports, digests, etc.--Kentucky. Court rules--Kentucky. Court rules--United States. LC Classification: KFK1245 .A19 1824c

Reports of criminal cases decided in the Appellate Courts of the state of New York and of other states, and in the Supreme Court of the United States: with notes / by Patrick H. Cowen. Published/Created: Albany: W.C. Little, 1884-1885. Related Authors: Cowen, Patrick H. (Patrick Henry) United States. Supreme Court. Description: 2 v.; 24 cm. Notes: Cases reported from 1867-1878. Subjects: Criminal law--New York (State) Criminal law--United States. Law reports, digests, etc.--New York (State) Law reports, digests, etc.--United States. LC Classification: LAW

Resource guide for organization design / developed for Administrative Office of the U.S. Courts, Office of Human Resources and Statistics, Human Resources Division. Published/Created: [Washington, D.C.]: The Division, [2000] Related Authors: United States. Administrative Office of the United States Courts. Human Resources Division. Description: 66, 4, 10, 3 p.: ill.; 29 cm. Notes: Cover title. Includes bibliographical references. Subjects: Court administration--United States. Courts--United States--Management. LC Classification: KF8732.Z9 R47 2000 Dewey Class No.: 347.73/13 21

Respect for law. Published/Created: Chicago, Ill. (77 So. Wacker Dr., Chicago 60606): American Bar Assiciation, Division of Communications, Special Events Dept., c1981. Description: 19 p.; 18 cm. Summary: Introduces the American legal and judicial system, lawsuits, court and appeal procedure, the Bill of Rights. Notes: Cover title. Subjects: Law--United States--Juvenile literature. Law. Courts. LC Classification: KF387 .R47 1981 Dewey Class No.: 349.73 347.3 19

Restructuring justice: the innovations of the Ninth Circuit and the future of the federal Courts / Arthur D. Hellman, editor. Published/Created: Ithaca, N.Y.: Cornell University Press, 1990. Related Authors: Hellman, Arthur D. Description: xvii, 385 p.: ill.; 23 cm. ISBN: 0801424054 (cloth: alkaline paper) 0801496861 (paper:

alkaline paper) Notes: Includes bibliographical references and index. Subjects: United States. Court of Appeals (9th Circuit) Courts--Judicial process--Court congestion and delay--United States. LC Classification: KF8700 .R47 1990 Dewey Class No.: 347.73/2 347.3071 20

Rice, Charles E. Reagan and the courts: prospects for judicial reform / Charles E. Rice; introduction by Daniel J. Popeo; foreword by Orrin G. Hatch. Published/Created: Washington, D.C. (1612 K St., N.W., Washington 20006): Washington Legal Foundation, c1980. Description: vii, 36 p.; 23 cm. Notes: Includes bibliographical references. Subjects: Reagan, Ronald. Courts--United States. LC Classification: KF8720 .R5 1980 Dewey Class No.: 347.73/1 347.3071 19

Richards, Walter Buck, 1863-1904. Genesis of the federal judiciary system; Published/Created: Richmond, Everett Waddey co., 1904. Description: 36 p. 24 cm. Subjects: Courts--United States. LC Classification: KF8700.Z9 R48 Microfilm LL 1217 KF

Richardson, Richard J. The politics of Federal courts; lower courts in the United States [by] Richard J. Richardson [and] Kenneth N. Vines. Published/Created: Boston, Little, Brown [1970] Related Authors: Vines, Kenneth Nelson, 1924- Description: xi, 180 p. illus. 21 cm. Notes: Includes bibliographical references. Subjects: Courts--Judges--United States. Law and politics. LC Classification: KF8700 .Z9R5 Dewey Class No.: 347.99/73

Richardson, William S. The judiciary: special report to the 1978 Constitutional Convention. Published/Created: [Honolulu: Supreme Court of Hawaii], 1978. Description: 86 leaves; 28 cm. Notes: Cover title. Includes bibliographical references. Subjects: Judges--Hawaii. Appellate Courts--United States. LC Classification: KFH513 .R5 Dewey Class No.: 347/.969/014

Riekes, Linda. Courts and trials: Riekes-Ackerly lessons in law for young people. Edition Information: 2d ed., for teachers. Published/Created: St. Paul: West Pub. Co., c1980. Related Authors: Ackerly, Sally Mahe, joint author. Description: 153 p.: ill.; 25 cm. ISBN: 082991028X Summary: Examines the United States courts, suggesting activities such as mock trials to illustrate the strengths and weaknesses of the system. Subjects: Courts--United States--Juvenile literature. Dispute resolution (Law)--United States--Juvenile literature. Mock trials--Juvenile literature. Courts. Trial practice. LC Classification: KF8700.Z9 R53 1980 Dewey Class No.: 347.73 19

Riekes, Linda. Courts and trials: Riekes-Mahe lessons in law for young people. Edition Information: Teacher's ed. Published/Created: St. Paul: West Pub. Co., c1975. Related Authors: Ackerly, Sally Mahe, joint author. Description: 139 p.: ill.; 25 cm. Summary: Examines the United States courts, suggesting activities such as mock trials to illustrate the strengths and weaknesses of the system. Subjects: Courts--Trial practice--United States--Juvenile literature. Courts. Trial practice. LC Classification: KF8700.Z9 R53 Dewey Class No.: 347/.73

Riekes, Linda. Juvenile problems and law / Riekes, Ackerly. Edition Information: 2nd ed. Published/Created: St. Paul, Minn.: West Pub. Co., c1980. Related Authors: Ackerly, Sally Mahe. Description: 127 p.: ill. (some col.); 25 cm. ISBN: 0829910255 (pbk.) Summary: Presents common situations of juvenile delinquency and discusses the basic concepts of justice to be applied. Offers discussion and group action on specific cases. Notes: "Lessons in law for young people." Subjects: Juvenile Courts--United States--Juvenile literature. Juvenile justice, Administration of--United States Juvenile literature. Juvenile delinquency. Law. Juvenile courts. Series: Law in action series LC Classification: KF9780 .R53 1980 Dewey Class No.: 345.73/08 347.3058 19

Riekes, Linda. Juvenile problems and law: lessons in law for young people / [Linda] Riekes [Sally Mahe] ackerly. Edition Information: 2d ed. for teachers. Published/Created: St. Paul: West Pub. Co., c1980. Related Authors: Ackerly, Sally Mahe, joint author. Description: 133 p.: ill.; 25 cm. ISBN: 0829910263 Summary: Presents common situations of juvenile delinquency and discusses the basic concepts of justice to be applied. Offers discussion and group action on specific cases. Subjects: Juvenile Courts--United States--Juvenile literature. Juvenile justice, Administration of--United States Juvenile literature. Juvenile delinquency. Law. Juvenile courts. LC Classification: KF9710 .R53 1980 Dewey Class No.: 345.73/08

Riekes, Linda. Juvenile problems and law: Riekes-Mahe lessons in law for young people. Published/Created: [St. Paul]: West Pub. Co., [1975] Related Authors: Ackerly, Sally Mahe, joint author. Description: 95 p.: ill. (some col.); 25 cm. Summary: Presents common situations of juvenile delinquency and discusses the basic concepts of justice to be applied. Offers discussion and group action on specific cases. Subjects: Juvenile Courts--United States--Juvenile literature. Juvenile justice, Administration of--United States. Juvenile delinquency. Law. LC Classification: KF9710 .R53 Dewey Class No.: 345/.73/08

Riekes, Linda. Juvenile responsibility & law / Linda Riekes, Steve Jenkins, Armentha Russell. Edition Information: 3rd ed. Published/Created: St. Paul: West Pub. Co., c1990. Related Authors: Jenkins, Stephen, 1946- Russell, Armentha. Riekes, Linda. Juvenile problems and law. Description: v, 203 p.: ill.; 26 cm. ISBN: 0314473637 Summary: Presents common situations of juvenile delinquency and discusses the basic concepts of justice to be applied. Offers discussion and group action on specific cases. Notes: Rev. ed. of: Juvenile problems and law. 2nd ed. c1980. Subjects: Juvenile Courts--United States--Juvenile literature. Juvenile justice, Administration of--United States Juvenile delinquency. Series: Law in action series LC Classification: KF9780 .R53 1990 Dewey Class No.: 345.73/08 347.3058 19

Rightmire, George Washington. Cases and readings on the jurisdiction and procedure of the federal courts, Published/Created: Cincinnati, The W. H. Anderson company, 1917. Description: xvi, 892 p. 24 cm. Subjects: Courts--United States. Jurisdication. LC Classification: KF8858 .R5

Ritz, Wilfred J. Rewriting the history of the Judiciary Act of 1789: exposing myths, challenging premises, and using new evidence / by Wilfred J. Ritz; edited by Wythe Holt and L.H. LaRue. Published/Created: Norman: University of Oklahoma Press, c1990. Related Authors: Holt, Wythe, 1942- LaRue, Lewis H. Description: xiii, 264 p.; 24 cm. ISBN: 0806122390 (alk. paper) Notes: Includes bibliographical references (p. 209-253) and index. Subjects: United States. Judiciary Act of 1789. Courts--United States. Jurisdiction--United States. LC Classification: KF8714.52.A16 R57 1990 Dewey Class No.: 347.73/1 347.3071 20

Robertson, Reynold. Appellate practice and procedure in the Supreme court of the United States: a chronological outline of proceedings necessary both in the Supreme court and in the lower courts on petition for a writ of certiorari, writ of error, or appeal, to review a decision in the Supreme court of the United States; and of steps necessary to be taken to file and conduct, or defend, a case in the Supreme court upon the granting of a writ of certiorari, writ of error, or appeal, or upon certified questions, with forms and citations to the applicable statutes, rules of court, and decisions, Published/Created: New York, Prentice-Hall, inc., 1928. Description: xxxix, 360 p. 24 cm. Subjects: United States. Supreme court. Writs. Appellate procedure--Courts-- Court rules--United States. Forms (Law)--United States. LC Classification: LAW

Robertson, Reynold. Appellate practice and procedure in the Supreme court of the United States: Published/Created: New York, Printice-Hall, inc., 1928. Description: p. cm. Subjects: United States. Supreme court. Appropriate procedure--United States. Writs--United States. Courts--United States. Court rules--United States. Forms (Law)--United States. LC Classification: KF9057 .R58 1928

Robinson, George Dexter, 1834-1896. The federal courts. Published/Created: Washington [Govt. print. off.] 1880. Description: 16 p. 21 cm. Subjects: Courts--United States. LC Classification: JK1591 .R66

Roche, John Pearson, 1923- Courts and rights; the American judiciary in action, by John P. Roche. Edition Information: 2d ed. Published/Created: New York, Random House [1966] Description: x, 143 p. illus. 19 cm. Notes: "Notes and references": p. [127]-134. Subjects: Civil rights--United States. Courts--United States. LC Classification: KF8700 .R6 1966 Dewey Class No.: 347.9973

Roche, John Pearson, 1923- Courts and rights; the American judiciary in action, by John P. Roche. Published/Created: New York, Random House [c1961] Description: viii, 117 p. 19 cm. Notes: Bibliographical references included in "Notes and references" (p.[106]-116) Subjects: Courts--United States. Civil rights--United States. Series: Studies in political science (New York, Random House); PS 36. LC Classification: KF8700 .R6 1961 Dewey Class No.: 347.9

Roe, Edward Thomas, b. 1847. Criminal procedure of United States courts, Published/Created: Chicago, Callaghan & company, 1887. Description: xiv, 274 p. 25 cm. Subjects: Criminal procedure--United States. Courts--United States. LC Classification: KF9619 .R6 Microfilm LL 1492 KF

Roe, Gilbert E. (Gilbert Ernstein), 1865-1929. Our judicial oligarchy / by Gilbert E. Roe; with an introduction by Robert M. LaFallette. Published/Created: New York: B.W. Huebsch, 1912. Description: xiv, 239 p.; 19 cm. Notes: Includes index. Subjects: Courts--United States. Recall. LC Classification: KF8700.Z9 R55

Root, Elihu, 1845-1937. Judicial decisions and public feeling, Published/Created: [n.p., 1937] Description: 23 p. 24 cm. Subjects: Courts--United States. Recall. LC Classification: KF8700.Z9 K6 1937

Root, Elihu, 1845-1937. Judicial decisions and public feeling: address by Elihu Root as president of the New York State Bar Association, at the annual meeting in New York City, January 19, 1912. Published/Created: [s. l.: s. n., 1912?] Related Authors: New York State Bar Association. Description: 26 p.; 24 cm. Notes: Cover title. Subjects: Courts--United States. Recall of judicial decisions. LC Classification: KF8700.Z9 R6 1912 Dewey Class No.: 347/.73/12

Rose, John Carter, 1861-1927 Jurisdiction and procedure of the federal courts, by John C. Rose ... Edition Information: 2d ed. Published/Created: Albany, N.Y., M. Bender, 1922. Related Authors: United States. Laws, statutes, etc. Description: ix, 790 p. 24cm. Notes: First edition published 1915 under title: An elementary treatise on the jurisdiction and procedure of federal courts. Subjects: Courts--Jurisdiction--United States. Civil procedure--United States. Criminal procedure--United States. LC Classification: KF8858 .R6

Rose, John Carter, 1861-1927. An elementary treatise on the jurisdiction and procedure of the federal courts, by John C. Rose ... Published/Created: Baltimore, King Brothers, 1915. Related Authors: United States. Laws, statutes, etc. Description: xxx, 406 p. 24 cm. Subjects: Courts--United States. Jurisdiction--United States. Civil procedure--United States. Criminal procedure--United States. LC Classification: KF8885 .R6 1915

Rose, John Carter, 1861-1927. Jurisdiction and procedure of the federal courts, by John C. Rose. Edition Information: 4th ed., rev. and enl. to date by Byron F. Babbitt ... with foreword by John C. Knox ... Published/Created: Albany, N.Y., M. Bender & company, incorporated, 1931. Related Authors: Babbitt, Byron Fenner, 1874- ed. Description: xxxix, 994, 102 p. 1 l. illus. (map) 26cm. Subjects: Courts--United States. Jurisdiction--United States. Civil procedure--United States. Criminal procedure--United States. Court rules--United States. Forms (Law)--United States. LC Classification: KF8858 .R6 1931

Rose, John Carter, 1861-1927. Jurisdiction and procedure of the federal courts, by John C. Rose. Edition Information: 3d ed. Published/Created: Albany, N.Y., M. Bender and company, incorporated, 1926. Related Authors: United States. Supreme Court. Description: xxxiv, 919 p. 27 cm. Subjects: Courts--United States. Jurisdiction--United States. Civil procedure--United States. Criminal procedure--United States. Court rules--United States. LC Classification: KF8858 .R6 1926

Rose, John Carter, 1861-1927. Jurisdiction and procedure of the federal courts / by John C. Rose; with foreword by John C. Knox. Edition Information: 4th ed., rev. and enl. / by Byron F. Babbitt. Published/Created: Albany, N.Y.: Matthew Bender & Company, 1931. Related Authors: Babbitt, Byron Fenner, 1874- United States. Supreme Court. Description: xxxix, 820, 102 p.; 22 cm. Notes: On cover: Students' edition. Subjects: Courts--Jurisdiction--United States. Civil procedure--United States. Criminal procedure--United States. Court rules--United States. LC Classification: KF8858 .R6 1931b

Rose, Marcus A., 1888- Law and the little man, Published/Created: [n.p., 1935] Description: [4] p. 28 cm. Subjects: Legal aid--United States. Law reform--United States. Courts--United States. LC Classification: KF390.5.P6 R6

Rose, Walter Malins, 1872- The case of Marbury v. Madison, 1 Cranch, 137; Published/Created: Albany, N.Y., Print of H. B. Parsons [c1898] Description: 1 p. l., 70 p. 24 cm. Subjects: Jurisdiction. Courts--United States. LC Classification: JK1541 .R6

Rose, Walter Malins, 1872-1908. A code of federal procedure. (Superseding Detsy's Federal procedure.) Embodying enactments of Congress, constitutional provisions, established principles, and court rules, in force December 1, 1906, and the Bankruptcy act of 1898, with amendments and orders, together with a collection of forms and precedents. By Walter Malins Rose. Published/Created: San Francisco, Bancroft-Whitney company, 1907. Related Authors: Detsy, Robert, 1827-1895. A manual of practice in the courts of the United States. United States. Laws, statutes, etc. United States. Courts. Description: 3 v. 24cm. Subjects: Courts--United States. Civil procedure--United States. Criminal procedure--United States. Court rules--United States. Bankruptcy--United States. Forms (Law)--United States. LC Classification: KF8840 .R63

Rose-Ackerman, Susan. Rethinking the progressive agenda: the reform of the American regulatory state / Susan Rose-Ackerman. Published/Created: New York: Free Press; Toronto: Maxwell Macmillan Canada; New York: Maxwell Macmillan International, c1992. Description: xiii, 301 p.; 25 cm. ISBN: 0029269156 : Notes: Includes bibliographical references (p. 251-275) and indexes. Subjects: Administrative law--United States. Administrative agencies--United States. Deregulation--United States. Judicial review--United States. Courts--United States. Social choice--United States. Progressivism (United States politics) Policy sciences. United States--Economic policy--1981-1993. LC Classification: KF5402 .R665 1992 Dewey Class No.: 342.73/0664 347.302664 20

Rosenberg, Gerald N. The hollow hope: can courts bring about social change? / Gerald N. Rosenberg. Published/Created: Chicago: University of Chicago, 1991. Description: xii, 425 p.: ill.; 24 cm. ISBN: 0226727025 (alk. paper) : Notes: Includes bibliographical references (p. 367-414) and index. Subjects: Courts--United States. Political questions and judicial power--United States. Sociological jurisprudence. Civil rights--United States. Women's rights--United States. Social change. Series: American politics and political economy. LC Classification: KF8700 .R66 1991 Dewey Class No.: 340/.115 20

Rosenberg, James N. (James Naumburg), b. 1874. Corporate reorganization and the federal court / by James N. Rosenberg, Robert T. Swaine, Roberts Walker. Published/Created: New York: Baker, Voorhis, 1924. Related Authors: Swaine, Robert T. (Robert Taylor), b. 1886. Walker, Roberts, b. 1874. Description: xxviii, 148 p.; 21 cm. Contents: A new scheme of reorganization / by James N. Rosenberg -- Reorganization by decree: recent noteworthy instances / by Roberts Walker -- The Aetna explosives case--a milestone in reorganization / by James N. Rosenberg -- Reorganization--the next step / by James N. Rosenberg -- Reorganization--the next step: a reply to Mr. James N. Rosenberg / by Robert T. Swaine -- Phipps v. Chicago, Rock Island & Pacific Ry. Co. / by James N. Rosenberg. Notes: "Appeared in the Columbia law review and the Cornell law quarterly during the last seven years."--Pref. Includes index. Subjects: Corporation law--United States. Courts--United States. LC Classification: KF1544.A75 R6

Rule of civil procedure for the United States District Courts as amended... Jan 1, 1955. Published/Created: [n.p., n.d.] Description: 223 p. cm. LC Classification: LAW

Rules governing the Courts of the State of New Jersey, 1969 revision, as amended. Published/Created: St. Paul, Minn., West Pub. Related Authors: United States. District Court (New Jersey) New Jersey. Supreme Court. United States. Court of Appeals (3rd Circuit) Description: v. 25 cm. Began in 1969. -1992. ISSN: 0193-967X Summary: Including New Jersey evidence rules and rules for United District Court, and rules for United States Court of Appeals. Notes: Subtitle varies. Supplements accompany some vols. SERBIB/SERLOC merged record Subjects: Court rules--New Jersey. Court rules--United States. LC Classification: KFN2329 .A196 Dewey Class No.: 347/.749/05

Rules governing the courts of the State of New Jersey. 1969 revision, effective September 8, 1969. Published/Created: St. Paul, West Pub. Co. [1969] Related Authors: United States. District Court (New Jersey) Description: vii, 837 p. 25 cm. Notes: With Rules of evidence. Also included are rules of United States District Court for the District of New Jersey. Subjects: Court rules--New Jersey. LC Classification: KFN2329.A317 A2 1969 Dewey Class No.: 347/.749/05

Rules of civil procedure for the District Courts of the State of New Mexico, adopted May 23, 1949, effective December 31, 1949, with amendments through August 1, 1962 and Rules of the New Mexico Supreme Court. Published/Created: St. Paul, Minn., West Pub. Co. [1962] Related Authors: New Mexico. Supreme Court. Rules. Description: vii, 153 p. 23 cm. Subjects: Court rules--New Mexico. Civil procedure--New Mexico. LC Classification: LAW

Rules of civil procedure for the District Courts of the United States. Documentary history, 1934-1938 ... Published/Created: [Washington, 1938] Description: 16 pts. in 1 v. 24 cm. Subjects: Court rules--United States. Civil procedure--United States. LC Classification: LAW

Rules of civil procedure for the District Courts of the United States: letter from the Attorney General transmitting the "Rules of civil procedure for the District Courts of the United States," adopted by the Supreme

Court of the United States pursuant to the Act of June 19, 1934, ch. 651. Published/Created: Washington: U.S. Govt. Print. Off., 1938. Related Authors: United States. Supreme Court. Description: xvii, 126 p.; 23 cm. Notes: Cover title. Subjects: Court rules--United States. Civil procedure--United States. District Courts--United States. Series: House document (United States. Congress. House). 75th Congress, 3rd session; no. 460. LC Classification: KF8816 .A2 1938e

Rules of criminal procedure for the District Courts of the United States / adopted by the Supreme Court of the United States. Published/Created: Washington: U.S. Govt. Print. Off., 1944. Related Authors: United States. District Courts. United States. Supreme Court. Description: 80 p.: forms.; 23 cm. Subjects: Court rules--United States. Criminal procedure--United States. LC Classification: LAW

Rules of practice, adopted by the Circuit and District Courts of the United States, for the sourthern district of Illinois, together with the rules in equity and admiralty, prescribed by the supreme court of the United States; the acts of Congress regulating fees and costs, etc., etc., etc. Published/Created: Springfield, Steam press of Baker and Phillips, 1864. Description: 103 p. cm. LC Classification: LAW

Rules of the District Courts of the State of New Mexico, adopted May 23, 1949, effective December 31, 1949, and Rules of the New Mexico Supreme Court. Published/Created: St. Paul, West Pub. Co. [1949]. Related Authors: New Mexico. Supreme Court. Rules. Description: vii, 139 p. 24 cm. Notes: New Mexico state doc. no.: J87.N6 B101.21, D61, 1949 Subjects: Court rules--New Mexico Civil procedure--New Mexico. LC Classification: LAW Dewey Class No.: 347.9

Rules of the Supreme and District courts of the state of Nevada. Published/Created: [Carson City, Nev., State printing office, J. Farnsworth, superintendent, 1926] Related Authors: Nevada. District courts. Description: 1 p.l., 31, [1] p. 23 cm. Subjects: Court rules--Nevada. LC Classification: LAW

Rules of the Supreme Court of the United States and rules of practice for the circuit and District Courts in equity and admiralty cases... Published/Created: Washington, G.P.O., 1866. Description: 87 p. cm. LC Classification: LAW

Rules of the U.S. Courts in New York. Published/Created: [St. Paul, Minn.]: West Group, c1998- Description: v.: forms; 25 cm. 1998 ed.- ISSN: 1537-9515 Notes: "Federal rules of Appellate procedure, U.S. Court of Appeals for the Second Circuit ... Southern, Eastern, Northern, and Western Districts." Continues the 2nd ed. of a loose-leaf publication issued under the same title, 1978-c1997. Subjects: United States. District Court (New York: Northern District)--Rules and practice. United States. District Court (New York: Southern District)--Rules and practice. United States. District Court (New York: Eastern District)--Rules and practice. United States. District Court (New York: Western District)--Rules and practice. Court rules--New York (State). Series: Federal practice (West Group) LC Classification: KF8821.N578 A197 Dewey Class No.: 347 13

Rules of the United States Circuit and District Courts for the Southern District of West Virginia, Fourth Circuit. Published/Created: [S.l.: s.n.], 1907. Related Authors: United States. Circuit Court (West Virginia: Southern District) District Court Description: 27, x p.; 24 cm. Notes: Cover title. Includes indexes. Subjects: Court rules--United States. Court rules--West Virginia. LC Classification: KF8816 .A2 1907a

San Francisco law journal. Published/Created: San Francisco: Baggett and Scofield, 1877-1878. Description: 1 v.; 23 cm. Vol. 1, no. 1 (Sept. 1, 1877)-v. 1, no. 26 (Feb. 23rd, 1878). Notes: Containing all the decisions of the Supreme Court of California, and of the United States Circuit and United States District Courts for the district of California; and important decisions of the United States Supreme Court, and higher Courts of other states. Subjects: Law reports, digests, etc.--California--United States. LC Classification: KFC47 .S26

Schramm, Gustav Lorch. A series of eight radio talks on The story of our Courts Published/Created: [Pittsburgh] 1927. Description: 82 p. 24 cm. Subjects: Courts--United States. LC Classification: JK1521 .S3

Small world: Douglas, Birkett, Voelker [Motion picture] Published/Created: [n.p.] Columbia Broadcasting System, 1960. Related Authors: Douglas, William Orville, 1898- Birkett, Norman Birkett, baron, 1883-1962. Voelker, John Donaldson, 1903- Columbia Broadcasting System, inc. Description: p. 28 min. sd. b&w. 16 mm. Notes: CREDITS: Producers and editors, Edward R. Murrow, Fred W. Friendly; cameramen, Leo Rossi, William K. McClure, Peter Garbrini, James Lillis; film editor, F. Howard O'Neill. SUMMARY: Supreme Court Justice William O. Douglas, Lord Birkett, and Judge John Voelker discuss the merits of election vs. appointment of judges, differences in judicial roles in England and America, historical changes in the role of the United States Supreme Court, and congestion and delay in the American Courts. Host, Joseph N. Welch. Subjects: United States. Supreme Court. Judges. Judicial process--United States. Judicial process--Great Britain. Court congestion and delay--United States.

Special masters' incidence and activity: report to the Judicial Conference's Advisory Committee on Civil Rules and its Subcommittee on Special Masters / Thomas E. Willging ... [et al.]. Published/Created: Washington, DC (One Columbus Circle, N.E., Washington, 20002-8003): Federal Judicial Center, 2000. Related Authors: Willging, Thomas E. Judicial Conference of the United States. Advisory Committee on Civil Rules. Judicial Conference of the United States. Subcommittee on Special Masters. Description: v, 125 p.: forms; 23 cm. Subjects: Referees--United States. District Courts--United States. Evidence, Expert--United States. LC Classification: KF8986 .S68 2000

Staff directories on CD-ROM [electronic resource]. Published/Created: Mount Vernon, VA: Staff Directories, Ltd., Description: computer laser optical discs; 4 3/4 in. ISSN: 1080-9546 Notes: Accompanied by: User's manual, issues for <1997- also includes control diskettes. Description based on: 1993/1 (June 1993); title from disc label. System requirements: IBM PC/AT or 100 % compatible; at least 640 KB real memory (at least 384 KB free memory); MS DOS 3.0 or higher; 20 MB hard disk drive; 1 CD-ROM drive with appropriate controller and interface cable from Hitachi or Sony, or any other CD-ROM drive with High Sierra or ISO 9660 compatible device driver. SERBIB/SERLOC merged record Contains in full-text format: Congressional staff directory; Federal staff directory; and: Judicial staff directory. Congressional staff directory 0589-3178 (DLC) 59013987 (OCoLC)1239097 Federal staff directory 0735-3324 (DLC) 82647381 (OCoLC)8152681 Judicial staff directory 1091-3742 (DLC) 87640790 (OCoLC)13238092 Subjects: United States. Congress--Directories--Databases. Government executives--Judges--United States--Directories--Databases. Courts--United States--Official and employees--Directories Databases. LC Classification: JK404 Dewey Class No.: 320 12

Standards relating to appeals and collateral review / recommended by the IJA-ABA Joint Commission on Juvenile Justice Standards, Irving R. Kaufman, chairman; Charles Z. Smith, chairman of Drafting Committee II; Michael Moran, reporter. Published/Created: Cambridge, Mass.: Ballinger Pub. Co., c1980. Related Authors: Moran, Michael C. IJA-ABA Joint Commission on Juvenile Justice

Standards. Juvenile Justice Standards Project. Description: xiv, 48 p.; 24 cm. ISBN: 0884102394 Notes: At head of title: Institute of Judicial Administration, American Bar Association, Juvenile Justice Standards. Spine title: Appeals and collateral review. Subjects: Appellate procedure--United States. Juvenile Courts--United States. LC Classification: KF9822 .S7 1980 Dewey Class No.: 345.73/08 19

Standards relating to Appellate Courts. Edition Information: 1994 ed. Published/Created: [Chicago?]: American Bar Association, Judicial Administration Division; [S.l.]: State Justice Institute, 1994. Description: vi, 134 p.; 26 cm. ISBN: 1570731640 Notes: "First approved by the American Bar Association House of Delegates in February 1977 and were amended ... in August 1994"--T.p. verso. Includes bibliographical references. Subjects: Appellate Courts--United States. Series: American Bar Association. Standards of judicial administration; v. 3. LC Classification: KF8750 .A944 1994 Dewey Class No.: 347.73/24 347.3073 20

Standards relating to Appellate Courts: approved draft / American Bar Association Commission on Standards Judicial Administration. Published/Created: [Chicago]: The Commission, 1977. Description: x, 111 p.; 23 cm. Notes: "The standards ... were approved by the American Bar Association House of Delegates in February, 1977." Includes bibliographical references. Subjects: Appellate Courts--United States. LC Classification: KF8750 .A95 1977 Dewey Class No.: 347/.73/24

Standards relating to Appellate Courts: tentative draft, 1976 / American Bar Association Commission on Standards of Judicial Administration. Published/Created: [Chicago]: The Commission, [c1976] Description: x, 124 p.; 24 cm. Notes: Includes bibliographical references. Subjects: Appellate Courts--United States. LC Classification: KF8750 .A95 Dewey Class No.: 347/.73/24

Standards relating to Appellate delay reduction / Appellate Delay Reduction Committee; chairperson, Ben F. Overton ... [et. al.]. Published/Created: Chicago, Ill.: Appellate Judges Conference, Lawyers Conference Task Force on the Reduction of Litigation Cost and Delay, American Bar Association: Copies available from American Bar Association, Order Fulfillment Dept., c1988. Description: v, 27 p.: ill.; 23 cm. ISBN: 0897073681 Subjects: Court congestion and delay--Appellate Courts--United States--States. LC Classification: KF8727.Z95 A66 1988

Standards relating to court organization / American Bar Association, Judicial Administration Division. Edition Information: 1990 ed. Published/Created: [Chicago]: The Association, 1990. Description: viii, 137 p.; 26 cm. ISBN: 0897075633 Notes: "First approved by the American Bar Association House of Delegates in February 1974 and were amended ... in February 1990"--T.p. verso. Includes bibliographical references. Subjects: Courts--Court administration--United States. Series: American Bar Association. Standards of judicial administration; v. 1. LC Classification: KF8720 .A43 1990 Dewey Class No.: 347.73/1 347.3071 20

Standards relating to court organization / American Bar Association Commission on Standards of Judicial Administration. Published/Created: Chicago: ABA, 1974. Description: 120 p.; 23 cm. Notes: Includes bibliographical references. Subjects: Courts--Court administration--United States. LC Classification: KF8720 .A44 1974 Dewey Class No.: 347/.73/13

Standards relating to court organization. Published/Created: [Chicago?] 1974. Description: 88 p. 28 cm. Notes: "Final draft." Includes bibliographical references. Subjects: Courts--United States. Court administration--United States. LC Classification: KF8719.3 .A44 1974 Dewey Class No.: 347/.73/13

Standards relating to court organization. Published/Created: [n.p.] 1973. Description: vii, 109 p. 23 cm. Notes: "Tentative draft." Includes bibliographical references. Subjects: Courts--United States. Court administration--United States. LC Classification: KF8720 .A44 1973 Dewey Class No.: 347/.73/13

Standards relating to trial Courts / American Bar Association Commission on Standards of Judicial Administration. Published/Created: [Chicago?]: The Association, 1976. Description: 141 p.; 23 cm. Notes: "Final draft." Includes bibliographical references. Subjects: Courts--United States. LC Classification: KF8720 .A445 1976 Dewey Class No.: 347/.73/1

Standards relating to trial Courts / American Bar Association Commission on Standards of Judicial Administration. Published/Created: [Chicago?]: The Association, 1975. Description: x, 136 p.; 23 cm. Notes: "Tentative draft." Includes bibliographical references. Subjects: Courts--United States. LC Classification: KF8720 .A445 Dewey Class No.: 347/.73/1

Standards relating to trial Courts / American Bar Association, Judicial Administration Division. Edition Information: 1992 ed. Published/Created: [Chicago]: The Division, c1992. Description: viii, 140 p.; 26 cm. ISBN: 0897077687 Notes: Includes bibliographical references. Subjects: Courts--United States. Series: American Bar Association. Standards of judicial administration; v. 2. LC Classification: KF8720 .A43 1992 Dewey Class No.: 347.73/1 347.3071 20

Standards relating to trial Courts as amended, 1976 and 1987 / American Bar Association. Published/Created: [Chicago]: The Association, c1987. Related Authors: American Bar Association. Committee on Standards of Judicial Administration. Description: 141 p.; 23 cm. ISBN: 0897073347 (pbk.) Notes: "Judicial Administration Division, Committee on Standards of Judicial Administration"--P. opposite t.p. Includes bibliographies. Subjects: Courts--United States. LC Classification: KF8720 .A46 1987 Dewey Class No.: 347.73/1 347.3071 20

State and local financing of the courts: tentative report. Published/Created: New York: Institute of Judicial Administration, 1969. Description: ii, 75, [141] p.; 29 cm. Notes: Cover title. Subjects: Courts--United States--States--Finance. LC Classification: KF8732.5.Z95 I57 Dewey Class No.: 347/.73/13

State Appellate court jurisdiction guide for statistical reporting: summary tables. Published/Created: Williamsburg, Va.: National Center for State Courts, Court Statistics and Information Management Project, 1985- Related Authors: National Center for State Courts. Court Statistics and Information Management Project. Conference of State Court Administrators. Description: v.: forms; 28 cm. 1984- Notes: "A joint effort of the Conference of State Court Administrators and the Court Statistics and Information Management Project of the National Center for State Courts." Chiefly tables. SERBIB/SERLOC merged record Subjects: Appellate Courts--United States--States--Statistical methods. Court administration--United States--States--Statistical methods. LC Classification: KF8736 .S73

State court caseload statistics. Published/Created: [Washington] Dept. of Justice, Law Enforcement Assistance Administration, National Criminal Justice Information and Statistics Service; [for sale by the Supt. of Docs., U.S. Govt. Print. Off.] Related Authors: United States. National Criminal Justice Information and Statistics Service. National Center for State Courts. National Court Statistics Project (U.S.) Description: v. ill. 26 cm. 1975- Notes: "Report of work performed by National Court Statistics Project, National Center for State Courts." Vols. for 1975-79 issued by the Dept. of Justice; 1980- by the National Center for State Courts. SERBIB/SERLOC merged record

Companion document to: State court organization, and Examining the work of state Courts. State court organization (DLC) 89659287 (OCoLC)8999028 Examining the work of state Courts 1096-164X (DLC) 97648371 (OCoLC)32371680 Subjects: Judicial statistics--United States--States--Periodicals. LC Classification: KF180 .S83 Dewey Class No.: 347.73/13 Govt. Doc. No.: J 26.10:SD-C-

State court journal. Published/Created: [Denver] National Center for State Courts. Related Authors: National Center for State Courts. Description: v. 28 cm. v. 1- winter 1977- Ceased with v. 20, no. 2 published in 1996. ISSN: 0145-3076 Notes: SERBIB/SERLOC merged record Indexed entirely by: Legal resource index 1980- Subjects: Court administration--United States--States--Periodicals. LC Classification: KF8732.A15 S73 Dewey Class No.: 347/.73/3

State court model annual report / National Court Statistics Project. Published/Created: Williamsburg, Va.: National Center for State Courts, c1980. Related Authors: National Center for State Courts. Description: ix, 88, 3 p.: ill.; 28 cm. ISBN: 0896560422 Notes: "National Center publication no. R0050." Subjects: Court administration--United States--States. Courts--United States--States--Statistical methods. Report writing. LC Classification: KF8732.Z95 N38 Dewey Class No.: 347.73/3

State court model statistical dictionary, 1989: a joint effort of the Conference of State Court Administrators and the National Center for State Courts. Published/Created: Williamsburg, VA (300 Newport Ave., Williamsburg 23187-8798): National Center for State Courts, c1989. Related Authors: Conference of State Court Administrators. National Center for State Courts. Description: xviii, 89 p.; 28 cm. Notes: Includes index. Subjects: Courts--United States--States--Statistical methods. Court administration--United States--States. Procedure (Law)--United States--Dictionaries. Series: Publication (National Center for State Courts); R111. LC Classification: KF8735 .S75 1989 Dewey Class No.: 347.73/3 347.3071 20

State court model statistical dictionary: a joint effort of Conference of State Court Administrators and National Center for State Courts / National Court Statistics Project. Published/Created: [Washington, D.C.]: U.S. Dept. of Justice, Bureau of Justice Statistics: For sale by the Supt. of Docs., U.S. G.P.O., 1980. Related Authors: Conference of State Court Administrators. National Center for State Courts. National Court Statistics Project (U.S.) United States. Bureau of Justice Statistics. Description: vii, 129 p., 4 p. of plates: forms; 28 cm. Notes: "NCJ-62320, SD-C-7." "July 1980." Includes index. Bibliography: p. [113]-115. Subjects: Courts--United States--States--Statistical methods. Court administration--United States--States. Procedure (Law)--United States--Dictionaries. LC Classification: KF8735 .S75 Dewey Class No.: 347.73/3 347.3071 19

State court organization / a joint effort of Conference of State Court Administrators and National Center for State Courts; U.S. Department of Justice, Bureau of Justice Statistics. Published/Created: Williamsburg, Va.: National Courts Statistics Project, 1982- Description: v.: ill.; 28 cm. 1980- Notes: Vols. for 1993- issued by: U.S. Dept. of Justice, Office of Justice Programs, Bureau of Justice Statistics. SERBIB/SERLOC merged record Companion document to: State court caseload statistics, and: Examining the work of state Courts. State court caseload statistics (DLC) 79644737 (OCoLC)5233996 Examining the work of state Courts 1096-164X (DLC) 97648371 (OCoLC)32371680 Subjects: Courts--United States--States--Periodicals. Court administration--United States--States--Periodicals. LC Classification: KF8736.A15 S7 Dewey Class No.: 347.73/3/05 347.307305 20 Govt. Doc. No.: J 29.9:

State court systems, by William E. Hannan, librarian, and Mildred B. Csontos, New York Legislative Reference Library. September, 1940. Published/Created: Chicago, Ill., The Council of State Governments [1940] Related Authors: Hannan, William Everett, 1878-1948. Csontos, Mildred B. Council of State Governments. Description: 3 p. l., 41 numb. l. 28 cm. Notes: Reproduced from type-written copy. Subjects: Courts--United States. LC Classification: JK2521 .N4 Dewey Class No.: 347.97097

State court systems. Published/Created: Chicago [n.d.] Description: v. 28 cm. Current Frequency: Series entry Notes: Serial. Subjects: Courts--United States--States. Judges--United States--States. LC Classification: JS308 .C6 subser.

State court systems. Published/Created: Chicago: Council of State Governments, 1950. Related Authors: Hannan, William Everett, 1878-1948. Csontos, Mildred B. Description: 29 leaves; 28 cm. Notes: "Revisions of similar tables prepared by Mr. Wm. E. Hannan and Miss Mildred B. Csontos of the New York Legislative Reference Library and published ... in 1940. They also include data from the Book of the states, 1950-51 edition." Subjects: Courts--United States. Judges--United States. Series: BX (Council of State Governments); 277 LC Classification: JS308 .C6 no. 277

State Courts and judicial federalism: a constitutional primer / edited by Stanley H. Friedelbaum. Published/Created: New Brunswick, N.J.: Edward McNall Burns Center for State Constitutional Studies, c1992. Related Authors: Friedelbaum, Stanley H. (Stanley Herman), 1927- Description: 81 [i.e. 80] p.; 28 cm. Subjects: Courts--United States--States. Federal government--United States. Series: Special educational report; no. 3 LC Classification: KF8736.Z9S7 1992 Dewey Class No.: 347.7/33 347.3073 20

State judiciary news. Published/Created: Lexington, Ky., Council of State Governments. Related Authors: Council of State Governments. Conference of Chief Justices. Conference of State Court Administrators. Description: v. 28 cm. v. 1- May 1975- ISSN: 0363-1362 Notes: Vols. for 1975- published for the members of the Conference of Chief Justices and the Conference of State Court Administrators. SERBIB/SERLOC merged record Subjects: Courts--United States--States--Periodicals. LC Classification: KF8736.A15 S8 Dewey Class No.: 347/.73/105

State of Louisiana: United States district courts / prepared by Department of Public Works; Dorothy L. Hammatt, cartographer. Published/Created: Baton Rouge, La.: The Department, 1961. Related Authors: Hammatt, Dorothy L. Description: 1 map: photocopy; 43 x 48 cm. Scale Information: Scale [ca. 1:1,150,000] (W 94°--W 89°/N 33°--N 29°). Notes: Blue line print. Subjects: United States. District Court. Louisiana (Eastern District)--Maps. United States. District Court. Louisiana (Western District)--Maps. District courts--Louisiana--Maps. LC Classification: G4011.F85 1961 .L6 Geographic Class No.: 4011

State of the federal judiciary: annual reports of the Chief Justice of the Supreme Court of the United States / edited by Shelley L. Dowling. Published/Created: Buffalo, N.Y.: W.S. Hein, 2000- Related Authors: Dowling, Shelley L. United States. Supreme Court. Description: 1 v. (loose-leaf); 27 cm. ISBN: 1575886243 (alk. paper) Subjects: Justice, Administration of--United States--History Sources. Courts--United States--History--Sources. Court administration--United States--History--Sources. LC Classification: KF8700 .S67 Dewey Class No.: 347.73 21

State supreme Courts: policymakers in the federal system / edited by Mary Cornelia Porter and G. Alan Tarr. Published/Created: Westport, Conn.: Greenwood Press, 1982. Related Authors: Porter, Mary Cornelia. Tarr, G. Alan (George Alan) Description: xxvii, 221 p.; 25 cm. ISBN: 0313229422 Notes: Includes index. Bibliography: p. 201-209. Subjects: Courts of last resort--United States--States. Series: Contributions in legal studies 0147-1074; no. 24 LC Classification: KF8736 .S8 1982 Dewey Class No.: 347.73/36 347.30735 19

State-federal judicial observer: a joint publication of the Federal Judicial Center and the National Center for State Courts. Published/Created: Washington, DC: The Centers, [1993- Related Authors: National Center for State Courts. Federal Judicial Center. Description: 17 v.: ill.; 43 cm. Issued two or three times a year. No. 1 (Jan. 1993)- Ceased with no. 17 (Feb. 1999). Notes: Title from caption. Not distributed to depository libraries in a physical form, 199 - Vols. for <1994- issued solely by: Federal Judicial Center. SERBIB/SERLOC merged record Ceased in paper format only; continued by an online version. Subjects: Courts--United States--Periodicals. Courts--United States--States--Periodicals. LC Classification: KF8700.A15 S73 Dewey Class No.: 347.73/3/05 21 Govt. Doc. No.: JU 13.13/2: JU 13.13/2:993/1-

Statistical tables for the federal judiciary. Published/Created: Washington, D.C.: Statistics Division, Administrative Office of the United States Courts, [1995- Related Authors: United States. Administrative Office of the United States Courts. Statistics Division. Description: v.; 28 cm. June 30, 1995- Notes: Vols. for 1995-1996 distributed to depository libraries in microfiche. SERBIB/SERLOC merged record Subjects: Judicial statistics--United States--Periodicals. LC Classification: KF180 .S84 Dewey Class No.: 347.73/1/05 21 Govt. Doc. No.: JU 10.21/2:

Structural and other alternatives for the Federal Courts of Appeals: report to the United States Congress and the Judicial Conference of the United States / Judith A. McKenna, project director. Published/Created: Washington, DC (Thurgood Marshall Federal Judiciary Building, 1 Columbus Circle, N.E., Washington 20002-8003): Federal Judicial Center, 1993. Related Authors: McKenna, Judith A. Federal Judicial Center. Description: v, 179 p.: ill; 28 cm. Notes: "The Federal Judicial Center prepared this report pursuant to the request of Congress in section 302(c) of the Federal Courts Study Implementation Act of 1990." Includes bibliographical references. Subjects: Appellate Courts--United States. Court congestion and delay--United States. Judicial process--United States. LC Classification: KF8750 .S77 1993 Dewey Class No.: 347.73/24 347.30724 20

Struggle for equal justice; a report on most critical problems of the lower courts, defined by judges [and] proposals for solutions, recommended by task force of judicial experts. Compilation by Albert B. Logan, project director. Edition Information: [1st ed.] Published/Created: Washington, 1969. Related Authors: Logan, Albert B., 1909- ed. Description: x, 135 p. 26 cm. Notes: Includes reports on the Judical Conference on Most Critical Problems of the Lower Court System, held at Rancho Tranquillo, Colo., in Aug. 1966, and on the meeting of a task force at Lake Tahoe, Calif., on Feb. 9-11, 1968. Bibliography: p. 131-135. Subjects: Courts--Criminal justice, Administration of--United States. LC Classification: KF9223 .A75J8 Dewey Class No.: 347.99/73

Study of the division of juisdiction between State and Federal Courts. Official draft[s]. Published/Created: Philadelphia, 1965- Description: v. 23 cm. Subjects: Jurisdiction--United States. Courts--United States. LC Classification: KF8735 .A94

Study of the division of jurisdiction between State and Federal Courts. As adopted and promulgated by the American Law Institute at Washington, D.C., May 18, 1965, and May 21-22, 1968. Published/Created: [Philadelphia, 1969] Description: xix, 587 p. 27 cm. Subjects: Jurisdiction--United States. Courts--United States. LC Classification: KF8735 .A95 Dewey Class No.: 347.99/73

Study of the division of jurisdiction between State and Federal Courts. Proposed final draft[s] no. 1- Submitted by the Council to the members of the American Law Institute. Published/Created: Philadelphia, 1965- Description: v. 23 cm. Subjects: Jurisdiction--United States. Courts--United States. LC Classification: KF8735 .A943

Study of the division of jurisdiction between State and Federal Courts. Tentative draft[s] Submitted by the Council. Published/Created: Philadelphia, 1963- Description: v. 24 cm. Subjects: Jurisdiction--United States. Courts--United States. LC Classification: KF8735 .A947 Dewey Class No.: 347.98

Suggestions for improving juror utilization in the United States District Court for the Eastern District of New York. Published/Created: New York, N.Y.: Institute of Judicial Administration, [1971] Related Authors: Institute of Judicial Administration. Description: 45 leaves: ill.; 28 cm. Notes: "Prepared under a contract with the Federal Judicial Center." "August 31, 1971." Subjects: United States. District Court (New York: Eastern District) Jury--United States. Court administration--United States. District Courts--United States. LC Classification: KF8972.Z9 S84 1971 Dewey Class No.: 347.73/752 347.307752 20

Summary of state and local justice improvement activities, 2001 / American Bar Association, Coalition for Justice. Published/Created: Chicago, IL: Office of Justice Initiatives, c2001. Related Authors: Coalition for Justice (American Bar Association) American Bar Association. Office of Justice Initiatives. Description: 184 p.: ill.; 28 cm. ISBN: 1570739935 Notes: Includes index. Subjects: Justice, Administration of--United States--States. Courts--United States--States.

Superintending democracy: the Courts and the political process / edited by Christopher P. Banks and John C. Green. Edition Information: 1st ed. Published/Created: Akron, Ohio: University of Akron Press, 2001. Related Authors: Banks, Christopher P. Green, John Clifford, 1953- Description: xii, 396 p.; 24 cm. ISBN: 1884836720 (alk. paper) Notes: "U.S. Supreme Court." Includes bibliographical references (p. 369-379) and index. Subjects: United States. Supreme Court. Political questions and judicial power--Election law--Campaign funds--Law and legislation--United States. Law and politics. Series: Series on law, politics, and society LC Classification: KF8742 .S55 2001 Dewey Class No.: 342.73/07 21

Supplement to the State court model statistical dictionary: a joint effort of Conference of State Court Administrators and National Center for State Courts. Published/Created: Williamsburg, Va. (300 Newport Ave., Williamsburg 23185): Court Statistics and Information Project, 1984. Related Authors: Conference of State Court Administrators. National Center for State Courts. Description: iv, 81 p.; 28 cm. Notes: Includes index. Subjects: Courts--United States--States--Statistical methods. Court administration--United States--States. Procedure (Law)--United States--Dictionaries. Series: Publication (National Center for State Courts); no. R-0088. LC Classification: KF8735 .S75 Suppl. Dewey Class No.: 347.73/3 347.3071 19

Symposium: Automation in the Courts; its impact on record-making and record-keeping, implications for the private citizen and the public. Published/Created: [New York, 1972] Description: viii, 65 p. 23 cm. Notes: Held at the House of the Association of the Bar of the City of New York on Nov. 5, 1971. "Planned and arranged by the Subcommittee on Automation and Administration of Court Records of the departmental committees of the Appellate Divisions, First and Second Departments [of the New York State Supreme Court]" Subjects: Information storage and retrieval systems--Court administration--United States. LC Classification: KF242.C69 S9 Dewey Class No.: 029/.9/3477313

Synopsis of legislative provisions for official reporters of the highest Courts in the United States: and letters of United States circuit judges and district judges favoring legislation for the appointment of an official reporter for the United States Circuit Courts of Appeals. Published/Created: Washington, D.C.: Gibson Bros., 1900. Related Authors: YA Pamphlet Collection (Library of Congress) Description: 48 p.; 23 cm. Notes: Cover title. Subjects: Law reporters--United States. Courts--United States--Officials and employees. LC Classification: YA 21207

Texas digest, 1840 to date, covering Texas reports and South western reporter, as well as Texas cases decided in the Federal circuit and District Courts, Circuit Court of Appeals and Supreme Court of the United States. Published/Created: St. Paul, West Pub. Co. [1935-<1979 Related Authors: West Publishing Company. Description: <42 v. 26 cm. Notes: "Key number system." Subtitle varies. Kept to date by current cummulative pocket service, supplementary pamphlets, and replacement vols. LC holdings recorded in Shelflist only as of Aug. 26, 1983. Subjects: Law reports, digests, etc.--Texas. Law reports, digests, etc.--Southwest, Old. LC Classification: KFT1257 .T45 Dewey Class No.: 345.32 19

Texas subsequent history table. Published/Created: St. Paul, Minn.: West Pub. Co., c1989- Related Authors: United States. Supreme Court. Texas. Court of Criminal Appeals. West Publishing Company. Description: v.; 25 cm. 1st ed. (1989)- ISSN: 1049-1198 Notes: Vols. cover cases of the Supreme Court, the Courts of Appeals and the Court of Criminal Appeals reported in West's South Western reporter, beginning with volume 20, in which there has been a subsequent proceeding by the state Courts or by the Supreme Court of the United States. SERBIB/SERLOC merged record Vols. supplemented daily by INSTA-CITE on WESTLAW and also weekly by the cumulative table in West's Texas cases advance sheets. West's south western reporter (DLC) 88647631 (OCoLC)17592356 Subjects: Annotations and citations (Law)--Texas. LC Classification: KFT1259 .T48 KFT1259 .T49 Dewey Class No.: 348 11

The administration of justice, Published/Created: Philadelphia, 1933. Related Authors: Moley, Raymond, 1886- ed. Wallace, Schuyler Crawford, 1898- joint ed. Description: p. cm. Subjects: Justice, Administration of--United States. Civil procedure--United States. Courts--United States. Law--United States--Study and teaching. LC Classification: H1 .A4 vol. 167

The Advocate. Published/Created: Falls Church, Va.: Defense Appellate Division, U.S. Army Legal Services Agency; [Washington, D.C.: Supt. of Docs., U.S. G.P.O., distributor, -1985. Related Authors: U.S. Army Legal Services Agency. Defense Appellate Division. Description: v.; 27 cm. -v. 16, no. 2 (Mar.-Apr 1984). Began with Mar. 1969. ISSN: 0094-2197 Summary: A journal for military defense counsel. Notes: Title from cover. Description based on: Vol. 11, no. 1 (Jan.-Feb. 79). Vols. for for 19 -19 published by the Defense Appellate Division, U.S. Army Judiciary; 19 - by the Defense Appellate Division, U.S. Army Legal Services Agency. SERBIB/SERLOC merged record Indexed by: Index to U.S. government periodicals 0098-4604 Indexed entirely by: Legal resource index 1980- Indexes: Vols. 1 (1969)-4, no. 3 (Aug. 1972) in v. 4, no. 3; Vols. 1 (1969)-7 (1975) in v. 7, no. 3; Vols. 1 (1969)-10 (1978) in v. 10, no. 6. Subjects: Courts-martial and Courts of inquiry--United States Periodicals. Military law--United States--Periodicals. LC Classification: KF7639.A1 A3 Dewey Class No.: 343/.73/0143 Govt. Doc. No.: D 108.109:

The American court system / edited with introductions by Marilyn McShane, Frank P. Williams III. Published/Created: New York: Garland Pub., 1997. Related Authors: McShane, Marilyn D., 1956- Williams, Franklin P. Description: xvii,

404 p.: ill.; 24 cm. ISBN: 0815325126 Notes: Includes bibliographical references. Subjects: Criminal justice, Administration of--United States. Law enforcement--United States. Criminal Courts--United States. Series: Criminal justice (New York, N.Y.); 5. LC Classification: KF9223 .A955 1997 Dewey Class No.: 345.73/05 21

The American Courts: a critical assessment / edited by John B. Gates, Charles A. Johnson. Published/Created: Washington, D.C.: CQ Press, c1991. Related Authors: Gates, John Boatner. Johnson, Charles A., 1948- Description: x, 534 p.: ill.; 23 cm. ISBN: 0871875411 Notes: Includes bibliographical references and index. Subjects: Courts--United States. Justice, Administration of--United States. Judicial process--United States. Judges--United States. LC Classification: KF8719.A2 A454 1991 Dewey Class No.: 347.73/1 347.3071 20

The American judiciary: critical issues / special editors of this volume, A. Leo Levin, Russell R. Wheeler. Published/Created: Beverly Hills: Sage Publications, c1982. Related Authors: Levin, A. Leo, 1919- Wheeler, Russell R., 1943- Description: 214 p.; 25 cm. ISBN: 0803918526: 0803918534 (pbk.) : Notes: Includes bibliographical references and index. Subjects: Courts--United States. Series: Annals of the American Academy of Political and Social Science; v. 462. LC Classification: H1 .A4 vol. 462 KF8719 Dewey Class No.: 320/.05 s 347.73/1 320/.05 s 347.3071 19

The analysis of judicial reform / edited by Philip L. Dubois. Published/Created: Lexington, Mass.: Lexington Books, c1982. Related Authors: Dubois, Philip L. Description: xiv, 221 p.: ill.; 24 cm. ISBN: 0669044806 Notes: Includes bibliographies and index. Subjects: Courts-- Justice, Administration of--United States. Series: Policy Studies Organization series (Unnumbered) LC Classification: KF8700 .A96 1982 Dewey Class No.: 347.73/1 347.3071 19

The Army lawyer. Published/Created: Charlottesville, Va.: Judge Advocate General's School, [1971- Related Authors: Judge Advocate General's School (United States. Army) United States. Dept. of the Army. Description: v.; 26 cm. Vol. 1, no. 1 (Aug. 1971)-v. 3, no. 2 (Feb. 1973); 3 (Mar. 1973)- ISSN: 0364-1287 Notes: Title from caption. Prior to Mar. 1977 issues had item nos. 348-D and 327 (Rev. 1969). Issued by: Headquarters, Department of the Army, SERBIB/SERLOC merged record Indexed by: Index to U.S. government periodicals 0098-4604 Indexed entirely by: Index to legal periodicals 0019-4077 Legal resource index 1980- Subjects: Army--Military law--United States--Courts-martial and Courts of inquiry--Periodicals. Series: DA pam; 27-50. LC Classification: KF7209.A1 A74 Dewey Class No.: 343/73/01 Govt. Doc. No.: D 101.22:27-50

The Attorneys' daybook. Published/Created: Newark, N.J.: Lawyers Diary and Manual, Related Authors: Lawyers Diary & Manual (Firm) Description: v.: ill.; 27 cm. Notes: Description based on: 93. SERBIB/SERLOC merged record Subjects: Lawyers--United States--Handbooks, manuals, etc. Lawyers--United States--Diaries. Courts--United States--Directories. LC Classification: KF319 .A88

The Bill of Rights, the Courts & the law: the landmark cases that have shaped American society, with essays and case commentary / by Lynda Butler ... [et al.]; edited by David Bearinger. Edition Information: 3rd ed. Published/Created: [Charlottesville, Va.]: Virginia Foundation for the Humanities and Public Policy, c1999. Related Authors: Butler, Lynda Lee. Bearinger, David. Virginia Foundation for the Humanities and Public Policy. Description: xx, 396 p.; 23 cm. ISBN: 0966891910 Subjects: United States. Supreme Court. Civil rights--United States--Cases. Judicial process--United States--Cases. LC Classification: KF4748 .B553 1999 Dewey Class No.: 342.73/085 21

The Bill of Rights, the Courts, and the law: case abridgements and commentary / by A.E. Dick Howard ... [et al.]. Published/Created: [Charlottesville, Va.]: Virginia Foundation for the Humanities and Public Policy, c1991. Related Authors: Howard, A. E. Dick. Virginia Foundation for the Humanities and Public Policy. Virginia Commission on the Bicentennial of the United States Constitution. Commission on the Bicentennial of the United States Constitution. Crestar Foundation. Description: xv, 227 p.; 28 cm. Notes: "In cooperation with the Virginia Commission on the Bicentennial of the United States Constitution, the Commission on the Bicentennial of the United States Constitution, and the Crestar Foundation." Subjects: United States. Supreme Court. Civil rights--United States--Cases. Judicial process--United States--Cases. LC Classification: KF4748 .B55 1991 Dewey Class No.: 342.73/085 347.30285 20

The ceremony at the laying of the corner stone of the new United States court house at the corner of Pearl, Park and Centre streets, New York city, on March 1, 1933, at 4 o'clock p. m. under the auspices of the Association of the bar of the city of New York and the New York county lawyers association. Published/Created: [New York, Tenny press, 1933] Related Authors: New York county lawyers' association. Description: [12] p. 23 cm. Subjects: New York (City) United States court house. Courts--United States. LC Classification: KF5775.Z9 A8

The changing borders of juvenile justice: transfer of adolescents to the criminal court / edited by Jeffrey Fagan and Franklin E. Zimring. Published/Created: Chicago: University of Chicago Press, c2000. Related Authors: Fagan, Jeffrey. Zimring, Franklin E. Description: xvi, 440 p.; 24 cm. ISBN: 0226233804 (cloth: acid-free paper) Notes: Includes bibliographical references and indexes. Subjects: Juvenile justice, Administration of--United States. Extenuating circumstances--United States. Transfer of cause--United States. Criminal Courts--United States. Series: The John D. and Catherine T. MacArthur Foundation series on mental health and development LC Classification: KF9779 .C435 2000 Dewey Class No.: 364.36/0973 21

The Commercial agency annual. Published/Created: New York, McKillop & Wood. Description: 18 cm. ISSN: 0092-7589 Notes: SERBIB/SERLOC merged record Subjects: Commercial law--United States--States. Courts--United States. LC Classification: KF890 .C59 Dewey Class No.: 346/.73/07

The Constitution and the Courts, Published/Created: Northport, N.Y., Edward Thompson company, 1924. Related Authors: Meigs, William Montgomery, 1852- Growth of the Constitution in the Federal convention of 1787. Calvert, Thomas Henry, 1868- Constitutional construction and notes on the Constitution. Thompson, Edward, company. Description: 3 v. 26 cm. Subjects: United States. Constitution. Law reports, digests, etc.--United States. United States--Constitutional history. United States--Constitutional law. LC Classification: KF4502 .C6

The Constitution, the Courts, and the quest for justice / Robert A. Goldwin and William A. Schambra, editors. Published/Created: Washington, D.C.: American Enterprise Institute for Public Policy Research, c1989. Related Authors: Goldwin, Robert A., 1922- Schambra, William A. Description: xi, 135 p.; 23 cm. ISBN: 0844736929 (pbk.) 0844736910 Notes: Includes bibliographical references. Subjects: Constitutional law--United States. Courts--United States. Judicial review--United States. Series: Constitutional studies AEI studies; 491 LC Classification: KF4550.A2 C655 1989 Dewey Class No.: 342.73 347.302 20

The Court manager: a publication of the National Association for Court Management. Published/Created: Williamsburg, VA: The Association, 1986- Related Authors: National Association for Court Management (U.S.) Description: v.:

ill.; 28 cm. Vol. 1, no. 1 (Mar. 1986)- ISSN: 1046-249X Notes: Title from cover. SERBIB/SERLOC merged record Subjects: National Association for Court Management (U.S.) Periodicals. Court administration--United States--Periodicals. LC Classification: KF8732.A15 C685 Dewey Class No.: 347.73/13 347.30713 19

The Courts and education / edited by Clifford P. Hooker; editor for the Society, Kenneth J. ReHage. Published/Created: Chicago, Ill.: National Society for the Study of Education: distributed by the University of Chicago Press, 1978. Related Authors: Hooker, Clifford P. Description: xxv, 389 p.; 24 cm. Notes: Includes bibliographical references and index. Subjects: Educational law and legislation--United States--Addresses, essays, lectures. Series: Yearbook of the National Society for the Study of Education; new ser., 77th, pt. 1. LC Classification: LB5 .N25 77th, pt. 1 KF4119 Dewey Class No.: 370/.8 s 344/.73/07

The Courts and the press in a free society [sound recording]. Published/Created: Santa Barbara, Calif.: Center for the Study of Democratic Institutions, 1982. Related Authors: Graham, Fred P. Lewis, Anthony, 1927- Fortas, Abe. Vanocur, Sander. Powe, L. A. Scot. Center for the Study of Democratic Institutions. Description: 1 sound tape reel (55 min.): 3 3/4 ips, 1/4-track; 5 in. Summary: Panelists discuss the shift in judicial interpretation of the First Amendment and the war between the press and the judiciary. Notes: Panel discussion. "Recorded by NPR." Recorded on both sides. Recorded Dec. 7, 1978, in Washington, D.C., at the center's national convocation: The William O. Douglas Inquiry Into the State of Individual Freedom, held in honor of Justice Douglas. Subjects: Freedom of the press--United States. Free press and fair trial--United States. Series: Douglas inquiry series; # 14 LC Classification: KF4774 RXA 0431

The Courts in American life: major historical interpretations / edited with an introduction by Kermit L. Hall. Published/Created: New York: Garland Pub., 1987. Related Authors: Hall, Kermit. Description: xii, 705 p.: ill.; 24 cm. ISBN: 082400132X (alk. paper) : Notes: Bibligoraphy: p. xii. Subjects: Courts--United States--History. Series: United States constitutional and legal history; v. 4. LC Classification: KF8719.A2 C72 1987 Dewey Class No.: 347.73/1 347.3071 19

The court's response to domestic violence / National Association for Court Management Comprehensive Public Information Programs Subcommittee. Published/Created: Williamsburg, VA (300 Newport Ave., Williamsburg 23187-8798): National Association for Court Management, [1997] Related Authors: National Association for Court Management (U.S.). Comprehensive Public Information Programs Subcommittee. Description: 44 p.: forms; 28 cm. Notes: "NACM mini-guide, December 1997"--Cover. Includes bibliographical references (p. 41-44) Subjects: Family violence--United States. Courts--United States. LC Classification: KF9322 .C68 1997

The courts, separation of powers: final report of the 1983 Chief Justice Earl Warren Conference on Advocacy in the United States / A.E. Dick Howard ... [et al.]; Edited by Bette Goulet; conference chairman, Michael F. Colley; sponsored by The Roscoe Pound-American Trial Lawyers Foundation, Washington, D.C. Published/Created: Washington, D.C. (1050 31st. St., N.W. Washington 20007): Roscoe Pound-American Trail Lawyers Foundation, 1983. Related Authors: Howard, A. E. Dick. Goulet, Bette. Colley, Michael, 1936- Roscoe Pound-American Trial Lawyers Foundation. Description: iv, 141 p.: ill.; 24 cm. Notes: Includes bibliographies. Subjects: Courts--United States--Congresses. Judicial power--United States--Congresses. Judicial review--United States--Congresses. Separation of powers--United States--Congresses. LC Classification: KF8700 .A17 1983 Dewey Class No.: 347.73/012 347.30712 19

The Courts, social science, and school desegregation / [Betsy Levin and Willis D. Hawley, special editors for this symposium]. Published/Created: Durham, N.C.: School of Law, Duke University, 1975. Related Authors: Levin, Betsy. Hawley, Willis D. Description: 2 v. (432 p.); 27 cm. Notes: Cover title. Includes bibliographical references. Subjects: Segregation in education--Law and legislation--United States--Addresses, essays, lectures. School integration--United States--Addresses, essays, lectures. Series: Law and contemporary problems; v. 39, no. 1-2 LC Classification: K12 .A9 vol. 39, no. 1-2 KF4155 Dewey Class No.: 340/.08 s 344/.73/0798

The Courts, social science, and school desegregation / edited by Betsy Levin and Willis D. Hawley. Published/Created: New Brunswick, N.J.: Transaction Books, c1977. Related Authors: Levin, Betsy. Hawley, Willis D. Description: 432 p.: ill.; 24 cm. ISBN: 0878551506 : Notes: Originally appeared in Law and contemporary problems, v. 39, no. 1-2, 1975. Includes bibliographical references. Subjects: Segregation in education--Law and legislation--United States. School integration--United States. LC Classification: KF4155.A2 C63 Dewey Class No.: 344/.73/0798

The Courts, the public, and the law explosion. Published/Created: Englewood Cliffs, N.J., Prentice-Hall [1965] Related Authors: Jones, Harry Willmer, ed. Description: viii, 177 p. 22 cm. Notes: "Under the editorial supervision of Harry Willmer Jones ... prepared as background reading for the Arden House Assembly." Subjects: Courts--United States--Addresses, essays, lectures. Judges--United States--Addresses, essays, lectures. Justice, Administration of--United States--Addresses, essays, lectures. LC Classification: KF8719 .A2A45 Dewey Class No.: 347.9973

The Courts, validity, and minimum competency testing / George F. Madaus, editor. Published/Created: Boston: Kluwer-Nijhoff, c1983. Related Authors: Madaus, George F. Description: xi, 292 p.: ill.; 24 cm. ISBN: 0898381134 Notes: Based on a Conference on the Courts and the Content Validity of Minimum Competency Tests, sponsored by the Ford Foundation and held at Boston College, Mass., on Oct. 13-14, 1981. Includes bibliographies and index. Subjects: Competency based educational tests--Law and legislation United States--Congresses. Series: Evaluation in education and human services LC Classification: KF4156.A75 C68 1983 Dewey Class No.: 344.73/077 347.30477 19

The Electronic church, Congress, the administration & the Courts [sound recording]. Published/Created: Los Angeles, Calif.: Pacifica Radio Archive, p1983. Related Authors: Pacifica Radio Archive. Description: 1 sound cassette (29 min.): analog. Summary: Presents an examination of the relationship between religious broadcasters and government, focusing on the Federal Communications Commission, state and federal justice departments, and the Supreme Court. Notes: Radio broadcast. Issued also on reel. Subjects: United States. Supreme Court. United States. Federal Communications Commission. Evangelists--Legal status, laws, etc.--United States. Radio in religion--Government policy--United States. Television in religion--Government policy--United States. LC Classification: KF2805 RYA 3903

The Federal Appellate judiciary in the twenty-first century / Cynthia Harrison and Russell R. Wheeler, editors. Published/Created: Washington, D.C.: Federal Judicial Center, 1989. Related Authors: Harrison, Cynthia Ellen. Wheeler, Russell R., 1943- Description: vii, 277 p.: ill.; 24 cm. Notes: "FJC-SES-89-1"--T.p. verso. Item 743-C-3 Includes bibliographical references. Subjects: Appellate Courts--United States. LC Classification: KF8750 .F43 1989 Dewey Class No.: 347.73/24 347.30724 20 Govt. Doc. No.: Ju 13.10/4:89-1

The federal cases [microform]: comprising cases argued and determined in the circuit and District Courts of the United States. Published/Created: St. Paul: West Pub. Co., 1894-1897. Description: 30 v.; 26 cm. Notes: Includes indexes. Microfilm. Dobbs Ferry, N.Y.: Trans Media Pub. Co., 1972. 16 microfilm reels; 35 mm. (American state reports prior to the National reporter system) Subjects: Law reports, digests, etc.--United States. Series: American state reports prior to the National reporter system. LC Classification: KF105 Microfilm LL-1712

The Federal cases: comprising cases argued and determined in the circuit and District Courts of the United States from the earliest times to the beginning of the Federal reporter, arranged alphabetically by the titles of the cases, and numbered consecutively. Published/Created: Buffalo, N.Y.: Hein, 1995. Description: 31 v.; 26 cm. Bk. 1-bk. 30. Notes: The reprint ed. has a bk. 31, comprising the Digest and Table of cases vols. of the original set. SERBIB/SERLOC merged record Reprint. Originally published: St. Paul: West Pub. Co. Subjects: Law reports, digests, etc.--United States. LC Classification: KF105 .F4292 Dewey Class No.: 348.73/046 21

The Federal cases: comprising cases argued and determined in the circuit and District Courts of the United States from the earliest times to the beginning of the Federal reporter, arranged alphabetically by the titles of the cases, and numbered consecutively. Published/Created: St. Paul: West Pub. Co., 1894-1897. Description: 30 v.; 26 cm. Bk. 1-bk. 30. Notes: Includes a digest of decisions vol. and table of Federal cases, with a table of citations vol. SERBIB/SERLOC merged record Subjects: Law reports, digests, etc.--United States. Series: National reporter system. United States series LC Classification: KF105 .F429

The federal court system in the United States: an introduction for judges and judicial administrators in other countries / Article III Judges Division, Office of Judges Programs, Administrative Office of the U.S. Courts. Published/Created: Washington, D.C. (Thurgood Marshall Federal Judiciary Bldg., 1 Columbus Circle, N.E., Washington 20544): The Division, 2000. Related Authors: United States. Administrative Office of the United States Courts. Article III Judges Division. Description: 58 p.: ill., maps; 28 cm. Notes: "Developed by the Administrative Office of the United States Courts"

The Federal court system in western Pennsylvania. Published/Created: [Pittsburgh? 1972] Description: [44] p. (incl. cover) illus., ports. 26 cm. Notes: Cover title. Subjects: United States. District Court. Pennsylvania (Western District)--Courts--Pennsylvania--History. Judges--Pennsylvania. LC Classification: KF8755.P4 A93 Dewey Class No.: 347/.73/22

The Federal Courts [Filmstrip] Published/Created: [n.p.] Encyclopædia Britannica Films, 1953. Related Authors: Encyclopædia Britannica Films, inc. Description: p. 55 fr., color, 35 mm. Notes: Government in action. Eastman color. Cartoon drawings. CREDITS: Associate producer, Oscar E. Sams, Jr.; collaborator, William Anderson. Subjects: Courts--United States. Series: Government in action [Filmstrip]

The federal Courts of the tenth circuit: a history / edited by James K. Logan with the assistance of J. Terry Hemming, Catherine McGuire Eason, Ruthann Rehnborg, and the tenth circuit library staff. Published/Created: [Denver, Colo.]: U.S. Court of Appeals for the Tenth Circuit, 1992. Related Authors: Logan, James K. Description: x, 548 p.: ill.; 29 cm. Notes: Includes bibliographical references and index. Subjects: United States. Court of Appeals (10th Circuit)--History. LC Classification: KF8752 10th .F43 1992 Dewey Class No.: 347.73/24 347.30724 20

The Federal Courts, yesterday, today, and tomorrow: a symposium commemorating the bicentennial of the federal Courts,

1789-1989 / speeches by A. Leon Higginbotham, Jr. ... [et al.]; panel discussion with the speakers and Marilyn Hall Patel, Ephraim Margolin, Stuart S. Taylor, Jr.; moderated by William W. Schwarzer; [contributions by Gerald Gunther ... et al.]. Published/Created: San Francisco: U.S. District Court for the Northern District of California Historical Society, 1990. Related Authors: Higginbotham, A. Leon (Aloyisus Leon), 1928Description: xi, 86 p.; 22 cm. ISBN: 0962790907 Notes: Cover title: The federal Courts, yesterday, today & tomorrow. Proceedings of a symposium held on Nov. 3, 1989 and sponsored by the United States District Court for the Northern District of California and its Historical Society. Subjects: Courts--United States--Congresses. LC Classification: KF8700.A1 F43 1990 Dewey Class No.: 347.73/2 347.3072 20

The Federal Courts. Published/Created: [Durham, N.C.] School of Law, Duke Univ., 1948. Related Authors: Duke University. School of Law Description: 243 p. 27 cm. Contents: Foreword, by Brainerd Currie.--Historical bases of the Federal judicial system, by J. P. Frank.--Federal Courts in foreign systems, by S. A. Riesenfeld and J. N. Hazard.--Federal criminal jurisdiction and prosecutors' discretion, by L. B. Schwartz.--Jurisdiction in bankruptcy, by W. E. Mussman and S. A. Riesenfeld.--The jurisdiction of Federal Courts in labor disputes, by Ray Forrester.--The function of the lower Federal Courts as protectors of civil liberties, by O. K. Fraenkel.--The influence of Federal procedural reform, by C. E. Clark.--The law applied in the Federal Courts, by F. W. Snepp.--The administration of the Federal Courts, by H. P.Chandler.--Federal judicial statistics, by Will Shafroth.--Federal jurisdiction and the revision of the judicial code, by Herbert Wechsler. Notes: Cover title. Subjects: Courts--United States. Series: Law and contemporary problems,, v. 13, no. 1, winter 1948 LC Classification: KF8719.A2 F4

The Federal reporter. Published/Created: St. Paul, West Pub. Co. Related Authors: Boyle, Peyton, ed. Goodwin, James Wells, ed. Desty, Robert, 1827-1895, ed. United States. Supreme Court. United States. Circuit Courts. United States. Courts of Appeals. United States. Commerce Court. District of Columbia. Court of Appeals. West Publishing Company. Description: 300 v. 23 cm. v. 1-300; Mar./May 1880-Sept./Nov. 1924. Superseded by: Federal reporter. Second series Summary: Includes cases argued and determined in the District Courts of the United States and, Mar./May 1880-Oct./Nov. 1912, the Circuit Courts of the United States; Sept./Dec. 1891-Sept./Nov. 1924, the Circuit Courts of Appeals of the United States; Aug./Oct. 1911-Jan./Feb. 1914, the Commerce Court of the United States; Sept./Oct. 1919-Sept./Nov. 1924, the Court of Appeals of the District of Columbia. Notes: Vols. 47-300 called "Permanent edition." At head of title: National reporter system. United States series. Title varies slightly. Editor: v. 1-7, 30-32, P. Boyle; v. 8-9. W. Goodwin; v. 10-23, R. Desty. Ultra fiche. St. Paul, West Pub. Co. [1974?] 300 sheets. 11.5 x 15 cm. Subjects: Law reports, digests, etc.--United States. LC Classification: Ultrafiche LL-F-19 KF105

The Federal reporter. Published/Created: St. Paul: West Pub. Co., 1880-1988. Related Authors: United States. Court of Claims. Description: 1130 v.: ill.; 26 cm. Vol. 1 (Mar.-May 1880)-v. 300 (Sept.-Nov. 1924); 2nd ser., v. 1, 2d (Nov. 1924-Jan. 1925)-v. 830 F.2d. Notes: "Cases argued and determined in the Circuit and District Courts of the United States" (varies). Bound vols. replace weekly advance sheets. SERBIB/SERLOC merged record Vols. 276, 2d- include Court of Claims cases which were formerly issued in the Federal supplement. Federal supplement (DLC) 33014431 (OCoLC)1569040 Subjects: Law reports, digests, etc.--United States. LC Classification: KF105 .F432

The First duty: a history of the U.S. District Court for Oregon / edited by Carolyn M. Buan; with contributions by Caroline P.

Stoel ... [et al.]. Published/Created: Portland, Or.: U.S. District Court of Oregon Historical Society, c1993. Related Authors: Buan, Carolyn M. Stoel, Caroline P. Description: xxv, 332 p.: ill., ports.; 24 cm. ISBN: 0963515608 : Notes: Includes bibliographical references and index. Subjects: United States. District Court (Oregon)--History. Courts--Oregon--History. LC Classification: KF8755.O7 F57 1993

The Future of federalism; the law center dedication lecture series [by] Robert C. Weaver [and others] Compiled and with an introd. by Samuel I. Shuman. Pref. by William Rea Keast. Published/Created: Detroit, Wayne State University Press, 1968. Related Authors: Weaver, Robert Clifton, 1907- Shuman, Samuel I., ed. Wayne State University. Law School. Description: 120 p. 23 cm. Contents: Federal executive action and States' rights, by R. C. Weaver.--The Supreme Court and the future of federalism, by P. A. Freund.--The Federal Courts and the nature and quality of State law--from the point of view of a Federal judge, by J. S. Wright.--The Federal Courts and the nature and quality of State law--from the point of view of a State judge, by C. S. Desmond.--The role of the Congress and the political vitality of State government, by T. H. Kuchel. Notes: Public lectures delivered 1966-67 to commemorate the Wayne State University Law School's first year in its new quarters. Includes bibliographical references. Subjects: Federal government--United States. Courts--United States. LC Classification: KF4600 .A75F8 Dewey Class No.: 340

The JAG journal [microform]. Published/Created: Washington, [Govt. Print. Off.] Related Authors: United States. Navy. Office of the Judge Advocate General. Description: v.; 24 cm. No issue published for Oct. 1947. Aug. 1947- Notes: Title varies slightly. Microfilm. Ann Arbor, Mich.: University Microfilms. microfilm reels; 35mm. Published by the Office of the Judge Advocate General, Department of the Navy. SERBIB/SERLOC merged record Indexes: Aug. 1947- Dec. 1950, with Aug. 1947- Dec. 1950. Aug. 1947- Dec. 1951. Subjects: Naval law--United States--Periodicals. Courts-martial and Courts of inquiry--United States Periodicals. LC Classification: Microfilm (o) 82/10073

The JAG journal. Published/Created: Alexandria, Va.: Office of the Judge Advocate General, Dept. of the Navy; Washington, D.C.: For sale by the Supt. of Docs., U.S. G.P.O., Related Authors: United States. Navy. Office of the Judge Advocate General. Description: v.; 23-26 cm. Numbering of some volumes incomplete due to irregular publication and combined issues. Began with: Vol. 1, no. 1 (Aug. 1947). ISSN: 0021-3519 Notes: Description based on: Vol. 31, no. 1 (summer 1980); title from cover. SERBIB/SERLOC merged record Indexed entirely by: Index to legal periodicals 0019-4077 Subjects: Naval law--Courts-martial and Courts of inquiry--Military offenses--United States--Periodicals. LC Classification: K14 .A88 Dewey Class No.: 359.133 Govt. Doc. No.: D 205.7:

The journal of Appellate practice and process. Published/Created: Little Rock, Ark.: University of Arkansas at Little Rock School of Law, c1999- Related Authors: University of Arkansas at Little Rock. School of Law. Description: v.; 26 cm. Vol. 1, no. 1 (winter 1999)- ISSN: 1533-4724 Notes: Title from cover. Subjects: Appellate procedure--Appellate Courts--United States--Periodicals. LC Classification: K10+ IN PROCESS K10 .O835 Dewey Class No.: 347 13

The Judges' journal. Published/Created: [Chicago, ABA Press] Description: v. ports. 28 cm. v. 10, no, 2- Apr. 1971- ISSN: 0047-2972 Notes: SERBIB/SERLOC merged record Indexed entirely by: Legal resource index 1980- Index to legal periodicals 0019-4077 Subjects: Courts--Law--United States--Periodicals. LC Classification: K10 .U27 Dewey Class No.: 347/.73/105

The Judicial Code and rules of procedure in the federal Courts. Edition Information: Students' ed. Published/Created: Brooklyn: Foundation Press, Related Authors: Meltzer, Daniel J., 1951- Shapiro, David L., 1932- Description: v.; 25 cm. Began: 1949. ISSN: 1055-727X Notes: Description based on: 1962 revision. Compilers <1989-1994: D.J. Meltzer, D.L. Shapiro. Published in: Westbury, N.Y., <1985- SERBIB/SERLOC merged record Subjects: Procedure (Law)--United States. Court rules--United States. Courts--United States. LC Classification: KF8815 .A198 Dewey Class No.: 347.73/05 347.30705 20

The Judiciary Act of 1789 / introduction by David Eisenberg ... [et al.]. Published/Created: Washington, DC: National Archives and Records Administration, 1989. Description: 32 p.: ill.; 28 cm. ISBN: 0911333746 : Notes: "Published for the National Archives and Records Administration by the National Archives Trust Fund Board"--T.p. verso. Includes bibliographical references (p. 32). Subjects: Courts--United States. Jurisdiction--United States. Series: Milestone documents in the National Archives LC Classification: KF8719 .J83 1989 Dewey Class No.: 347.73/1 347.3071 19

The Judiciary fair employment practices annual report for ...: Judicial Conference report. Edition Information: Conference ed. Published/Created: Washington, DC: Administrative Office of the U.S. Courts, Employee Relations Office, [1999- Description: v.: ill.; 28 cm. Oct. 1, 1998 to Sept. 30, 1999- Subjects: Courts--United States--Officials and employees Periodicals. Discrimination in employment--United States--Periodicals. Courts--United States--Officials and employees--Statistics Periodicals. Discrimination in employment--United States--Statistics Periodicals. LC Classification: KF8770 .A83

The Judiciary in a democratic society / edited by Leonard J. Theberge. Published/Created: Lexington, Mass.: Lexington Books, c1979. Related Authors: Theberge, Leonard J. National Legal Center for the Public Interest. Description: xv, 216 p.; 24 cm. ISBN: 0669015083 Notes: "Based on papers presented at the national conference on the role of the judiciary in a democratic society held at the Georgetown University Law Center in Washington, D.C., on September 30 and October 1, 1977." "Sponsored by the National Legal Center for the Public Interest." Includes bibliographical references and indexes. Subjects: Courts--United States--Congresses. Political questions and judicial power--United States Congresses. LC Classification: KF8700.A75 J83 Dewey Class No.: 347/.73/1

The Judiciary: digest of appropriations / prepared by the Administrative Office of the United States Courts. Edition Information: Mar. 1991 ed. Published/Created: [Washington, D.C.?]: The Office, [1991] Related Authors: United States. Administrative Office of the United States Courts. Description: 1 v. (various pagings); 28 cm. Subjects: United States. Administrative Office of the United States Courts--Appropriations and expenditures. Courts--United States--Finance. LC Classification: KF8732.5 .A85 1991 Dewey Class No.: 347.73/13 347.31073 20

The Justice machine [Motion picture] Published/Created: [n.p.] Group W (the Westinghouse Broadcasting Co.) in cooperation with the Operation Government Committee of Washington, D. C. Released by Westinghouse Broadcasting Co., 1968. Related Authors: Westinghouse Broadcasting Company, inc. Description: p. 29 min. sd. color with b&w sequences. 16 mm. Notes: The Government story, no. 36. L. C. has b&w print. CREDITS: Producer, Alfred Kelman; narrators, Stephen Horn, Paul Long; consultant, Ronald L. Goldfarb; music, Jess Soraci. SUMMARY: A profile of the Federal Court system, including its organization, relationship to State Courts, and the concept of judicial review. Gives a history of key Supreme Court cases, including the Marbury case which produced the concept of judicial review. Subjects: Courts--United States. Judicial review--United States. Series: Government story [Motion picture] no. 36.

The Kentucky statutes containing all general laws including those passed at session of 1898, with notes of decisions of the Court of appeals, prefixed by the Magna charta, the Declaration of independence, Articles of confederation, Constitution of United States, naturalizationn laws of United States, laws relating to removal of actions and prosecutions to United States courts, compact with Virginia, act admitting Kentucky into Union, and constitutions of Kentucky. Edition Information: 2d ed. Prepared by John D. Carroll. Published/Created: Louisville, The Courier-Journal Job Printing Company, 1899. Related Authors: Carroll, John Dennis, 1854-1927, ed. Kentucky. Court of Appeals. Description: 3 p. l., 1783 p. 27 cm. LC Classification: KFK1230.1899 .A22

The Kentucky statutes, containing all general laws not included in the codes of practice. With full notes of decisions of the Court of appeals to June, 1903, prefixed by the Magna charta, the Declaration of independence, Articles of confederation, Constitution of United States, naturalization laws of United States, laws relating to removal of actions and prosecutions to United States courts, compact with Virginia, act admitting Kentucky into Union, and constitutions of Kentucky. Edition Information: 3d ed. Prepared by John D. Carroll ... Published/Created: Louisville, The Courier-Journal Job Printing Company, 1903. Related Authors: Carroll, John Dennis, 1854-1927, ed. Kentucky. Court of Appeals. Description: 3 p. l., 1848 p. 27 cm. LC Classification: KFK1230 1963 .A213

The Law and the New Deal / edited, with an introduction, by Melvyn Dubofsky and Stephen Burwood. Published/Created: New York: Garland, 1990. Related Authors: Dubofsky, Melvyn, 1934- Burwood, Stephen. Description: 329 p.: ill.; 24 cm. ISBN: 0824008995 : Notes: Articles originally published 1969-1986. Includes bibliographical references. Subjects: Roosevelt, Franklin D. (Franklin Delano), 1882-1945. War and emergency legislation--United States--History. Courts--United States--History. New Deal, 1933-1939. United States--Economic policy--1933-1945. Series: The Great Depression and the New Deal; 7 LC Classification: KF6011.Z9 L38 1990 Dewey Class No.: 342.73/042 347.30242 20

The Law of administrative tribunals: a collection of judicial decisions, statutes, administrative rules and orders and other materials / by E. Blythe Stason and Frank E. Cooper. Edition Information: 3rd ed. Published/Created: Chicago: Callaghan, [1957]. Related Authors: Stason, E. Blythe (Edwin Blythe), 1891-1972. Cooper, Frank E., 1910- Description: xxix, 747 p.; 26 cm. Notes: Bibliography: p. xix-xx. Subjects: Administrative Courts--United States--Cases. Administrative procedure--United States--Cases. Judicial review of administrative acts--United States Cases. Series: National casebook series. LC Classification: KF5417 .S7 1957 Dewey Class No.: 353

The Law of administrative tribunals: a collection of judicial decisions, statutes, administrative rules and orders and other materials for use in courses on administrative law / by E. Blythe Stason. Edition Information: 2nd ed. Published/Created: Chicago: Callaghan, 1947. Related Authors: Stason, E. Blythe (Edwin Blythe), 1891-1972. Description: xxxi, 731 p. 26 cm. Notes: Includes bibliography and index. Subjects: Administrative Courts--United States--Cases. Administrative procedure--United States--Cases. Judicial review of administrative acts--United States Cases. Series: National casebook series LC Classification: KF5417 .S7 1947

The laws of Alaska; embracing the Penal code, the Code of criminal procedure, the Political code, the Code of civil procedure, the Civil code, with the treaty of session, and all acts and parts of acts relating to the district, annotated with references to decisions by the Courts of the United States and the Supreme court of Oregon. Published/Created: Chicago, Callaghan and company, 1900. Related Authors: Carter, Thomas Henry, 1854-1911, ed. Oregon, Supreme court. United States. Laws, statutes, etc. United States. Courts. Description: xxxix, 533 p. 27 cm. LC Classification: KFA1230.1900 .A425

The lawyer's guide, containing a complete table of Missouri cases, overruled, reversed, modified and distinguished by the United States court, the Supreme court of Missouri and the Missouri Courts of Appeals. Published/Created: Joplin, Mo., Carthage, Mo. [etc.] Mooneyham, Shepherd & Crane, 1909- Related Authors: Crane, Herbert Stanley, comp. Description: 1 v. 20 x 12 cm. Notes: PREMARC/SERLOC merged record LC Classification: LAW

The legal system and American constitutional democracy / editors, Maria Frankowska and Albert P. Melone. Published/Created: Sofia: St. Kliment Ohridski University Press, 1993. Related Authors: Frankowska, Maria. Melone, Albert P. Southern Illinois University Carbondale. American-Bulgarian Symposium on American Courts and the Protection of Democracy and Human Rights (1992: Carbondale, Ill.) Description: 172, 216 p.: 4 maps; 22 cm. Notes: "...consists of twelve studies...prepared under a grant of the United States Information Agency for the American-Bulgarian Symposium on American Courts and the Protection of Democracy and Human Rights. The symposium took place on the SIU-C campus from May 26 to June 6, 1992."--T.p. verso. Subjects: Law--Courts--Justice, Administration of--Civil rights--Constitutional law--United States. LC Classification: KF385.A4 L48 1993 Dewey Class No.: 349.73 21

The Los Angeles daily journal presents with its compliments the following court rules and rules of practice ... Published/Created: [Los Angeles, The Los Angeles daily journal, 1929?] Related Authors: California. Superior court (Los Angeles co.) California. Judicial Council. California. Superior Courts. California. Supreme court. California. District Courts of appeal. United States. District court. California (Southern district) Los Angeles. Municipal court. Long Beach, Calif. Municipal court. United States. Courts. United States. Supreme court. Description: 254 p. 22 cm. Subjects: Court rules--California--Los Angeles co., Calif--United States. Court rules--Los Angeles--Long Beach, Calif. Equity pleading and procedure--Admiralty--United States. LC Classification: KFC992 .A2 1929

The magistracy in England & America. Published/Created: [London, R. Barrett & sons, printers, 1874?] Related Authors: Tallack, William, 1831-1908. Description: 4 p. 22 cm. Subjects: Courts--United States. Courts--Great Britain. LC Classification: HV6327 .H75

The Martindale-Hubbell law directory. Published/Created: New York: Martindale-Hubbell Law Directory, Inc., 1931- Related Authors: Martindale-Hubbell Law Directory, Inc. Martindale-Hubbell, Inc. Martindale-Hubbell (Firm) Description: v.; 26 cm. Each year issued in several vols. arranged by states. 63rd year (1931)- ISSN: 0191-0221 Notes: "Complete legal directory service." Place varies: 1942- <1991: Summit, N.J. Includes unnumbered Alphabetical index and Areas of practice index vols. Supplements accompany some issues. Vols. for 1931-1933 published by Martindale-Hubbell Law Directory, Inc.; for 1934-1990 by Martindale-Hubbell, Inc.; for 1991- by Martindale-Hubbell. SERBIB/SERLOC merged record Formed by the union of: Martindale's American law directory, and: Hubbell's legal directory, and continues the ed. numbering of the former. Vols. for 1990- available also as CD-ROM computer file. Continued in part in 1991 by: Martindale-Hubbell law digest, formerly vol. 8 of the directory; also by: Martindale-Hubbell international law directory. In 1998, the corporate law departments section of this directory was continued by: Martindale-Hubbell corporate law directory. Martindale-Hubbell law directory 1071-7455 (DLC) 93648872 (OCoLC)28698801 Subjects: Lawyers--United States--Directories. Lawyers--Canada--Directories. Law--United States--Digests. Law--Canada--Digests. Patent lawyers--United States--Directories. Patent lawyers--Canada--Directories. Courts--United States--Directories. Courts--Canada--Directories. LC Classification: KF190 .H813

The National directory of Courts of law. Published/Created: Arlington, Va.: Information Resources Press, 1991- Description: v.; 29 cm. 1991- ISSN: 1054-9471 Notes: SERBIB/SERLOC merged record Subjects: Courts--United States--Directories. LC Classification: KF8700.A19 N363 Dewey Class No.: 347.73/1/025 347.3071025 20

The New amendments to the Federal rules of civil procedure / chairman, Paul F. Rothstein. Published/Created: New York (757 3rd Ave., New York 10017): Law & Business, Inc., c1983. Related Authors: Rothstein, Paul F., 1938- United States. Supreme Court. Amendments to the Rules of civil procedure for the U.S. District Courts. 1983. Description: v, 484 p.: ports.; 22 cm. Notes: "Amendments to the Rules of civil procedure for the U.S. District Courts":p. 179-261. Subjects: Civil procedure--United States. Court rules--United States. LC Classification: KF8841 .N48 1983 Dewey Class No.: 347.73/5 347.3075 19

The Pacific law magazine. Published/Created: San Francisco: F. Clarke, 1867. Related Authors: California. Supreme Court. Description: 1 v.; 22 cm. Vol. 1, no. 1 (Jan. 1867)-v. 1, no. 6 (June 1867). Summary: Consists of two parts, the first composed of original essays, important decisions of the Courts, abstracts of recent decisions, notes, reviews and notices of law books, etc., the second composed of decisions of the Supreme Court of California, with notes. Notes: Title from cover. Subjects: Law--United States--Periodicals. Law--California--Periodicals. LC Classification: K16 .A263

The pioneers of judicial behavior / edited by Nancy Maveety. Published/Created: Ann Arbor: University of Michigan Press, 2003. Related Authors: Maveety, Nancy. Description: p. cm. ISBN: 0472098225 (cloth: alk. paper) 0472068229 (paper: alk. paper) Contents: The study of judicial behavior and the discipline of political science / Nancy Maveety -- C. Herman Pritchett: innovator with an ambiguous legacy / Lawrence Baum -- Glendon Schubert: the judicial mind / Jeffrey A. Segal -- S. Sidney Ulmer: the multidimensionality of judicial decision making / Robert C. Bradley -- Harold J. Spaeth: the Supreme Court computer / Sara C. Benesh -- Joseph Tanenhaus: the "learned discipline" of public law / Robert A. Carp -- Beverly Blair Cook: the value of eclecticism / Lee Epstein and Lynn Mather -- Walter F. Murphy: the interactive nature of judicial decision making / Lee Epstein and Jack Knight -- J. Woodford Howard Jr.: fluidity, strategy, and analytical synthesis in judicial studies / Nancy Maveety and John Anthony Maltese -- David J. Danelski: social psychology and group choice / Thomas G. Walker -- David Rohde: rational choice theorist / Saul Brenner -- Edward S. Corwin as public scholar / Cornell W. Clayton -- Alpheus Thomas Mason: piercing the judicial veil / Sue Davis -- Robert G. McCloskey, historical institutionalism, and the arts of judicial governance / Howard Gillman -- Robert Dahl: democracy, judicial review, and the study of law and Courts / David Adamany and Stephen Meinhold -- Martin Shapiro: anticipating the new institutionalism / Herbert M. Kritzer. Notes: Includes index. Subjects: Judicial process--United States. LC Classification: KF8775 .P56 2003 Dewey Class No.: 347.73/1 21

The Political role of law Courts in modern democracies / edited by Jerold L. Waltman and Kenneth M. Holland. Published/Created: New York: St. Martin's Press, 1988. Related Authors: Waltman, Jerold L., 1945- Holland, Kenneth M. Description: ix, 237 p.: ill.; 23 cm. ISBN: 0312003838 : Contents: Introduction / Jerold L. Waltman -- The Courts in the United States / Kenneth M. Holland -- The Courts in Australia / Roman Tomasic -- The Courts in Canada / Carl Baar -- The Courts in the Federal Republic of Germany / Kenneth M. Holland -- The Courts in England / Jerold L. Waltman -- The Courts in France / Dallis Radamaker -- The Courts in Italy / Giuseppe Di Federico and Carlo Guarnieri -- The Courts in Sweden / Joseph B. Board -- The Courts in Japan / Hiroshi Itoh -- The Courts and political change in post-industrial society / Jerold L. Waltman. Notes: Includes bibliographies and index. Subjects: Courts. Political questions and judicial power. Judicial process. LC Classification: K2100 .P65 1988 Dewey Class No.: 347/.01 342.71 19

The Politics of judicial reform / edited by Philip L. Dubois. Lexington, Mass.: LexingtonBooks, c1982. Related Authors: Dubois, Philip L. Description: xi, 187 p.; 24 cm. ISBN: 0669044784 Notes: Includes bibliographies and index. Subjects: Courts--United States. Series: Policy Studies Organization series (Unnumbered) LC Classification: KF8719 .P64 1982 Dewey Class No.: 347.73/1 347.3071 19

The Presentence investigation report. Edition Information: Jan. 1978 (rev. Sept. 1978, Apr. 1984) Published/Created: Washington, D.C.: Division of Probation, Administrative Office of the U.S. Courts, 1984. Description: vii, 61 p.: forms; 28 cm. Notes: Item 729 Subjects: Pre-sentence investigation reports--United States. Series: Publication (United States. Administrative Office of the United States Courts); 105. LC Classification: KF9685 .A875 1984 Dewey Class No.: 345.73/0772 347.305772 19 Govt. Doc. No.: Ju 10.2:P 92/2

The Press and the Courts: competing principles: held on October 3, 1978, and sponsored by the American Enterprise Institute for Public Policy Research, Washington, D.C. / John Charles Daly, moderator; Jack C. Landau ... [et. al.]. Published/Created: Washington: The Institute, c1978. Related Authors: Daly, John Charles, 1914- Landau, Jack C. American Enterprise Institute for Public Policy Research. Description: 37 p.; 21 cm. ISBN: 0844721425 : Subjects: Freedom of the press--United States. Crime and the press--United States. Series: American Enterprise Institute for Public Policy Research. AEI public policy forum; 23. LC Classification: KF4775.Z9 P74 Dewey Class No.: 342/.73/085

The Problems of juvenile Courts and the rights of children / [edited by] Monrad G. Paulsen. Published/Created: Philadelphia: American Law Institute-American Bar Association, Committee on Continuing Professional Education, c1975. Related Authors: Paulsen, Monrad G. Description: xii, 176 p.; 22 cm. Notes: Bibliography: p. 173-174. Subjects: Juvenile Courts--United States. LC Classification: KF9709 .P76 Dewey Class No.: 345/.73/08

The Process of government; lectures by Simeon S. Willis [and others. Published/Created: Lexington] Bureau of Govt. Research, University of Kentucky, 1949. Related Authors: Willis, Simeon S., 1879-1965. University of Kentucky. Bureau of Government Research. Description: 63 p. 23 cm. Contents: The judicial process and the executive function, by S. S. Willis.--The judicial process in Federal District Courts, by M. Swinford.--The majority leader in the legislative process, by A. W. Barkley.--The administrative process: Federal and local, by W. W. Wyatt. Subjects: Legislative bodies--United States. Justice, Administration of. United States--Politics and government--20th century. LC Classification: JK273 .P74 Dewey Class No.: 320.4

The public image of courts: highlights of a national survey of the general public, judges, lawyers, and community leaders: state courts, a blueprint for the future March 19-22, 1978 / prepared for the National Center for State Courts by Yankelovich, Skelly and White, inc. Published/Created: [Denver]: National Center for State Courts, c1978. Related Authors: National Center for State Courts. Yankelovich, Skelly, and White, inc. Description: iii, 65 p.; 28 cm. Notes: Cover title. Subjects: Courts--United States--Public opinion. Public opinion--United States. LC Classification: KF8700.Z9 N28 1978 Dewey Class No.: 301.15/43/347731

The Reporter: containing decisions of the Supreme and circuit Courts of the United States, Courts of last resort in the several states, and the English Courts. Published/Created: Boston, Houghton, Mifflin and company; Cambridge, The Riverside press; [etc., etc., 1876]-88. Related Authors: Ellis, Howard, 1834-1902, ed. Cox, Rowland, ed. Description: v. 26 cm. Subjects: Law reports, digests, etc.--United States. Law reports, digests, etc.--Great Britain. LC Classification: KF105 .R46

The Restatement in the Courts / American Law Institute. Edition Information: 2nd ed. Published/Created: [St. Paul]: The Institute, 1935. Description: 354 p.; 23 cm. Notes: Cover title. Includes bibliographical references. Subjects: Law--United States--Digests. LC Classification: KF395 .A3 1935

The revised statutes of South Carolina ... Published/Created: Columbia, S.C., C.A. Calvo, jr., state printer, 1894. Related Authors: Maher, John J., b. 1827, ed. Breazeale, John E., ed. South Carolina. Supreme Court. South Carolina. Circuit Courts. Description: 2 v. 24 cm. Contents: v. 1. The Civil statutes, approved by the General assembly of 1893.--v. 2. The Code of civil procedure, and the Criminal statutes. Approved by the General assembly of 1893. Also the constitutions of the United States and of the state, and the rules of the Supreme and of the Circuit Courts of the state. Notes: Revision begun by John J. Maher, completed by John E. Breazeale. Subjects: Court rules--South Carolina. LC Classification: LAW

The Role of Courts in American society: the final report of the Council on the Role of Courts / principal editor, Jethro K. Lieberman. Published/Created: St. Paul, Minn.: West Pub. Co., 1984. Related Authors: Lieberman, Jethro Koller. Council on the Role of Courts (U.S.) Description: xiii, 171 p.; 25 cm. Notes: Includes bibliographies. Subjects: Courts--United States. Judicial power--United States. Public policy (Law)--United States. Sociological jurisprudence. LC Classification: KF8700 .R63 1984 Dewey Class No.: 347.73/1 347.3071 19

The Significance of judicial structure: the effect of unification on trial court operations / research team, Thomas A. Henderson ... [et al.]. Published/Created: Washington, D.C.: U.S. Dept. of Justice, National Institute of Justice, 1984. Related Authors: Henderson, Thomas A. Description: iiii, 187 p.; 28 cm. Notes: "Supported by grant numbers 79-NI-AX-0075 and 80-IJ-CX-0095, awarded to the Institute for Economic and Policy Studies, Inc. by the National Institute of Justice, U.S. Department of Justice"--T.p. verso. "March 1984." Item 718-A Bibliography: p. 180-187. Subjects: Courts--Court administration--United States--States. Series: NIJ research report LC Classification: KF8736 .S6 1984 Dewey Class No.: 347.73/3 347.3073 19 Govt. Doc. No.: J 28.2:J 89

The sourcebook of federal Courts, U.S. district and bankruptcy: the definitive guide to searching for case information at the local level within the federal court system. Edition Information: 2nd ed. Published/Created: Tempe, Ariz.: BRB Publications, 1996. Related Authors: BRB Publications. Description: 410 p.: maps; 28 cm. ISBN: 1879792257 Subjects: Courts--District Courts--Bankruptcy--United States--Directories. Series: The public record research library LC Classification: KF8700.A19 S65 1996

The sourcebook of federal Courts, U.S. district and bankruptcy: the definitive guide to searching for case information at the local level within the federal court system. Published/Created: Tempe, Ariz.: BRB Publications, c1993. Related Authors: BRB Publications. Description: 1 v. (various pagings): maps; 28 cm. ISBN: 1879792109 Subjects: Courts--United States--Directories. Bankruptcy--United States--Directories. Series: The public record research library LC Classification: KF8700.A19 S65 1993 Dewey Class No.: 347.73/2/025 347.307205 20

The sourcebook of local court and county record retrievers: the national guide of information retrievers who pull files and documents from US, state, and local Courts and from county agencies. Published/Created: Tempe, Ariz.: BRB Publications, c1993. Related Authors: BRB Publications. Description: xv, 431 p.; 28 cm. ISBN: 1879792095 Notes: On spine: A PRRL sourcebook. Subjects: Court records--Research--United States--Directories. Public records--Research--United States--Directories. Legal research--United States--Directories. Series: The public record research library LC Classification: KF8700.A19 S66 1993 Dewey Class No.: 025.5/24/02573 20

The third branch. Published/Created: [Washington, D.C.: Federal Judicial Center, 1968- Related Authors: Federal Judicial Center. United States. Administrative Office of the United States Courts. United States. Administrative Office of the United States Courts. Office of Legislative and Public Affairs. United States. Administrative Office of the United States Courts. Office of Congressional, External, & Public Affairs. United States. Administrative Office of the United States Courts. Office of Public Affairs. Description: v.: ill.; 28 cm. Vol. 1, no. 1 (Dec. 1968)- ISSN: 0040-6120 Notes: Title from caption. Not distributed to depository libraries in a physical form, May 2001- Vols. for -19 issued by: Administrative Office the U.S. Courts; <1990-199 by: Administrative Office of the U.S. Courts, Office of Legislative and Public Affairs; <1996-199 by: Administrative Office of the U.S. Courts, Office of Congressional, External & Public Affairs; Administrative Office of the U.S. Courts, Office of Public Affairs. SERBIB/SERLOC merged record Subjects: Courts--United States--Periodicals. LC Classification: KF8700.A16 T45 Dewey Class No.: 347.99/73 Govt. Doc. No.: JU 10.3/2:

The Trial of a civil action in the federal Courts and the prosecution and defense of federal criminal cases [sound recording]. Published/Created: Philadelphia, Pa.: American Law Institute-American Bar Association Committee on Continuing Professional Education, p1978. Related Authors: American Law Institute-American Bar Association Committee on Continuing Professional Education. Association of the Bar of the City of New York. Description: 36 sound cassettes. Summary: Presents a judge's overview of helpful techniques and skills in a civil action. Other speakers discuss avenues to speedy disposition, significant pretrial efforts in a civil action, federal rules of evidence, the trial of a commercial case, the trial of a corporate and an environmental action, special problems of grand jury investigations, communicating with the judge in a civil nonjury trial, and other aspects of the topic. Notes: American Law Institute-American Bar Association Committee on Continuing Professional Education: V436-V453. Lectures and discussions. "Second series." Recorded in the House of the Association of the Bar of the City of New York, Jan.-June, 1978. LC copy imperfect: 14 cassettes wanting. Subjects: Trial practice--United States. LC Classification: KF8915 RYA 2381-2400, 2411-2412

The Trial of an action in the federal Courts [sound recording] / Association of the Bar of the City of New York. Published/Created: Philadelphia, Pa.: American Law Institute-American Bar Association Committee on Continuing Professional Education, c1979. Description: 9 sound cassettes. Contents:

session no. 1. Recent developments under the federal rules of evidence 3/21/79 (2 cassettes) -- session no. 2. Complex litigation 3/26/79 (2 cassettes) -- session no. 3. Techniques of trial and Appellate proceedings 4/19/79 -- session no. 5. The expedited trial 5/9/79 (2 cassettes) -- session no. 6. Handling the expert witness 5/16/79 (2 cassettes) Notes: Lectures and discussion. In loose-leaf binder with study materials (29 cm.) Intended audience: Lawyers. Recorded in New York City, Mar.-May, 1979. Subjects: Procedure (Law)--United States. Evidence (Law)--United States. LC Classification: KF8841 RZA 0036

The United States Court of Appeals for the Federal Circuit: a history, 1982-1990. Published/Created: [Washington, D.C.?]: United States Judicial Conference Committee on the Bicentennial of the Constitution of the United States, 1991. Description: xxi, 369 p.: ill. (some col.); 29 cm. Notes: Distributed to some depository libraries in microfiche. Shipping list no.: 91-478-P. Item 734 Includes bibliographical references. Subjects: United States. Court of Appeals (Federal Circuit) History. Appellate Courts--United States--History. Judges--United States--Biography. LC Classification: KF8751 .U55 1991 Dewey Class No.: 347.73/24/03 347.3072403 20 Govt. Doc. No.: Ju 7.2:H 62/2

The United States Courts of Appeals: reexamining structure and process after a century of growth: report of the American Bar Association Standing Committee on Federal Judicial Improvements. Published/Created: [Chicago]: American Bar Association, c1989. Related Authors: American Bar Association. Standing Committee on Federal Judicial Improvements. Description: ii, 51 p.; 23 cm. LC Classification: MLCM 98/02495 (K)

The use/nonuse/misuse of applied social research in the courts / edited by Michael J. Saks, Charles H. Baron. Published/Created: Cambridge, Mass.: Published for the Council for Applied Social Research by Abt Books, c1980. Related Authors: Saks, Michael J. Baron, Charles H., 1936- Description: ix, 189 p.: ill.; 24 cm. ISBN: 0890115443 : Notes: Includes bibliographies and index. Subjects: Social sciences--Research--United States. Courts--United States--Sociological jurisprudence--Social psychology--Psychology, Forensic--Congresses. LC Classification: KF4280.S6 C66 1978 Dewey Class No.: 347.73/1/0724 347.30710724 19

The Utah legal directory. Published/Created: Dallas, Tex.: Legal Directories Pub. Co., c1996- Description: v.; 24 cm. 1996- ISSN: 1094-4796 Notes: SERBIB/SERLOC merged record Subjects: Lawyers--Utah--Directories--Periodicals. Courts--United States--Directories--Periodicals. Courts--Utah--Directories--Periodicals. LC Classification: KF192.U8 U82 Dewey Class No.: 340/.025/792 21

Traffic court justice. Published/Created: [Chicago, Ill.]: Traffic Court Program, American Bar Association, [1958- Related Authors: American Bar Association. Traffic Court Program. Description: 14 v.: ill.; 32 cm. [Vol. 1, no. 1] ([July 1958])- Ceased publication: v. 14, no. 1 (Jan. 1973). Notes: Title from caption. Subjects: Traffic Courts--United States--Periodicals. LC Classification: KF2232.A73 T7

Traffic officer in court. Edition Information: 3rd ed. Published/Created: Evanston, Ill. (555 Clark St., Evanston 60204): Traffic Institute, Northwestern University, 1981. Related Authors: Northwestern University (Evanston, Ill.). Traffic Institute. Description: 7 p.: ill.; 28 cm. Notes: Includes bibliographical references. Subjects: Traffic Courts--United States. Traffic police--United States. Series: Traffic law enforcement series; no. 552 LC Classification: KF2232.Z9 T7 1981 Dewey Class No.: 347.73/66 347.30766 19

Trial court performance standards and measurement system / Bureau of Justice

Assistance. Published/Created: Washington, DC: The Bureau, [1997] Description: ix, 34 p.; 28 cm. Notes: "Prepared by the National Center for State Courts"--P. [2] of cover. Shipping list no.: 97-0369-P. "July 1997." Includes bibliographical references (p. 17-19). Subjects: Courts of first instance--United States--States Standards. Courts of first instance--United States--States Evaluation. Series: Program brief (United States. Bureau of Justice Assistance) LC Classification: KF8736 .T75 1997 Dewey Class No.: 347.73/13 21 Govt. Doc. No.: J 26.31:T 73

Trial court performance standards and measurement system implementation manual / Bureau of Justice Assistance. Published/Created: Washington, DC: The Bureau, [1997] Description: 1 v. (various pagings): forms; 28 cm. Notes: "Prepared by the National Center for State Courts"--Verso t.p. Shipping list no.: 97-0067-S. "July 1997." Includes bibliographical references. Subjects: Courts of first instance--United States--States Standards. Courts of first instance--United States--States Evaluation. Series: Monograph (United States. Bureau of Justice Assistance) LC Classification: KF8736 .T752 1997 Dewey Class No.: 347.73/1 21 Govt. Doc. No.: J 26.30:T 73/2

Trial court performance standards with commentary / Bureau of Justice Assistance. Published/Created: Washington, DC: The Bureau, [1997] Related Authors: United States. Bureau of Justice Assistance. National Center for State Courts. Description: xi, 50 p.: ill.; 28 cm. Notes: "Prepared by the National Center for State Courts"--P. [2] of cover. Shipping list no.: 97-0366-P. "July 1997." Includes bibliographical references (p. 35-37). Subjects: Courts of first instance--United States--States Standards. Series: Monograph (United States. Bureau of Justice Assistance) LC Classification: KF8736 .T753 1997 Dewey Class No.: 347.73/13 21 Govt. Doc. No.: J 26.30:T 73

Trial evidence and techniques in federal and state Courts: a clinical study of recent developments: ALI-ABA course of study materials. Published/Created: Philadelphia, Pa. (4025 Chestnut St., Philadelphia 19104): American Law Institute-American Bar Association Committee on Continuing Professional Education, c1983. Related Authors: American Law Institute-American Bar Association Committee on Continuing Professional Education. Description: xi, 247 p.; 28 cm. Notes: Spine title: Trial evidence in federal and state Courts. "ALI-ABA course of study, trial evidence and techniques in federal and state Courts, January 13-14, 1983, Los Angeles, California"--P. v. "C708." Includes bibliographical references. Subjects: Evidence (Law)--United States. LC Classification: KF8935.Z9 T74 1983 Dewey Class No.: 347.73/6 347.3076 19

Trial evidence and techniques in federal and state Courts: a clinical study of recent developments: ALI-ABA course of study materials. Published/Created: Philadelphia, Pa. (4025 Chestnut St., Philadelphia 19104): American Law Institute-American Bar Association Committee on Continuing Professional Education, c1983. Related Authors: American Law Institute-American Bar Association Committee on Continuing Professional Education. Description: xv, 323 p.; 28 cm. Subjects: Evidence (Law)--United States. LC Classification: KF8935.Z9 T74 1983a Dewey Class No.: 347.73/6 347.3076 19

Trial evidence and techniques in federal and state Courts: a clinical study of recent developments: ALI-ABA course of study materials / cosponsored by the Committee of Continuing Legal Education of the Virginia Law Foundation. Published/Created: [Philadelphia, Pa.] (4025 Chestnut St., Philadelphia 19104): American Law Institute-American Bar Association Committee on Continuing Professional Education, c1983. Related Authors: Virginia Law Foundation. Committee on Continuing Legal Education. American Law Institute-American Bar Association Committee on

Continuing Professional Education. Description: xii, 353 p.; 28 cm. Notes: "ALI-ABA course of study ... December 8-9, 1983, Arlington, Virginia"--P. v. "C776." Subjects: Evidence (Law)--United States. LC Classification: KF8935.Z9 T74 1983b Dewey Class No.: 347.73/6 347.3076 19

Trial evidence and techniques in federal and state Courts: a clinical study of recent developments: ALI-ABA course of study materials / cosponsored by the Michigan Institute of CLE. Published/Created: Philadelphia, Pa. (4025 Chestnut St., Philadelphia 19104): American Law Institute-American Bar Association Committee on Continuing Professional Education, c1984. Related Authors: Michigan Institute of CLE. American Law Institute-American Bar Association Committee on Continuing Professional Education. Description: xii, 366 p.; 28 cm. Notes: "C886." "August 16-17, 1984, Southfield, Michigan"--P. v. Subjects: Evidence (Law)--United States. LC Classification: KF8935.Z9 T74 1984 Dewey Class No.: 347.73/6 347.3076 19

Trial evidence and techniques in federal and state Courts: a clinical study of recent developments: ALI-ABA course of study materials / cosponsored by the South Carolina Bar. Published/Created: [Philadelphia, Pa.] (4025 Chestnut St., Philadelphia 19104): American Law Institute-American Bar Association Committee on Continuing Professional Education, c1982. Related Authors: South Carolina Bar. American Law Institute-American Bar Association Committee on Continuing Professional Education. Description: xii, 345 p.; 28 cm. Notes: Held in Charleston, S.C. Sept. 30-Oct. 2, 1982. "C688." Includes bibliographical references. Subjects: Evidence (Law)--United States. LC Classification: KF8935.Z9 T74 1982 Dewey Class No.: 347.73/6 347.3076 19

Trial evidence and techniques in federal Courts: a clinical study of recent developments: ALI-ABA course of study materials / cosponsored by California Continuing Education of the Bar. Published/Created: [Philadelphia, Pa.] (4025 Chestnut St., Philadelphia 19104): American Law Institute-American Bar Association Committee on Continuing Professional Education, c1982. Related Authors: American Law Institute-American Bar Association Committee on Continuing Professional Education. California Continuing Education of the Bar. Description: xii, 233 p.; 28 cm. Notes: Course held Feb. 25-27, 1982, in San Franciso, Calif. "C644." Subjects: Evidence (Law)--United States. LC Classification: KF8935.Z9 T743 1982 Dewey Class No.: 347.73/6 347.3076 19

Trial evidence in federal and state Courts [sound recording]: ALI-ABA course of study / [panelists, Frederick B.] Lacey ... [et al.]. Published/Created: Philadelphia, Pa.: American Law Institute-American Bar Association Committee on Continuing Professional Education, c1980. Related Authors: Lacey, Frederick B. American Law Institute-American Bar Association Committee on Continuing Professional Education. Villanova University. School of Law. Description: 7 sound cassettes + 1 blank cassette. Summary: Discusses federal rules of evidence, relevancy, unfair prejudice, witnesses, sequestration of witnesses, doctor-patient privilege, hearsay, sample evidence, etc. Notes: Sponsored with the cooperation of Villanova University School of Law. In loose-leaf binder with study materials (29 cm.) Intended audience: Lawyers. Recorded on June 19-20, 1980, at the ALI-ABA course of study: Civil practice and litigation in federal and state Courts, held June 16-20, 1980. Subjects: Evidence (Law)--United States. LC Classification: KF8935 RZA 0055

Trial evidence in the federal Courts: problems and solutions in the '90s: ALI-ABA course of study materials: July 21-22, 1994, San Francisco, California / cosponsored by California Continuing Education of the Bar. Published/Created: Philadelphia, PA (4025 Chestnut St., Philadelphia 19104-

3099): American Law Institute-American Bar Association Committee on Continuing Professional Education, c1994. Related Authors: Continuing Education of the Bar--California. American Law Institute-American Bar Association Committee on Continuing Professional Education. Description: xii, 115 p.; 28 cm. Notes: "C914." Subjects: Evidence (Law)--United States. LC Classification: KF8935.Z9 T763 1994 Dewey Class No.: 347.73/06 347.3076 20

Trial evidence in the federal Courts: problems and solutions in the '90s: ALI-ABA course of study materials: June 17-18, 1993, Washington, D.C. / cosponsored by George Washington University, National Law Center. Published/Created: Philadelphia, PA (4025 Chestnut St., Philadelphia 19104-3099): American Law Institute-American Bar Association Committee on Continuing Professional Education, c1993. Related Authors: George Washington University. National Law Center. American Law Institute-American Bar Association Committee on Continuing Professional Education. Description: xii, 595 p.; 28 cm. Notes: "C829." Subjects: Evidence (Law)--United States. LC Classification: KF8935.Z9 T76 1993 Dewey Class No.: 347.73/6 347.3076 20

Trial evidence in the federal Courts: problems and solutions in the '90s: ALI-ABA course of study materials: June 6-7, 1996, San Francisco, California / cosponsored by California Continuing Education of the Bar. Published/Created: Philadelphia, PA (4025 Chestnut St., Philadelphia 19104-3099): American Law Institute-American Bar Association Committee on Continuing Professional Education, c1996. Related Authors: Continuing Education of the Bar--California. American Law Institute-American Bar Association Committee on Continuing Professional Education. Description: x, 93 p.; 28 cm. Notes: "SA55." Subjects: Evidence (Law)--United States. LC Classification: KF8935.Z9 T763 1996 Dewey Class No.: 347.73/6 347.3076 20

Trial evidence in the federal Courts: problems and solutions: ALI-ABA course of study materials: July 23-24, 1998, San Francisco, California / sponsored with the cooperation of the ABA Section of Litigation. Published/Created: Philadelphia, PA (4025 Chestnut St., Philadelphia 19104-3099): American Law Institute, c1998. Related Authors: American Bar Association. Section of Litigation. American Law Institute. Description: xxiv, 261 p.: ill., forms; 28 cm. Notes: "7/98"--Spine. "SD05." Subjects: Evidence (Law)--United States. LC Classification: KF8935.Z9 T763 1998 Dewey Class No.: 347.73/6 21

Trial evidence in the federal Courts: problems and solutions: ALI-ABA course of study materials: June 5-6, 1997, Charleston, South Carolina. Published/Created: Philadelphia, PA (4025 Chestnut St., Philadelphia 19104-3099): American Law Institute-American Bar Association Committee on Continuing Professional Education, c1997. Related Authors: American Law Institute-American Bar Association Committee on Continuing Professional Education. Description: xx, 134 p.; 28 cm. Notes: "SB67." Subjects: Evidence (Law)--United States. LC Classification: KF8935.Z9 T763 1997 Dewey Class No.: 347.73/6 21

Trial evidence, civil practice, and effective litigation techniques in federal and state Courts: ALI-ABA course of study materials. Published/Created: Philadelphia, PA: American Law Institute-American Bar Association Committee on Continuing Professional Education, Related Authors: American Law Institute-American Bar Association Committee on Continuing Professional Education. Description: v.; 28 cm. Vols. for 1988-<1989 issued in two vols. ISSN: 1045-2176 Notes: Description based on: 1985. Supplements accompany some issues. SERBIB/SERLOC merged record Subjects: Evidence (Law)--United States. Civil procedure--United States. Actions and defenses--United States. LC Classification: KF8935.Z9 T75 Dewey Class No.: 347.73/6/05 347.307605 20

Trial judges news / National Conference of State Trial Judges. Published/Created: Chicago: The Conference, 1981- Description: v.; 28 cm. Vol. 1, no. 1 (Oct. 1981)- Notes: Caption title. SERBIB/SERLOC merged record Beginning in summer 1998, only available as a section of: Judicial Division record. Subjects: National Conference of State Trial Judges. Judges--Courts--United States--States--Periodicals. Courts--Justice, Administration of--United States--States. LC Classification: KF8785.A15 T75 Dewey Class No.: 347.73/14/05 347.3071405 19

Trial of an administrative case / chairman, William J. Kolasky, Jr. Published/Created: New York: Law & Business, Inc., c1985. Related Authors: Kolasky, William J. Law & Business, inc. Description: iii, 112 p.: ill.; 22 cm. Notes: "CO3999"--P. [4] of cover. Subjects: Administrative Courts--United States. Trial practice--United States. LC Classification: KF5417.Z9 T75 1985 Dewey Class No.: 342.73/0664 347.302664 19

Trow's legal directory and lawyers' record of the United States:bcontaining a convenient and comprehensive digest of the laws of the several states touching subjects of commercial law, laws relating to estates of decedents and descent of property, and the insolvent laws of the several states, blank legal forms and instructions for taking depositions; Published/Created: New York, A. S. Barnes & co. [etc., c1872-] Related Authors: Trow, John Fowler, 1810-1886. Ulma, Hezekieth Charles, ed. Description: v. 25 cm. Notes: Serial. PREMARC/SERLOC merged record Subjects: Lawyers--United States--Directories. Courts--United States. Forms (Law)--United States. Commercial law--United States Inheritance and succession--United States. LC Classification: KF190 .T76

Twenty years of courthouse design revisited: supplement to the American courthouse / the American Bar Association, Judicial Administration Division, the National Center for State Courts, State Justice Institute. Published/Created: Chicago, IL: American Bar Association, c1993. Related Authors: American Bar Association. Judicial Administration Division. National Center for State Courts. State Justice Institute (U.S.) Description: xv, 232 p.: ill., plans; 28 cm. ISBN: 0897077601 Notes: "This project is supported by a grant (No. SJI-88-05X-B-072) to the National Center for State Courts from the State Justice Institute." Includes bibliographical references (p. 230-232). Subjects: Courthouses--United States. Courthouses--Designs and plans. LC Classification: NA4471 .T93 1993 Dewey Class No.: 725/.15/0973 20

U.S. court cases / edited by the editors of Salem Press. Published/Created: Pasadena, Calif.: Salem Press, c1999. Related Authors: Salem Press. Description: 2 v. (xvi, 614 p.): ill.; 24 cm. ISBN: 0893564222 (set: alk. paper) 0893564230 (v. 1: alk. paper) 0893564249 (v. 2: alk. paper) Notes: Includes bibliographical references (p. 573-593) and index. Subjects: Law--United States--Cases. Courts--United States. Series: Magill's choice LC Classification: KF385.A4 U15 1999 Dewey Class No.: 347.73/1 21

Uncertain justice: politics and America's Courts: the reports of the Task Forces of Citizens for Independent Courts. Published/Created: New York: Century Foundation Press, 2000. Related Authors: Citizens for Independent Courts. Century Foundation. Description: xi, 242 p.: ill.; 24 cm. ISBN: 087078448X (pbk.) Contents: Justice held hostage: politics and selecting federal judges: the report of the Citizens for Independent Courts Task Force on Federal Judicial Selection -- Choosing justice: reforming the selection of state judges: the report of the Citizens for Independent Courts Task Force on Selecting State Court Judges -- Balancing act: legislative power and judicial independence: the report of the Citizens for Independent Courts Task Force on the Role of the Legislature in Setting the Power and Jurisdiction of the Courts -- Defending justice: the Courts, criticism, and intimidation: the report of the Citizens for Independent Courts Task Force on the Distinction Between Intimidation and Legitimate Criticism of Judges. Notes: "A publication of Citizens for Independent Courts, a project of the Century Foundation." Includes bibliographical references and index. Subjects: Judicial process--United States. Judges--Selection and appointment--United States. Law reform--United States. Law and politics--United States. LC Classification: KF8775 .U52 2000 Dewey Class No.: 347.73/1 21

Understanding reversible error in criminal appeals: final report / submitted to the State Justice Institute by National Center for State Courts; Joy A. Chapper, co-project director, Roger A. Hanson, co-project director. Published/Created: Williamsburg, Va.: The Center, c1989. Related Authors: Chapper, Joy A. Hanson, Roger A. National Center for State Courts. State Justice Institute (U.S.) Description: x, 50 p.; 23 cm. ISBN: 0896560953 Notes: Cover title: Three papers on understanding reversible error in criminal appeals. Includes bibliographical references (p. 49-50). Subjects: Appellate procedure--United States. Criminal procedure--United States. Judicial error--United States. Series: Publication (National Center for State Courts); R113. LC Classification: KF9690 .U53 1989 Dewey Class No.: 345.73/05 347.3055 20

Understanding the federal Courts. Edition Information: 2nd ed. Published/Created: Washington, D.C.: Administrative Office of the U.S. Courts, [1996?] Related Authors: United States. Administrative Office of the United States Courts. Description: 27 leaves: ill., map; 22 x 28 cm. Notes: Cover title. Shipping list no.: 96-0340-P. Subjects: Courts--United States. Court administration--United States. LC Classification: KF8700 .U53 1996 Dewey Class No.: 347.73/2 21 Govt. Doc. No.: JU 10.2:C 83/3/996

Understanding the federal Courts. Published/Created: [Washington, D.C.?]: Administrative Office of the U.S. Courts, [1992?] Related Authors: United States. Administrative Office of the United States Courts. Description: 27 leaves: ill.; 22 x 28 cm. Notes: Item 0729 Cover title. Shipping list no.: 92-0548-P. Subjects: Courts--United States. Court administration--United States. LC Classification: KF8700 .U53 1992 Dewey Class No.: 347.73/2 347.3072 20 Govt. Doc. No.: Ju 10.2:C 83/3

Understanding the law: equal justice for all [Motion picture] Published/Created: [n.p.] Encyclopædia Britannica Films, 1953. Related Authors: Encyclopædia Britannica Films, inc. Description: p. 12 min., sd., b&w, 16 mm. Notes: With teacher's guide. SUMMARY: Describes the operation of the United States court system and explains the principles which guarantee protection to every citizen through due process of law. Includes scenes of staged courtroom trials in which legal procedures and demonstrated. CREDITS: Associate producer, Milan Herzog; collaborator, Robert K. Carr. Subjects: Courts--United States. Justice, Administration of--United States.

Uniform traffic ticket and complaint and Model rules governing procedure in traffic cases; a guide designed to assist traffic judges in court and police aspects. Published/Created: [Lansing, Mich., Weger Governmental Systems, 1958] Related Authors: National Conference of Commissioners on Uniform State Laws. Description: 21 p. forms. 28 cm. Notes: Model rules governing procedure in traffic cases were approved by the National Conference of Commissioners on Uniform State Laws in 1957. Subjects: Traffic violations--Traffic Courts--United States. LC Classification: KF2230.Z95 A44 Dewey Class No.: 345/.73/0247

United States Courts in the Second Circuit: a collection of history lectures delivered by judges of the Second Circuit. Published/Created: New York, N.Y. (145 E. 49th St., New York 10017): Federal Bar Council Foundation, 1992. Description: iv,

164 p.; 28 cm. Notes: Includes bibliographical references. Subjects: United States. Court of Appeals (2nd Circuit)--History. LC Classification: KF8752 2nd .U55 1992 Dewey Class No.: 347.7324 347.3072 20

United States District Courts sentences imposed chart. Published/Created: Washington, D.C.: Administrative Office of the United States Courts: [Supt. of Docs., U.S. G.P.O., distributor, [1977-1990?] Description: 14 v.; 28 cm. For the 12 month period ended June 30, 1977- Ceased with 1989/1990 issue. Notes: Title from cover. SERBIB/SERLOC merged record Statistics for earlier years included in the D series of: United States. Administrative Office of the United States Courts. Annual report of the Director for the twelve month period ending ... United States. Administrative Office of the United States Courts. Annual report of the Director for the twelve month period ending ... (DLC) 74648849 Subjects: Sentences (Criminal procedure)--United States--Statistics Periodicals. Criminal statistics--United States--Periodicals. LC Classification: KF183 .A37 Dewey Class No.: 345/.73/077 Govt. Doc. No.: Ju 10.18:

United States lawyers reference directory. Published/Created: Los Angeles: Legal Directories Pub. Co., Description: v.; 24 cm. Issues for <2000-2001- published in 5 vols. 1967- Ceased with 2001 ed. Notes: Some vols. issued in a loose-leaf format. Published: Dallas, Tex., 1991- SERBIB/SERLOC merged record Subjects: Lawyers--Courts--United States--Directories. LC Classification: KF190 .U5 Dewey Class No.: 340/.025/73

United States. Bureau of labor statistics of the United States series. Published/Created: Washington, Govt. print. off., 1913- Related Authors: United States. Bureau of labor. United States. Laws, statutes, etc. Description: v. fold. tab. 24 cm. Subjects: Labor laws and legislation--Courts--United States. LC Classification: HD8051 .A62

Update on the Courts / American Bar Association Special Committee on Youth Education for Citizenship. Published/Created: [Chicago, IL]: The Committee, [1992- Related Authors: ABA Special Committee on Youth Education for Citizenship. Description: v.: ill.; 28 cm. Began with v. 1, no. 1 in 1992. ISSN: 1066-0194 Notes: Description based on: Vol. 3, no. 2 (winter 1995); title from caption. SERBIB/SERLOC merged record Subjects: Justice, Administration of--Courts--United States--Periodicals. LC Classification: KF8700.A16 U63 Dewey Class No.: 347.73 347.307 20

Views from the bench: the judiciary and constitutional politics / collected and edited by Mark W. Cannon and David M. O'Brien; with introductions by David M. O'Brien; foreword by Warren E. Burger. Published/Created: Chatham, N.J.: Chatham House Publishers, c1985. Related Authors: Cannon, Mark W. O'Brien, David M. Description: xxii, 330 p.: ill.; 23 cm. ISBN: 0934540330 (pbk.): 0934540349 (hard) : Notes: Includes indexes. Bibliography: p. 303-316. Subjects: Judicial process--Courts--Political questions and judicial power--United States. Series: Chatham House series on change in American politics LC Classification: KF8775.A75 V53 1985 Dewey Class No.: 347.73 347.307 19

Virgin Islands reports: containing opinions of Courts of record, and others, relating to the Virgin Islands. Published/Created: Orford, N.H.: Equity Pub. Corp., c1959- Description: v.; 24 cm. Vols. 1-3 issued together; v. 2 (1940-1953); v. 3 (1954-1958); v. 4 (1959-1964). Report year irregular. Vol. 1 (1917-1939)- Notes: Imprint varies. Includes opinions of the District Court of the Virgin Islands. SERBIB/SERLOC merged record Kept up-to-date by: Virgin Islands reports. Current cases, issued irregularly to be interfiled in loose-leaf binder, replaced by bound vol. at end of court session. Subjects: Law reports, digests, etc.--Virgin Islands of the United States. LC Classification: KGZ13 .A21917

Want's Federal-state court directory. Published/Created: Washington, D.C.: WANT Pub. Co., c1984- Related Authors: Want Publishing Company. Description: v.; 28 cm. 1984 ed.- ISSN: 0742-1095 Notes: SERBIB/SERLOC merged record Has companion publication: Directory of state court clerks & county courthouses. Directory of state court clerks & county courthouses 1042-4172 (DLC) 90660208 (OCoLC)19037975 Subjects: Judges--Courts--United States--States--Directories. Series: Know your government series LC Classification: KF8700.A19 F42 Dewey Class No.: 347.73/025 347.307025 20

Women in the Courts / edited by Winifred L. Hepperle and Laura Crites. Published/Created: Williamsburg, Va.: National Center for State Courts, 1978. Related Authors: Hepperle, Winifred L. Crites, Laura L. Description: xviii, 232 p.: ill.; 23 cm. Contents: Oliver, M. The female in the trial court.--Ginsburg, R.B. Women, men, and the Constitution.--Cook, B.B. The Burger court and women's rights.--Cook, B.B. Women judges.--Hepperle, W.L. and Hendryx, J.L. Women in court administration.--Mahoney, A.R. Sexism in voir dire.--Hoffman, B. Changes in domestic relations court.--Crites, L. Women in the criminal court.--Gates, M. Victims of rape and wife abuse.--Nader, L. and Collier, J. Justice, a woman blindfolded? Notes: Includes bibliographical references. Subjects: Women--Legal status, laws, etc.--United States--Addresses, essays, lectures. Sex discrimination against women--Law and legislation United States--Addresses, essays, lectures. Courts--United States--Officials and employees--Addresses, essays, lectures. Series: Publication (National Center for State Courts); R0037. LC Classification: KF390.W6 W64 Dewey Class No.: 344.73/01761347/0088042 347.30417613470088042 19

Women, the Courts, and equality / edited by Laura L. Crites, Winifred L. Hepperle. Published/Created: Newbury Park: Sage, c1987. Related Authors: Crites, Laura L. Hepperle, Winifred L. Description: 256 p.: ill.; 23 cm. ISBN: 0803928114 0803928122 (pbk.) Notes: Includes bibliographies. Subjects: Women--Legal status, laws, etc.--United States. Sex discrimination against women--Law and legislation United States. Courts--United States--Officials and employees. Series: Sage yearbooks in women's policy studies; v. 11 LC Classification: KF390.W6 W65 1987 Dewey Class No.: 342.73/0878/0269 347.3028780269 19

Word processing in the Courts / jointly sponsored by the National Center for State Courts and the Bureau of Justice Statistics. Published/Created: Williamsburg, Va.: National Center for State Courts, c1984. Related Authors: National Center for State Courts. United States. Bureau of Justice Statistics. Description: v, 59 p.: ill.; 28 cm. ISBN: 0896560775 (pbk.) Notes: Bibliography: p. 43. Subjects: Court administration--United States--Data processing. Word processing--United States. Series: Publication (National Center for State Courts); R091. LC Classification: KF242.C68 W67 1984 Dewey Class No.: 347.73/0285 347.3070285 19

Working papers and subcommittee reports, July 1, 1990 / Federal Courts Study Committee. Published/Created: Philadelphia, Pa.: The Committee, [1990] Description: 2 v.; 28 cm. Notes: Includes bibliographical references. Subjects: Courts--United States. Court congestion and delay--United States. Justice, Administration of--United States. LC Classification: KF8719 .P48 1990 Dewey Class No.: 347.73/13 347.31073 20

AUTHOR INDEX

A

B

C

D

E

F

G

H

M

N

O

P

R

S

T

U

V

W

SUBJECT INDEX

A

B

C

P

R

S